Back to Britain

The Holiday Journals of a G.I. Bride

Back to Britain

The Holiday Journals of a G.I. Bride

MARGARET H. WHARTON

in collaboration with

CHRISTOPHER J. WHARTON

England's green & pleasant land
William Blake 1757–1827

ALAN SUTTON PUBLISHING LIMITED

First published in the United Kingdom in 1995 by
Alan Sutton Publishing Ltd
Phoenix Mill · Far Thrupp · Stroud · Gloucestershire

British Library Cataloguing in Publication Data

Wharton, Margaret H.
    Back to Britain: Holiday Journals of a G.I. Bride
    I. Title II. Wharton, Christopher J.
    914.10485

    ISBN 0–7509–0830–0

Typesetting and origination by
Alan Sutton Publishing Limited
Typeset in Bembo 11/12pt
Printed in Great Britain by
Ebenezer Baylis, Worcester.

CONTENTS

List of Illustrations   vii
Foreword   viii
Notes   ix
Chapter One   London   1
Chapter Two   The South   27
Chapter Three   The West   61
Chapter Four   Wales and Scotland   105
Chapter Five   The North   132
Chapter Six   The Midlands   163
Chapter Seven   The East   186
Chapter Eight   Wiltshire   241
Chapter Nine   1992   315
Chapter Ten   Postscript – 1994   340

For my husband
David:
travel companion
photographer
chauffeur

LIST OF ILLUSTRATIONS

Hampton Court	93
Moat Garden at Windsor Castle	94
Mayor and Town Crier of Weymouth at VE Day ceremony 1945	95
Slapton Sands, South Devon where many Americans were killed in pre-invasion exercises	95
Statue of King Alfred at Wantage, thought to be his birthplace	96
Shadowed arches at Winchester Cathedral	96
Hardy's Cottage at Little Bockhampton, Dorset where he was born	97
Corfe Castle towers over the village	97
Bath – the Abbey and the Roman Baths	98
Statue of Sir Francis Drake stands on Plymouth Hoe	99
Clovelly – stepped main street leads down to the harbour	100
Wells Cathedral	101
Wild Ponies on Dartmoor	101
John Knox's house on the Royal Mile in Edinburgh	102
Statue of David Lloyd George, World War I prime minister in Caernarvon	103
Conway Castle, North Wales	104
Railway to Snowdon Summit	104
York Minster	159
Sanctuary Knocker on the door of Durham Cathedral	159
Fountains Abbey	160
Whitby Abbey	160
Haworth, home of the Bronte Family	161
Wharton Hall, Westmorland. Half eroded Coat-of-Arms	161
Wharton Effigies in the church at Kirkby Stephen	162
Sheep on the road – a hazard in rural Yorkshire	162
Great Gate at Blenheim Palace, Oxfordshire	230
Chester – the Rows and Black and White Architecture	230
Washington Old Hall, Durham	231
Sulgrave Manor, Northamptonshire. Homes of George Washington's Ancestors	231
Coventry Cathedral – the Old and the New	232
Newstead Abbey – home of Lord Byron	232
Tunbridge Wells – the Pantiles	233
Flatford Mill and Willy Lott's Cottage	233
Canterbury Cathedral	234
Sissinghurst – home of Harold Nicholson and Vita Sackville-West	235
American Cemetery at Cambridge	236
Marlborough High Street	236
Marlborough College – famous public school	237
Tottenham House – ancestral home of the Marquess of Ailesbury in Savernake Forest	237
Devizes – Market Place, Bear Hotel and Corn Exchange	238
Castle Combe – often called the prettiest village in England	238
Stonehenge	239
St David's Cathedral, South Wales	239
Fettiplace Tombs at Swinbrook in the Cotswolds	240

FOREWORD

I wrote my first travel journal on a trip to eastern Canada in 1972. I found it a most rewarding experience. Since then, wherever we have gone in the world I have recorded a daily account of the places we have visited, along with my own thoughts and observations.

This book contains excerpts from journals of 11 trips my husband David and I, usually travelling alone but sometimes with others, made to England between 1973 and 1992. Though the journals have been edited by my son Christopher and are arranged regionally rather than chronologically, they remain to a large extent as I wrote them, making notes on the spur of the moment in all kinds of places, then putting them into narrative form either late at night or early the next morning. Occasionally I have incorporated into the journal entries thumbnail sketches of places that seem to deserve more than a passing mention.

I trust that my observations, impressions and reflections will refresh and perhaps amplify the memories of those who have already visited the British Isles and that they will encourage others to do so and come to know and understand in some small measure England's treasure house of history.

Chapter One

LONDON

'. . . there is in London all that life can afford.'
Samuel Johnson 1709–1784

So wrote Dr Samuel Johnson in September of 1777. It is no less true today, for there is in London something for everyone. To go to 'Town,' as Britons say, is a great thrill for natives, and all foreign visitors want to visit London. Many arrive in the turmoil and welter of the airports, make their way to the city, and never venture into the England beyond, finding in London 'all that life can afford.'

London was first a rudimentary settlement of the ancient Britons. Because of its position at a ford across the River Thames it grew in importance with the Roman occupation of Britain in the first century after Christ. In AD 61, the hordes of Boadicea, queen of the Iceni tribe that lived to the north and east, overran and sacked the Roman settlement, but ultimately the Romans defeated her and rebuilt and walled their city to prevent further attacks.

Little is known of London during the early days of the Saxons, but by AD 604 it had become the capital of the East Saxons. In AD 730 the Venerable Bede wrote that it was becoming 'the mart of many nations', and it is mentioned frequently in existing accounts of Danish raids. The later Saxons established their capital at Winchester in Hampshire, but in 1052 Edward the Confessor, last but one of the Saxon kings, began building an abbey at Westminster. Fourteen years later William the Conqueror was crowned there, and London became the residence of kings and nobility and eventually the seat of government. Since William's time, all of England's monarchs, except for Edward V, have been crowned in Westminster, a city within the greater London of today.

One of the first things William the Conqueror did after his victory at Hastings in 1066 was to grant the citizens of London a royal charter in return for their allegiance and support. Then he built the White Tower to demonstrate his conquest and serve as a warning to Saxon rebels. It is one

GREATER LONDON

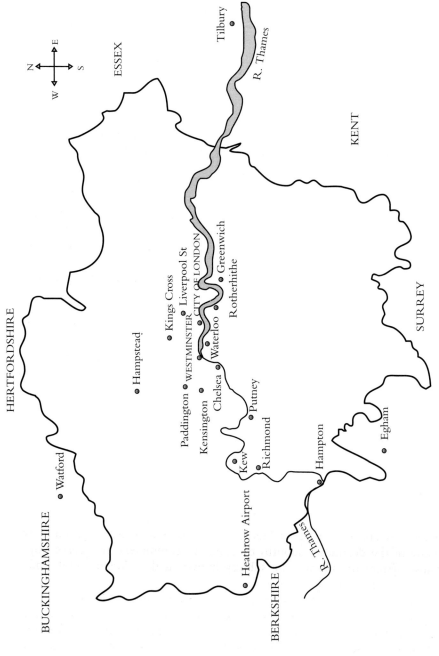

BUCKINGHAMSHIRE

HERTFORDSHIRE

ESSEX

KENT

SURREY

BERKSHIRE

N
E
S
W

Watford

Hampstead

Kings Cross

Paddington

WESTMINSTER

Liverpool St

CITY OF LONDON

Waterloo

Greenwich

Rotherhithe

Kensington

Chelsea

Putney

Kew

Richmond

Hampton

Heathrow Airport

Egham

Tilbury

R. Thames

R. Thames

London   3

of the oldest buildings in London and remains the central keep of the Tower of London, a much greater fortress built piecemeal over the centuries.

In the Middle Ages the city government headed by the Lord Mayor became very rich and powerful, as did the city guilds. London became a great port, trade with the Continent grew apace, and the city became very wealthy.

In 1665 and 1666 two great calamities befell the prosperous city. First an epidemic of bubonic plague decimated the population. It was followed a year later by fire that destroyed much of mediaeval, Tudor and Stuart London. A great rebuilding followed with Sir Christopher Wren as chief architect. London resumed its rapid growth, and in the Georgian and Regency periods, streets, terraces and crescents of rows of graceful stucco houses were laid out in the symmetrical architecture of the times.

Phenomenal growth continued during the reigns of Victoria and Edward VII, and London was the capital not only of England but of the far-flung Empire. It became the biggest city in the world, with an estimated population of seven million in the 1930s. It has grown considerably in number and diversity of people since then, though it can no longer claim to be the world's largest city.

Badly battered in World War II, London is now rebuilt. Slums were swept away, damaged landmarks restored and parks created where bombs had devastated wide areas. Modestly high skyscrapers have appeared on the skyline to the chagrin of some. Clean air legislation has outlawed the use of soft coal and so pollution is slowed. The erosion of stone buildings has been halted, and London fogs likewise are almost a thing of the past.

London has always been a cosmopolitan city. Since the war there has been an influx of immigrants from Pakistan, India, the Middle East, Africa, and the West Indies, as well as from many European countries. London's population today is truly multiracial.

It is difficult to know where London begins and ends for it has encroached far into the surrounding countryside. Greater London, covering some 650 square miles, is the vast conglomeration of streets, houses and factories along both banks of the Thames. It includes the whole of Middlesex and large parts of Hertfordshire, Essex and Kent, and embraces many of the dormitory suburbs of London's commuters. It is served by a transit system of railways, the subway known as the Underground, and a great fleet of red double-decker buses.

Inside Greater London is the administrative County of London, which consists of 27 boroughs and two cities, the City of London and Westminster. Each borough has its own mayor and council, as do the two cities, and each borough is represented in London's governing body, the London County Council. Some of the boroughs as well as parts of Greater

London were at one time separate villages, and some have retained their rural characteristics.

The historic 'Square Mile' of the City of London lies to the east and stands on the north bank of the river. It was the original walled city of the Romans. It is the capital of trade and finance and home of the Bank of England and the city craft and trade guilds formed in the Middle Ages. The monarch may not enter the City without the Lord Mayor's permission, and at griffin-guarded Temple Bar he or she is handed the keys of the city and is received as an honoured guest. The city is crowned by St Paul's Cathedral atop Ludgate Hill, while below winds the Thames crossed by innumerable bridges.

Westminster, the other separate city, lies to the west. It is the seat of government centred around the Houses of Parliament and Whitehall. Westminster merges into what has become the 'best' part of London, the West End. Here are parks and palaces, theatres, shops, and residential areas for the wealthy. The south bank tends to attract the young upper-middle classes, while the north and especially the east are the homes of working men and women. The latter is the domain of the Cockneys, Londoners born within the sound of the 'Bow Bells' of Bow Church, one of Wren's churches in the very heart of the city. Here are the docks and some of the great markets for which London is so famous. This is the part of London that was most heavily damaged in the war, and today neat blocks of flats have replaced the slums of old.

For myself I have fond memories of childhood visits to London. Some were day trips by train, for Paddington Station – the terminus of the Great Western Railway – was within a 2-hour ride of my Wiltshire home. On my first trip at the age of 5, I went to the British Empire Exhibition at Wembley, and I can still remember buying a pot of guava jelly, being introduced to the tropical bird known as the toucan, and seeing a statue of the then Prince of Wales carved in butter. Subsequent visits took us to most of London's high spots, including Madame Tussaud's wax museum. Twice we were taken to pantomimes, the very British theatre productions for children at Christmastime. Sometimes we spent longer periods in London, staying with an uncle in Hampstead. For two years just prior to the war I was a student at Whitelands College, a teacher training college in Putney near the Thames in the southwest of London. During that time I was introduced to opera, theatres, concerts, with many of the tickets for students free, provided they went to matinees and sat high in the 'gods,' the least desirable seats. We studied ancient history in the British Museum and made a special study of the Wren churches in the City, many of which were to be damaged or destroyed in air raids during the war. After I had met the American soldier who would become my husband, London was the most convenient place for us to meet, and so we had a little experience of wartime there – the city blacked out, the constant threat of bombs, services in short supply, and soldiers crowding in from all the Allied countries, especially America. We became engaged in London and spent part of our honeymoon in the Dorchester Hotel.

Since those days we have visited London many times from the United States, often combining business with pleasure, though rarely staying long. Since retirement we are in the habit of picking up a rented car and heading west to my home county and leaving London to the younger generation to enjoy what it has to afford.

1973

with Thomas & Margaret McKnight

SERVICES IN WESTMINSTER ABBEY

SUNDAY, JULY 15TH

We left the hotel for the short ride to Westminster Abbey, where morning services were to begin at 10.30. Admittance to Sunday services is for worshippers only, with the great church open to sightseers at other times. As we entered we passed the Tomb of the World War I Unknown Soldier framed in Lord Haig's red poppies, its sight stirring in me some long-ago memories of listening as a child to solemn Armistice services on the wireless. Nearby is the Abbey's memorial to Winston Churchill. The marble slab set in the floor reads:

> Remember Winston Churchill –
> in accordance with the wishes of the Queen
> and Parliament the Dean and Chapter placed
> this stone on the twenty-fifth anniversary
> of the Battle of Britain
>
> 15 September 1965

Earlier we had seen the solid, robust, though controversial statue of Churchill in Parliament Square, just another of London's many tributes to the great war leader.

We sat in Poets' Corner among the many memorials to nationally acclaimed writers, artists and musicians, and listened to the glorious music. The rich tones of the organ swelled in the great church and the ethereal voices of the choirboys floated down from the vaulted roof. We followed the Order of Matins in the Book of Common Prayer. There was much chanting and singing of psalms, and the prayers and sermon were intoned in the beautifully modulated accents of the clergy. They seemed remote and removed from the ordinary people and their problems, however. The congregation took little part, and I wondered if this may not be one reason for the falling attendance the Church of England is facing today.

The final hymn, 'Be Thou My Vision,' reminded me of the baccalaureate service at Brown University in Roger Williams' church in Providence, Rhode Island, where we had heard it sung the previous summer at our younger son's graduation. We were reminded in the prayers and collect that today is St Swithin's Day. He was a mediaeval saint and early bishop of Winchester, and legend has it that if it rains on his day it will rain every day for the following 40. Dying in 862, he asked to be buried outside the cathedral so his parishioners could walk over his grave, but on July 15th, AD 971, his remains were exhumed and moved inside. At that time, the legend tells us, 'the heavens opened and wept copiously.' This gave rise to the rhyme:

> St Swithin's Day if thou dost rain
> For forty days it will remain.
> St Swithin's Day if thou be fair
> For forty days 'twill rain no mair.

We took this very seriously when we were children.

After the service we walked around the cloisters, thinking of the monks of old who walked daily around the grassy enclosure in prayer and contemplation, or sat illuminating their manuscripts with rubric and gold to the glory of God. As we left the Abbey a few raindrops fell and soon a heavy downpour developed. I certainly hoped that this St Swithin's Day shower did not augur rain for our very special holiday.

1975

WHITEHALL – WESTMINSTER – ST MARTIN'S IN THE FIELDS – OXFORD STREET – KEW GARDENS – HAMPSTEAD – HAMPTON COURT – THE WALLACE COLLECTION – A JEWISH SABBATH

SUNDAY, JULY 6TH

After an uneventful night flight from New York, we landed at Heathrow at 8 a.m. and were driven to our hotel, the Royal Trafalgar in Trafalgar Square. After lunch and a short rest we took a walk which turned out to be longer than we had expected.

All London lay basking in the warm sunshine of a golden July afternoon. We admired the stone lions and the fountains playing merrily around Nelson's lofty column in the middle of the square, which, as usual, was swarming with pigeons. The square is named for Lord Nelson's greatest and final victory at Trafalgar on October 21st 1805. His fleet utterly destroyed the French fleet, and Napoleon was thus unable to invade England. Nelson, however, was killed in the battle.

We walked to Whitehall, the heart of British government. It runs from Trafalgar Square to Westminster and is named for a royal palace of which today only the banqueting house remains. Designed by Inigo Jones and completed in 1622, it is a fine example of the Italian classical style of architecture that became popular in England at that time. It contains a magnificent ceiling painted by Rubens. We came to Downing Street, a short street lined with unpretentious houses. Its entrance was guarded by a policeman, for No. 10 has been the official residence of the Prime Minister since 1732, when George II offered the house to Sir Robert Walpole. A little further on is the Cenotaph, a marble obelisk which is the national war memorial. We passed the Horse Guards, the blue-clad mounted sentries who guard St James Palace, site of a leper colony in the thirteenth century. Inside the courtyard is the chapel where Charles I took Holy Communion before his execution in 1649. We reached the Thames Embankment, a walkway and street paralleling the east bank of the river. Constructed during Victoria's reign – and sometimes known as the Victoria Embankment – it takes the walker on a scenic path north to Westminster Bridge and the Houses of Parliament. Reaching the bridge we saw that today, as in Wordsworth's time, 'Earth has not anything to show more fair...' We saw Boadicea, queen of the Iceni, 'huge of frame, and terrifying of aspect'. Warlike in her chariot, she still seems to guard the river crossing from the Romans.

We walked along the length of the vast complex of buildings that make up the Houses of Parliament. They are Gothic structures, designed and built between 1840 and 1860 by Sir Charles Barry and A. W. Pugin. They are located on the site of the old Palace of Westminster, Parliament's customary meeting place until a fire almost entirely destroyed it in 1834. The House of Commons was badly damaged in World War II but has been entirely restored. After much discussion the small size of its meeting chamber was retained on Winston Churchill's recommendation that a small space favoured 'good House of Commons speaking'. The clock tower by the House of Commons is famous for its deep-toned bell Big Ben. The bell rang for the first time on April 10th 1858. It was named for Sir Benjamin Hall, Chief Commissioner of Works at Westminster. I remember how its tolling heralded the 9 o'clock evening news and how during the war it seemed the very symbol of Britain's resistance to tyranny.

We went into the Victoria Tower Gardens and rested on a shady bench, next to a statue of the suffragette Emmeline Pankhurst. Walking further into the gardens we admired Rodin's beautiful statue of the besieged burghers of Calais, those starving heroes saved from death by the entreaties of Edward III's queen Philippa of Hainault during the Hundred Years' War. We next came to the Jewel Tower of Westminster, a Norman structure and one of two buildings that survived the fire of 1834. It is partially surrounded by a moat in which were growing the most lovely waterlilies. Westminster Hall, the other building to survive the fire, is noted for its incomparable hammer-beam roof. Passing St Margaret's Church, site of many society weddings, we came to Westminster Abbey itself. The great church was founded in the eleventh century by Edward the Confessor, second-to-last of the Saxon kings. Only the cloisters were open for visitors during our visit, but strolling around them we discovered an exhibition of historical finds tracing the Abbey's long history. We passed into the Little Cloister which encloses a small green lawn with a fountain at its centre. Surrounding the fountain were herbaceous borders of many flowers, among them giant hollyhocks and enormous fuchsias. We saw the Westminster School where the boy choristers receive their education.

Very tired, we took a cab back to the hotel. After a short rest we attended Evensong at St Martin's-in-the-Fields, one of the old historic churches of London. Its name derives from its original location in the fields outside the small mediaeval town that London once was. The church has long been noted for the fervour of its ministers and the high calibre of their preaching. One of the best known was Dick Shepherd, whom I remember hearing preach in the early days of radio. He was a popular and much decorated padre in World War I. After a few years at St Martin's he died of cancer, still a young man. Right up to his death he wrote an inspirational column in the *Sunday Express*. My mother never missed listening to him on the radio or reading his column, and his death was like a great personal loss to her, as it was to thousands of others.

The church is now the seat of the Academy of St Martin's-in-the-Fields, a musical group headed by Sir Neville Marriner and noted for its performances and recordings of classical music. The present building, designed in classical style and fronted with six huge Corinthian columns, was built by James Gibbs in 1726. It is undergoing extensive repair and renovation. Steel scaffolding was in place in the interior and portions of the ceiling were newly painted in mediaeval fashion with bosses of bright gold, white, blue and red.

A young bearded minister led the service, for which a large crowd had assembled. The prayers seemed interminable, the singing difficult to follow with little participation by the congregation. The sermon was given by a priest from Belfast and told a tragic tale of misunderstanding, reprisal and bloodshed.

MONDAY, JULY 7TH

David was off to the London office early, but I was able to sleep late as my niece Rachel was not expected to arrive at the hotel from Weymouth till about 10.30. I found she had grown up considerably since I had last seen her: she was taller, slimmer and very pretty. She was dressed in a print dress that accentuated her small waist and curvaceous figure. She was wearing the high platform-soled shoes that all the young English girls seem to be wearing this year. She was in high spirits, all ready for a shopping spree with her aunt from America.

Oxford Street was crowded with shoppers for the July sales, and many people were in search of bargains. We stopped at Marks and Spencers and then went on to Selfridge's for lunch, after which we found an outfit Rachel wanted for playing squash. We returned to the hotel in time for tea and went for a walk along the Thames Embankment. David took some pictures of us and we had dinner in the floating restaurant called the 'Hispaniola' which Rachel found very exciting. Afterwards we took a cab to Waterloo Station where Rachel caught a train back to Weymouth. We promised to see her there later on our way to Winchester.

TUESDAY, JULY 8TH

'Go down to Kew in lilac time,' wrote the poet Alfred Noyes. It isn't lilac time but I wanted to see Kew again, and Esther Borkum promised to go with me. Esther is a friend of many years. She and her late husband Jack came to London from South Africa, and David's business association with him in textiles ripened into friendship. The business in London is being carried on by Jack's son and son-in-law, and Esther continues to live in their apartment in Clifton Gardens. Since her husband's death she has taken up sculpture and is doing some fine work which is showing in the West End and developing an enthusiastic clientele.

We caught a bus to Kew, sitting on the top level for the best view. We went through Kensington and eventually got off at the Lion's Gate entrance to the famous gardens. The entrance fee was one penny, surely one of the great bargains anywhere.

Before the city encroached on it, Kew was a village on the Thames outside London. It was built around a church and triangular green with houses in the elegant style of the early eighteenth century. The Hanoverian kings built a palace here, and in 1759 Princess Augusta laid out botanic gardens landscaped by Capability Brown. Brown was a much sought-after designer of gardens who acquired his nickname because of his habit of telling landowners that their estates had great capabilities. He lived from 1716 to 1783 and judging from the number of gardens he laid out he must have been in great demand and very busy. The gardens cover 300 acres and contain some 45,000 varieties of plants and trees, some indigenous, some from far exotic places. There are many beautiful plantings and flower gardens, yet the main purpose of Kew was and remains the study of horticulture and botany. After much experimentation, for example, Kew supplied the seeds for the rubber trees of Malaya and Ceylon and the cinchona trees and shrubs of India, the source of quinine. Both of these species were indigenous to South America. Kew was described by the Wiltshire writer Richard Jefferies as 'a great green book whose broad pages are illuminated with flowers – a place where the peace of green things reigns.'

There are many greenhouses, the most impressive the curved and domed Palm House, which has a visitors' gallery. The greenhouses are full of tropical plants, and in the humid heat one can almost see leaves and buds unfolding. In a pool in one of the houses grew water plants with flat leaves like huge green trays and cup-like blossoms of pale hues. A party of schoolchildren about eleven years old had gathered around the pool making earnest sketches of the plants. They were completely absorbed in their task, and I could not help but contrast their behaviour with that of American students out on a field trip.

The weather was good. Some clouds remained in the sky after an earlier rain, but we were grateful for them in view of all our walking. On our way to the restaurant we passed some rose beds, but the blooms were past their best. We had a picnic-style lunch outside and then walked to the Chinese pagoda, a Kew landmark. It is a folly erected in the Chinoiserie period of the Georgians when there was a craze for anything oriental. We went through the park and came to the main gate, passing the palace on the way. We crossed Kew Bridge to wait on the pier for a boat back to London. It was a long walk and we were grateful for the river trip, although it was very slow. We made a stop at Putney, which reminded me of my college days at Whitelands. We finally disembarked at Westminster about 5 and made our separate ways to home and hotel.

I just had time for a quick wash and change before Esther's son Brian arrived to take David and me to his house in Hampstead for cocktails. Like Kew, Hampstead was once a village outside the city. It developed into a popular resort for the rich when mineral springs believed to have therapeutic value were discovered. The nearby high, open and sandy Hampstead Heath increased its popularity.

Many famous people have been associated with Hampstead. John Keats lived here for a while in a small Regency house, writing most of his best poetry while carrying on a love affair with Fanny Brawne. John Constable lived here, painted the village and heath, and is buried in the churchyard. Another great artist, George Romney, also lived here, as for a while did novelist John Galsworthy. The poet Shelley is said to have sailed boats with his children on Whitestone Pond, and nearby is Jack Straw's Castle, an inn known to Dickens and Thackeray. Perhaps its name comes from one of the men in Wat Tyler's peasant revolt of 1381. The wild heathland was ideal for the nefarious activities of highwaymen, and Dick Turpin is believed to have visited the Spaniards Inn to conspire with the innkeeper about ambushing the coaches of the rich for their gold and jewels. The inn is thought to have once been the residence of a Spanish ambassador – hence its name. Nearby is Kenwood House, designed by Robert Adam with its grounds merging into the heathland. I visited this house and the heath as a child, for I had an uncle who lived in Hampstead.

Brian was nice enough to drive us round for a quick look at Hampstead's famous places before taking us to his gracious home. Hampstead is now a beautiful residential area. We drove through the 'village' out on to the high wild heath with the great city spread beneath. It is hard to realize that this lovely open area is in the very heart of London.

At Brian's home we had drinks in the garden, a riot of colour in full summer bloom. We then drove to the Carlton Towers for dinner. An opulent hotel in one of London's squares, its restaurant is known for its fine food and impeccable service. A tremendously fat man in a black parson's suit was sitting alone at the table next to us. His face looked vaguely familiar, and when Brian asked if he wasn't a famous American actor, I knew immediately it was Orson Welles. He appeared to be waiting for someone and was whiling away the time eating rolls and butter, strawberries and cream, and drinking glass after glass of wine. Just as we were about to leave his expected guests arrived.

We had a lovely meal of soup and roast beef and enjoyed the company of Brian and his wife Jan, a very attractive American girl. She loves her life as a prosperous young matron in London.

WEDNESDAY, JULY 9TH

David left early for the office in Great Titchfield Street, and I set out to do some shopping. I walked along the narrow streets leading into Waterloo Place and Regent Street and thence to Bond Street and Piccadilly. In Regent Street I went to a shop called the Needlewoman, which I always visit for embroidery supplies. Bond Street, one of the most exclusive streets in the world, is lined with small very expensive shops, many of them patronized by royalty. Burlington Arcade, built in 1819 by Lord George Cavendish, is a small enclosed mall. It was modelled on similar shopping areas Cavendish had seen on the continent. Uniformed beadles kept the arcade free of crime so the wealthy and privileged could shop in safety, protected from pickpockets as well as the weather. Even today men are employed to give shoppers any aid or assistance needed.

I then rode the underground to Selfridge's where I met Esther and her friend Sadie, also from South Africa. We had lunch and then went to Manchester Square and Hertford House. The latter is the home of the Wallace Collection, the richest privately formed art collection in London and now the property of the nation. Its most valuable and famous picture is the *Laughing Cavalier* by Frans Hals.

When I told David later that I had visited the Wallace Collection, he said it is mentioned in the book he is reading, Nigel Nicolson's *Portrait of a Marriage*, the story of the strange union between his parents Sir Harold Nicolson and Victoria (Vita) Sackville-West. Later in this trip we hope to visit both Knole, where Vita grew up, and Sissinghurst, the home and garden the Nicolsons created between them.

THURSDAY, JULY 10TH

More shopping! There seems time for little else. Sales are on so bargains can be found if one can cope with the crowds. I first went to Harrod's in search of a Wedgwood teapot for a friend but found it out of stock. Service was bad and slow, the sales personnel conveying the impression that they were conferring a great favour on the customer. Perhaps they resent some of our American accents! There has been a sad deterioration from pre-war standards in this respect. An American, buying china on a large scale for export, was so annoyed at the constant telephone interruptions that he removed the receiver and said in no uncertain voice, 'Finish waiting on me!' Quite a contretemps ensued, and the manager was called. The Yank triumphed, I am glad to say. This rather epitomizes my dilemma – I am both critical and defensive of British shortcomings.

I went to the food halls to feast my eyes on their delights. Meats, fish, poultry and game were displayed. Some were prepared for the oven, but others still in fur or feather dripped an occasional spot of blood on the sawdust spread amidst the marble pillars and tiled walls. In another section baked goods and confectionery were on view in mouth-watering arrangements. The food halls are scheduled for renovation and work has already begun in some departments. Harrod's was once described as a cross between an ocean liner and an oriental bazaar, and the description certainly applies to the cavernous food halls.

My friend Nancy Pennefather, whose sister I know in New Jersey, met me in time for lunch, which we enjoyed in one of the Harrod's restaurants. We then took a boat up the Thames to Hampton Court, where we took a guided tour. The great Tudor palace, begun by Cardinal Wolsey and given by him to Henry VIII, became that king's favourite residence. Of his queens, Anne Boleyn honeymooned and Jane Seymour died in childbirth here, while the ghost of beheaded Katherine Howard haunts the gallery to the chapel. The palace is said to have cost Wolsey 200,000 gold crowns. When finished, it was described as 'more lyke unto a paradise than any earthly Habitation.' Henry later enlarged it, and it was again added to by Sir Christopher Wren in the seventeenth century. Of the original palace only the great gatehouse and some of the courts survive. The patterned brickwork shades from rose to crimson, and the tall spirally carved chimneys are distinctive Tudor features. The great hall, with its carved and decorated beamed roof, is one of the finest anywhere. Perhaps Shakespeare once acted here with his troupe as entertainment after one of the frequent sumptuous banquets. We saw the famous astronomical clock built by a French clockmaker. It is still in working order. We saw too the court where the portly king played tennis, a game imported, like the clock, from France. He was accustomed to joust in another court and hunt in the extensive park surrounding the palace. The immediate environs of the building are planted with formal gardens, very beautiful today in the July sun. There is a pond garden, a knot garden planted entirely in herbs, and most fun of all the Maze of tiny bushes of sweet-smelling box planted after Henry's time in 1714.

We returned to Nancy's apartment in Hampton, where David met us for drinks, and then we went to dinner at a riverside inn nearby. We returned to the hotel by the Underground, an unexpectedly unnerving experience as we were alone in the car except for a group of Pakistanis who were arguing and flashing knives. Hitherto I had always thought of London as the safest city in the world!

FRIDAY, JULY 11TH

I finished my shopping this morning, finding the teapot for my friend in Chinacraft and stopping at Liberty's. Like Harrod's, it is another shopping landmark. The store, housed in a huge black and white mock Tudor building, now seems less exclusive than formerly, and I could find nothing to suit my taste. It is ironic that now that I can afford to shop in Liberty's, Liberty's no longer suits me.

After a hairdo and manicure I took a bus tour of the City of London, the square-mile city proper bounded by the old Roman walls. We passed the

Tower, St Paul's, the Bank of England and the column marking the start of the Great Fire of 1666. The tour was enjoyable but, like most tours, could offer only a cursory view.

In the evening we drove to the Hampstead home of Peter and Linda Charad, Esther Borkum's son-in-law and daughter, for Sabbath dinner. In accordance with Jewish law the meal was cold. The men and boys wore yarmulkes and prayers were intoned. It was a new experience for me and very impressive, and I felt very privileged to be a guest. Four children were present, Peter's son and daughter and their two cousins. A Colombian au pair girl lives with them, as seems to be popular among rising young couples in England today. After the meal we went for a long walk on the heath, stopping at some of the sights we had passed in a car a few days ago.

1976

HEATHROW – ST PAUL'S

FRIDAY, JULY 9TH

We left New York from Kennedy at the end of a week busy with Bicentennial celebrations. We were in the midst of a heat wave and hoping it would be cooler in England, though weather reports told of unprecedented heat and drought there as well. I stayed up late last night to watch the State dinner at the White House hosted by the Fords for British royals, so was tired starting the trip. We found it very busy at Kennedy and the plane was full, but that is only to be expected in the height of summer.

We landed at Heathrow very early in the morning after a short but sleepless night. We found it even busier than Kennedy. Tremendous crowds in long lines were inching towards the immigration booths. We have often commented that it seems as if every plane in the world lands in London at 8 a.m. on any given morning. The crowds hold some fascination for me. People of all races, colours and creeds, polyglot and cosmopolitan, were there, some of them insouciant holidaymakers, others anxiously waiting to start a new life. Middle and Far Easterners predominated – beautiful doe-eyed sari-clad women from India, prosperous-looking Arabs, brash youngsters with a veneer of Western civilization, and pitifully bewildered old people laden with the humble possessions of a lifetime. My heart lifts thinking that London is still the Mecca for many people, but then I wonder how a small island can absorb all these immigrants.

SUNDAY, JULY 18TH

After a few days in East Anglia and a visit with friends living in Norfolk, we were on our way to London by 11 a.m., enjoying the lovely Suffolk and Essex countryside before reaching the outlying sprawl of London and going through the Dartford Tunnel under the Thames. We turned the car in and went by taxi to the St George's Hotel.

Our few days in London were principally taken up with business for David and shopping and seeing friends for me, but we did spend an afternoon at St Paul's Cathedral and took a day trip down the river to Greenwich.

Since the war St Paul's has stood as a symbol of the very survival of London, for while the streets and buildings of the city all around were well-nigh levelled, the great church itself sustained only minor damage. Prior to the war the cathedral had been encroached on by buildings of all kinds, but now it proudly stands in cleared open space. It has been cleaned of the accumulation of decades of London soot so that its warm Portland stone now glows as it did when it was completed in 1675.

The mediaeval cathedral which once stood on the site was destroyed in the Great Fire of 1666, and Christopher Wren, the Wiltshire-born and Oxford-educated mathematician and architect, was commissioned to build a replacement. Modelled on the Italianate design of St Peter's in Rome, St Paul's became his masterpiece. The cathedral was completed in 1710, and when Sir Christopher was a very old man he showed Queen Anne around the great structure. Her surprising comment was 'awful, artificial, and amusing', and even more surprising was Wren's pleasure at the remark. For what she meant was 'awe-inspiring, artistic, and amazing' – an indication of the changes the language has undergone in the last two hundred and fifty years.

Since the war the stained glass windows, shattered by explosions during the Blitz, have been replaced by clear glass and enhance the cool spaciousness of the vast interior as Wren had originally planned. On the inside of the dome – undoubtedly the outstanding feature of the design – are paintings by Sir James Thornhill. We climbed to the Whispering Gallery, where we experimented with a whisper which went round and round before dying away, and thence to the Stone Gallery, from where we got a panoramic view of the city spread below. Descending to the body of the cathedral, we saw the choir stalls and organ case delicately carved by that master of the art Grinling Gibbons. We saw Flaxman's statue of Lord Nelson and the monument to Dr John Donne, onetime Dean of St Paul's and famous poet who posed in his shroud for his unusual memorial.

We went into the choir room and sat in briefly on the rehearsal of the boys' choir, the pure, innocent, flute-like tones belying the sparkle of mischief in the boys' eyes. In the crypt, which is almost like another church in itself, we saw the massive tombs of the victorious leaders of the Napoleonic Wars, Lord Nelson and the Duke of Wellington. There too is the enormous funeral carriage which bore the duke's body to St Paul's in 1852. Best of all we saw the tablet bearing Christopher Wren's epitaph *'Si monumentuam requiris circumspice'* – 'If you seek his monument, look around you.'

1977

THE TOWER OF LONDON – NOSTALGIC RETURN TO WHITELANDS COLLEGE, PUTNEY

TUESDAY, OCTOBER 18TH

We went first to a part of London called Little Venice, a secluded basin of the Grand Union Canal, where we planned to get a boat to the London Zoo in Regents Park. London's canals fell into disuse after their heyday in the nineteenth century but have recently revived with the introduction of pleasure trips. We were disappointed, however, as the barges to the Zoo have been out of service since October 1st. We had lunch at a pub called the Hansom Cab, which had a Victorian air to it and where the sun was warm enough for us to eat outside in the secluded garden. We then took the long subway ride to the Tower of London.

The weather was beautifully clear, and when we emerged from the subway we got an excellent view up and down the river. To the east of the Tower rose the shipping cranes of the great dock system that lies where the Thames begins to widen. The Tower is at the eastern edge of the square mile of the City proper, so to the west lay the City, from here appearing as a maze of modern buildings – banks and office blocks – over which the great dome of St Paul's stands out. The square mile of the City is defined by the second-century Roman wall, only traces of which remain today, though excavation is constantly uncovering more. Hard by the Tower can be seen a stretch of the wall, and the river here is spanned by the Tower Bridge, the most scenic of all the Thames bridges but something of an anachronistic bottleneck for today's traffic.

The Tower itself is a distillation of one thousand years of history. The central tower, known as the White Tower because it was whitewashed in 1241, was built by William the Conqueror to ensure his hold on London. Building then went on sporadically until the nineteenth century. Over the years it has been fortress, palace and prison. One of the earliest prisoners was Charles, Duke of Orleans, who was captured by Henry V at Agincourt in 1415. Foul deeds have been committed within its walls. Perhaps the murder of the two little princes during the Wars of the Roses took place here, though definitive evidence thereof is lacking. Certainly many traitors or enemies or those who otherwise displeased the ruler lost their heads on the execution block on Tower Green – among them two wives of Henry VIII, Anne Boleyn and Katherine Howard; Lady Jane Grey, who was queen for less than a week; the Earl of Essex, the fallen favourite of Elizabeth I; and the Duke of Monmouth, the seventeenth-century pretender to the throne. They were brought to the Tower in dead of night by boat up the river to enter the fortress by the waterside entry known as Traitor's Gate. Most were brought for summary execution, though a few were held prisoner for many years before meeting their death by the headsman's axe. These captives often engraved their names and messages on the stone walls of their prison, their words still visible to our prying eyes.

We joined a tour led by one of the Beefeaters, the Yeomen Wardens of the Tower. He was clad in the dark blue Elizabethan uniform of long tradition and was a good guide, obviously well-steeped in the long history of the great fortress. He pointed out a row of guns facing the river and told us they had been captured from the French at Waterloo. We also saw the jet-black ravens pecking around the Tower Green. These birds, their wings clipped, are closely guarded, for it is generally believed that if the ravens leave the Tower then London and England will fall to an enemy. Clipping their wings of course ensures that they remain in the Tower, but it also inhibits their mating rituals so replacements are often hard to come by and the population must be replenished and maintained with captured birds from outside. At the beginning of World War II, their numbers were very low, and they were very jealously watched over during the ensuing years.

We ended our visit by going to the Armoury, which houses an impressive collection of weapons from many centuries past. I thought the most amazing exhibit was a complete suit of armour for an elephant used at Clive's great victory at Plassey in India in 1757. We joined the queue to see the closely guarded Crown Jewels, walking through so quickly that we simply could not do justice to the wealth of gold, silver and jewels magnificently crafted into crowns, coronets, tiaras, necklaces, bracelets, brooches and rings that make up the trappings of the British monarchy.

We caught a bus to Leicester Square – the traffic was appalling – where we got an indifferent meal. We cancelled plans to go to the theatre from sheer exhaustion and also because my foot had become swollen and painful. Dr Johnson once said that he who is tired of London is tired of life. I love both, but I am tired! Perhaps Dr Johnson would feel the same after a hot day's sightseeing in twentieth-century London, especially with a sore foot!

WEDNESDAY, OCTOBER 19TH

There is much talk of an airline strike that perturbs us, as our return is imminent. David thinks he will investigate the possibility of changing to Freddie Laker's service as that is not affected by the strike. Today I planned to spend time with Betty Glover, an old college friend, who is coming down from Ipswich to see us. David had planned to spend the day with the Borkums and possibly take in a museum.

I caught the Underground to Liverpool Street to meet Betty, whose train was on time, and we went into the North Eastern Railway Hotel to decide what to do. We found a quiet corner for a chat that went on and on till lunchtime. It suited me to stay off my feet and, as Betty often comes to London, she was not overly interested in seeing the sights. We had an excellent meal in the old-fashioned elegance of the hotel – both service and food were impeccable. Today in the waning days of rail popularity the railway hotels struggle hard to maintain their past standards of luxury and service. In the heyday of rail travel, every large station had its hotel run by the railway line serving that station, and I remembered how my mother used to enjoy the Great Western Railway Hotel at Paddington.

After lunch we took a nostalgic trip to Whitelands College, the teacher training college in Putney where we had met over 40 years ago. It looked quite different to us – small and to me not very imposing after the huge college and university buildings I have grown used to in the States. Although small by these standards, the college was well-equipped even when Betty and I arrived as students in 1936. The buildings were still rather new, standing amidst gardens and playing fields entered by a drive at the head of which was a porter's lodge. Originally housed in cramped quarters in Chelsea, the college had moved into fine brick buildings designed by Sir Gilbert Scott in a modified Byzantine style. The small chapel was especially beautiful. There was an elegantly furnished common room and a dining room set up in refectory style with tables for 10 and a raised dais for visitors and staff. There were lecture rooms, labs, craft and music rooms, and small and large auditoriums and gymnasiums. Students' rooms, arranged in corridors named for Chelsea streets, were private and well-furnished. The college sustained some damage during the Blitz but has been restored and enlarged to accommodate the student body, which numbered less than 200 when we were there but has since grown considerably.

Today Betty and I were greeted by the porter and walked down the Red Corridor, the central hall leading to the lounge, where we met the principal, a youngish man who was a far cry from the elderly and intimidating Miss Counsell of our day. The college is coeducational now, and we saw young men and women in casual clothing that would not have passed muster when we were students. The chapel seemed unchanged – small and peaceful in blue and gold – and I wondered if attendance is still compulsory.

We took a taxi back to the station for Betty's train, and David met us there with the news that he had booked us on Laker on Saturday leaving from Gatwick. We would have to be there early as seats would be first come, first served. Back at the hotel we made calls to the U.S. announcing our change of plans and making arrangements to be met. Then after dinner at a nearby restaurant we were early to bed.

1982

ARRIVAL – BUSINESS CALL – DOLPHIN SQUARE

TUESDAY, MAY 11TH

We got off the plane at Heathrow and after completing formalities and collecting our luggage got an airport bus marked Paddington Station. There was a long wait in the bus, and when it finally started we experienced one of the longest, slowest, most detour-filled trips imaginable. We were tired and impatient, but the journey was made bearable by the beauty of the countryside and the cool, crisp, blue and sunny weather. Heathrow is far to the west of the city, and we rode through rural and then suburban and built-up areas. I had forgotten how beautiful England can look early on a bright morning in the merry month of May. Every tree and shrub seemed to be in bloom or full leaf – white and pink may and hawthorn, horse chestnuts with great candle-like flowers of white and red, white and purple lilac, heavy yellow chains of laburnum, orange and red wallflowers, tulips, and bluebells. Lawns were green as only English lawns can be, playing fields were closely mown to a velvety texture, and pastures were yellow with buttercups and dotted with white daisies. All the glory of spring was on display in the meadows of the countryside and the gardens and parks of suburb and city.

When at last we reached our hotel, we were quite disappointed. What had once been a gracious residence of Georgian design is being converted into a hotel with renovations not nearly complete, and is a far cry from the description given us when we made our reservation in New York. We are on the third floor, but no lifts are in operation and no hall porter was in evidence when we arrived. Nor are any meals served except for a continental breakfast. We are not happy, but the location near Marble Arch is good, and we only plan to spend one night here.

We went for lunch to the Mount Royal Hotel next door and had a passable meal though service was slow. We then walked up Oxford Street to a bank and then proceeded to Great Titchfield Street to see Peter Charad, a former business associate of David's and friend of long standing. As we walked along Oxford Street, the busiest of all London's shopping streets, we encountered great crowds of shoppers even though there were no special sales and it was only a Tuesday afternoon. The shop windows were full of high-priced goods, but as far as we could tell the quality looked inferior to similar goods in the U.S. The huge bulk of Selfridge's had marvellous window displays, and Marks and Spencers was crowded with bargain hunters. We saw several women collecting money for sailors' charities, but other than the gloom and doom of newspaper placards there was little to indicate that Britain is at war with Argentina. The fruit stalls standing on every corner were displaying fine wares – green and red apples, luscious crimson strawberries, white and purple grapes, and bright oranges – but the prices seemed shockingly high, especially to Americans like us who after adjusting pounds to dollars are shocked even more.

We reached the old building in which Peter has his office and found the cage-like elevator that worried me five years ago still in wheezing operation. Peter's secretary, a coal-black girl from Uganda, greeted us and later brought us tea and biscuits while we talked to Peter. His mother-in-law, a close friend, is visiting in the U.S. so we will unfortunately not get to see her.

We returned to the hotel and after some difficulty with the phone lines called my friend Betty Glover in Ipswich to tell her we would be arriving there by train at 11.45 a.m. tomorrow. We then called Sam and Millie Farb, friends from North Carolina who are in London on a tour, arranged to meet them for dinner, and caught a taxi to the huge apartment complex where they are staying in Dolphin Square near the river in Chelsea. The complex is completely self-contained and equipped with a swimming pool, shopping mall and tennis courts. It is surrounded by lovely green lawns and gardens well-planted at this time of year with yellow, orange, white, and dark red and rust wallflowers. Their soft sweet scent, especially noticeable on a damp warm evening, brought back my childhood. The flat itself was well-appointed and nicely furnished, making an altogether pleasant place for two Americans to stay on their first visit to London.

I was by this time very tired and so very happy to relax over a drink and bask in their welcome. Sam has discovered a good restaurant nearby, but we caught a taxi for a little sightseeing on the way. We went through Hyde Park and past hotels which held wartime memories for us, especially the Dorchester. Our taxi driver was talkative and told us he had plans for a 10-week trip in the States later in the summer. Our dinner was very good and we enjoyed being together. Nevertheless we were glad to return to our hotel and get to bed.

1983

ST JAMES' CHURCH – PICCADILLY – BUS FROM PICCADILLY TO ROTHERHITHE – SHOPPING AT HARROD'S

MONDAY, JULY 11TH

On then from Bath to London on the last leg of our trip with the choir. We travelled a road new to me, since it is to the south of the route David and I normally use from Marlborough to London. We went though some pretty country. On a lake I saw a pen, or mother swan, swimming with her four little cygnets, ugly ducklings indeed. But most of our group were too tired from the heat or too excited at the prospect of London shopping to pay much attention to scenery or old buildings.

The heat in London was intense, and the Forum Hotel, a high-rise of some 27 storeys, seemed the antithesis of everything English. Noise, bustle, confusion, crowds, inadequate lift service, was followed by a meal that left much to be desired. We took a walk around the environs of the hotel. It had once been an elegant part of Georgian London, but today the terraced houses are subdivided into flats occupied by Indians, Pakistanis, Arabs and people from every part of the globe except England.

It was hot and airless in our 24th-floor room, and riding the elevators was a nightmarish experience. But at last weariness caught up with us and we slept the sleep of sheer exhaustion.

TUESDAY, JULY 12TH

The heat persists, intensified by London's crowds of tourists and bargain hunters in the July sales. After breakfast we were taken by bus to St James' Church in Piccadilly. The church is one of Christopher Wren's originals. After the Great Fire of 1666 destroyed much of the city, Wren was commissioned to design and rebuild many of the churches, St James' among them. He considered it one of his most successful parish churches. Like many of London's churches, it was so badly damaged in World War II that almost total reconstruction was needed. This has been done well and faithfully, and today the church and its yard provide a quiet oasis amidst the hurly-burly of Piccadilly. It is cool, balanced and symmetrical in design with gilt ornamentation that appears at once both lavish and restrained. Today there were beautiful blue and yellow flower arrangements in the church for an afternoon wedding. The organ appeared magnificent though it was unfortunately inoperative, a big disappointment to the organists in the group. This was the church in which William Blake, mystic, poet, painter and visionary of the eighteenth century, was baptized. Yesterday I read his poem 'Jerusalem' on the bus when I referred to the legend that Christ had once visited the west of England.

The church itself is on Piccadilly but nearby is St James' Square, an example of an important architectural innovation introduced in London in the century following the restoration of Charles II to the throne in 1660. The squares were mostly built by noblemen interested in property speculation, and St James' was one of the first in the West End. Built by the Earl of St Albans and once the home of dukes and earls, it now houses private clubs and business firms. There is an equestrian statue of William of Orange at its centre and many plane trees grow in the gardens.

After our practice, we broke up into individual groups going separate ways, though about half of us, including David and I, decided to take the bus tour offered by our driver as the best way to see a lot in a short time with a minimum of effort. A minister friend of one of our leaders offered his services as guide, and he added a great deal of information in a whimsically humorous fashion. Threading his way skilfully through the London traffic, our driver took us down Piccadilly to Piccadilly Circus where five roads converge. In the centre is a fountain topped by the statue of Eros, Greek god of love, even though the sculptor Sir Alfred Gilbert intended it to be an angel of Christian charity. Piccadilly takes its name from an eighteenth-century club whose members wore frilled neckwear or collars known as 'piccadils,' which were manufactured in a house nearby.

Piccadilly Circus is London's Times Square and entertainment hub, and at night is lit up with huge commercial neon signs. We passed the great movie houses of Leicester Square and the street called Haymarket because in days gone by market cattle were fed hay here. We entered Trafalgar Square, where a statue of Lord Nelson, the one-armed, one-eyed hero of the great naval victory, stands atop the lofty column guarded by Sir Edwin Landseer's bronze-sculpted lions. For all their ferocious demeanour, the lions fail to deter the hordes of ever-present pigeons fouling and desecrating the monument. The National Gallery with its rich collection of paintings overlooks the square from the north and close by is the church of St Martin-in-the-Fields. Looking through Admiralty Arch and down the straight tree-lined Mall we caught a glimpse of Buckingham Palace fronted by an impressive statue of Queen Victoria.

We entered Whitehall, the administrative centre of the country. In 1649 it was the scene of the execution of Charles I, the monarch who pushed Parliament and the people too far in his quest for supreme power. As he stepped from an upper window on to the scaffold, the poet Andrew Marvell described the scene thus:

> He nothing common did or mean
> Upon that memorable scene ...
> But bow'd his comely head
> Down as upon a bed.

On the right we passed Downing Street and a little further on, in the middle of the street we saw the Cenotaph, the national monument to the dead of the two world wars.

The Cenotaph stands in the middle of Whitehall. I remember when it was erected in the early 1920s and the considerable controversy its plain and simple rather than ornate design aroused. Solemn ceremonies were at first held there at 11 a.m. every Armistice Day, November 11th. The day of the ritual has since been changed to Remembrance Day, the Sunday before November 11th, with the Queen placing a wreath of red poppies at the foot of the memorial 'lest we forget'.

Whitehall leads into Parliament Square, and on our right was Westminster Abbey. Recently cleaned, the familiar edifice rose sparkling in the morning sun. Housed in the separate city of Westminster, it is the scene of most royal ceremonial services. Coronations always take place here, with the monarch seated in the coronation chair in which rests the Stone of Scone, a flat slab of rock on which the ancient kings of Scotland were crowned. This stone was brought to England in 1296 by Edward I, a symbol of the union of the two countries, though the crown was not actually united until the 1603 accession of James Stuart, and the two parliaments did not unite until 1707. Most, though not all, royal funerals and weddings take place in the abbey, a recent exception being the marriage of Prince Charles and Diana, which was held at the larger St Paul's in order to accommodate more people.

The majestic Gothic buildings of the Houses of Parliament were scaffolded for cleaning, but we were able to distinguish the great face of Big Ben. Many statues stand in the area around Parliament, among them one of Richard Coeur-de-Lion on horseback with sword held aloft, and one of Abraham Lincoln.

From Westminster Bridge, the Thames below was alive with boats of all kinds, its banks crowded with pedestrians, and adjacent streets were choked with traffic with the big red buses standing out among the cars and lorries. Across the river stands London's County Hall, home to the mighty city's bureaucracy. In front of it stands an ominous sign bearing in gigantic figures the number of London's unemployed – 350,557 as of today.

We passed Somerset House where every birth, marriage and death in the country is recorded and then proceeded into the Strand, so-called because it was once a beach on the Thames. We passed King's College, part of the great complex of the University of London, and the Savoy Hotel, where

David and I met once unexpectedly when he was on a short leave from France. We then came to 'legal' London – the Temple and the beautiful Inns of Court set in manicured grounds – and then on to the griffin-manned entrance to the original one-square-mile City of London proper.

Presided over by the Lord Mayor who lives in the eighteenth-century Mansion House, the city is the business and financial centre of London. The buildings of modern enterprise within still follow the dense mediaeval street plan of old. Here is the Bank of England, known as the Old Lady of Threadneedle Street. The bank was founded in 1694 and has been protected by a detachment of guards every night since rioters threatened it in 1780. The city contains 110 churches, 50 of them designed by Christopher Wren to replace those destroyed by the fire of 1666. In their turn many of Wren's churches were destroyed or damaged in the Blitz. One of the city churches held the bells that induced the poor boy Dick Whittington to return to the city after it first rejected him, ringing out their message, 'Turn again, Whittington, thrice Lord Mayor of London'. St Clement's of the nursery rhyme 'Oranges and Lemons' is another of the city's churches. Only a shell remains of St Magnus', the burning of which in 1666 Samuel Pepys so vividly described. St Olave's is another church often mentioned by the diarist. We saw the column marking the spot in Pudding Lane where the fire began. While indeed a disaster, it should be noted the fire did not destroy only the good and beautiful but also killed the lingering germs from the Great Plague of the year before.

We passed the new London Bridge that replaces the old one purchased several years ago by Arizona. We then went up Ludgate Hill for a quick look at St Paul's Cathedral.

We went on to Fleet Street where most of London's newspapers are published, past Dr Johnson's house, and past the Cheshire Cheese, his favourite eating place and still a famous restaurant. We came to Billingsgate, home for many years to London's fishmarket, and then on to the Tower of London. We got a good view of the tremendous fortress and its four-turreted keep. We crossed the Thames at Tower Bridge, the most picturesque of the river's many bridges. It was originally a drawbridge, but big ships no longer come this far upriver because to raise the bridge would throw local street traffic into unthinkable confusion and delay.

Once across the river we passed into the East End, a name synonymous for many years with docks and slums. Heavily bombed in the Blitz, the slums have been largely cleared and replaced with neat but modest housing developments. We were bound for Rotherhithe, once a separate port and seafaring town but now part of the great city complex. In particular we were going to St Mary's Church, a sailors' church of special interest to Americans. Its most famous son is Christopher Jones, master of the

Mayflower, who is buried here along with three of the ship's four owners. Many of the Mayflower crew were from Rotherhithe, and it was from here that the ship sailed to rendezvous with the Pilgrims at Plymouth for the voyage to America. There is a beautiful organ in the church and some woodcarving in the reredos done by Grinling Gibbons. As usual he 'signed' his work with a carving of an open peapod.

The choir singers present grouped and sang 'Come Ye Who Love the Lord' – it has almost become our signature tune – and the rector, a fat jolly man who reminded me of Friar Tuck, played the organ. We then left in a hurry as we were due back at the hotel by 1 p.m.

People were free for the afternoon to shop, explore, see museums, and so on. David and I found once more the old Victorian pub called the Hansom Cab where we had an excellent lunch. Dinner was early and we were at the church in good time for the concert. It went well in spite of the extreme heat. It was our swan song and a beautiful ending to a memorable choral experience.

WEDNESDAY, JULY 13TH

All commitments fulfilled and all planned activities over, we were free to do as we pleased on Wednesday, the group's last full day in England. Many swelled the crowds of shoppers in search of bargains in Harrod's and Selfridge's, while some went on sightseeing tours or visited the art galleries and museums. Those who went to Hampton Court by boat were delayed getting back by an unusually strong tide. Many had theatre or concert plans for the afternoon and evening. Later we were to hear rave reviews of the Royal Shakespeare Company's production of *Much Ado About Nothing*, performed in the new theatre in the Barbican. This area, named for the barbicans, or watchtowers, built into mediaeval city walls, was levelled in the Blitz and has become one of London's most notable redevelopment schemes. It aims to bring citizens back to live in the City by creating a centre of cultural life with theatres, concert halls, museums, art galleries, and the like.

As for ourselves we went to Harrod's – the store that advertises that it has everything any customer requests. Everybody seemed to be there, but everything was not. Airless and packed with people, the shop failed to provide a smocked dress (surely traditionally English!) for my baby granddaughter and a pith helmet for my husband to wear in his garden in the hot North Carolina sun. I thought the latter an indication that the sun over the British Empire has indeed set! David, always a reluctant shopper, was surprisingly patient but mightily relieved to find a cool basement wine bar where we had a good lunch. Later in the day we had tea and dinner with Esther Borkum, a very old friend, a widow of one of David's former business associates. We returned to the hotel in good time to get our packing done.

On Thursday morning the hotel foyer was a bustling place with many tour groups scheduled for early morning departure. We had to keep our luggage separate from the others' since we were going to the airport only to pick up a car for the rest of our stay and not for the flight to the States with the rest of the group. At the airport we said our goodbyes and made promises to write, and we felt some sadness that the trip was over. Our friends were soon swallowed up in the milling crowds of the airport and we were on our own.

Chapter Two

THE SOUTH

'... chalk should somewhere be warmly hymned
and praised by every man who belongs to the
south of England for it is the meaning of good land.'
Hilaire Belloc 1870–1953

This section of my journals mainly describes our travels in Hampshire and Dorset, though on occasion we venture into Berkshire, Oxfordshire and Buckinghamshire. My home county of Wiltshire can be considered part of either the South or the West of England, but because I write so much about it I have given it a section of its own. The southern counties of Surrey, Sussex and Kent I have chosen to consider as part of England's East.

Much of the southland is dominated by chalk, whence come the distinctive white horses and other figures on the barren uplands, or downs as they are generally called. Their wide expanses are broken only by the many beech copses planted by farmers to act as windbreaks. This land was the heart of Saxon Alfred's Wessex, the land of the West Saxons. From early times the area has remained largely agricultural, with sheep on the downs, cattle in the lowlands, and rich arable land in the sheltered valleys formed by crystal clear chalk streams and rifts in the hilly downs. There is still some virgin soil, mainly scrub land, and much woodland, of which the New Forest in Hampshire is the largest expanse.

The South Coast, washed by the waters of the English Channel, is one of the great playgrounds of England. Bournemouth is the hub of the resort area, Southampton the great commercial port, and Portsmouth the site of a very important naval base. Many of the county towns are very beautiful and have long histories. The cathedral town of Winchester is among the finest in England. There are countless villages, many of which boast fine old churches, gracious manor houses, and stories of historical significance. Here in this land are many traces of prehistoric Britain – barrows, cromlechs, stone circles and temples – so that it can, along with the West, be called the very cradle of British civilization.

THE SOUTH AND WEST

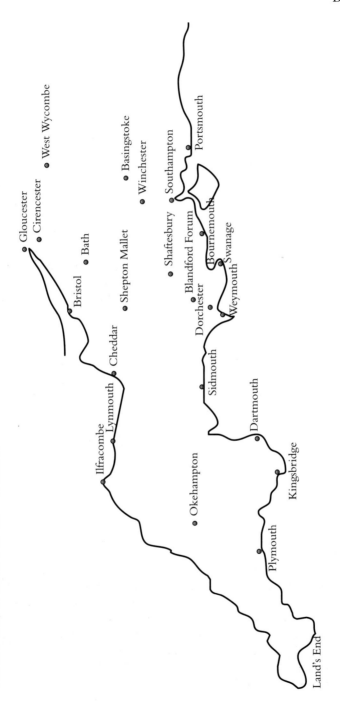

Gloucester
Cirencester
West Wycombe
Basingstoke
Winchester
Southampton
Portsmouth
Bristol
Bath
Shepton Mallet
Shaftesbury
Blandford Forum
Bournemouth
Swanage
Cheddar
Dorchester
Weymouth
Lynmouth
Sidmouth
Ilfracombe
Dartmouth
Kingsbridge
Okehampton
Plymouth
Land's End

1973

with Thomas & Margaret McKnight

THE NEW FOREST – BOURNEMOUTH – THE PORTLAND PENINSULA TO WEYMOUTH AND SOUTHAMPTON – FERRY TO FRANCE

THURSDAY, JULY 19TH

Yesterday was a quiet day with the McKnights in Banbury on business of their own. David and I visited friends and shopped in the vicinity of Marlborough.

Today we had a trip planned and were rather disappointed by heavy morning rain. Nevertheless we set out for our destination Bournemouth, a large resort 54 miles away on the south coast. Bournemouth is the nearest seaside resort to Marlborough, and when I was a child a day trip there with my parents or the Sunday School was a rare treat. It never ceases to amaze me that fifty years ago a trip to Bournemouth or Bath, Salisbury or Stratford, was a big adventure. Today, all these places can be reached from Marlborough easily in an hour or less.

We went across Clench Common to get the lovely view of Pewsey Vale from Martinsell, but it was obscured by rain and mist. We passed through Pewsey where the Salisbury Avon rises and where there is a statue of King Alfred, then through Amesbury and Salisbury, and so through the New Forest to Lymington. This is as lovely an area as any, and, being younger than Savernake, the forest has suffered less from the depredations of time. William the Conqueror developed the once wild area into a hunting preserve that became a favourite retreat for the sport of many future kings. It came to be known as the New Forest, with beautiful glades of beech and oak interspersed with sweeps of moor covered with heather, scrub, and occasional patches of bog. With Winchester at that time the capital of the country, the New Forest was truly the heart of Norman England.

Today yellow broom was in full bloom but the prickly gorse was over and the purple heather not fully out. Wild ponies wandered freely, and we saw them along the roadside and even in the road obstructing traffic. Little towns are tucked away and remain largely unspoiled despite the sightseers they attract. It was raining hard by the time we found a nice little pub where we got a good lunch. Afterwards we went on to Christchurch, once a very important Channel port at the mouth of the Avon. It is the site of a big Norman priory church, and we had a good view of its strong squat tower across the watermeadows.

We were slowed to a snail's pace through Christchurch by heavy coastal traffic but eventually reached Bournemouth. It was cold and windy, but the rain had stopped and the sun began to peep out now and then. Bournemouth is situated on a lovely bay enclosed by steep cliffs known as the Chines, where pine trees grow with many walks winding among them. The town seems sadly changed, however, its gardens somewhat neglected and lots of new buildings cheek by jowl with older, far more attractive ones. Many of the South Coast resorts have suffered economically since cheap air travel takes British vacationers – desperate for sun – to Mediterranean haunts. Bournemouth in the past attracted well-to-do people and was popular with retired high-ranking military personnel, but it is obviously less prosperous and exclusive than it used to be. Tom had been in Bournemouth during the war and he shared my disappointment in the way it has changed. Today, in spite of the weather, a lot of trippers were there. A few brave souls were in the water but most were walking briskly or huddled in deck chairs making the most of the sea air.

We took another route back to Marlborough, going through Romsey. The brief sun had disappeared completely and chilling rain was falling fast. We detoured from the main road to see the Rufus Stone. Set in a beautiful glade of giant trees, it marks the spot where William II, known as Rufus because of his red hair, fell dead from an arrow from the bow of his henchman Sir Walter Tyrell while hunting in the forest. Son of William the Conqueror, he ruled from 1087 to 1100. A harsh tyrannical king, his death was more likely murder than accident, though Tyrell's excuse of a deflected arrow was accepted and he went free. Because of the very heavy rain, we did not stop either at the famous old abbey in Romsey or at Broadlands, the home of Lord Louis Mountbatten. In typically English fashion the sun then came out as we rode down leafy lanes and back roads through Tidworth and the Collingbournes, where Tom had visited a farm family during the war. At last we came to Axford in time for a late supper and a gathering of friends.

MONDAY, JULY 23RD

A maid failed to appear for work at the hotel, the Oxenham Arms in South Zeal, this morning, which made our breakfast and departure later than we had anticipated. The sun was shining in a desultory fashion, and we left South Zeal, just within the Devonshire border, and drove east for Weymouth hoping for good weather. Traffic was moving very slowly, accumulating behind lorries and caravans on the hilly twisting road. As we neared the coast we caught glimpses of the sea between the chalk hills covered in soft green grass. The water was grey rather than blue but smooth as glass. The sun was shining on the red-banded lighthouse at the very tip of the rocky hook-shaped promontory called Portland Bill, and we pulled off the road at a couple of spots to enjoy marvellous views of pebbly Chesil Beach and its lagoon. A curved reef of 16 miles, Chesil Beach (or Bank) is something of a geological phenomenon. Because of the action of storms and prevailing winds and tides, the pebbles of the shingle that carpet the beach get larger towards the eastern part of the bank. It forms a natural seawall enclosing a strip of calm brackish water known as the Fleet. The word 'chesil' comes from the old English word for 'shingle,' and pebbles taken from the bank were used as ammunition by the Iron Age defenders of nearby Maiden Castle.

The narrow rugged Portland peninsula was called the Gibraltar of Wessex by Thomas Hardy. The peninsula is formed of rock that came to be known as Portland stone and has been used in the construction of many of London's important buildings, including St Paul's Cathedral. Today Portland is the site of a naval base and prison, and it is still a centre for stone-quarrying.

The traffic grew very heavy as we approached Weymouth, and I began to despair of ever getting through the town. We dropped Tom and Margaret off in the Esplanade and drove up the steep hill to Portland to see my niece Jenny and her husband Michael. We all drove down into Weymouth after taking some photographs of the views. We had a wild ride down the hill following Michael and then had a long search for a parking place. Finally we met up with the McKnights and all had lunch together. The town was crowded with holidaymakers, for it is one of the most popular resorts on the South Coast. A colourful painted statue of George III – the 'discoverer' of Weymouth who turned it into a well-known seaside resort – stands prominently in the Esplanade, and an equestrian figure of the town's royal patron cut in the chalk hills at Osmington welcomes all comers. In his reign were built the beautiful Georgian buildings that border the Esplanade as it follows the curve of the bay, which is enclosed at each end by impressive white cliffs.

After lunch we went to see a mural of D-Day soldiers embarking for the Normandy beaches from Weymouth, one of many South Coast ports that served as staging points for the invasion. Weymouth was Tom's embarkation point on that dawn of June 6th 1944. As we were about to leave, the Channel Islands ferry came in, for Weymouth is the terminus for this service.

We encountered a massive traffic jam getting out of Weymouth, but once off the main road we made good time through the pretty little towns of Wool, Bere Regis, Wimborne Minster and Ringwood. We had been in this part of the New Forest earlier in the week but it had been raining then.

Today the sun was out and things looked quite different, bright, cheerful and green.

Southampton lies at the head of the Solent, a narrow waterway between the mainland and the Isle of Wight, with the island protecting the town from the rough Channel waters. It is the most important commercial port on the south coast. Its docks are the only ones large enough to accommodate ocean liners such as the Queen Mary and Queen Elizabeth. The town has a very long and distinguished history. Armies sailed from here during the Hundred Years' War and the Napoleonic Wars, and from here expeditions of discovery, commerce and colonization have set forth. The Pilgrim Fathers stopped here en route to Plymouth and America. It was heavily bombed in World War II but has now been largely rebuilt. Famous people born in Southampton include Isaac Watts, poet and hymn writer; artist Sir John Millais; and Lord Jellicoe, a mercantile sea captain's son who became Admiral of the Fleet in World War I and defeated the German fleet at the Battle of Jutland.

We found our way to the Dolphin Hotel. It is very old and one of the few Southampton landmarks to escape the Blitz during the war. It has associations with many celebrities, including Nelson and Thackeray. The rooms are spacious and furnished with fine antiques. We had an excellent dinner and after a brief walk around the hotel environs retired early, ready for embarkation to France tomorrow.

TUESDAY, JULY 24TH

After breakfast David and I turned the car in, having a pleasant early morning ride through the streets of Southampton. We recalled how I had come to meet him here during the war and how he had been unexpectedly shipped off to France. I remember well how shocked I was then at the devastation in the town, which had been battered by intensive bombing over a prolonged period. Now it is rebuilt and revitalized and shows much growth and change since those grim days.

Back at the hotel we packed and went out to change money into francs. Then we went to Holyrood Church, very close to the Dolphin. Built in 1320, the church was burned in the Blitz so that now only a shell remains. What was once the nave has been made into a garden of remembrance – a lovely quiet spot for prayer and contemplation and recollecting the past. A huge anchor stands there, a reminder – if one needs reminding – that Southampton is a great port and that her people are those who 'go down to the sea in ships.' In one corner there is a fountain, subscribed for by widows, orphans, parents and friends of the crew of the Titanic, the 'unsinkable' ship that sailed in 1912 from Southampton on her maiden voyage and met a watery grave in the North Atlantic. We walked down to the Bargate, the great Norman doorway cut in the strongly fortified wall that protected the mediaeval city. The gate and parts of the wall survived the Blitz. Perhaps it was here that Henry V harangued his brave knights and archers before setting sail for France and victory at Agincourt in 1415.

We boarded the ferry for Cherbourg in the early afternoon. The water both in the Solent near the mainland and beyond in the Channel proper was smooth as a millpond. We stood on deck to watch the coast of England recede as we sailed past the Isle of Wight. Although it is summer the day soon became cold and windy, and we were glad to retreat to the warmth of the cabin and dining room. I was reminded of that other time almost 30 years ago when I sailed for a new land and a new life. Then it was February, bitterly cold but calm and sunny, and we G.I. brides stayed on deck till there was nothing left of land to see, our hearts filled with emotion and love for the country we were leaving.

1975

WEYMOUTH AND WINCHESTER

WEDNESDAY, JULY 16TH

We were up early for the two-hour ride to Weymouth. It was the usual pleasant trip through Salisbury, Blandford Forum and Dorchester.

Blandford Forum, as its name suggests, was important in Roman times. Celia Fiennes, the well-born lady who travelled around England on horseback between 1685 and 1704 and kept comprehensive journals of all she saw, called it 'a pretty neate little town.' After fire destroyed the old town in 1731, Blandford was rebuilt by two local architects (with the rather unfortunate name of Bastard and known as the Bastard brothers) in Georgian style reminiscent of Bath. We drove through the centre of the town, its beauty and elegance temporarily diminished by construction of a bypass.

Closer to Dorchester we passed Maiden Castle, one of the most famous, best-preserved, and possibly the largest of England's Iron Age forts. Dorchester is a pleasant old town, known chiefly for its associations with Thomas Hardy, who distilled the essence of the Dorset past into literature. He lived nearby, and the town figures in his novels under the name of Casterbridge. At Dorchester the road to Weymouth veers off to the south, a bottleneck approach to the town at the end of the peninsula. There was little traffic, and, as the road descended through the steep chalk hills to the bay, we were struck by the beauty all around us.

We found Rachel's house without difficulty and then drove to Portland for my other niece Jenny. We went for lunch to a restaurant called the Pennsylvania Castle, a castellated house built of stone quarried nearby. The house perches on cliffs overlooking Portland Bay, and we sat on a terrace above the garden with the sea beyond blue and sparkling in the sunshine. We then drove the girls back to their respective homes and set out for Winchester.

We went through the beautiful country of Dorset and Hampshire, stopping briefly at Bere Regis and remembering its associations with *Tess of the D'Urbervilles*. Hardy buried his heroine here in the ancestral church of the Norman family of the D'Urbervilles. At Wimborne Minster we saw the tower of the great church and then went through the green glades of the New Forest to Romsey, where there is an important abbey. Unfortunately we had no time for more than a passing glance at these treasures.

We arrived in Winchester at the 5.30 rush hour, and it is a very crowded and confusing town for an American newcomer to drive in. Eventually we found the Royal Hotel, where we had a reservation. After dinner we took a stroll around the cathedral close and in the evening dusk the huge grey church with its square Norman tower looked very impressive.

THURSDAY, JULY 17TH

Winchester is full of history. Important in Roman times, it grew to be the capital of Saxon England and vied with London for that position even after the Normans came. It lost much of its importance when England lost her possessions in France after the Hundred Years' War. Its location just north of Southampton, the port for France, was strategic only as long as England ruled Normandy and Aquitaine. Even after London became the capital, Winchester was often the meeting place for Parliament when kings hunted in the New Forest, and Henry VII's oldest son Arthur was christened in the cathedral.

The city is built on the River Itchen, a crystal clear stream that winds its way through the city. The river is famous for its trout fishing and was one of Izaak Walton's favourite fishing streams. The oldest public school in England, named Winchester after the town, is here. It was founded by William of Wykeham in 1382, who gave it its motto 'Manners Makyth Man.' There is an impressive statue of King Alfred in the main street of Broadway. It was Alfred's capital, as it was of the Danish king Canute who ruled England from 1016 to 1035. Many of the King Arthur legends are connected with Winchester, and in the castle hall hangs a representation of the Round Table of his knights.

On the street we saw several elderly men in ruffed caps and flowing gowns. There are ancient almshouses here known as the Hospital of St Cross, and the men clad so strangely are pensioners there. Everyday at the hospital a 'Wayfarer's Dole' of bread and ale is given to visitors who request it. We had neither the time nor the inclination to sample the fare, but I was reminded that Winchester was an important stop for pilgrims from the continent who came to worship at the shrine of St Swithin on their way to Canterbury.

The cathedral at Winchester is one of the largest in England and its nave is the longest. Its Norman origins are evident in the strong squat tower. Many famous people are buried here, among them King Canute, Izaak Walton and Jane Austen. We spent an hour or so in the cathedral and the close, which is very green and beautiful and ringed by houses where the clergy dwell. There are seven chapels in the cathedral, mediaeval wall paintings, fine stained glass, a black marble font, and the library contains a copy of Bede's *Ecclesiastical History*.

1976

ROMAN REMAINS AT SILCHESTER – THE VYNE – WEYMOUTH

SATURDAY, JULY 10TH

We left Marlborough early for Basingstoke in Hampshire, our ultimate objective a National Trust house called the Vyne. We chose a circuitous route through Highclere and Silchester. The day was warm and sunny, and I settled down to enjoy the ride through 'my' part of England. We viewed Highclere Castle from a distance as it was not open to the public. It is the seat of the Earls of Carnarvon, an old fortress rebuilt in 1842 to plans drawn up by Sir Charles Barry, the architect of the Houses of Parliament. On the summit of a high hill just outside the village is the grave of the fifth and most famous earl, an archaeologist and Egyptologist who in 1922 and '23 excavated the tomb of Tutankhamen – 'King Tut' – and sent its treasures to the British Museum in London. While the work in Egypt was still in progress he died under mysterious circumstances, giving rise to the belief that Tutankhamen's curse would fall upon anyone who disturbed the ancient king's grave. As a child I heard much of this story from my Aunt Nellie, who once worked as a housemaid in the castle.

We did not linger in Highclere but drove on to Silchester, travelling for some miles along the Portway, the Roman road connecting Sarum (Salisbury) and Calleva Atrebatum (Silchester), a very important Roman encampment. Silchester had been a tribal centre before the Claudian conquest began in AD 43. Under the Romans it developed into a military station. There has been a complete excavation of the site, revealing traces of the defences and the outline of an amphitheatre. The great wall is the most striking evidence, however. It extends for some two miles, with a later mediaeval church built inside and adjoining it. We went in the church, where the organist was playing. The music hovered in the summer air mingling with the scent of flowers newly arranged on the altar in preparation for tomorrow's services. We stopped briefly in the fine museum, unable to take in more than a tiny fraction of all that is displayed, for like most Americans we are in a hurry and time is short.

Before driving on to Aldermaston we had lunch in a nice pub called the Butt. Aldermaston used to be a sleepy village in the watermeadows of the Kennet, its most exciting product watercress. Now, however, it is the site of a very important and top-secret nuclear research station. It seemed as if we drove for miles past its fenced and heavily guarded boundaries.

We avoided Basingstoke, an old market town growing by leaps and bounds under the press of industrialization, coming at last to the very imposing Tudor manor house located just outside the tiny village of Sherborne St John and known as the Vyne. In all its long history this mansion has been in the possession of only two families, the Sandyses and the Chutes. It was built in the sixteenth century on the banks of a clear-flowing river for a Lord Sandys, who for a brief time was chancellor to Henry VIII. Its construction is of warm diapered brick in the Tudor style. A handsome Greek portico was added to the house later. One enters an unusual and imposing stone gallery, above which is a corresponding one of wood panelled in oak carved in the linenfold pattern. This latter gallery is considered to be one of the finest to be found anywhere. A Palladian staircase, designed by one of the Chute family, leads to the upper floor. A small sitting room is known as the Print Room, because it is papered in eighteenth-century prints. Though a favourite haunt of the owner, it is always open to the public because it is so unusual. The chairs are mostly covered in needlepoint of rare design, and I learned that it was done by several ladies of the house as well as the present owner, a man who includes needlework among his hobbies. The house has its own private chapel, a lovely peaceful sanctuary. Because of the drought the lawns and gardens were not at their best, though some of the herbaceous borders were managing to bloom. The lawns sloped down to the river where many ducks were swimming and eagerly snapping up any titbits thrown to them. Tea was being served in an outbuilding which had once been a brewery, and we sat outside and enjoyed tea and cakes in the sunshine.

SUNDAY, JULY 11TH

Just a week from the Bicentennial celebrations back home when we sang the Moravian Psalm of Joy in Ridgewood.

We had a day trip planned to Weymouth to see my niece Rachel and her fiance. I had some reservations about going there on a summer Sunday, because it is a popular seaside resort at the end of a peninsula that acts as a bottleneck to traffic. My fears were ungrounded, however, and we had an easy run through the beautiful countryside of southern Wiltshire and Dorset. The weather was sunny, and though the hills were less green than usual, the sea was blue and sparkling. We found our niece and her fiance, whom we met for the first time, well and happy and eagerly looking forward to their forthcoming wedding. I sensed her disappointment that we would not be there, and I am sorry too for I am her only older relative.

Surprisingly Weymouth was not crowded. We had lunch in a fine restaurant in Portland from which we got a view of the curve of pebbly Chesil Beach and westward to the Purbeck Hills. An old lighthouse looks out to sea, though it is no longer needed to warn ships of coastal hazards.

1977

THE AUSTEN AND WHITE HOMES IN HAMPSHIRE – WEYMOUTH AND WEST TO KINGSBRIDGE IN DEVON

TUESDAY, OCTOBER 4TH

We slept late and spent the rest of the morning shopping in Marlborough's wide High Street, something I always enjoy doing. After lunch we set off for Chawton in Hampshire, home of Jane Austen for many years. We then planned to go on to Selborne to see the home of the famous naturalist and journal writer Gilbert White.

Our route took us through Andover and Basingstoke, both busy market towns with the latter showing further signs of industrial growth since I last passed through two years ago. The weather, as so often in England, was unsettled, with alternating clouds and sunshine interspersed with heavy but mercifully short rainstorms. Two of these were followed by bright rainbows, with the implied promise of better weather ahead.

We meandered down leafy Hampshire lanes in search of the tiny village of Chawton. Our perseverance was rewarded when we arrived at the rather commodious red brick farmhouse where Jane Austen took up residence in 1809 and remained almost until her death in 1817. Born in Steventon, a Hampshire village where her father was the rector, Austen moved several times during her life and spent some months in Bath before moving to Chawton. At Chawton she wrote her most famous novels, including *Pride and Prejudice, Persuasion, Emma*, and *Mansfield Park*. A few weeks before her death, she went again to Winchester, possibly for medical treatment, and died there at the age of 41 of Bright's disease.

The house at Chawton is now a museum, preserved and restored to its appearance during Austen's lifetime. Many of her personal belongings are here, and the house reflects the personality of this rare genius. Austen's inspiration for her quiet books about rural England and the spa town of Bath came from the daily lives of the inhabitants of these settings, and the characters in her books are drawn from the people of the places where she lived. Though a spinster, she had a busy family life, the centre of which was the parlour. Like the majority of women writers of her day, her writing was done secretly and was secondary to her domestic responsibilities. The parlour door at Chawton was said to creak, warning her to hide her manuscript when family members came into the room. The visit here reminded me of how much as a student I enjoyed her novels – even as required texts at both school and college, they were nothing but a pleasure to read.

Leaving Chawton for Selborne, we drove a few miles in a southeasterly direction down deep sunken Hampshire roads and came to the home of Gilbert White, village rector, philosopher, naturalist, and journal keeper. He was born in Selborne in 1720, the oldest son of a family of small landowners. He went to school in Basingstoke and came under the tutelage of the Reverend Thomas Warton, a fine scholar and father of two distinguished sons, one who became Master of Winchester School and the other a poet and professor at Oxford. White himself went on to Oxford, where he took Holy Orders. He then returned to serve in his native region, first as curate in a neighbouring village and later as rector of Selborne. He stayed at Selborne the rest of his long life, spending most of his time in the study of nature. He recorded his observations faithfully in comprehensive journals of literary excellence about all that took place in the world around him, interlarding his observations with philosophical comment. We are told that he lived 'tranquil and serene with scarcely any other vicissitudes than those of the seasons.' He was however somewhat neglectful of his parish duties, and his preoccupation with nature was at times misunderstood and resented by the villagers. When he died his only eulogy came from a parishioner – 'he was a still quiet body and there wasn't a bit of harm in him, there wasn't indeed.'

Though he had no thought of a book when he was writing his journals – perhaps much of their charm and freshness is due to this fact – they did eventually become *The Natural History of Selborne*, published in 1789. It has been described as the best book of natural history in the language and was praised alike by Charles Darwin, Thomas Carlyle, and James Russell Lowell.

Coming into the village we stopped first at the village green, called, for reasons unknown to me, the Plestor. Hard by is the church, a fine old edifice, where we saw a memorial window given in honour of White. It shows St Francis surrounded by the wildlife of the Hampshire countryside against a background not of Assisi but of a village that looks remarkably like Selborne. White's grave is in the churchyard, and growing nearby is a tremendous yew tree – quite the largest I have ever seen. Its trunk is surrounded by a seat from which we enjoyed the view of the long village street, parts of it lined with pollarded lime trees. The October sun was warm, and in the distance we could see the Hanger just tinged with the first colours of autumn. The Hanger is a beech wood growing on a hill of chalk. It was one of White's favourite haunts, and we are told it is bisected by a zigzag path cut by White and his brothers. It is best described in White's own words:

> The high path to the south west consists of a
> vast hill of chalk rising 300 ft. above the valley
> and is divided into a sheep down, the high wood
> and a long hanging wood called the Hanger. The
> covert of this eminence is altogether beech, the
> most lovely of all forest trees. The down or sheep
> walk is a pleasing park like spot commanding a very
> engaging view. At the foot of this hill lies the
> village which consists of one long straggling street.

We walked up the 'long straggling street' to the Wakes, the house where White lived. It is a gracious house set in a garden of green lawn and herbaceous borders and is now a museum open to the public. The rooms are filled with antiques, several of heavily inlaid Dutch design that glow with the patina of age and constant care. The windows look out on to the garden, and French doors permit access to the grounds. White's books and other memorabilia are on display. Upstairs the rooms are devoted not to White but to Captain Oates, a member of Scott's ill-fated 1912 South Pole expedition. Thus the museum memorializes two men, one who earned undying fame in the native village that he never left, and another who died a hero's death vainly trying to save his companions in the farthest reaches of the earth.

MONDAY, OCTOBER 10TH

It is always fun to go to Weymouth, for it brings back pleasant memories of Sunday School day trips by coach to that beach resort on the Dorset coast. Now my newly married niece lives there, and it is a change of pace for us to be visiting young people. We got there very quickly.

We left Marlborough about 10 a.m. with some sadness, as I always wonder if this will be our last visit. The weather was sunny and bright and the drive was pleasant. We skirted the towns of Salisbury, Blandford and Dorchester before heading south down the main and virtually only road to Weymouth, the town built on a promontory of land sticking out into the Channel. We found Rachel's house and met her husband Barry, as well as a large collie named Sabrina and a very tiny and playful tabby kitten. Rachel had a good lunch waiting for us, and afterwards we took a walk along the front and up to the Promenade Gardens. At this time of year they are planted with a marvellous show of full-blooming dahlias of all varieties and colours.

Later we had tea and then went out to dinner at a very nice restaurant. It seemed a day of nonstop eating. We had a lot to talk about – family, old friends and of course their wedding. From the restaurant we watched a ferry boat from the Channel Islands come in and unload at their Weymouth terminus. Returning home, we noticed it had become very cold. We missed the central heating we have become accustomed to but slept well all the same.

TUESDAY, OCTOBER 11TH

We were up early and after a good breakfast said goodbye to Rachel and Barry and were on our way to Devonshire. We went west along the coast road, the scenery magnificent on a bright sunny morning. We detoured at Portisham to drive to the high spot on the downs where Hardy's monument is located. The tall granite column is not a memorial to the poet and novelist Hardy, as most people think, but to Admiral Hardy, a Dorset man from a prominent Weymouth family who was Nelson's second-in-command at Trafalgar. It was in his arms that Nelson died with the enigmatic words, 'Kiss me, Hardy', on his lips. The view from this high spot was magnificent and extended to the sea, but the gale-like winds forced us to enjoy it only from the car. The wild heathland was covered in gorse in yellow bloom, which surprised me as I thought the gorse only flowered in May.

We drove next to Abbotsbury, a village of stone and thatch famous for a swannery established by Benedictine monks in the fifteenth century as a source of birds for their table. The monks also built the large tithe barn, which has an unusual thatched roof that is remarkably well preserved. The village is built at the edge of the salt water lake protected by the Chesil Bank and known as the Fleet. It is here that the swans nest and breed. The swannery was closed, but we could see some of the large white birds swimming on the water among the reeds. Nearby are ruins of an old chapel dedicated to St Catherine, patron saint of spinsters.

Outside of Abbotsbury we stopped to climb a hill and take pictures of the view below of the coast, Chesil Beach and the Channel itself, its bright blue waves foam-tipped and choppy. On the opposite side of the road we watched the energetic antics of a sheepdog as he rounded up and drove away a flock of sheep, the shepherd standing idly by leaning on his crook and puffing meditatively on his pipe. We then stopped at a wayside inn called the Three Horseshoes for lunch. In spite of its unprepossessing appearance, the little hostelry served an excellent ploughman's lunch, and David enjoyed a pint of the local brew.

After lunch we left the main road to go to Sidmouth, a very attractive seaside resort with many Regency and early Victorian buildings and a favourite spot for well-to-do retirees. In 1819 the Duke and Duchess of Kent stayed here with their infant daughter Princess Victoria. The town is built around a beautiful bay ringed with cliffs, red-gold in colour as this is no longer chalk country. We explored the very fine gardens and took pictures of the dahlias, fuchsia and Michaelmas daisies that were flowering in profusion. It was hilly, cold and windy, however, and we were soon on our way again.

Our destination was Kingsbridge, an old market town that stands at the head of a tidal estuary. We had made a reservation from the States at an old inn called the King's Arms but found it, and the town, disappointing. The town seemed depressed and unkempt, while the inn did not live up to the glowing account we had been given of it. We took our room nonetheless and went for a walk up the hilly main street. Everything seemed closed up for the winter, and all we could find was a cup of coffee at the local bus stop! We saw the very old church and in front of it a row of recently restored mediaeval houses called the Shambles. The town rises up from the estuary in a series of hills and terraces in a rather attractive fashion, but the water of the river looked dirty with only a few swans and ducks swimming in it. We returned to the hotel rather dejected and had a drink in the depressing Long Bar. Then a mediocre meal in the dining room and to bed in a large fourposter, the mattress of which had a tendency to sag towards the middle.

1982

A DAY IN WEYMOUTH – THROUGH DORSET TO TOLPUDDLE

TUESDAY, MAY 18TH

Yesterday we left Devizes and drove to Weymouth, a leisurely trip with brief stops in Blandford and Dorchester. We came to visit my nieces Rachel and Jenny. Rachel lives in Weymouth, while Jenny came from her home in

Portland to see us. Both are married, Rachel for the second time, with a little girl named Sharon.

Rachel brought us tea about eight, and we saw it was a bright sunny morning. Shortly after breakfast Jenny and her husband Michael arrived, and we set out for a day of sightseeing. First we took a walk along the waterfront paralleled by the Esplanade. The air was cool but the sun warm, and the sea was calm and very blue. The grey symmetry of the houses was brightened by many coloured flowers blooming in window boxes, hanging baskets, and in pots set out on stoops. Leaving the seaside we crossed the Esplanade to a shopping mall where we got coffee and ice cream and went to a bank. We then drove out to a popular pub called the Elm Tree for lunch. It was a delightful place serving excellent food, and we ate in the garden. The 'Englishness' of the setting was complete when we had to beat a hasty retreat to the car because of a sharp and very sudden shower. It was fortunately brief, and in a few moments the sun was shining as brightly as ever.

We stopped briefly in a pretty village called Portisham where we walked up the village street and, to Sharon's delight, came upon a motley flock of ducks and ducklings swimming in the clear water of a spring head. The street was lined with blossoming trees and shrubs growing in the cottage gardens. One huge lilac tree which had just been trimmed had scattered its purple flowers over the street making a carpet for our feet. In one of the gardens we saw hutches containing rabbits, some with babies, and Sharon liked these too. Leaving Portisham we drove up to Hardy's monument. On the way up we passed acres of bluebells growing through what appeared to be stubble. Less attractive than when they grow in deep woods, they were nevertheless quite spectacular. The hilltop affords a great sweeping view of the area. We all then returned to Rachel's house and went out to dinner at a very fine restaurant on the Esplanade.

WEDNESDAY, MAY 19TH

We were up and away from Weymouth by 10 a.m. for our return to Marlborough, hoping to stop on the way at Wilton House later in the day. The weather was quite warm, though it was cloudy with intermittent sprinkles through which a watery sun now and then appeared. We had been given directions to a famous drive in the Puddletown Woods in Dorset known as the Rhododendron Mile. Unfortunately the huge shrubs with their shiny evergreen leaves were not in full bloom, though some were showing signs of the glorious pink, white, purple and red blossoms to come. We entered the 'mile' through a beech copse, the huge grey-trunked trees in full leaf of pale spring green with soft emerald grass around their bases. It was dim and hushed as in a cathedral.

We detoured a few miles to the fertile valley of the Piddle to see Tolpuddle, a small village which would have remained in obscurity except for dramatic events in the 1830s. For a few brief weeks in 1830, villages in southern and eastern England were ablaze with farmworker riots – fearful events graphically described by Mary Mitford in *Our Village*. Labourers were protesting against poor wages, bad living conditions and the introduction of machinery they feared would make them redundant. On December 9th 1833 a group of six Dorset men led by a Methodist lay preacher named George Loveless met in Tolpuddle to establish a trade union as a vehicle for voicing complaints peacefully. The organizers wanted to link labourers in the surrounding area's villages to prevent their already low wages from being cut further. The six were arrested, charged as a 'secret society,' tried, and, in spite of an impassioned yet dignified plea from Loveless, sentenced to seven years' transportation to Australia. All over the country a massive outcry arose at the injustice, and within two years the men were pardoned and returned to England. They have since become known as the Tolpuddle Martyrs.

The huge sycamore tree under which the men met still stands on the village green, its limbs propped up against advancing age. Nearby is a memorial given by the National Trust to mark the centenary of their action. The village hosts a trade union march every year to remember them, though, as deeply religious men, they had no wish to be glorified as heroes or martyrs. Some of them emigrated to Canada to escape the glare of publicity.

We made a brief stop in Blandford Forum, then left the main road to look for a pub for lunch before pressing on for Wiltshire. We found one in a tiny remote village called Swallowcliffe. Here we sat in the bar of the Royal Oak and enjoyed a ploughman's lunch of bread, local 'blue vinny' cheese, pickled onions, beer and cider. Our highly polished table had a slight cant to it so that our glasses slid toward us, and we had to watch them carefully. Our fellow diners were village locals, and we tried to decipher their broad accents as they joked with each other and teased the buxom barmaid.

1983

THE HARDY COUNTRY OF DORSET

(ONE DAY IN LATE JULY)

[After the choir trip of 1983 was over, we spent some additional time in Marlborough. We had a lovely 10 days visiting friends and relatives, using the Castle and Ball as our headquarters for seeing friends and attending to business connected with the publication of my book. We made one long trip to Westmorland to seek out some information about Wharton family roots and one trip to Weymouth. Worn out with writing I did not keep a regular journal but could not resist making notes that I put into narrative form after we got back home.]

One day en route to Weymouth to visit my niece, we stopped for several hours in the Hardy country of Dorset, reminding us both of a bus tour of the area we had taken in 1945 while David was on leave from France. In this corner of Dorset, not many miles from Dorchester, there is a cluster of three tiny hamlets – Stinsford and Upper and Lower Bockhampton – known collectively in Hardy's poems and novels as Mellstock. The cottage in which Hardy was born in 1840 is in Upper Bockhampton. A sickly child, he grew up here in the cottage built by his great-grandfather. His family were local masons and builders and had become relatively prosperous, so the house was enlarged and improved over the years. Heavily thatched, the long low building only one room deep is built in front of deep woods.

In one of his earliest poems Hardy described the family cottage:

> It faces west and round the back and sides
> High beeches, bending, hang a veil of boughs,
> And sweep against the roof. Wild honeysucks
> Climb on the walls, and seem to sprout a wish
> (If we may fancy wish of trees and plants)
> To overtop the apple trees hard by.

And his grandmother, from whom he may have inherited his talent, had earlier described it when she went there as a young bride:

> In days by gone –
> . . . Our house stood quite alone, and those tall firs
> And beeches were not planted. Snakes and efts
> Swarmed in the summer days and nightly bats
> Would fly about our bedrooms. Heathcroppers
> Lived on the hills and were our only friends;
> So wild it was when first we settled there.

It was hard to reconcile this description with the lovely thatched cottage approached by paths winding through flower beds brimming with the old-fashioned blossoms of country gardens. We could see and smell lavender, mignonette, pinks and stocks, while wild roses, syringa and honeysuckle clustered around the door and climbed the walls and windowsills. The whole garden was alive with bees humming busily as they collected pollen and nectar.

Hard by the cottage however is the desolate moorland known in his books as Egdon Heath. The wild heathland is never far away in Hardy's writing, and of the 'majestic, watchful, haggard' Egdon Heath he wrote:

Heath and furze
Are everything that seems to thrive
Upon the uneven ground. A stunted thorn
Stands here and there, indeed; and from a pit
An oak uprises, springing from a seed
Dropped by a bird a hundred years ago.

This is the locale of the tragic *Return of the Native*, and it is where in another book the mayor of Casterbridge dies a broken man.

In 1912 the Hardy family left the cottage in Upper Bockhampton and moved closer to Dorchester, where in his latter years Hardy built himself a dour, forbidding house called Max Gate. In Dorchester's main street there is a fine statue of Hardy in a seated pose looking towards the countryside where he grew up.

Just down the road from Upper Bockhampton we came to Stinsford and St Michael's Church in the valley of the Frome. When Hardy was a boy there was a musicians gallery in the church, though today it has been removed and replaced by an organ. Hardy himself had a plaque placed in the church in memory of his father and uncles who performed as string players in the choir. His mother and father are said to have fallen in love as she in the congregation watched him play fiddle in the gallery, a romance Hardy described in a sonnet in which he calls his father a 'minstrel ardent, young and trim.'

In the churchyard members of the Hardy family are buried in a neat row. Only the heart of writer Thomas is here, however, for his ashes are interred in Westminster Abbey in the company of other literary greats. Nearby is the grave of the noted poet C. Day Lewis, who was such an admirer of Hardy that he elected to lie forever beside his hero's heart. Yet another famous man is buried here as well, though he is unconnected with the Hardy family. T. E. Lawrence – Lawrence of Arabia – in his later years lived nearby at Cloud's Hill under the name T. E. Shaw and was buried here in 1935 after his fatal motorcycle accident.

We drove on to Weymouth to the seafront hotel kept by my niece Rachel and her husband. Here we met up also with Dick and Emily Aumiller who had been on the choir tour with us. They too had spent some time exploring the Hardy country. Rachel provided us with an old-fashioned English tea, and we admired her two little girls, the youngest only a few weeks old. Very tiny and blond, she looked like a little doll.

1985

WYKE IN DORSET – WEST ALONG THE COAST:
SWANAGE, CORFE, WEYMOUTH, LYME REGIS,
SIDMOUTH – NEWBURY IN BERKSHIRE

SUNDAY, APRIL 28TH

After lunch we drove to Wyke in Dorset, going through Devizes, Warminster, Trowbridge and Mere. Crossing the county border into Dorset, we arrived at a nearby town called Gillingham where we asked directions to Wyke. Gillingham, at one time a rather nice old town, seems now to have become a centre for tourists and caravanners, so that on a Saturday afternoon it was very crowded. There are some fine Georgian houses here and an old silk mill that John Constable delighted in painting. The surrounding countryside, much praised by the great artist, is very beautiful.

We reached Wyke shortly and found our way to my cousin Victor Sharpe's house without difficulty. Victor lived for many years in Canada, first in Montreal and later in Vancouver, where he made something of a name for himself as a watercolourist. Having long wanted to retire in England, he was shocked at the price of property in the South and was disappointed at having to buy in Dorset instead of Wiltshire, from whence both his parents hailed and which he would have preferred. We too are surprised at the high cost of even modest housing in and around Marlborough and other choice locations in the South. We understand that houses are much cheaper in the Midlands and the North, reflecting the economic imbalances among regions.

Wyke is a rather unprepossessing village, home to a large brewery that gives off a distinctive odour. But Vic's house is quite large, and he has been able to set up a fine studio. He also has a big and pleasing garden. We had a delightful evening, a very good dinner and lots of talk before we left for the rather long ride back to Marlborough along unfamiliar country roads.

FRIDAY, MAY 3RD

Leaving Ipswich after a very large breakfast we took to the road. My cold had considerably worsened, which somewhat blunted my pleasure in the beautiful countryside we passed leaving Tunbridge Wells. We went from Kent to Surrey to Sussex and Hampshire. Many of the roads were wooded, and those close to the bigger towns were lined with affluent-appearing houses. We saw some fine rhododendron in full bloom in all shades from palest pink to deep purple, and many gardens had fine displays of daffodils, narcissus and tulips. In uninhabited stretches of the road we saw primroses, cowslips and lavender cuckoo flowers growing along the banks and hedgerows.

We drove around Petworth, where the old buildings of the town huddle right up to the grey walls of Petworth House, the lovely eighteenth-century mansion built by a duke of Somerset. We were disappointed that it was not open to the public, but with time being short perhaps it was just as well. The house is famous for its art collection, particularly its Turners. One of Turner's most famous paintings is a view of Petworth from across its lake. We did get a passing glimpse of the house and saw a herd of deer grazing in the grounds around it.

We then came to Cowdray Park, a lovely area of grass and trees surrounding the ruins of an old Tudor mansion. The property was once owned by a titled family named Browne, who were said to be cursed by a monk's prophesy that the family would suffer through fire and water. The mansion was burned down in 1793, and in the same year the 8th viscount was drowned. Near the gaunt and spectral ruins there is a large field where important polo matches are held, with the ruins an impressive backdrop for the games. Nearby is Midhurst, a quaint little town of oak-beamed, stucco-fronted Tudor houses with overhanging upper storeys. It has an old grammar school where H. G. Wells was once a pupil. The small town was represented in Parliament by two other famous men – the opponent of slavery Charles James Fox, who was elected in 1768 and kept his seat till his death in 1806, and Sir William Hamilton, husband of Lord Nelson's notorious mistress Emma. We stopped in the town and took a short walk up the main street to make a few purchases at a Boots and cash a cheque at a bank.

Driving on we got on a heavily travelled motorway around Southampton and then went through part of the New Forest, stopping at Lyndhurst for a most enjoyable pub lunch. Our next stop was Lymington, now vastly changed from the quiet little seaside town it used to be. In mediaeval times it had some importance as a port, at one time rivalling Southampton. It also produced most of the country's salt until much larger deposits were found in Cheshire.

We went through the New Forest from Lyndhurst to Lymington, an area of verdant woodland interspersed with wild sandy heath covered with yellow gorse and purple heather. Wild ponies roam at will over the heath. As one nears the ocean the air has a fresh salty tang. The ride brought back my adolescent love affair with Arthur Conan Doyle's historical novels *Sir Nigel* and *The White Company*, in which the forest is home to the archers and men-at-arms whose exploits fill the pages.

Leaving the commercial area of Lymington we went on to the car ferry at Sandbanks to cross to the Isle of Purbeck and the little town of Swanage. The ferry, sort of an engineering anachronism, saved us many miles, and arriving at Swanage we found our bed and breakfast accommodation with no trouble. It was in an old Victorian house, a type that abounds here, and though our room was small it was comfortable and well-appointed.

Swanage is a small town. Originally Saxon, it developed a reputation in Victorian days as a quiet seaside resort set among beautiful cliffs. We once stayed here at the Grosvenor Hotel on a brief leave during the war. I remembered little about it except for the spectacular view across the bay. We decided to have dinner there, and it was a fine choice – good food, memories and still the view as twilight deepened into dusk. It was still light enough after dinner to take the short walk on the cliffs going down to the Coast Guard Station. We then rode out to Durston and its recently developed country park, promising ourselves to return in the morning before going on to Weymouth.

SATURDAY, MAY 4TH

We woke to a sunny morning and stopped in the town for postcards, stamps and Kleenex, which I use at an incredible rate because of my persistent dripping cold. We saw the Town Hall, its facade designed by Christopher Wren. We drove up to Durston Castle, a Victorian version of a mediaeval castle built by a wealthy tycoon. We walked around the grounds and went down the cliff walk to where a great stone globe and a plaque listing much geographical trivia overlooks the sea. We spent a few moments at the information centre at the park, finding a lot of interesting facts about the local flora, fauna and geology. There were several groups of Boy Scouts and Cub Scouts in the centre being instructed by their leaders.

We left for Corfe Castle about 11 o'clock in bright sunshine, though a keen wind offset the sun's warmth. In the south of Dorset near the old port of Wareham, Corfe is one of the most spectacular ruins anywhere in England, and its state of ruin and history of murder, cruelty, blood and siege heighten its menacing aspect. It stands on a great hill guarding the road to the coast at a gap in the Purbeck Hills. The ruins stand atop the eminence silhouetted against the sky, frowning down upon the pretty little village huddled at its base.

Today we unfortunately were unable to enter the castle, but its history is well worth recounting. Strategic use of the site predates the Norman Conquest. It was first fortified during a time of constant wars and insurrections between rival Saxon warlords and between the Saxons and their common enemy the Danes. In AD 876 Wareham was seized and occupied by the Danes, but the invaders were repelled at Corfe and driven back to Wareham. Subsequently their fleet was destroyed at Swanage.

Corfe was a favourite residence and hunting lodge of the Saxon kings who succeeded Alfred the Great. The castle was enlarged and greatly strengthened by King Edgar who died an early death. Edgar left Corfe to his second wife Elfrida, but the throne went to Edward, son of his first wife. Edward, a devout Christian, promised to be a strong king, but Elfrida had coveted the throne for her son Ethelred. On March 18th, AD 978, in the fourth year of his brief reign, Edward went to Corfe to hunt and visit his stepmother and half brother. Elfrida met him at the gate with a chalice of wine in the classic gesture of welcome, but as he raised the stirrup cup to his lips one of Elfrida's henchmen stabbed him to the heart. In his mortal agony the king spurred his horse and falling from the saddle was dragged to the gate where he died. His body was hidden in a well but was later removed to the religious house at Wareham and taken eventually to Shaftesbury Abbey for burial.

Edward was canonized by the Pope and was henceforth known as St Edward the Martyr. Many legends and myths grew up around him. One tells that the body was hidden in a room in the house of a blind woman before being thrown into the well. At midnight the room was filled with a heavenly radiance and sight was restored to the woman. Another legend says that the body was discovered in the well when a ray of celestial light pointed to it and that ever afterwards the water possessed healing properties. The well became known as St Edward's Fountain. Yet another tells that when Elfrida set out to ride in the sad procession from Wareham to Shaftesbury, her horse refused to move. She changed mounts several times, always with the same result.

Edward was followed on the throne by Elfrida's son Ethelred. Known as the Redeless or Unready, he turned out to be the weakest and most foolish of all the Saxon kings. During his reign most of the areas of England that Alfred had freed from the Danes returned to their control. Perhaps it was a case of divine retribution for the sins of his mother.

The Normans quickly recognized the importance of Corfe and strengthened and enlarged the castle, so that some of the ruins we see today are of Norman origin. In the civil war lasting from 1135 to 1154 between Stephen and Matilda, nephew and daughter of Henry I, Corfe was held throughout by Matilda in spite of frequent attacks by Stephen's forces. It later became a favourite hunting spot for King John. In 1326 the weak and debauched Edward II was imprisoned in the castle by his wife Isabella, called the 'she-wolf of France' by the poet Gray. He was later transferred to Berkeley in Gloucestershire, where he was murdered.

Corfe remained in the Royal Family until Queen Elizabeth I sold it to

Sir Christopher Hatton who in turn sold it to Sir John Banks in 1635. Sir John was a supporter of Charles I, and when the Civil War broke out he spent most of his time in London with his monarch. The castle was left in the capable hands of Lady Banks and was besieged for 13 weeks before being relieved by the Royalists, who spent much time and money to fortify it further. It was subjected to a later siege that went on for many weeks until at last Lady Banks and her family surrendered and were given safe conduct by Cromwell's troops. Sir John died in London during the siege, but Lady Banks lived to see the Restoration. Under orders from Cromwell that the castle be destroyed, the great fortress was reduced to a pitiable ruin, and the Banks family made their home in another of their houses. The castle nonetheless has remained in the family to this day. Much restoration has been carried out to bring the spectacular ruins the appearance they have today.

Today we arrived shortly before lunch and after browsing around the National Trust shop – as usual full of fascinating merchandise – we went into a tiny pub called the Fox for lunch. The inn was crowded with sightseers and trippers, but we were able to find a place in the walled garden where in the shade of an apple tree we enjoyed the sunshine and our food sheltered from the wind. After lunch ominous clouds arose to block out the sun and the wind grew fiercer and much colder. We reluctantly decided against attempting the steep rough climb to the castle in view of my cold and the deteriorating weather. I was here once as a child but felt David missed a rare experience and a spectacular view both landward and seaward.

So instead we left for Weymouth, making a stop at the old town of Wareham, an important port in mediaeval times at the mouth of the Frome and Piddle rivers. It is also the site of a priory and famed religious house. We detoured to see Creech Grange, a beautiful house set in magnificent wooded grounds but found it closed. Climbing a very steep hill we entered an area that is given over to military manoeuvres and so is not often open to the public. We drove into a village named Tyndale, a casualty of war games, its inhabitants evacuated and buildings damaged by tanks and pocked by shells – what national sacrifices some people are called upon to make! On one side lay the sea, sparkling in intermittent sun with foam-tipped waves whipped by the wind, while on the other side was a huge valley laid waste by tank exercises.

We descended a steep hill into the village of West Lulworth and then went on to the famous beauty spot of Lulworth Cove. Parking the car we walked down to the almost circular cove. It was my first visit though I had heard my mother speak of it many times. The tide was out, and we were not able to get a good look at the round hole in a great spur of rock known as the Durdle Door.

We then went on to Weymouth where we were warmly received by my niece Rachel and her family.

SUNDAY, MAY 5TH

My niece Rachel and her second husband Rob are the proprietors of a hotel that looks out to sea from the Esplanade, and we were happy to be their guests for two nights. Their life is a busy one, especially in 'the season.'

The day dawned cold and grey, with drizzling rain that now and then developed into brief heavy downpours. Weymouth was holding its VE anniversary celebrations today rather than on May 8th, so of course the rainy weather was a disappointment. The services and wreath-laying ceremonies were held at the Cenotaph, the marble obelisk on the Esplanade that is Weymouth's war memorial. In spite of the weather David walked the hundred yards from the hotel to the ceremonies, but I stayed and got only an oblique view from a balcony, unable to hear much of the prayers or singing. The lady mayor and town corporation in their ceremonial robes led the parade through the streets, followed by a military band, colour bearers, veterans, and British soldiers, sailors and airmen marching in formation. The surpliced, cassocked rector of Weymouth intoned the prayers, and the mayor and heads of veterans organizations such as the British Legion laid wreaths of poppies. A few Americans were there, some of whom embarked from Weymouth for Omaha Beach on June 6th 1944 and had come to mourn comrades lost on that day. In spite of the rain the ceremony was conducted with all the sad panoply the British muster on such occasions, and at the end – just as voices were raised in 'O God, Our Help in Ages Past' – the rain stopped and the sun came out and shone brilliantly.

After lunch the weather improved, and we left Rob to man the hotel and drove with Rachel and the girls to Abbotsbury to see the recently restored and expanded subtropical gardens. We were here today to see the gardens created two centuries ago by the Countess of Ilchester. By some quirk of climate camellias flourish here in the shelter of walls. There are many other types of bushes and big trees of all varieties and colours. Today the blossoms were at their best. There were also many rhododendrons, and they too were in bloom with flowers of purple, pink, white and deep red. Some formal beds were planted with tulips and daffodils, but there were also whole areas where wildflowers such as primroses and bluebells grew haphazardly. The children especially liked the peacocks, white ones as well as blue-green ones, that mixed freely with the visitors around the restaurant area.

Returning to Weymouth we took Rob and Rachel out to dinner at a very nice restaurant some distance around the Esplanade, walking in the cold wind to reach it. Navy ships in the harbour were firing salvos to mark VE Day, and on one of the piers a huge bonfire was lit, around which a celebratory crowd had gathered. We were fortunate to find a taxi to take us back to our hotel.

MONDAY, MAY 6TH

The day again dawned cold and grey and threatened rain, but we got an early start westward along the Dorset coast. The scenery was beautiful – cliffs, beaches and wind-tossed waves on our left while landward lay hilly green fields and hedgerows. We made a short stop at a tiny hamlet on the shore to watch fishermen casting their nets into the grey rolling sea, their enthusiasm not yet blunted by the weather. We then drove on to Lyme Regis where we walked around and had lunch, though the inclement weather quite spoiled our enjoyment of this historic old town.

Lyme Regis earned its royal title long ago in the reign of Edward III, who used the harbour for his ships before invading France in the fourteenth century. The harbour is sheltered by an unusually long and massive breakwater called the Cobb, which provided a dramatic backdrop for some of the action in the recent filming of *The French Lieutenant's Woman*. It was here that the Duke of Monmouth landed for his ill-fated attempt to capture the throne of England in 1685, and at that time Lyme Regis rang to shouts of 'A Monmouth! A Monmouth! The Protestant Religion!' The town became a centre for smuggling in the eighteenth century but later regained respectability as a popular seaside resort where bathing in the sea was encouraged. Jane Austen liked the town and visited here often, staying in an old house that can still be seen. Here she wrote some of her novel *Persuasion*, and part of its action takes place in Lyme Regis. In World War I survivors from a torpedoed battleship were brought ashore and fed and clothed by the people of Lyme Regis. Today the old town appears on the verge of toppling into the ocean due to erosion of the base of the cliffs on which it is perched.

Bundled in raincoats, hats and scarves we walked out on to the Cobb. The wind was blowing hard and we returned to a restaurant crowded with visitors seeking, as we were, shelter from the rain and wind. After an indifferent lunch we took a quick look at the town gardens but found them disappointing after those at Abbotsbury and then returned to the car for the drive to Sidmouth.

The sun was shining brightly when we crossed into Devon and arrived at the delightful resort of Sidmouth. The beach is pebbled and drops off sharply into the ocean, making it uninviting for families with young children but ideal for the elderly who want sea air and peace in beautiful surroundings. Sidmouth became a very popular holiday spot in the days of Queen Victoria and attracted many well-to-do retired people to make their home there. The town is old and charming with many small but exclusive shops.

We drove along the front past many fine hotels looking seaward. One, the

Riviera, attracted us with its well-kept look and symmetrical bay-windowed facade, and we were pleased that a room was available. The semicircular window had a fine view of the ocean, and the room was beautifully appointed and decorated in pink toile, very cool and feminine-looking. We enjoyed a Devon cream tea in the lounge and after a brisk walk by the sea had a fine dinner in the elegant dining room. It so happened that the hotel proprietors were named Wharton, and so our arrival caused quite a stir. We certainly got the best of service, the staff perhaps assuming we were long-lost cousins from America.

TUESDAY, MAY 7TH

After a walk on the beach and a quick look at the town we left Sidmouth reluctantly. The road as far as Honiton led through beautiful country, typical of Devon with red soil and the land a patchwork quilt of fields, hedges, and orchards today in full bloom. As we crossed into Somerset we stopped at Shepton Mallet for lunch in a pleasant inn called Downside. Shepton Mallet is an old grey stone town with narrow twisting streets and a market place with a stone poultry cross in its centre. It takes its name from the sheep that supported its early economy, while Mallet was the name of the Norman family that was granted the town and land at the time of the Conquest. It has long been a working-class town and is the site of a county prison.

1987

A REUNION IN BOURNEMOUTH

SUNDAY, AUGUST 2ND

It so happens that one of my dear English friends from New Jersey, Florence McLellan, is visiting a friend in Bournemouth, the town she lived in for many years before marrying the Canadian Roy McLellan. We had arranged to meet and spend a few hours with her and her friend.

The day dawned bright and sunny, and we enjoyed the ride through Salisbury and the New Forest. Bournemouth is one of the most prosperous and popular of the many South Coast resorts – a place where day trippers visit, where families take their annual 'fortnight' by the sea, and where the well-to-do, many retired from the armed services, choose to spend their later years. The sands are superb, the climate mild, and every form of entertainment sought by visitors and residents is available.

The town has grown up around the mouth of the small River Bourne, which empties into a bay of exceptional beauty sheltered by 100-foot cliffs that are backed by pine forests. It has grown tremendously since the days when I visited as a child and in so doing seems to have lost some of its exclusivity. At the same time it seems, paradoxically and like other English resorts, to have lost some of its prosperity.

In prehistoric times the cove at Bournemouth provided an entry into Britain for Celtic tribes from the mainland of Europe. Hengistbury Head, which forms the eastern arm of the bay is most likely named for Hengist, the early Saxon leader who is thought to have landed about AD 450 somewhere along the south coast. While the towns of Poole and Christchurch on either side of the bay grew and prospered in Norman and mediaeval times, Bournemouth's site remained a wilderness area of moorland, sandy wastes and pine forests until, some two hundred years ago, its potential as a vacation spot was realized. The first house was not built until 1810, but from that time construction proceeded apace with the development of pine forests into gardens, parks and walking areas. Two fine piers were built and furnished with a variety of entertainments. With the later establishment of a symphony orchestra, Bournemouth became a cultural centre with concert halls and theatres.

But we had come to see an old friend, not to investigate Bournemouth's history or sample her many attractions. We met at an inn outside the city and followed Florence and her friend Margaret through lovely tree-lined suburban streets to a block of retirement flats where Margaret lives. As we are considering moving shortly to a retirement complex in Chapel Hill, it was of special interest to us to see what England has to offer in this way. There were several blocks of three-storeyed flats in the complex, which was surrounded by manicured lawns and well-tended flower beds and rose gardens. We entered Margaret's building through a gracious foyer and a lift whisked us up to her apartment. We found it spacious, light, airy and equipped with all modern conveniences. Its several rooms made a lovely backdrop for Margaret's fine antiques and lovely china and bric-a-brac. In answer to our enquiries we learned that a security guard is always on duty, but there is no provision for the medical services that in the U.S. are called 'continuing care.' Apart from that, we were most impressed with the facilities. As in the U.S., however, the cost is high and affordable only to the well-to-do.

After coffee we left for a ride through the lovely surrounding countryside, stopping at a very old inn called 'The Silent Woman.' The painted inn sign pictured a headless woman with her head tucked underneath her arm. This is a common inn sign that appears in towns and villages throughout England. The inns are sometimes called 'The Quiet

Woman.' The sign suggests that the only way to silence a nagging wife is to behead her. Some think the sign is a reference to Anne Boleyn, second wife of Henry VIII whom he executed partly for her alleged infidelity and partly for her failure to produce a son. Sometimes the inn sign bears the verse,

> Here is a woman who has lost her head,
> She's quiet now because she's dead.

With great glee David arranged his three loquacious companions beneath it and took our photograph.

1989

WEST WYCOMBE AND THE HELL-FIRE CLUB – TO WEYMOUTH AND BACK

FRIDAY, SEPTEMBER 15TH

We wished to visit the Buckinghamshire village of West Wycombe because of the eighteenth-century Hell-Fire Club, founded there by the first and only Duke of Wharton. The name piqued our interest, and research and visits to Wharton Hall in Westmorland lead us to suppose there may be some tenuous family connection.

The story of the Hell-Fire Club is an interesting one. It was founded about 1719 by Philip, Duke of Wharton, and a group of immediate friends to promote sacrilege among highborn ladies and gentlemen. Its president was the devil, and a vacant chair at all meetings represented his invisible presence. The meetings were held at a small tavern in London called the Greyhound. Fumes of burning brandy and sulphur created an illusory Hell, three members represented the Holy Trinity, and others were patriarchs, prophets and martyrs. Their activities seem to have been largely innocuous – gambling, feasting on special food to which they gave devilish names, and drinking Hell-Fire punch. When ladies were present they met in private homes, as taverns were off-limits to females. No prostitutes were ever admitted to the club's ranks.

Thirty years later a similar club met under the leadership of Lord Sandwich and Sir Francis Dashwood of West Wycombe. About the former the following lines were once written:

> Nature designed him in a rage
> To be the Wharton of his age,
> But having given all the sin
> Forgot to put the virtue in.

At West Wycombe the club met in caves on the Dashwood estate now known as the Hell-Fire Caves. Here at dead of night Black Masses were held and sexual orgies with ladies dressed as nuns were said to take place. Much of this is largely myth, but the name Hell-Fire stuck to Sir Francis' activities. The caves – actually nothing more than Dashwood's disused chalk mines – are unimpressive and because they seemed an undistinguished locale, the club later moved its meetings to a ruined abbey in the nearby village of Medmenham, and members became known as the monks of Medmenham. Today it is believed that the chief aim of the club was less to practise a satanic cult and allied nefarious rites than to proclaim contempt for established thought on morality, theology and religion.

We were disappointed to wake to rain this morning, as we had planned this rather long trip through countryside largely new to us. We left Marlborough about 10 o'clock, making a stop in Hungerford. We drove next to Wantage through downland country with many grazing sheep and some enormous newly ploughed fields. It was very misty and a light rain continued to fall so that the surrounding country appeared as in an impressionistic painting. Nearing Wantage we descended a very steep hill lined with lofty beech trees, their leafy tops meeting so that we appeared to be in a dim green tunnel dripping from the rain. Wantage marketplace is the busy hub of the ancient stone town and centred by a fine statue of King Alfred, said to have been born here.

Next we came to Didcot, once a very important railway junction with many maintenance shops and yards and now site of a railway museum. The town has now been overshadowed industrially by Harwell, site of Britain's most important and advanced nuclear station and research centre. The great steaming cooling towers are landmarks for miles, and their electric pylons and wires are the largest and thickest I have ever seen. The complex seems alien in rural England, and the spectre of power held so far in check but not yet fully understood casts something of a pall over the surrounding countryside. Surprisingly enough, however, very close to this mighty symbol of the nuclear age are acres and acres of very fine orchards, their trees at this time of the year loaded and bowed down under a bumper harvest. The trees were mostly apple and pear, and the ground around was scattered with fallen fruit. Near the orchards were some very large and beautiful houses, and I noticed one delightful-looking hotel.

Approaching by now Thames country, we drove on to the old river town of Wallingford, where we encountered such heavy traffic that we turned around and retraced our steps to the Red Lion, a delightful pub in a village called Brightwell-cum-Sotwell some miles from the main road down narrow flowery lanes. When we reached it we found it everything an English country pub should be – thatched, beflowered, cosy and welcoming. Here we enjoyed a lunch of hot soup, sandwiches, beer and lemonade served by a friendly landlord. Road directions were given by an elderly gentleman with a black Labrador, and a youngish couple from London talked to us in Cockney accents, the woman asking me if I married ''im' during the war. We drove back into Wallingford, an old town of narrow streets on the Thames, crossing the river by a one-way stone bridge, very scenic but the cause of much traffic delay. The rain had stopped and a watery sun had come out to add to the beauty of the river, which at this point was quite wide between wide grassy banks built up with charming riverside houses. It made a lovely idyllic sight reminiscent of *Wind in the Willows* and *Three Men in a Boat*.

Leaving Wallingford we took some narrow roads, made a wrong turn at a small town called Wallington, and altogether got thoroughly lost. We drove past an immense walled estate that we believed was Stonor Park. The walls seemed to go on forever, shielding us from as much as a glimpse of what lay within. We then went on through a section of the Chiltern Forest, a beautifully preserved and maintained woodland area set aside for picnickers and travellers. The dry chalk flinty country is not good for agriculture, but its glory is its beechwoods, which have given rise to a flourishing furniture – especially chairmaking – industry.

We eventually found the main road and drove into West Wycombe, a long village strung out along the road and now under the care of the National Trust to preserve its beauty. The park is the magnificent home of the Dashwood family, built in the Palladian-Adam style and standing in grounds designed by Capability Brown and further developed by Humphrey Repton, who opened up the vista with a lake and elaborate plantings that now front the gracious house. We were disappointed to find the mansion closed, but, trespassing, we drove far enough along the driveway to catch a glimpse of its magnificence. We then crossed the main road and drove up the steep escarpment of the Chilterns, passing the caves en route but finding no parking outside them or nearby. Continuing up a steep and narrow road, we reached the top from which we had a most far-reaching view of the surrounding countryside, partially obscured of course by the continuing mist and drizzle. The place was quite deserted, though I am sure it is popular on summer weekends when the weather is right.

We parked nearby to explore West Wycombe's famous and unusual village church dedicated to St Laurence. From early Saxon times there has been a small church on this hilltop. The present church was rebuilt, greatly enlarged and redesigned by the same Sir Francis Dashwood who engaged in devil worship – a paradox indeed! However, he chose as his architect a man named Nicholas Revett, a member of the Dilettante, or Hell-Fire, Club in London. The result is different, lavish, and from the beginning controversial. Revett succeeded in creating an avant-garde building at considerable cost, only retaining the walls of the chancel and the lower part of the tower of the original church. The finished body of the church, with furnishings chosen by Revett and Dashwood, looks more like an elegant drawing room than a place of worship. The chancel was remodelled and the tower completely reconstructed, heightened considerably and crowned with the church's distinguishing feature, a golden ball. The tall slender tower is a landmark for miles. It houses eight bells ranging in age from 70 to 400 years. Rising above the belfry is the 'new' part of the tower, and from its 80-foot height a fine view can be obtained. The whole is crowned by the famed Golden Ball. This is hollow, made of wood and covered with gilded fabric. It once seated 10 people but is not in use now.

An announcement of the opening of the church stated, 'It is reckoned the most beautiful country church in England.' Inside, the roof is supported by 16 giant columns with richly carved capitals, and the ceiling is painted with the Italian artist Giovanni Borgnis' conception of the Last Supper. The altar and choir stalls, lectern, and pulpit follow the Chippendale style, while the font is unique – a slender carved mahogany pillar around which a serpent, symbol of evil, is entwined. This supports a priceless silver gilt bowl to hold the holy water, though this is stored for safety and only brought out when baptisms are performed. On both sides of the chancel are Dashwood and le Despenser monuments, as Sir Francis later became Baron le Despenser. The design of the nave was taken from the Temple of the Sun at Palmyra, and the floor of the church is paved with marble in a variety of patterns, lending the church something of an Oriental or Byzantine air. The ceilings, though flat, appear to be in relief due to the skill with which they were painted, and Borgnis' painting of the Last Supper is quite beautiful in its fading pastel sensitivity.

The church was locked when we first reached it, but an elderly countrywoman fortuitously appeared carrying two buckets of water and cleaning materials. She let us in, explaining that no water had ever been laid on in the church because of its hilltop elevation and that she had undertaken the cleaning chores in spite of the labour and inconvenience involved. She knew a lot about the church and was very willing to share her knowledge with two Americans, the only visitors on this damp afternoon in the early fall.

The hilltop churchyard is full of graves, many of which are very old, though some recent ones indicate that burials still take place here. Close by is a tremendous circular construction of grey stone, unroofed and open to the sky. It is the mausoleum of the Dashwoods and le Despensers, and the individual urns containing the ashes of the departed nobles can be seen in niches in the walls. The whole effect is eerie and weird and lends some credence to the tales of Hell-Fire rituals.

We returned to a parking lot at the bottom of the hill, debating whether time would allow us to walk back up the very steep road to the caves. We decided against it as we had been told there was little to see, it was still raining slightly, and I was tired. It was still a long way back to Marlborough, and we had a date with friends in Pewsey. A minor snafu occurred before we could leave the parking lot – we had no 10p. coins needed to put in the machine to let us out of the parking lot, so David had to walk to a shop in the village for some change. We made better time on the way home avoiding the roads where we had lost our way earlier. In spite of heavy traffic we were in Marlborough by 5 p.m. and Pewsey by 6 p.m. We had dinner in an inn in Milton Lilbourne called the Three Horseshoes. This is a common inn sign generally denoting a nearby forge where a lost horseshoe can be replaced while the horseman refreshes himself at the inn.

THURSDAY, SEPTEMBER 21ST

Shortly after leaving Yeovil we passed from Somerset to Dorset, coming to Dorchester, the county town, important in Roman times and featured as Casterbridge in Thomas Hardy's novels. Here, as we have so often on past trips, we headed south for Weymouth. We could smell the sea as we approached and got our first view of the blue foam-tipped waves. We drove along the front to the gracious curved Esplanade, crowded like the beach on this beautiful warm day. We had some difficulty finding the restaurant owned by my niece Rachel and her husband, but two metermaids helped us get located and parked. We met Rachel's three daughters and caught up with family news. We ate dinner in the restaurant that night, treated like honoured guests and enjoying a delicious meal.

FRIDAY, SEPTEMBER 22ND

We slept in Rachel and Rob's bedroom on the fourth floor of the old Georgian building. Its wide window looked far out over the bay and ocean so that we could see the white faces of the cliffs called the Seven Sisters, the jetty, and a large stationary ship that blew its horn all night in the fog. This morning the fog had dissipated with the dawn and the rising of a brisk wind, and on the far green hillside we could make out the equestrian chalk figure of George III. On the beach a man huddled in a hooded anorak zipped tight against the biting wind was running on the beach with his dog.

At breakfast we saw the three little girls ready to go to school. The older two were in neat uniforms – what a good idea school uniforms are – and even ebullient three-year old Lizzie, her hair neatly confined in pigtails, was

clad in a sweatsuit for a morning in play school. We said goodbye to them –
they are very sweet children.

We would have liked a walk on the beach, but the wind was approaching
gale proportions and it was cold in spite of the bright sun. Instead we
walked a few yards to the local Marks and Spencers, one of England's
premier stores, and bought well-made skirts, sweaters and slacks to take
with us back home.

We left Weymouth about noon. Our last view of the sea was of foamy
waves rolling on to the beach, the water green in the distance but changing
to bright blue close to shore. We were able to bypass Dorchester and
Blandford Forum since new roads have been built. Though we saved time I
missed the close look at these lovely old towns. At Blandford we took a
road towards Warminster that was new to us. The lovely scenery
encompassed the fields, farms and hills of Dorset leading into the high wild
downland of Wiltshire. We went through many pretty villages each with its
own pond or stream built around an old church and big house. Perhaps the
most interesting was East Knoyle, the birthplace of Christopher Wren. His
father was the rector of the village, but because of a fire at the rectory the
birth took place in a room over a grocery store. It is still known today as
Wren's store, and we took note of it as we passed. Just outside Shaftesbury
we stopped for lunch at a large hotel called the Royal Chase. We then drove
through the crowded streets of the small town, seeing pedestrian signs to
the ancient abbey of which only traces remain. At Mere we passed into
Wiltshire and thence to Warminster, a pleasant market town. Warminster
was at one time an important wool town and has a famous grammar school
that produced two pupils of note, the writer Joseph Addison and Thomas
Arnold, the educational pioneer who was headmaster of Rugby and father
of the poet Matthew Arnold.

We returned to Marlborough through Westbury and Devizes. After a
short rest we met friends and went to the Red Lion at Axford for dinner.

Chapter Three

THE WEST

'An' dreamin' arl the time of Plymouth Hoe'
Sir Henry Newbolt 1862–1938

I have chosen to consider the West as the three counties of Cornwall, Devon and Somerset, counties that form a claw-like peninsula sticking far out into the Atlantic. Its northern rocky shore is pounded constantly by the rough waves of the open sea, while the gentle southern coast is washed by the waters of the English Channel.

Cornwall lies farthest west, separated from Devon by the River Tamar, which for many years isolated Cornwall from the rest of England. It was not until 1859 that famed engineer I. K. Brunel completed a railway bridge across the river at Plymouth, while a road bridge followed almost a century later.

The Cornish people are descended from Celts and Britons who fled west first before the Romans and later before the Saxons. Racially they are more akin to the Welsh and Irish than the English. Until the late Middle Ages they spoke a Celtic language, traces of which still remain in the dialects of remote inland areas.

This heritage makes Cornwall a mysterious land of legend and half-forgotten lore, and ruins from the Neolithic, Bronze and Iron ages can be seen in its barrows, cairns, standing stones and circles. Legendary King Arthur may or may not have held court in Camelot or Tintagel, and perhaps the Scilly Isles were once joined to the mainland to form the ancient kingdom of Lyonesse, where Tristan of Tristan and Isolde fame was born.

All our travels in Cornwall took place in my pre-journal writing days. My introduction to Cornwall was in the wartime days of 1944, when my husband was briefly stationed near Bude on the northern coast. Years later we spent an enchanting few days in Mousehole (pronounced 'Mowzal'), a tiny fishing village tucked away in the south of Cornwall's claw, and from there explored the land nearby. Of course we went a few miles away to

Land's End, the westernmost promontory of the rocky coast that is ceaselessly battered and eroded by the cruel sea and bitter winds. Like all tourists we had our picture taken at the signpost pointing seaward to America, three thousand miles away. Just east of Land's End the narrow peninsula is only about five miles across, and it is possible to walk from one coast to the other, although the going is rough because of the rocky terrain. Today the little fishing villages on Cornwall's south coast have become haunts for artists and vacationers, while the north tends to attract hikers, climbers, and those in search of history and mystery.

The interior of Cornwall is today a region of marginal farming. The copper and tin mines that once brought it prosperity are largely outworked, their lonely half-ruined stacks sadly punctuating the landscape. Before the birth of Christ, Phoenicians came for these precious metals, followed by Romans and a succession of miners from England. Today most of the mining is for kaolin or china clay, from which much of England's fine porcelain and pottery is manufactured in the Midlands. Outside the mining towns I remember seeing the distinctive white pyramids of the residual clay.

Devon lies east across the Tamar and is one of England's largest and loveliest counties. Like Cornwall it stretches from north to south across the peninsula, much wider here, and to the east abuts the counties of Somerset and Dorset. Devon's south coast boasts an almost Riviera-like climate with many lovely beaches and vacation resorts. Plymouth is the great port, while Dartmouth is the site of the Royal Naval College. The northern shore is a continuation of Cornwall's rocky coast.

Much of the interior of Devon is taken up by the great granite upland of Dartmoor, a wild outcropping of rock, heath and bog that hides delightful small towns and villages in its sheltered valleys. Away from the moorland the soil of Devon is red and very fertile, and the landscape often presents a patchwork of colour and shape seamed with the green of hedgerows. Many of the roads serving the small villages are narrow, banked and hedged, forming green tunnels where one meets at risk an oncoming car.

Devon came into its own during the age of discovery and exploration, when sailors, fishermen, smugglers and adventurers turned to the newly found continent across the Atlantic and challenged Spain for its riches. Drake, Grenville and Raleigh were among these men, and each is considered one of the great heroes of the English.

To the east, Devon merges into Somerset. The great port of Bristol, which also grew in importance with the settling of America, lies where the rocky coast meets the Severn estuary. Just inland lies the moorland of Exmoor, much like Dartmoor though smaller and less rugged.

Most of Somerset is lush and agricultural and much of it is devoted to dairy farming. Historically it is part of the old kingdom of Wessex, the land of the West Saxons. In Somerset one finds beautiful villages, towered churches, old castles, sacred ruins, Wells Cathedral, the Abbey Church of Bath, the geological wonders of Cheddar and Wookey Hole, and the Roman remains and Georgian elegance of Bath. The legend that Christ and Joseph of Arimathea visited Glastonbury still persists, and Arthur along with his queen Guinevere is said to be buried there. Some people believe Glastonbury was Avalon, the kingdom 'where rains not hail nor any snow' to which Sir Bedivere carried Arthur's wounded body. With more certainty we know that Alfred the Great hid out in AD 878 in the swamps of Athelney, burning the goodwife's cakes while forming plans to defeat the Danes. And it was at Sedgemoor near Bridgwater that the Monmouth Rebellion failed in 1685 in the last battle to be fought on English soil.

1973

with Thomas & Margaret McKnight

WEST TO DEVON – SOUTH ZEAL – LYDFORD GORGE – PLYMOUTH – DARTMOOR

SATURDAY, JULY 21ST

The party last night in the Red Lion at Axford left little time for sleep and we all awoke feeling not very well rested. We said a fond farewell to Oscar, Joan, and their helpers Mrs Kirby and Angela, and finally got away about 10.30. From Marlborough we headed up Granham Hill and got a last look from its summit at the little red-roofed town sheltering in the valley – the town that is home to me. We went through Pewsey and Amesbury and took the main road west towards Honiton in Devon. This town seems now to be little more than an important road junction, but for many years it was world-renowned for the lace that was made there. Queen Victoria's wedding veil was made of Honiton lace, and my mother, at her wedding, carried a handkerchief edged with it, a handkerchief which I own today.

Traffic was very heavy and the weather a mixture of rain and watery bright intervals. After stopping for lunch in the busy little town of Wincanton, we inched our way into Devon, leaving the main road after Honiton and following leafy lanes banked with hedgerows. It was slow going and after six when we reached South Zeal. There we had reservations at the Oxenham Arms, a very ancient stone inn that had at one time been part of a monastery. Later it became a dower house – a sort of extra house for the local manor generally occupied by a dowager – and eventually an inn. The first building on the site had been planned around an ancient granite obelisk, perhaps of Druidic consequence though its actual origin is unknown. The inn's associations are not only historical but also literary, for it plays an important part in Eden Philpotts' book *The Beacon*.

We entered our room by climbing two extremely steep and narrow stone steps to a massive oak door heavily studded with iron nails. Both of us had to bend down to pass through, David practically double – men of a thousand years ago were definitely shorter than they are today. Our window overlooks the garden, pretty though a little overgrown, then across fields and out to the grim brooding moor. In spite of its antiquity the hotel is very comfortable, modernized without disturbing the charm of age. The furniture is well-polished and has the sheen and patina of time and constant care, and there is much shining brass and copper around, something we have come to associate with old English hotels. Loose casual flower arrangements of both wild and cottage flowers are everywhere.

After unpacking and freshening up we took a walk through the village. A tiny chapel stands in the middle of the street, its churchyard full of ancient graves and headstones. I was reminded of St Peter's in Marlborough, which stands in the High Street surrounded by its coffin-shaped churchyard. For dinner we ate in the oak-panelled dining room, enjoying a good meal abundant with country fruit and vegetables. Shortly afterwards we retired to our rooms as we were all very tired.

SUNDAY, JULY 22ND

Breakfast at 8.30 was very good and afterwards we started out for Plymouth. Hotel guests last night had suggested we go to Lydford Gorge. I remembered my mother had talked of going there long ago, and so we decided to stop there since it would not be far out of our way. The gorge is formed by two small rivers, one of which is 'captured' by the other. Potholes formed by swirling water have joined together to make a stream that cuts deeply through the rock creating magnificent scenery. We walked along the edge of the gorge, which was dripping wet but so sheltered we could not tell whether the moisture came from rain or condensation. Everything was green – moss, lichens, ferns – and all bathed in an unearthly light.

Reluctantly we left the gorge and after a very cursory glance at the old castle in the town went on to Plymouth. The early morning sun had given way to rain so the harbour and the Hoe were grey, wet and uninviting. (What a difference the sun makes! It had been a beautiful day when David and I were here two years ago.) We walked out on to the wet slick surface of the Hoe, no longer grassy as in Drake's day. It was hard to imagine the admiral playing bowls and finishing the game before going out to defeat the

Spanish Armada in 1588. To escape the rain we stopped in at the tents of a dairy show, where flower beds planted with bright red geraniums made the only splash of colour in the grey misty scene.

We went on to the Mayflower Hotel where we had drinks and lunch in the bar overlooking the harbour, surely one of the finest in the world. By then it had stopped raining and we drove around the town in search of the Crownhill Barracks, where Tom had spent 10 months training in preparation for D-Day. The city has changed greatly because it was badly bombed and has been rebuilt with many changes. After enquiries we found what was left of the old barracks – two old red brick halls in one of which Tom had lived.

We then struck out across Dartmoor, which on this grey rainy day lived up to its reputation of mysterious desolation. A high, windswept, bleak mass of solid granite, it is the largest tract of open country left in southern England. The area comprises mountains, moors, combes (valleys), dense woods, remote villages and a few central market towns. In summer, cattle, sheep and wild ponies wander at will, but agriculture is confined to the sheltered river valleys. Dartmoor is rich in minerals, especially tin, which has been mined from time immemorial. Though most tin mining has now ceased, granite and china clay are still quarried. Today in the summer Dartmoor draws many tourists seeking a return to primeval nature and a wild unspoiled tract of land.

We stopped at Princetown in the very heart of the moor for a look at the notorious maximum security prison there. The prison is the only reason for the town's existence. The desolate spot was chosen to house French prisoners from the Napoleonic Wars and Americans from the War of 1812, and was named Princetown because the Prince of Wales – later George IV – gave the land for the prison. For many years it was almost unguarded, as the mists, bogs and impassable thickets were considered sufficient deterrents to escape. Today, however, fences and guardhouses ring its boundaries. We drove through the main street of the town, the population of which is almost entirely made up of wardens and other prison employees. The country in the immediate locality is used for agricultural and construction programmes aimed at prisoner rehabilitation. We stopped again to take pictures at the Post Bridge, making friends with a mare and foal, two of the wild ponies. The bridge is actually two bridges, a very old one of granite slabs and a more modern one (none the less five hundred years old!) beside it.

Before setting out for South Zeal we had a cream tea in the warm dry comfort of a hotel in Moretonhampstead. Here we saw two houses of great charm, one dated 1637, and an old stone cross in front of an oak tree outside a dwelling called Cross Tree Cottage. We were back in South Zeal by 6.30. The rain had stopped and we sat in the garden before another very good dinner.

1977

Salcombe – Wanderings in Devon – Ilfracombe – The Exmoor Region

Wednesday, October 12th

Before leaving Kingsbridge we did a little shopping and stopped in at the museum, which is housed in a room of the old grammar school founded in 1670. The museum is named after William Cookworthy, the town's favourite son, one of the school's most distinguished pupils, and developer of the process of making china clay into porcelain. Local artifacts were displayed in a large panelled room of dark oak, the walls much carved with the initials of past pupils. The master's desk, canopied and raised on a dais, dominated the room, and it too has its share of carved names and initials. The lady in charge of the museum was very pleasant and knowledgeable and told us much of interest about this part of Devon.

About 11 o'clock we left Kingsbridge for Salcombe, Britain's southernmost resort at the mouth of the Kingsbridge estuary. The small town looked very pretty around its harbour, and since the season is over there were not many tourists around. After parking the car we walked up the narrow twisting main street and went to the Salcombe Hotel to obtain a room and have a light lunch. A sudden storm came up and kept us marooned for a while, but it quickly cleared and the sun shone more brilliantly than ever.

Salcombe was known to the Romans, who obtained their salt from drying seawater in the valleys – or combes – nearby, from which procedure the settlement derived its name. Today it is a popular fishing and sailing centre and resort. The climate is mild and balmy, and some of the vegetation is semitropical. Poets, writers and artists have stayed here and gained inspiration from its peace and beauty. A sandbar across the estuary inspired Tennyson in 1889 to write an oft-quoted poem, 'Crossing the Bar':

> Sunset and Evening Star
> And one clear call for me
> And may there be no moaning of the bar
> When I put out to sea.

Salcombe's part in World War II is commemorated on a tablet in Normandy Way. Men of the U.S. Navy 'passed this way to embark for the Normandy beaches there to assault the enemy on D-Day, Tuesday the 6th of June 1944.' On the corner of the quay is the Salcombe Life Boat House, and we could see the lifeboat offshore. The Custom House is nearby, and sailors and men of the sea could be seen strolling or talking in knots on the harbourside.

We walked around and then went further afield in the car. We went out to Bold Head, a rocky promontory of land, and eventually came to the Sharpitor House gardens and museum. The Victorian house is full of the oddities that rich people of that era liked to collect, and outside has a beautiful cliffside garden full of semitropical plants and trees. The driveway approaching the house is lined with palm trees, and we were further surprised to find banana trees, orchids and bougainvillaea growing in the garden, surprising plants to survive in the temperate climate of England. Walking around the point we got a fine view of the harbour with boats anchored offshore and the pastel-coloured cottages gay with the last flowers of summer. We stopped in a tiny restaurant for tea and then after a further drive around the environs returned to the hotel to rest before dinner.

THURSDAY, OCTOBER 13TH

We had gone to bed early but were awakened by a very loud noise and then the clatter of feet running down the staircase to the ferry right outside our bathroom wall. From our balcony we could see flashing blue lights and a state of great confusion at the harbourside. All kinds of imaginings flashed through my mind – pirates, smugglers, shipwreck and rescue by lifeboat – but the weather was calm and I recalled that this is the twentieth century. Nonetheless it took me a long while to fall back into a fitful sleep, and I was glad of the appearance of tea at 7.45 this morning.

We had planned to go just across the Cornish border to Cotehele, a National Trust property famous for its gardens, but got lost in the maze of narrow lanes that pass for roads in this part of the country. In the vicinity of Plymouth we saw a sign to Saltram House, also belonging to the National Trust, and decided to stop there. We were very glad we did so. The house and property of the Earl of Morley, the estate was left to the National Trust with all furnishings intact in lieu of death duties. The small original house of Tudor origin remains as the core of the Regency House built around it. The mansion is elegant and beautifully situated in a vast park that, alas, has recently been bisected by a new express road leading to Plymouth. The house was designed by Robert Adam, and the rooms bear the unmistakable signs of his classical style. The walls of the formal rooms are washed in the pale colours he loved and decorated with oval designs, wreaths, and garlands of white plaster. The white ceilings are adorned in similar fashion and all the rooms have fireplaces. Line and symmetry are all important, and the whole effect is of balance and pale perfection. The house contains some valuable paintings, among them several portraits by Sir Joshua Reynolds.

We bought some items in the National Trust Shop, then set out for Cotehele only to get lost again. Tired and dispirited we stopped just before closing time at a small pub called the Miners' Arms where we got some food. The inn sign told us we were in a section of Cornwall where mining was once very important. Signs of it are still evident in the ruins of stacks and engine houses.

We never did find Cotehele and returned rather disgusted to Salcombe, going through a wild barren part of Dartmoor where we saw some wild ponies. We detoured into Buckland Monachorum and saw the house owned first by Sir Richard Grenville and later by Sir Francis Drake. The charming village grew up around an abbey founded in 1278, from which it added 'Monachorum', meaning 'of the monks', to its name. After Henry VIII's dissolution of the monasteries the abbey was converted into a mansion by Sir Richard Grenville, grandfather of the Elizabethan seaman of the same name who went down in the Revenge in a blaze of glory in 1591. Drake bought the property from the Grenvilles. It is now a National Trust property and maritime museum but unfortunately was not open today. I wondered if Tennyson got his inspiration here for his ballad of 'The Revenge', a poem of derring-do and high adventure that I have read to many schoolchildren and dearly love myself.

Back at Salcombe we took a walk before dinner and then got to bed quite early. We learned that the commotion that disturbed us last night was a lifeboat drill conducted regularly and very realistically.

For some reason I feel depressed – homesick, an unusual state of affairs for me especially when in England. Perhaps this trip has come too soon after an exhausting and emotionally draining summer – retirement from teaching, our son's overseas marriage, the wrenching move from New Jersey to North Carolina, the unusually bad heat and humidity. My foot hurts and my heart aches, but tomorrow is another day.

FRIDAY, OCTOBER 14TH

We were up early to pack, breakfast and set out on the long ride to Ilfracombe across the widest part of the Devon peninsula. It was a beautiful day – so lovely that we hated to leave Salcombe – but the good weather was to follow and remain with us. We had found on the map a road that zigzagged across Dartmoor but we missed it and went instead through the pretty little towns of Bovey Tracey and Moretonhampstead. We could see the tall tower of the church at Bovey, pronounced 'buvvy', and the china clay deposits on which the local economy is based. As we did some years ago on a previous visit, we stopped for a little refreshment in Moretonhampstead. We then detoured across the moor and as ever were thrilled with the wide open desolation, and the occasional sheep, rough cattle and wild ponies grazing among the heather and gorse. Here and there we could see a few acres under the plough, and in one spot a field of yellow mustard stood out sharply among the prevailing greens and browns. From the high areas a wide expanse of the moor lay before us.

In high summer and on a perfect day Dartmoor is mysteriously enticing, but more often it appears as the sinister wilderness of marsh, hill and forest that it really is, stretching nearly halfway across the county. Great boulders lie strewn over it, and ancient inhabitants have left their stone relics. Many are the cromlechs and menhirs that survive, and many of the tors or hills have rock basins at their summits. Here and there the narrow fast-flowing streams of brownish water are crossed by clapper bridges of rough slabs of uneven stones. The spirit of the savage inhabitant of the primeval moor still seems to brood over the place. The moor of course has to some extent been infringed upon by the towns at its edges, but the core remains untouched and inviolate, and in spite of the sunlight we sensed the underlying mystery and remote desolation.

We pressed on in the direction of Okehampton, but when we saw a sign to South Zeal we detoured to have lunch at the Oxenham Arms, where we stayed in 1973 with cousins Tom and Margaret McKnight. The old inn was attractive as ever and the food was equally good. We bypassed the old town of Great Torrington and crossed the Torridge at Bideford over an ancient arched bridge. Bideford was a prosperous port in days gone by and in the sixteenth century was home port for naval commanders like Sir Richard Grenville, under whom 'men of Bideford in Devon' sailed the Spanish Main. Charles Kingsley wrote most of *Westward Ho!* here. Silting has caused the town to decline in modern times.

Next we came to Barnstaple at the head of the Taw estuary. The estuary is now so silted up that Barnstaple can no longer be considered a port. It is one of the oldest towns in England and was an important 'staple,' or market, for the wool that was the backbone of West England's economy before the Industrial Revolution.

Late in the afternoon we arrived in Ilfracombe and were much taken by the rugged majestic beauty of the cliffs that enclose the harbour around which the houses of the town are grouped. The headlands drop sheer to the sea, and jagged rocks stick up through the waves, presenting a hazard to ships and boats. On this early fall day with the sun sinking westward, the town seemed at its very beautiful best.

The resort is larger than it first appears. Many of its houses are Victorian in style, for it was during that queen's reign that the town became a fashionable holiday spot. It was also much in favour with Edward VII and has preserved an old-fashioned air of those days. We parked the car and walked around the harbour. The tide was out, and boats of many colours lay stranded and useless, their naked masts giving them a pitiful appearance. We spotted an old square-built hotel overlooking the harbour, its sign telling us it was the Royal Britannia, and there we obtained accommodation. Plainly built and furnished accordingly, it had a smack of the sea about it, and the wavy glass of the windows indicated it has been here for many years. We learned later that Lord Nelson stayed here on several occasions. We were shown our bedroom, modestly comfortable with the bed made up with linen sheets redolent of lavender. A pretty, soft-spoken young lady told us she would take care of all our needs. I shall call her Cinderella.

We took a long walk in the darkening evening, stopping for tea at a little cafe crowded with people enjoying the warm autumn day. Upon leaving we found that a brisk wind had sprung up, and I felt the need of a coat. We returned to the hotel and enjoyed drinks in the cosy bar, the dark interior brightened by a fine collection of highly polished brass and copper. We went out for an excellent meal at a restaurant called the Smugglers' Rest, its decor in keeping with the name. When we came out to the street we were surprised to see the waves of the incoming tide, whipped by the wind, breaking over the seawall and covering parts of the sidewalk. The boats were now all afloat straining at their moorings, and ducks were bobbing about like corks. Back at the hotel the barman told us that water becomes quite deep in the streets when winter storms blow in.

Our bedroom proved rather noisy due to a dart game going on in the room below us, but exhaustion triumphed and in spite of it we slept very well.

SATURDAY, OCTOBER 15TH

Cinderella brought in early morning tea, and we followed it with a full English breakfast in the dining room. Then we drove to the heights overlooking the harbour and strolled in the cliff gardens, with David taking many pictures of the beauty around us. The cliffs near the town are crisscrossed by walking paths, with seats placed in strategic spots so that people may both rest and admire the view. Some of the walks pass through tunnels to avoid the steepest slopes. The environs of most British resorts are well-landscaped, reflecting the times when holidaymakers perforce spent their time in or very close to one place. In addition the formal gardens add to the loveliness of nature and give expression to the English love of gardening. Here on the cliffs above Ilfracombe, the landscaping expresses as well the Englishman's appreciation of the beauty of sea and shore.

Back in the car, we drove to a high lookout point and were well rewarded by the vista before us on this clear sunny morning. We then drove along the winding roads and lanes on the other side of town. Much of the countryside is and will remain unspoiled as it is under the auspices of the National Trust.

Almost every house in the town and surrounding countryside – whether a small cottage or a large mansion – is a hotel or boarding house, so that a wide variety of accommodations to suit all pocketbooks is available. At this season most have 'Vacancy' signs and some are closed up tight, their owners maybe repairing to the warmer winters of the Mediterranean. Some shops also are closed for winter. Most of the tourists at this time of year are elderly and taking advantage of lower prices and fewer people.

We left midmorning to go to the twin towns of Lynmouth and Lynton, though on the advice of a fellow resident in the hotel we took a detour to Trentishoe and Hunters' Inn. We were very happy we did so for they were indeed a high spot in a day full of loveliness. We drove along narrow, winding, and in places very steep roads through the wilds of Exmoor, the moors descending here and there to the sea. The sky above, the seas and gulls on one side, and the moors with a few baaing sheep and curlews wheeling overhead on the other presented a rare picture of essential unspoiled nature.

At a fork in the road we took a track marked 'Unfit for Motor Vehicles' that brought us without mishap to the isolated hamlet of Trentishoe, nothing more than a few tiny cottages and a grey stone church. We had come to the end of the road so there was nothing to do but return to the fork and take the more travelled arm, which led us to Hunters' Inn. Down, down we went winding around a craggy tor to enter a woodland glade green with ferns and moss, discovering at the bottom of the valley a very proper English garden surrounding a green-shuttered, grey stone inn. Its unexpected formality contrasted with its surroundings and combined with the beautiful weather to make perfection – heaven on earth if you will. Many people were dining and drinking at outside tables basking in the hot sun. In the flowering dahlia bed in front were four strutting peacocks, one unfurling his fan of a tail as if on cue, and a little later a hen appeared proudly leading her brood of tiny chicks. We ordered lunch and struck up a conversation with a couple from Watford and made friends with their beautiful golden retriever. As we reluctantly left, they gave us directions to Lynmouth.

We left by way of a very narrow road almost impassable at times, coming by way of Parracombe into Lynmouth through a green forest full of ferns. Lynmouth is a small port at the mouth of the River Lyn that was almost destroyed by a devastating flood in 1952. It has been rebuilt and restored in the style of the old town. On this sunny afternoon the tide was out, and despite distant fog we could see well out into the Bristol Channel. The town called Lynton is built on the clifftop high above Lynmouth, and the two towns are connected by a cliff railway that in its day was considered a masterpiece of engineering. We parked the car and rode the railway up, with David especially interested in its workings. We had a quick look around the Victorian town of Lynton and from the top got a marvellous view both landward and seaward.

Back on low ground we followed National Trust signs to Watersmeet, a beautiful spot in the woods where the Lyn is joined by one of its tributaries. We drove along a road between towering cliffs, parked the car, and then went by foot down tortuous winding paths into the valley. The rivers cascade down to their confluence and form a triangle of land where sits a restaurant and National Trust shop surrounded by the greenest lawn and shaded by a huge cedar tree. We enjoyed a cream tea on a table in the dappled sunshine and were fascinated by the flocks of birds, chaffinches I thought, flying around in search of crumbs.

Leaving this pleasant green glade, we went back towards Ilfracombe through the Valley of the Rocks, a huge outcropping of boulders in an area of Exmoor jutting out to sea. The rocks are eroded into weird fantastic shapes. We walked along the cliffs with the sea, calm today, several hundred feet below us. On a clear day South Wales is visible, but today a distant haze blocked this view. Goats were feeding on the steep rocky slopes, and David took a picture of them. We were in Lorna Doone country.

We returned to Ilfracombe by the main road, going through the straggling village of Martin with the setting sun in our faces. We reflected that it had been a perfect day in every respect.

SUNDAY, OCTOBER 16TH

We had not intended to return to Marlborough, but a call last night from Oscar suggested that we break our journey to London by staying with them. As we would pass very close to Marlborough on our return, we made plans accordingly.

At breakfast we met the pleasant lady who had directed us to Hunters' Inn. She was bubbling over with ideas of other places we might see, among them Arlington Court, which was in the general direction in which we would be going. As we ate we enjoyed the view of the harbour in the sunshine and thought of the past excitements this old hostelry had experienced, for it was once a headquarters for 'private venture commerce,' better known as smuggling.

We left regretfully about 10 a.m., heading for Arlington Court, a National Trust property about 20 miles distant. Built between 1820 and 1823, it is a rather plain house of yellow stone with a pillared portico and wings of grey stone added later. It belonged to the Chichester family of the famous yachtsman Sir Francis Chichester, though the house was actually last owned by Miss Rosalie Chichester. It is set off by velvet lawns dotted with enormous trees where peacocks strut and flocks of spotted Jacob's sheep graze. Through the trees one can see lovely old stables and, beyond, the towered church and the few scattered houses of the small hamlet of

Arlington. Miss Chichester died in her eighties in 1949 and left the house and all its contents to the National Trust. Inside, the house is gracefully proportioned with an especially fine hall and staircase. It is literally stuffed with treasures, many of them gathered by Miss Chichester who was an inveterate collector of china, snuff boxes, model ships, shells, paintings, and photographs. She herself was a painter, and many of the oils and watercolours on display are her works. She was also a keen photographer who developed her own pictures at a time when photography was in its infancy. Some of the model ships were made by French prisoners incarcerated during the Napoleonic Wars in the prison at Princetown. They used bones from their meagre rations to carve the ships and strands of their own hair for riggings. We saw Arlington's greatest treasure, a watercolour by William Blake called *Cycle of the Life of Man*. On the staircase was a display of nineteenth-century dresses worn by the Chichester ladies.

We left the house and walked through the grounds to the stables, where there was a fine collection of horse-drawn vehicles. Nearby was a bank covered by nasturtiums in full bloom, the yellow orange and red flowers almost covering the pretty green leaves and giving off their pungent and distinctive odour.

Leaving Arlington we took a road east across Exmoor rather than the shore road which would have been more scenic but longer. I was sorry to miss Porlock Hill, one of the steepest hills in the country. Many are the tales of the challenge it presented to drivers in the early days of motoring. According to my father, some motorists tackled it in reverse! We have been there previously – otherwise I would have insisted on that route today.

Exmoor is much like Dartmoor only gentler and less rugged. Some of the moor scenery was hidden as many of the narrow roads are sunken and lined with high hedges. We came at last to Exford in time for a late lunch. This village was built by a ford across the river Exe, a ford now replaced by a pretty stone bridge. It is a centre for stag-hunting and fishing and is in the heart of the moor within walking distance of Dunkery Beacon, the highest point of Exmoor. We pulled into an attractive-looking inn, though its pleasant exterior belied its inside gloom. The food was good and the meal enlivened by a salty old gentleman preoccupied with keeping his two Jack Russell terriers under control. They were very lively, and, like two owned by a cousin of mine, seemed not to like each other. He called them working fox terriers and told us how they are sent down rabbit holes to flush out the rabbits.

Next we came to Bridgwater, a large industrial town once a busy port on the River Parrett. Robert Blake, admiral for Cromwell, was born here in 1599, and the town figured prominently in the Monmouth Rebellion of 1685. It was here that the Duke of Monmouth was proclaimed king, and the town was his headquarters before his defeat at Sedgemoor dashed his hopes of attaining the throne. Just east of the town is the low-lying marsh where the battle took place, a flat depressing area still waterlogged in spite of drainage canals and reclamation projects. Next, past Glastonbury and Bath and on to Marlborough in time for tea, dinner at the Castle and Ball, and a featherbed at Oscar's.

1983

with the West Side Presbyterian Church Choir of Ridgewood N.J.

BATH

SUNDAY, JULY 10TH

I will never advise anyone about the English weather ever again! Who would have expected a heat wave of such intensity in cool damp England?

We enjoyed a good breakfast in the gracious Georgian dining room of the Francis Hotel, though our large numbers caused some overcrowding. Then we set out for the Central Reformed Church where we were to sing three anthems at morning worship. The church was only a 5-minute walk away and to get there we had to cross the famous Pulteney Bridge, designed by Robert Adam and unusual for the shops which line the sides of the road crossing it. As we walked across, it looked just like any other shop-lined street, though rather nicer than most because of its Georgian architecture. It only looks like a bridge from the river, from whence the full beauty of the structure can be appreciated. Here the Kennet and Avon Canal joins the river in a series of mini-cataracts, and the river banks are lined with pleasure gardens where in former days the rheumatic rich strolled to take the air as well as the waters.

The church was an old, large and somewhat dilapidated building dated 1790. Architecturally it was more like a colonial or early American church than the typical English place of worship. There are many denominations in the west of England other than the established Anglican church, for it was in this area that John Wesley led his powerful crusade for reform. In many places these 'free' churches have united to pool people and money in an attempt to compensate for the drop in church attendance.

Today the large building was hot and airless, though I suspect it would be cold and draughty in winter. The balcony from which we were to sing was stuffy and stifling. We received a nice welcome, and after positioning and a short rehearsal we repaired to an adjacent room for rest and refreshment. Meanwhile Jack had announced the arrival of two cousins of mine who live in nearby villages and whom I had invited to hear us sing and meet our friends. I was delighted to see them and have them share in a service in which we were participating.

The liturgy was most interesting and much more akin to the order of worship followed in the Presbyterian service than the Anglican. In a short address to the young people the minister cleverly wove in references to the red oak tree, the violet and the goldfinch – all symbols of the state of New Jersey from which we hailed and now linked to the Bath church by the universal power of the Cross. The sermon was a fine one, followed by our rendition of the Thompson 'Alleluia'. As in Earl's Colne we felt a deep gratitude for such a warm coming together, bridging distance and cultural differences with Christian love. The service concluded with an organ postlude by Jack that made 'the welkin ring.'

After a coffee reception David, my cousins, and I returned to the hotel for lunch while the rest of the party enjoyed a meal prepared by the ladies of the church. I spent the afternoon visiting with my guests, while others took guided tours of the city. Since I often visited Bath as a child and for a brief period during the war taught in a school here, I know the city well, and so I preferred the quiet time with my cousins whom I had not seen for a considerable time.

Later in the evening we took a walk, although the weather had cooled only slightly. Bath is noted for its humid climate, for the air is trapped in the hollow of the Mendip Hills in which the city is built, with the houses of mellow Bath stone ascending a series of terraces up the steep hills above the river. Invalids used to call the air relaxing and believed it and the water from the area's mineral springs were therapeutic. For Bath is the site of England's only hot springs, springs that have long been believed to have curative properties when drunk and bathed in.

The springs were known to early man, and legend has it that Bladud, son of a British king, was cured of leprosy after bathing in the waters. Later, it is said, he returned to the area and built baths around the springs, thus laying the foundations of the first city of Bath. The hot springs were later known to Phoenician traders who came to the British Isles in search of tin and copper before the birth of Christ. The waters were also used by Celts who began arriving from the continent to make their homes in the islands about 700 BC.

It was the Romans, however, who first developed the town as a spa, using it as a cultural centre and place for rest and relaxation for weary Roman troops. They occupied the area around Bath early on in their conquest of Britain, which began in the reign of Claudius in AD 43. They built a town which they called Aquae Sulis – the waters of Sul, the Celtic goddess of the springs, whom the Romans identified with Minerva. The town was on the Fosse Way, one of the main Roman roads, and was fortified with a wall.

The Romans built a series of very beautiful baths and also a temple to Sul-Minerva. The baths remain as the finest and most visible relic of the Roman occupation, and there is a reconstruction of the temple in the

Sydney Gardens. After the Romans withdrew from Britain early in the fifth century the baths fell into disuse. They silted up and disappeared under accumulated soil and rubbish so that later buildings were constructed over them. They remained hidden until the early nineteenth century when they were accidentally discovered. They were remarkably well-preserved, much in the way the ruins of Pompeii were preserved by volcanic dust.

In post-Roman times Bath regained some of its former importance under the Saxons. An abbey was founded there in AD 973. Under the Normans Bath became an important religious centre, though a great rivalry grew up with its neighbouring see of Wells. Eventually a compromise was reached, and in 1245 the sees were combined with the bishop becoming the Bishop of Bath and Wells. At this time the baths were used by the monks and clergy and by pilgrims who brought sick people to partake of the waters.

In the Middle Ages Bath became the very prosperous centre of the West Country woollen industry. The fame of Bath's cloth was immortalized by Chaucer's Wife of Bath:

> Of clothe-making she hadde wiche an haunt
> She passed hem of Ypres and Gaant.

Bath became a national centre of healing, culture, fashion and entertainment in the early eighteenth century. This was due largely to four men – Ralph Allen, the architects John Wood Senior and Junior, and Beau Nash. It became popular for the gout-ridden rich to seek relief from their pain by taking the waters. More baths, the pump room, assembly rooms, and gardens were planned and built. The Woods directed the construction of beautiful terraced houses of Georgian style laid out in a plan of crescents and circuses. Concerts and plays were held, and gambling was allowed according to strict rules laid down by Beau Nash. Although Nash heartily disliked John Wesley (who considered Bath a sink of iniquity!), he did require visitors to attend the abbey daily, a surprising demand from a man who for much of his life was a fop, dandy and libertine.

Bath became immensely popular. Queen Anne took the waters and many famous people resided there or visited regularly. Among them were Pitt the Elder, Gainsborough, Nelson and Lady Hamilton, Mrs Siddons and General Wolfe, Alexander Pope, and David Garrick. Bath gave its name to an invalid chair and also to a famous biscuit, the Bath Oliver. Other delicacies associated with the city are the Sally Lunn cake, Bath buns, and the boiled, breaded pigs' heads known as Bath chaps. Bath's period of prosperity has been enshrined in literature by Fielding, Jane Austen and Dickens.

With its popularity as a health spa declining somewhat as new treatments for gout and rheumatism developed, Bath turned to industrial growth in the nineteenth and twentieth centuries, especially in the period between the wars. In 1942 the beautiful city was heavily bombed by the Germans in a series of sharp raids that caused some loss of life and destroyed or damaged some of Bath's architectural treasures.

Today Bath is well-restored, a prosperous centre of light industry, and a very popular tourist centre which hosts an annual cultural festival as well as an important agricultural show. It is surrounded by the beautiful country of Somerset and has some interesting museums, including the only American museum in England. It is a centre of culture and attracts many well-to-do people for retirement. It remains England's most perfect Georgian city.

On our walk this evening, we crossed Milsom Street, the famous shopping thoroughfare, but all the stores were closed for Sunday. We wandered around the abbey, scene of the crowning of Edgar in AD 973 as first king of all England. We remembered being there 1,000 years later with our dear old friend George Garside from Marlborough, the last time we were to see him. We strolled beside the Avon, the lovely parade grounds closed, alas, to prevent vandalism. We watched the rippling pattern in the river below Pulteney Bridge where the canal flows in and watched swimmers cavorting in the rather murky waters. We returned to the hotel by some of Bath's narrow streets and arcades. On the site of the rooms where the rich were wont to drink the water and take hot baths to ease the pain of gout and rheumatism, there is now a clinic where such diseases are treated with more modern methods.

1986
with Jane Sockwell & Betsy Newland

GLOUCESTER – DARTMOUTH AND PLYMOUTH – DARTMOOR – THE SOUTHWEST COAST – DUNSTER – GLASTONBURY – WELLS

TUESDAY, SEPTEMBER 9TH

We left Marlborough very early on a nice bright morning and enjoyed the ride through Swindon, Cirencester and Birdlip before reaching Gloucester. We were mostly on straight roads first laid down by the Romans, and the countryside looked very pretty with the harvest just in and the first colours of autumn tinting the trees. Cottage gardens were rife with the flowers of fall: Michaelmas daisies, asters and masses of tall yellow daisy-like blooms. When we saw a signpost on the right pointing to Down Ampney we made the detour to see the village where the composer Ralph Vaughan Williams was born in the rectory and to see the church where his father had been rector. The village was very pretty, the gardens of the stone cottages gay with flowers and shaded by many large trees. A narrow country lane took us to the church, which stands next to a large farmhouse. Entering the churchyard through a lych gate, we saw many very old graves, for the church dates from early mediaeval times and is of great antiquity. Although Williams' father died when he was only four and the family left Down Ampney, the village remained very dear to the composer, and he named one of his best-known hymn tunes Down Ampney after it. The church contains some memorabilia pertaining to his musical composition, and perhaps his love for and interest in the village inspired him to revive many of the folk tunes and dances of old England. We stopped at the village shop to buy postcards of the church, one of which I sent to our organist in Chapel Hill, for Vaughan Williams is one of his favourite composers.

We stopped next at a large hotel at Birdlip and then again about half a mile further on for the view from the top of famed Birdlip Hill. We could see Cheltenham in the distance.

We then came to Gloucester in good time for our appointment with my publisher. Gloucester cannot be called a pretty city, but it has a long and important history starting from the time when the Romans called it Glevum. Strategically, the city guarded the approaches to Wales at the lowest place where the Severn can be crossed. Early kings often called Parliament to meet in Gloucester, and the city gave England the hunchback King Richard III, the last of the Yorkist rulers who met his fate at Bosworth Field in 1485 to end the Wars of the Roses. Gloucester is the site of a great cathedral, sister church to Worcester and Hereford. The cathedral is famous for the architecture of its choir, the first example of the Perpendicular style in England, and for the fine fan vaulting used in the roof of the cloisters. The stained glass also is very fine, and one large window commemorates the victory won against the French at Crecy by Edward III in 1346.

In the nineteenth century Gloucester developed into a fine inland port due to the construction of a canal in 1827. Brunel's engineering feats figure prominently in Gloucester's commercial development. After our visit to Alan Sutton we had lunch in a restaurant also named for Brunel, took a quick look in the cathedral, and then set out for Marlborough.

On the way we made another detour to a small isolated village called Miserden. This village was home for many years to an uncle of mine who was the head gamekeeper for a member of the Wills tobacco family who lived in the big house of the village. My uncle lived in a remote cottage isolated in a deep valley hemmed in by high hills. I remember visiting him in my childhood during bad weather, with my mother nervous that we would not be able to negotiate the steep unpaved track leading to his house. Miserden is a pretty little village tucked away in the hills. The houses are grouped around an old market cross opposite the village inn. The ancient village church is nearby, and two of my uncles are buried in the grassy graveyard shaded by big trees. The big house is no longer privately owned, and its gardens are operated commercially. We had driven for miles along narrow twisting lanes to reach the village, but I was happy that we did so.

Pleased with our day of sightseeing, and with our business satisfactorily concluded, we returned to Marlborough in time for dinner with friends.

SUNDAY, SEPTEMBER 14TH

In the charming dining room of our hotel in Limpley Stoke, we breakfasted at a table set in a bay window overlooking the garden, a bit overgrown but delightfully haphazard. Yesterday's rain had stopped but its drenching prevented us from exploring the steep hillside garden, though Jane and David took photographs against a backdrop of brilliant green Somerset hills.

We took the road to Bath and got a fine view of the terraced Georgian city as we skirted it. We continued west towards Weston-super-Mare and then veered south towards Exeter where we took a road leading south to the Devon shore. We passed through the beautiful country of Avon, Somerset and Devon. One marshy area near Bridgwater was the site of the Battle of Sedgemoor in 1685.

We went through many villages with gardens a riot of colour, and sometimes we followed walls shielding large estates from the outside world, getting only occasional glimpses of the big houses within. The large and generally towered churches were the focal points for most of the villages. We saw many sheep grazing on the hillside, while in the lush valley pastures we saw many dairy cattle, mostly of the black and white Friesian breed, fat and sleek.

Almost at the coast we stopped at a pub called The Smugglers' Cove for lunch. It was built at the head of a secluded inlet, so that it was easy to imagine smugglers landing their kegs of brandy by night and sending them on the perilous road to London. We were by this time well into Devon, and we noted the dark red soil and the hedgerows dividing the landscape into a quilt of many shades of green, brown and harvest gold, while to our south we caught occasional glimpses of the sea. Much of the time the roads we followed were narrow twisting lanes lined by high hedged banks. We stopped at one parking place overlooking the Channel where we bought ice cream cones from a mobile cafe and watched local tourists taking in the view and the exhilarating air in their camp chairs and the comfort of their newspapers, steaming hot tea and picnic fare.

A few miles further on we came to the Torbay area, then around the once very exclusive resort of Torquay and the more plebeian one of Paignton, the two towns running together in a vast conglomeration of houses, hotels and bed-and-breakfast establishments. In Torquay, with its

Riviera-like climate, we saw palm trees growing in a sheltered area. Looking out to sea we could see several large ships and a motley assembly of smaller craft. We took a road leading down to the point of land where the little town of Brixham is built. Here in 1688 William of Orange landed to take the throne abdicated by James II and rule jointly with his wife Mary, James' daughter, for the next 18 years. A statue of the diminutive Dutch prince stands in the spot where he debarked.

Going on to Kingswear we caught the ferry across the mouth of the River Dart to Dartmouth. As we waited for it we could see the narrow opening of the estuary guarded by the twin castles of Kingswear and Dartmouth. In times of war a heavy chain was stretched between the forts to prevent enemy ships from entering the harbour. It was last used in World War II.

We found our hotel near the Upper Ferry right on the riverfront with its own marina. It is rather disappointing, for we are two flights up with no lift and no porter. There is no ambience to compensate for the inconvenience, for our room is small and cheaply furnished, though it does have a little balcony that would be nice if the weather is kind.

After partially unpacking and getting settled we took a walk along the quay and into the town. It is very old and interesting historically, built in a series of terraces up a very steep escarpment overlooking the river. Narrow passages and odd stairways between many of the houses made me imagine pirates, smugglers, and attacks in the dead of night in days long gone. There is an old fort built in 1519 in fear of Spain, and we saw a stone marking the departure of the Pilgrim ships from Dartmouth where they had put in for repairs before going on to Plymouth and the perils of the Atlantic. We discovered an old inn called the Cherub bearing the date 1380 and resolved to return later for drinks before dinner. We found it low-ceilinged, the beams black with age and smoke from the blazing logs in the enormous hearth. The cadaverous-looking barman with hooked nose and sunken purplish cheeks could have stepped right out of the pages of a Dickens novel.

MONDAY, SEPTEMBER 15TH

We awoke to a wet world, with scudding rain and gusty wind – a bit surprising perhaps after yesterday's nice weather, though no weather is really surprising on this peninsula sticking out into the Atlantic between the English Channel to the south and the Bristol Channel to the north. The rain made us revise our plans to drive to Plymouth and cross the Tamar into Cornwall, and we decided to explore the environs of Dartmouth rather than undertake a long drive through rain, wind and cold.

We enjoyed a good breakfast as we watched small ferry boats chugging between the opposite shores, boats laden with cars, buses, lorries and pedestrians. We looked quickly at the guidebooks available and went first to Dartmouth Castle. We drove along ever-narrowing streets wet and slippery from the rain in the face of much approaching traffic. Grass and trees never seemed greener, lush and heavy with falling raindrops. Many of the steeply sloping gardens had beautiful hydrangeas, their blossoms a medley of pink, blue and lavender cascading over stone walls or verdant banks. The road descended sharply to the castle and we parked as closely as we could. Bundled in raincoats and hoods, our umbrellas rendered useless by the high wind, we went cautiously down a descending walkway of slopes and steps into the castle built in the fifteenth century to guard the entrance to the harbour. Important since Roman times, the harbour has launched many naval expeditions over the centuries, one of the most famous that of 1347 when Edward III sailed with a vast fleet to take part in the siege of Calais.

The guide on duty today took us into a huge round room, its thick stone walls pierced by arrow slits. It struck damp and chill on this wet morning. It contained two huge fireplaces, and in one corner was the garde robe or latrine. A narrow winding staircase led up to a central tower surrounded by parapets that allow a fine view on clear days.

Leaving the castle we walked to the nearby church dedicated to St Petrock. 'Petrock' is most likely a Celtic version of 'Patrick' and indicates that once a very old church stood here, later replaced first by one of Norman design and then by the present Gothic building completed in 1641. The interior was chill, dank and piercingly cold, but impressive in an austere ascetic way. There were some very old gravestones set in the floor of the aisles and one local name, Holdworth, appeared over and over through the ages. The War Memorial to Dartmouth men, most of them sailors who lost their lives in the two world wars shows their names carved into a wooden panel of exquisite workmanship. Dartmouth naturally has a long connection with the sea and is the home of the Royal Naval College, where many of Britain's most famous seafarers have received their training. The college is a huge red brick mass of buildings high on a hill above the town and is only open to the public on rare occasions. Outside the church, the graveyard, contained in a stout wall, sloped steeply down to the water, many of the headstones leaning at odd angles produced by erosion and the passage of time.

Returning to the town, by now full of traffic and wet shoppers and sightseers, we were fortunate to find a parking place right outside the Castle Inn. We spent a pleasant hour in the town museum, located in a row of houses known as the Butterwalk, one of Dartmouth's architectural treasures. Damaged by bombs in the Second World War, the row has now been fully restored. The houses are half-timbered with mullioned windows and are built on a row of sturdy granite pillars. The museum contained much naval and historical material relating to the town and area, and featured the engineering and railway accomplishments of one Thomas Newcomen, a resident of Dartmouth. There was also a fine collection of Victorian watercolours done by a reclusive local lady about whom little is known. From the museum we went to the Castle Inn, an old coaching establishment for lunch.

In spite of the rain we felt we should go to Plymouth, largest port in the southwest and very important historically to both English and Americans. We took the coastal road thinking it would be more scenic but it proved very slow going. We made one stop at Slapton Sands – a wide expanse of yellow sand ringed on this day by a surface boiling from the wind of almost gale force. Here American soldiers practised landings and attack tactics in preparation for D-Day. Many lost their lives when German E-boats penetrated the defences and torpedoed some of the craft engaged in the exercises. This was not revealed at the time because of the need for secrecy, and only recently has it come to light due to the discovery of bodies buried near the shore. Prior to D-Day several nearby villages were evacuated to accommodate the soldiers in training, and there is a monument on the sands given by the U.S. Army to honour the sacrifices made by the inhabitants. David took a picture of the monument, the wind so fierce that it took his hat and he was lucky to retrieve it.

We went on to Plymouth finding the approaches to the city quite unattractive. We followed signs to the Hoe, the flat-topped hill overlooking the harbour where Sir Francis Drake was playing bowls in 1588 when news came that the long-expected Spanish Armada had at last been sighted. Legend has it that he uttered the words, 'Time to finish the game and beat the Spaniards too!' The weather must have been fair on that long-ago day, unlike today's wind and rain, and yet later it was just such a storm that led to the final destruction of the defeated Spanish ships. Today the grass of the Hoe is replaced by asphalt, but a statue of Drake still looks out to sea ever watchful for enemy ships, perhaps true to his promise to return when and if England needs him.

We did not linger long nor did we on this occasion see the spot from which the Mayflower set sail in 1620. We were tired and the weather was not conducive to further sightseeing. We returned to Dartmouth by the main road making very good time.

We warmed up over a cup of tea and changed into dry clothes for dinner. We decided to drive to Dunster on the north shore of Somerset tomorrow and David made reservations at the Luttrell Arms Hotel in that town.

TUESDAY, SEPTEMBER 16TH

I slept poorly and was glad to be packed up and ready to leave. The rain had stopped though dark clouds were still scudding across the sky. We drove north towards Dartmoor going through Totnes and Newton Abbot. Totnes is a charming old town set on a steep hill above the River Dart, and at the northern end stands the keep of an eleventh-century castle, a solid round tower that is all that remains of the building. On a previous occasion many years ago David and I had climbed to the top and got a marvellous view of the surrounding country. But today we had no time and the weather was not cooperative. We went north and west across the edge of the moor to the quaint little town of Moretonhampstead and from there cut diagonally across Dartmoor to Postbridge and Princetown.

The high windswept plateau of Dartmoor, its slopes mistily purple with heather was a fascinating sight for David's sisters. We could see a circle of weatherworn stones, perhaps of Druidic consequence and later an old Celtic cross standing in isolation.

About this time the sun broke through the clouds and the forbidding landscape suddenly appeared softer and gentler. We stopped at prehistoric Post Bridge, while traffic crosses the river by a 'new' three arched bridge built in the thirteenth century. There is an excellent information centre near the bridge, and we spent a few minutes there examining the wealth of material assembled about Dartmoor and its geology, history, flora and fauna.

We passed through Princetown, getting a good view of the notorious prison there, and then through Tavistock and Launceston, the former a large market town for many years part of the estate of the Russell family, the dukes of Bedford. During the war David was briefly stationed near Launceston, a town just across the Devon border in Cornwall. Here we took a very lonely deserted road with few villages or even houses that eventually led us to a main road where we found a delightful inn that provided a good lunch.

Our next stop was Clovelly on the north coast of Devon – we had crossed the peninsula from south to north. Clovelly has long been one of the show places of Britain, a fishing village built on a steep cliff descending into the harbour. Cars cannot enter the village for the main – indeed only – street is very steep, cobbled and in places stepped. It lies in a lush narrow combe between high cliffs, and the street is lined with flower-bedecked houses and tiny shops. In olden days all supplies were brought in by donkey, and there was one such animal on display for photographs. The cobbled steps lead right down to the water's edge, the waves today a brilliant turquoise in the bright sunshine and white-capped in the stiff breeze. A scene of postcard colour and perfection, Clovelly has been called the most Mediterranean-like fishing village in England. Our, especially David's, appreciation of it was somewhat spoiled by the hazards of the descent for ladies with poor eyesight and the wrong shoes. We were glad to take advantage of the Land Rover service to get us back to our starting point.

We stayed for many miles on A39. Part of the way it followed the spectacular scenery of the coast.

Passing Lynmouth and Lynton the road now became very steep. We negotiated Porlock Hill, one of the steepest gradients in England, with care. Looking across the Bristol Channel we could see the Welsh mountains mistily purple in the distance. We were skirting Exmoor, the country of Lorna Doone, and at last we came to Dunster, our destination on the eastern edge of the moor. Dunster was once an important cloth town, and its old octagonal yarn market still stands in the centre of the main street. At one end of this street is a tower built in 1775 as a landmark for shipping, for until the river silted up Dunster was an important port. At the opposite end stands the castle frowning down upon the town. It was first built by the Normans and added to down the centuries, though it has been owned by only two families, the Luttrells and the de Mohuns.

We found the Luttrell Arms Hotel, a square stone building of great antiquity covered in Virginia creeper turning from green to crimson in the early autumn. Parking was a problem, but at last we entered the cool dim reception area and were shown to very charming rooms overlooking the main street.

WEDNESDAY, SEPTEMBER 17TH

Dunster is a charming town of great antiquity and history, and I am sorry we had to give it such a cursory inspection. The hotel is very comfortable, with every modern convenience incorporated without destroying its ancient charm, and there are still dark passages and uneven stone steps in unexpected places. The inn was once part of the monastery belonging to the abbots of Cleeve, and the abbots' kitchen remains. The inn is named for the Luttrell family who have owned the castle for centuries.

The main street is very wide, wide enough in fact to accommodate diagonal parking on one side, but the ingress and egress to the street are so extremely narrow that traffic jams are the norm. At the west end traffic has to go around the octagonal yarn market, and at the eastern end the road divides, the part going to the church so narrow that a one-way traffic system controlled by lights is in place to manage it. Lovely shops line the main street, and we visited the church, a very large and handsome building dating from the fifteenth century. Since the church served both town and monastery, the nave was divided into two parts by a very beautiful carved rood screen to separate the laity and the men of God. There are many handsome tombs, mostly those of de Mohuns and Luttrells, the two families connected with Dunster Castle. The tower of the church is exceptionally high and wide. Such towers distinguish many of the churches in this part of the West Country, so that they have come to be known as Somerset towers. 'Wool' money contributed to the size and beautification of the church. Beside the church was a memorial garden, and we strolled through it and had our pictures taken outside a lovely old stone house that was once part of the nunnery. We drove through the castle grounds, but the castle itself was closed to the public for television crews filming a forthcoming programme. The castle, still owned and occupied by the Luttrells, is considered one of the finest in the country and houses a priceless collection of furniture and art.

Leaving Dunster we set out for Glastonbury and Wells. We stopped in Glastonbury and had lunch at the George and Pilgrims Inn. This is one of the oldest and most famous hostelries in England, but it was crowded and service was slow. Down the centuries it has been the place for rest and refreshment for the legions of pilgrims visiting the shrine and monastery at Glastonbury.

Many legends have arisen around Glastonbury. Joseph of Arimathea is believed to have come here and planted his staff in the ground, the staff then growing into the thorn of Glastonbury that blooms at Christmas. Christ himself in the minds of some people also came here. Certainly Blake refers to that belief in his famous apocalyptic poem 'Jerusalem,' which begins, 'And did those feet in ancient time ...'. Glastonbury is also thought to be the burial place of King Arthur, himself a legend, and perhaps Avalon and Camelot were nearby. With its aura of mystery, it became the site of the great monastery that was closed by order of Henry VIII, the great buildings then falling into the massive spectacular ruins we see today.

On then to Wells, the little cathedral city tucked away in a remote corner of Somerset. We could see the towers of the huge cathedral long before we reached the town. We found it was market day, with the market place full of stalls and the roads choked with traffic. The stalls went right up to the cathedral walls, and we felt it must have been just like this on every market day since the Middle Ages. We went to the Crown Inn, where Sybil Beard had made reservations for David and his sisters while I was to spend the night at her cottage in East Harptree. One of several in the market place, the Crown appeared very old-fashioned with little attempt at modernization and somewhat shabby, though in a comfortable sort of way. It has been in operation as an inn since 1450. Like Glastonbury, Wells was an important religious shrine, site of a great cathedral and a moated bishop's palace. Both palace and cathedral are entered from carved gates that open directly on to the marketplace, for in true mediaeval fashion the secular and religious exist side by side.

David and his sisters set out for a tour of the cathedral and then went back to Glastonbury to explore the abbey ruins, while I awaited Sybil. She arrived promptly and we met for the first time, though our long correspondence, which had begun when she read *Recollections of a G.I. War Bride*, made us feel we knew each other well. We drove the few miles to East Harptree, talking all the way. The village is the site of the ruins of a castle that played a part in the twelfth-century civil war between Stephen and Matilda, nephew and daughter respectively of Henry I, and the church is old with a Norman porch and many ancient tombs.

Sybil and Norman live in the centre cottage of a group of three known as the Dower Cottage, which leads me to suppose they were once one house belonging to the nearby mansion, known as the Court, for the use of a dowager. Though it appears small from the outside, it is surprisingly roomy inside and decorated to provide maximum light. Sybil has it furnished impeccably with beautiful antiques of the right size and shape and all glowing with the lovely patina of age. Norman is Scottish, younger than Sybil, and a very attentive husband. Though with his ruddy complexion he appears the picture of health, he suffered a severe heart attack two years ago. He owns a nursery where he grows conifers and heathers, and since his illness has learned to repair antique china professionally so that he can earn money in a less physically demanding way. The third member of the family is Giba, a Borzoi or Russian wolfhound. She is a very tall thin dog with a long aristocratic nose and a thick curly silk coat that shades from creamy white through reddish tan to silver grey. Shy with strangers, she appeared to take to me, and I was touched when she offered her paw to me to shake. It signified acceptance.

David, Jane and Bet came about six, and we had drinks and a lovely four-course dinner, cooked and served by Norman. Prior to the meal we looked at the tiny walled garden, marvelling at the fine green grass and the number of flowering plants growing against the old brick wall. We also admired the flower arrangements in the house that were the work of Sybil. Roast beef at dinner was followed by the old English sweet known as syllabub, pure cream flavoured with liqueurs. About 10.30 the Wharton siblings left for the Crown, while Sybil, Norman and I sat and talked around the fire till the wee hours. I slept what remained of the night in a featherbed in a Laura Ashley-decorated room under the eaves, with a hot water bottle I didn't need. It was British hospitality at its best and warmest.

THURSDAY, SEPTEMBER 18TH

I was up about seven and breakfasted in the cosy well-equipped kitchen. Norman was once more the cook. The others arrived from Wells about 9, and we said goodbye to our kind hosts. Norman gave us directions to Bristol where we could pick up the motorway north. The weather was bright and sunny, and we went through pretty pastoral country before reaching the urban sprawl of Bristol. This city is one of the most important ports in England and has a long history of trade with the Americas in wine, sugar and bananas. At one time it was one of the chief centres of the slave trade. It was heavily bombed in World War II but has been largely restored. We skirted the main part of the city though we encountered heavy traffic on the road to Worcester. Once on the motorway the traffic thinned out and we maintained a high speed though at the expense of attractive scenery.

1987

EAST HARPTREE – SOMERSET SIGHTSEEING

WEDNESDAY, AUGUST 5TH

We left Marlborough early to go to East Harptree and spend a couple of days with Sybil and Norman Beard, friends whom we first met a year ago. The weather was delightful and the drive through Wiltshire and Somerset (or, I should say, the newly created county of Avon) showed the English countryside at its best.

Arriving before lunch we had time to sit out in the tiny walled garden of the Beards' cottage. The entrance way to the house is hung with baskets of begonias, geraniums, lobelia and fuchsia, the latter hanging low with red and purple blossoms looking like tiny ballerinas. We were introduced to Candi, a sleek black greyhound who has replaced Giba, the aristocratic Russian wolfhound who died suddenly and unexpectedly. Candi was a racing dog who was injured in her prime and rescued by the Beards. Tall and thin, almost emaciated-looking, this breed is closer to the hunting dogs of the Middle Ages than any other. Certainly the dogs of the Normans and Saxons portrayed in the Bayeux Tapestry look very much like greyhounds. These dogs are highly intelligent, very trainable and almost without exception very friendly. Candi quickly made friends with us and gives every indication she recognizes her good fortune in being adopted by the Beards.

We had lunch in a nearby village where Norman rents land for his horticultural business, and we enjoyed seeing his many varieties of conifers in various stages of growth. Later we drove to Chew Valley Lake, a reservoir created by damming the Chew River. The surrounding land has been made into a park and wildlife refuge, and we saw quite a variety of waterfowl, including ducks, geese, herons, moorhens and snipe. Back at the cottage Norman prepared dinner – he is a man of many talents, gourmet cooking among them.

THURSDAY, AUGUST 6TH

After taking care of some banking in a village a few miles from East Harptree called Stanton Drew, Sybil led us across the road, up a lane and to a field where cows stood grazing amidst a large circle of sarsen stones something like a miniature Avebury. Legend has it that the devil disguised as a fiddler played for a wedding party here long after the Sabbath had dawned. When the devil departed the bride, groom and guests were changed into stones in punishment for breaking the Fourth Commandment.

We had a special lunch at the cottage to celebrate Sybil's and my seventieth birthdays, which both occur in August within a few days of each other. Then all four of us left for an afternoon of sightseeing. We drove first to Axbridge, taking a lonely road past an isolated inn called the Castle of Comfort where miners from nearby Priddy Common were accustomed to meet. Not far away are traces of a Roman road and four earthwork rings known as the Priddy Circles. Axbridge is a grey stone town built around a spacious square from which many narrow streets, barely more than lanes, radiate. It has been a borough – a town incorporated by a royal charter – since before 1066. A great church approached by a timeworn stone staircase broods over the central square. In the square there is a large Elizabethan building called King John's hunting lodge, although that monarch in fact had no connection with the place. This old building houses a very interesting museum that contains among other artifacts wooden stocks and a 'bull anchor' used in the ancient and cruel sport of bull-baiting.

We spent a little time here and then walked a few of the streets, stopping in several antique stores but finding nothing we wanted to buy. The town was quite deserted, and it seemed a place where time had stood still while the rest of the world passed it by. There are many such old towns in England. While some like Marlborough have grown and prospered, others, though remaining centres for local farmers, seem to have withered on the vine with nothing more than interesting anachronisms to show the few visitors who find them. Such places lack proximity to the great arteries of transportation and do not possess a particular natural attraction or historical event, building, or institution to draw sightseers. Many have suffered from the decline of the railways and closure of rural stations.

We then went on to Cheddar, site of the famous gorge and limestone caves where great wheels of the local cheese ripen, and found the main street of the village packed with people, cars, bicycles, and caravans. Since we had all visited the caves before we contented ourselves with driving through the gorge and going on to the smaller ravine at Burrington Combe. We stopped at the cleft in the rocks where Augustus Toplady is said to have written the famous hymn 'Rock of Ages.' Toplady was the curate of a neighbouring village and while wandering through the hills was caught in a violent thunderstorm from which he sheltered in this cave-like hollow.

This is the country of the Mendip Hills, which lie in a broad band across the county. They are composed of limestone covering red sandstone, and it is the effect of water on limestone which has led to the formation of caves, gorges and holes. We would like to be able to explore more here, for it is a region full of surprises, and events here have moulded much of our history. Prehistoric lake villages, built on stilts amidst water and swamps for protection from wild animals and human enemies, flourished long before the Romans arrived, and Phoenician traders came here. Bladud, the father of King Lear, is said to have founded the first settlement at Bath long before the Romans and the Georgians made that city into the gem it is today. Legend suggests that Glastonbury may have played host to Joseph of Arimathea, perhaps even Christ himself, as well as King Arthur. Later King Alfred hid in the swamps of Athelney and, while sheltered in a charcoal burner's hut and preoccupied with plans to defeat the Danes, burned the goodwife's cakes. Centuries later, in 1685 at Sedgemoor, James II crushed the Duke of Monmouth's bid to take the English throne. The village of Mells gave rise to the nursery rhyme 'Little Jack Horner' – the 'plum' he pulled out of the pie the deeds to the family estates threatened by the king in the days of the Reformation. And few cathedrals can rival Wells.

1989

EAST HARPTREE – BRISTOL – WELLS CATHEDRAL
TUESDAY, SEPTEMBER 19TH

The day dawned bright and cheerful for our trip to Somerset. We left Marlborough about 11 o'clock heading west across the downs. We have travelled this road several times in the past week but always in rain or cloud. Though downs look somehow right when mist, fog, and rain heighten their bleak loneliness, it was good to see them clean and sparkling against a clear intensely blue sky.

We by-passed Chippenham and went on past Corsham and Box, seeing in the chequered landscape a pattern of bright yellows, green and brown, very different from the muted shades of last Saturday. It took us awhile to get through the outskirts of Bath, but we got a good view of the Georgian symmetry of its terraced hills centred around the mediaeval bulk of the great abbey. We passed some of Bath's famous public gardens, on this bright morning a riot of fall colour with beds of blossoming begonias and impatiens. We followed road signs to Wells, driving for the most part down narrow hedge-lined roads, eventually arriving at East Harptree to be warmly welcomed by our friends Sybil and Norman Beard.

They took us to lunch at a very ancient pub called the King's Arms in the nearby village of Litton. The uneven floors were stone-flagged, the ceilings low with dark oak beams, and the doorways very low, a menace to my tall husband. The food was good and we caught up with our private news. Sybil is looking much slimmer and consequently more elegant since her bout with a recurring virus and subsequent diligent dieting. Norman has the ruddy complexion of the Scotsman who leads an outdoor life, as indeed he does in his business of growing conifers and heathers.

Back at the cottage we were greeted by Candi, their sleek black greyhound. Though the sun was bright, the wind was too cool and brisk to sit in the walled garden still aflame with blooms of begonia, fuchsia, and chrysanthemum, the rosy brick a backdrop for the massed border flowers. Inside, the house was full of flowers, great loose shaggy arrangements of chrysanthemums and autumn leaves in huge brass and china bowls. In our bedroom we found the last sweet peas of summer, the delicate pastel-hued blossoms giving off a faint fragrance.

Sybil and I spent a lazy afternoon talking while Norman and David walked to the garden. After a delicious dinner prepared by Norman we were early to bed with the sound of the country – baaing of sheep, lowing of cows, and crowing and clucking of cocks and hens – all around us and a full moon shining. We were however chagrined to hear on television of the devastation wrought in the southern U.S. by Hurricane Hugo and hoped that Chapel Hill would be spared the full fury of the storm.

WEDNESDAY, SEPTEMBER 20TH

Bright sunshine awoke us and we had a real English breakfast in the large kitchen, modern yet retaining its country atmosphere. Again Sybil and I spent a lazy morning, taking a short walk through the village and sitting briefly in the warm sun in the sheltered garden, while David and Norman went to the local manor house where Norman rents land for his garden. Candi went with them and I was told demonstrated what remains of her racing skill. They came back to the house for lunch and then left for Bristol where they visited the restored S.S. *Great Britain*, designed in 1843 by Brunel and the first propeller-driven iron ship to cross the Atlantic. Altered now in many ways she ended her career as a sailing cargo ship and was virtually abandoned in the Falkland Islands. In 1970 she was brought back to Bristol for restoration to the very dock from which she was first launched. Later the two men walked across the Clifton Suspension Bridge spanning the Avon Gorge. It was built to Brunel's design, though he did not live to see it completed. They drove around the city and took a walk across the downs in bright sunshine and a wind of gale-like strength. It was an outing they both enjoyed tremendously.

Sybil and I meanwhile stayed at the cottage to entertain Babs Honey, a very old friend of mine who happened to be visiting nearby. Babs and I played together as children sixty-odd years ago and were pupils together at Marlborough Grammar School. Over tea we talked and talked mostly of Marlborough and old family members and friends.

In the evening we drove to Wells for dinner. Norman took a road across a high wild expanse of land known as Priddy Common. Mining for iron, Fuller's earth and tin has been carried on here since prehistoric times. It is well-known that Phoenician traders came to the West Country for tin, so perhaps Joseph was among them, as Cornish miners have long chanted 'St Joseph was a tinman' when molten tin flashes in the pan. Approaching Wells the floodlit cathedral came into view and from the Gatehouse restaurant we got an excellent view of it. After a fine meal we returned by another road in bright moonlight.

THURSDAY, SEPTEMBER 21ST

The day dawned bright and sunny – it really seems as if summer has returned. We were up by 8 o'clock and after packing walked to Norman's garden at the manor house. We passed Brook Cottage and stopped to admire its lovely garden complete with stone-arched bridge over a gurgling stream. We walked through the cutting garden of the manor, a grey stone mansion built in symmetrical Georgian style. The herbaceous borders against an old brick wall were planted with a melange of many plants, among them purple Michaelmas daisies, many coloured carnations, pinks and marigolds. Opposite the wall the path was bordered with a wide bed of very dark red roses, still in magnificent bloom at summer's end. Norman's section of the garden was planted in neat rows of small coniferous trees varying in size and type, their foliage ranging in colour from yellow to deep blue green. The little trees stand straight and evenly spaced in rows like soldiers on parade. The heathers grow in and near the greenhouse and run the gamut of shades from white to deep purple. We then walked back to the house and said goodbye to our gracious friends.

We drove through the lush green chequerboard Somerset countryside to Wells, which was very busy and bustling. Shoppers, mothers pushing baby carriages, some sadly handicapped elderly folk and a few tourists crowded the narrow pavements and streets so that it was difficult to make progress. Wells reminds me of Freiburg in the Black Forest, partly because the cathedral walls abut on to the marketplace so that trading is carried on in the very shadow of the great church, and partly because the streets are lined with culverts down which streams of water merrily run. The town is built on a number of underground springs and wells from which it gets its name. We found a couple of bookshops and made enquiries about my book to no avail, but in the second one, dealing mainly in old and used books, we talked to a tiny wizened old gnome of a man who was most courteous and promised to look out for the book and send us any copies he comes across.

Before leaving we visited the cathedral – dominating, majestic, triumphant. A bishop named Jocelyn began building it in the thirteenth century, but the carvers who fashioned the figures adorning the west front are unknown. Newly cleaned, the west front looked today more magnificent than usual. We watched the knightly figures of the ancient clock go through their ritual jousting as twelve o'clock struck and then went into the dim and cloistered interior where I found my favourite place – the curving flight of stone steps worn smooth by the feet of countless pilgrims leading from the nave to the chapter house. We then strolled down the Vicar's Close of small stone houses reserved for clergy, each with a tiny garden gay with many-hued impatiens, and then to the moated Bishop's Palace, which we could only view through the iron gates. The water in the moat was muddied and the surface covered with waterlilies. There was only one swan swimming among many ducks, and he declined to ring the bell for food as the Wells swans have been trained to do. No doubt too many kind people feed him these days so that he does not need to ask in the time-honoured way. Underneath a spreading Lebanon cedar I saw a pure white dove nestling, perhaps a symbol of peace in a place hallowed by faith that has survived the passage of time.

Back we then went to the car and on through Glastonbury.

Slowed by road works we reached Somerton in time for a late pub lunch. Somerton today is rather a sad little town, though once long ago it was for a brief time the capital of Saxon Wessex. The attractive marketplace ringed by several inns and an old church was quite deserted and though it was refreshing to go into a town not choked with traffic and people, I realized it spelled a poor economy and poverty. We ate a hurried lunch in the White Hart Hotel, where we were the only customers, and then stopped to look at the octagonal market cross and the War Memorial commemorating the dead of the two wars. Added to the list were the names of several civilians who were killed in an air raid in September 1942. I suppose the Germans were trying to bomb the nearby airfield and stray bombs hit the town.

The next town of any size we came to was Yeovil, which, as the centre of an important agricultural district, appeared thriving and prosperous. In addition Yeovil has for many years manufactured gloves. Years ago gloves were cut out of leather in factories and then sent out in bundles to women in the surrounding villages to be stitched by hand. I had an aunt who stitched gloves in her spare time from the time she was a girl till she was an old lady. I have been told that she never sat down without a glove to stitch in her hand.

Hampton Court

Moat Garden at Windsor Castle

Mayor and Town Crier of
Weymouth at VE Day ceremony
1945

Slapton Sands, South Devon where
many Americans were killed in
pre-invasion exercises

Statue of King Alfred at Wantage,
thought to be his birthplace

Shadowed arches at Winchester
Cathedral

Hardy's Cottage at Little Bockhampton, Dorset where he was born

Corfe Castle towers over the village

Bath – the Abbey and the Roman Baths

Statue of Sir Francis Drake stands on Plymouth Hoe

Clovelly – stepped main street leads down to the harbour

Wells Cathedral

Wild Ponies on Dartmoor

John Knox's house on the Royal Mile in Edinburgh

Statue of David Lloyd George, World War I prime minister in Caernarvon

Conway Castle, North Wales

Railway to Snowdon Summit

Chapter Four

WALES AND SCOTLAND

I have put journal entries from Wales and Scotland together because our time in these countries has been unfortunately brief. Also, Wales and Scotland seem to be quite different nations from England and to have more in common with each other than with England.

In contrast with the English and their predominantly Saxon origins, the Welsh and Scottish peoples have somewhat similar Celtic heritages. Although historical developments in the two countries have differed considerably, both are somewhat isolated and have been relatively uninfluenced by the history and cultures of continental Europe. Topographically the regions are similar with high mountains, fertile lowlands, and jagged indented coastlines, and both have rich deposits of coal and iron. Both countries have contributed many distinguished men of science, art and politics to the British Isles and to the world. Both peoples have retained to some extent their original Celtic languages, cultures, and customs – of which they are fiercely proud – and in both countries there is some desire and agitation for independence from England. In neither, however, does this seem a likely prospect for the foreseeable future, and each today remains part of the United Kingdom, represented in the Westminster Parliament, and under the English monarch as nominal ruler.

WALES

'Lovely the woods, waters, meadows, coombes, vales
All the air things wear that build this world of Wales.'
Gerard Manley Hopkins 1844–1889

Though Wales was conquered militarily by the Romans, many of the original people fled to the mountains and were thus largely untouched by Roman civilization. During the fifth-century Saxon invasion of Britain, many Romanized Britons fled to Wales, but at the same time considerable migration from Ireland to Wales helped to maintain the Celtic strain in the population. There was much border warfare between England and Wales during Saxon times, and the Saxon king of Mercia named Offa constructed a great defensive ditch or dike along the border, traces of which still remain.

Prior to the Norman conquest, Wales was ruled by a number of princes, one of whom, Llewellyn (1039–1063), succeeded in becoming master of all Wales. Border warfare continued after the Normans came to England, and at this time many forts and castles were built by both the Welsh and English along the Welsh marches. The English king Edward I (1272–1307) finally conquered Wales after long and arduous campaigns in which he borrowed the longbow from the Welsh and turned it to great effect against them. Edward was driven by his belief that the whole island should be united under one king, and he built eight strong castles to hold down his conquests. One of these, Caernarvon, was the birthplace of his son, later Edward II, whom he presented to the Welsh people as the first Prince of Wales.

Wales was only superficially conquered, however, and rebellions arose during the reigns of the weak kings who succeeded Edward. The most famous of these revolts was led by Owen Glendower, who in 1404 was crowned King of Wales at Machynlleth. His reign was short-lived but he remains a great hero to the Welsh.

Disorder persisted in Wales through the fourteenth- and fifteenth-century Wars of the Roses. The conflict finally ended in 1485 when the Welsh prince Henry Tudor led the Lancastrians to victory and became Henry VII of England. In the reign of his son Henry VIII, Wales and England were formally united by acts of Parliament in 1536 and 1542. With these acts Wales came under English law and English became the official language.

Religiously Wales became Protestant at the time of the Reformation. Methodism later grew in influence, and today most Welsh churchgoers belong to Nonconformist churches.

Welsh prosperity during the Industrial Revolution was connected primarily to the coal and iron found in South Wales. Towns like Cardiff and Swansea grew rapidly. The mines are largely worked out today, and the southern region has experienced hard economic times ever since World War I. North Wales, however, has remained relatively prosperous thanks to growing tourism.

In the face of continued agitation for independence, parliamentary concessions to Wales have been made in recent years. These are most conspicuous to the visitor in the realm of language, with both Welsh and English appearing on public signs. Welsh is taught in the schools as well.

1983

with the West Side Presbyterian Church Choir of Ridgewood N.J.

LLANGOLLEN IN WALES – THROUGH WALES TO BATH
FRIDAY, JULY 8TH

We returned to the hotel in Chester by taxi for a brief rest before an early dinner. We then met at the buses for the 25-mile journey to Llangollen and the Eisteddfod. It was a pretty ride in the cool of the evening, the land becoming increasingly hilly with rushing rocky streams and many sheep in the fields. The Shropshire Union Canal ran beside the road for several miles, and we saw barges and pleasure craft on its serene but murky waters. Using its money and political power, the county of Cheshire was instrumental in the development of the canals, including the Manchester Ship Canal.

We passed a delightful old mill dated 1681 around which stood a group of ancient stone cottages and outbuildings with gardens gay with flowers. In one place mine tippings intruded upon the pastoral scene, reminding us that coal is found in North as well as South Wales, and that these fields are really continuations of the vast deposits in Cheshire and Lancashire.

Llangollen is a small, very old grey town that comes to life during the weeks of the Eisteddfod international folk and music festival that has been held here since 1947. We passed the fourteenth-century stone bridge built by a bishop of St Asaph and considered one of the seven wonders of Wales. The town is also famous for a black and white timber-framed house that was the home of Lady Eleanor Butler and Miss Sarah Ponsonby, two Irish aristocrats who lived there for 50 years with their maid and entertained

WALES

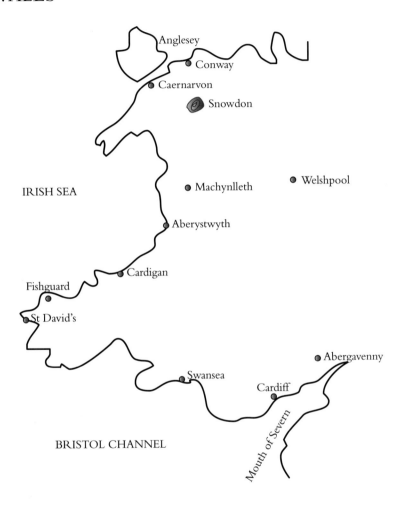

Anglesey

Conway

Caernarvon

Snowdon

IRISH SEA

Machynlleth

Welshpool

Aberystwyth

Cardigan

Fishguard

St David's

Abergavenny

Swansea

Cardiff

BRISTOL CHANNEL

Mouth of Severn

distinguished nobility and intellectuals. Wordsworth and the Duke of Wellington were among their guests.

We were not able to see the house, however, as we had to hurry to the parking lot and find our seats in the enormous tent that houses the Eisteddfod. Unfortunately the performance rather disappointed us, partly because of its slow pace and partly because we were all very tired. Choirs from many parts of the world participated, a Japanese violinist played, and we heard baritone and alto soloists. I think really we had expected traditional Welsh singing and music. At intermission there was a unanimous decision to return to the hotel. We drove back fast down the winding roads in dusk deepening into night, glad for the earlier than expected return in view of tomorrow's long journey.

SATURDAY, JULY 9TH

The day dawned bright but promised to be overcast – a blessing for the long bus trip. We left Chester and the amenities of the Abbot's Well Hotel with some regret, for our short stay had permitted only a small taste of the city's attractions.

Our original travel plans had to be revised. To take in Caernarvon and drive through Snowdonia and then on south to Bath was just too much on a hot Saturday when the roads of this popular resort area would be full of holidaymakers. So Conway Castle was substituted for Caernarvon, and we would barely skirt the mountains of central Wales. We would take a loop from Chester to Conway, go southeast to Bettys-y-Cwed for lunch, and then on east till we connected with the motorway.

The road following the northern coast of Wales was very scenic as we went through the huge resort area of Colwyn Bay and approached Llandudno. As expected there was a lot of traffic on the roads, but fortunately we encountered no major tie-ups on our way to the castle at Conway.

Wales has many castles in various stages of preservation. The strongest and finest of them were built by Edward I. Other castles, particularly those in the borderland between Wales and England known as the Welsh Marches, were built piecemeal by strong barons in the reigns of weak kings. These lords fought constantly among themselves though they would unite against the marauding Welsh.

Conway Castle is built on the heights above the estuary of a river of the same name. It is approached by a suspension bridge built by Thomas Telford, the famous engineer of the nineteenth century. We spent about an hour wandering around the fortifications, clambering up the steep steps of the battlemented towers, looking through arrow slits at the harbour below, peering down the deep well and exploring the deepest dungeons. We wondered how such a fortress could be built at the king's behest in the short space of four and one-half years. The secret lay in the master craftsmen and an inexhaustible supply of workers.

Leaving Conway we drove through hilly almost mountainous country. We passed a partially ruined church and a circle of Druid stones. Everywhere the flowers left us gasping in admiration. By 12.30 we arrived at the Royal Oak Hotel in Bettys-y-Cwed – the name means Chapel-in-the-Woods – a holiday town first popularized by artists in the nineteenth century. We enjoyed an excellent lunch of roast beef and Yorkshire pudding followed by strawberries and cream. We then started on the long drive through Wales and Shropshire to link up with the motorway at Cannock in Staffordshire. The countryside was very pretty and there was much to see, but many, sated with good food and lulled by heat and motion, nodded off and lost themselves in sleep.

We skirted Shrewsbury (pronounced 'shrowsbury'), the county town of Shropshire. For some miles we followed a stream, broad even at this considerable distance from the ocean. It was the Severn, the longest river in England. For some way it is the boundary between England and Wales and flows in a broad estuary into the Bristol Channel.

After we reached the motorway we made one brief stop for rest and refreshment. Then we went on at high speed through the industrial Midlands which gradually gave way to flat agricultural lands. We passed the fruit orchards of Worcestershire and saw pigs, sheep and fine herds of cattle in the pastures.

As we descended a steep hill the city of Bath at last lay before us, cupped in its sheltering hills. We all perked up like horses approaching the stable, but at the last moment we were balked by, of all things, a carnival procession. We tumbled, dirty and exhausted, out of our buses into a wall of heat, unusual and unexpected, to walk the last distance into the elegant Francis Hotel. There we thankfully found our rooms comfortable and attractive but lacking the air-conditioning to which we are accustomed. A drink and a fine meal restored us, and after a brief stroll and a cool bath, bed and sleep followed very quickly.

1986
with Jane Sockwell & Betsy Newland

RHAYADER – CAERNARVON – THE TRAIN UP SNOWDON
THURSDAY, SEPTEMBER 18TH

Continuing on through the lovely country of Herefordshire we passed from England into Wales near Rhayader. All road signs were in Welsh though subtitled in English. The letter groupings in the long names seemed very strange and to us appeared quite unpronounceable. The road ran through a wide valley, very green with a clear bubbling stream at its bottom, and sheep were everywhere wandering the steep hillsides with no fences to contain them. Cattle were conspicuous by their absence, however. Though there appeared no sign of mining in the immediate vicinity, the landscape brought to mind the book and movie *How Green Was My Valley.*

We stopped briefly in Rhayader, a rather depressed-looking grey town on the upper Wye, to get our bearings and buy fruit and drinks. Then we went on towards Aberystwyth on the coast, though we turned north to Machynlleth before reaching the shore.

We arrived at the Wynnstay Hotel in Machynlleth about 4 p.m. The town, though extolled in guidebooks as a regional centre, struck us as rather sad and lacking prosperity. The main street is wide and lined with shops, but the merchandise seemed unattractive and displayed poorly. A rather impressive clock tower stands at one end of the street, and there are some very old buildings. The most notable of these is the ancient Welsh Parliament house where Owen Glendower was crowned king in 1404. It is a dour forbidding building of heavy dark grey stone, blackened with soot, with tiny barred windows. Jane, Betsy and I walked the length of the main street feeling depressed and disappointed in the town. Returning to the hotel we cheered up in the bright warmth emanating from huge fires of good Welsh coal glowing in the grates of the public rooms. We had an excellent dinner in the restaurant where we were served by a pretty rosy-cheeked girl whose singsong Welsh accent charmed and delighted us. Our bedrooms overlooking the main street are comfortable, though it takes many uneven stairs to reach them.

FRIDAY, SEPTEMBER 19TH

Another beautiful day dawned. Getting off to a rather late start we set out for Snowdon, having decided in view of the good weather to take the train trip to the summit. Snowdon, at 3,560 feet above sea level, is the highest peak of the Cambrian mountain massif of central Wales, which boasts the highest peaks in Britain south of the Scottish border.

The drive from Machynlleth via Dolgellau and Bettys-y-Cwed to Llanberis, where we would board the train, was very scenic, though slow due to twisting mountain roads and repairs being undertaken upon them. The steep mountain slopes were dotted with sheep and clear tumbling streams ran gurglingly along at the bottom of valleys beneath towering peaks. The few towns we passed were drab and sombre, and I imagined how grey and depressing they would appear on the rainy days so frequent in Wales. The low row houses hugged and cowered into the ground with front doors opening directly onto the roads. We went through the large town of Blaenau Ffestiniog, where rows of identical houses climbed the mountainside in a series of terraces. It appeared very poor and depressed, understandable when we learned that it had once been the centre of very profitable slate mining until manmade tile replaced slate for roofing. Everywhere around we saw evidence of slate and slate quarries, and there was a sign indicating the largest slate mine in the world, now nothing but a museum and tourist attraction. The town itself was built of the dark grey slate that was the very reason for its existence.

The next town, Bettys-y-Cwed was very different. Situated in a very beautiful valley, its prosperity is built on tourism. Today the town was full of people and the streets lined with fine houses and many hotels. We passed the Royal Oak where we stopped for lunch with the West Side choir group three years ago.

We came next to Llanberis where we were to take the train to Snowdon's peak. We booked seats on the 2.30 train and then drove the eight miles or so into the lovely coastal town of Caernarvon so Betsy and Jane could see the castle. David and I had lunch in a hotel and did some shopping at the Welsh Wool Shop, as we had been to the castle several times before.

The castle brooding over the pretty little town is one of the most spectacular, and most visited, in the country. It was built by Edward I during the wars that united Wales and England and was the birthplace of that king's oldest son in 1284. Legend has it that in an inspired gesture the king placed the newborn infant in the hollow of his shield and from the battlements of the castle presented him to the Welsh people assembled below as their own prince, proclaiming to them, 'Here is your prince.' Since that day the male heir to the British throne has borne the title of Prince of Wales, though the title is not conferred by birth but in a ceremony known as investiture, which takes place when the young man reaches a mature age. The ceremony is conducted in the central courtyard of the castle and last took place in 1969 when Queen Elizabeth II invested Prince Charles with the title in a glittering pageant of pomp and circumstance.

Caernarvon was the political base of David Lloyd George, a fierce orator and champion of Welsh interests and one of the most able as well as controversial prime ministers in history. His Liberal government brought World War I to its conclusion in 1918 but was afterwards defeated by the Conservatives. My parents admired Lloyd George greatly but, out of regional loyalty and tradition, never deserted the Conservative ranks of the rural west of England to vote for him. He died in 1945, his passing barely noticed in the closing days of World War II, though his work had been carried on to some extent by his daughter Megan Lloyd George, who inherited his temperament and gift of oratory. A statue of the fiery Welshman stands just opposite the castle. Before Lloyd George, the nineteenth-century Liberal prime minister Gladstone had connections with Caernarvon through his wife.

After Jane and Betsy concluded their sightseeing, we drove fast back to Llanberis, only to have a long wait for the train because one car had derailed and was blocking the line. When at last we were able to start, every seat was taken and the heavily laden little train went chugging up the mountainside. The views on either side on this remarkably clear day were magnificent. We saw huge oak trees with mossy roots growing in twisted shapes from fine-textured grass of the greenest hue, rowan trees laden with bunches of bright red berries, and babbling brooks of the clearest purest water. As we got higher the trees became stunted with limbs tormented and distorted by the prevailing westerly winds. We caught a glimpse of a spectacular waterfall. There were many hikers out in the lovely September weather, as this is considered the best month for exploring Snowdon. Many had no doubt ridden the train up and were walking back. One young couple had a bouncing baby strapped on Daddy's back. We saw a few remote and isolated farmhouses in the lower reaches, and as we went higher we saw tumbledown grey stone shelters that were once used in the summer by herders or shepherds who took their animals up to the high mountain pastures in the fashion of Swiss Alpine villagers.

The train reached its terminus to deposit us almost at the summit. We climbed the remaining short distance to see the plaque marking the very top of the mountain but did not linger, for despite the sun the wind was very cold. We stayed long enough to enjoy a cup of tea before getting back on the train for the descent. Sitting beside us was a man from Lancashire who had sold cotton-spinning machinery to Cone Mills in North Carolina, the firm for which David and his father before him had worked. This gentleman had actually been to their hometown of Greensboro and stayed at the Oaks Hotel just a stone's throw from the house on Summit Avenue where David and his sisters were born. It seemed a great coincidence that added something to our enjoyment of the trip.

We returned to our hotel by a different and quicker route. Driving fast and furiously in the twilight, we followed a spectacular sunset to arrive in time for dinner, after which we retired thankfully to bed.

SCOTLAND

'Oh, Scotia! my dear, native soil!
For whom my warmest wish to Heaven is sent!
Long may thy hardy sons of rustic toil
Be blest with health, and peace, and sweet content!'
Robert Burns 1759–1796

Scotland has never been conquered by either the Romans or the English. The Romans did not advance beyond their Antonine Wall, the fortification they built across the narrow waist of Scotland, and in fact remained there but a short time. They instead withdrew south back to Hadrian's Wall, along which line they were able to stand firm against incursions of the wild northern tribes known as the Picts and the Scots. Hadrian's Wall became the northernmost outpost of the Roman Empire in Britain and effectively kept the fierce Celtic groups bottled up in the north.

The Saxons made little attempt to conquer the Scots, who retained their national identity as an independent kingdom ruled by their own kings. For centuries, however, there was bitter warfare along the border between the Scots and their equally warlike English neighbours.

After his success in Wales, Edward I turned his attention to Scotland. At first he hoped to achieve union peacefully by marrying his son to the heiress to the Scottish throne, a young princess known as the Maid of Norway. But en route from Norway to Scotland the young girl drowned in a shipwreck, foiling Edward's strategy. Edward then gathered a large army and set out for Scotland. After initial successes, he met strong opposition from John Balliol, William Wallace, and Robert the Bruce, and was unable to achieve complete victory before his death in 1307. He was succeeded by his son Edward II, a weak and debauched king who in 1314 was utterly overwhelmed and defeated at Bannockburn. With this defeat, England had to give up its attempt at conquest, and Scotland allied with France, England's traditional enemy.

At the death of Elizabeth I in 1603, the crown of England passed to her cousin James VI of Scotland, who became James I, the first of England's Stuart kings. Under James I, the two countries were united for the first time under one king, although relations between the two countries remained bad. They worsened further when the second Stuart king Charles I was beheaded at the end of the seventeenth-century civil war, during which Oliver Cromwell laid waste to parts of Scotland in a cruel campaign.

The restoration of the Stuart monarchy in Charles II improved relations somewhat between the Scots and the English, but the English later became disenchanted with his brother James II and forced him to abdicate in 1688. His successor, William of Orange, endeavoured to come to terms with Scotland. Although he was blamed for the terrible massacre at Glencoe in 1692, he achieved the formal union of England and Scotland in the parliamentary Act of Union of 1707.

Restoration of the Stuart monarchy remained the goal of many Scots, resulting in the Jacobite rebellions of 1715 and 1745. The '45 rebellion against the English was led by the Scottish hero 'Bonnie' Prince Charlie and ended with the decisive battle at Culloden, where the Scots were crushed completely. Many Scots have never accepted the defeat as final, however, and a movement towards independence is still active in Scotland.

Religiously, the islands of Scotland, Iona in particular, were the home of early Celtic Christianity. During the Reformation, Scotland moved from this devout mystical Catholicism to one of the strictest forms of Protestantism. The changes did not come easily, and the religious wars in Scotland were long, bitter and costly. They brought the Presbyterian Church to power as the church of Scotland. Its first leader was John Knox, one of the most famous of all Scotsmen. Knox was strongly influenced by John Calvin and was a bitter enemy of the Catholic Mary, Queen of Scots.

Scotland is basically a poor country of mountains, unproductive land, and harsh, unrelenting climate. The growing use of coal and iron during the Industrial Revolution brought prosperity to the country's southern region, however, and Glasgow developed into Britain's second city with shipbuilding its greatest industry. Edinburgh, Scotland's capital, also prospered, becoming an intellectual and cultural centre and attracting tourists from all over the world.

Scotland's greatest wealth, however, lies in the character of her people. Ever since the days of discovery and the growth of the British Empire, Scots have gone all over the world as engineers, administrators, soldiers, doctors, lawyers, missionaries, and teachers. Generations later, wherever they live, they yet retain fond and close ties to the dour land of their ancestors. They keep the old Scottish traditions in their diverse homes, wearing the kilt and playing the bagpipes on ceremonial occasions faithfully observed, organizing their clans in recreations of Highland games, celebrating Hogmanay at New Year, and marking the January 25th birthday of Robert Burns with song, dance and readings of his verse while feasting on haggis washed down with good Scotch whisky. And it is the dream of every transplanted Scot to see for himself the lovely, romantic land his forefathers left.

SCOTLAND

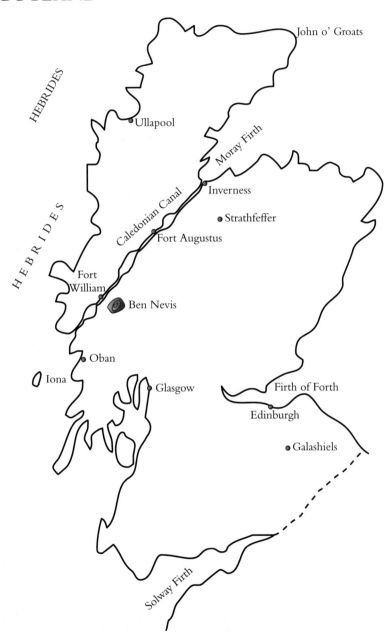

John o' Groats

HEBRIDES

Ullapool

Moray Firth

Inverness

HEBRIDES

Caledonian Canal

Strathfeffer

Fort Augustus

Fort William

Ben Nevis

Oban

Iona

Glasgow

Firth of Forth

Edinburgh

Galashiels

Solway Firth

1973

with Thomas & Margaret McKnight

BY TRAIN FROM LONDON TO EDINBURGH – HIGH SUMMER IN EDINBURGH – WEST AND NORTH THROUGH SCOTLAND: FORT WILLIAM, STRATHPEFFER, ULLAPOOL, INVERNESS, CULLODEN

SUNDAY, JULY 29TH

At Charing Cross we transferred to King's Cross, where a West Indian porter found our seats on the train for the 10-hour trip to Edinburgh. Tea was served and later we had a fine dinner graciously served in the dining car. We followed the course of the journey on a map. The train stopped at Doncaster and York, where we glimpsed the Minster, England's second cathedral. From the station at Durham we got a fine view of the fortress-like cathedral. We crossed into Scotland at Berwick, and from here we could just discern far out to sea the Holy Isle of Lindisfarne, cradle of Celtic Christianity.

And then at last we reached Edinburgh. Perhaps because it was Sunday we had to wait for a taxi, but finally we reached our hotel. On the way we found the cool air brisk and refreshing. We drove down Princes Street past the Scott Monument, the gardens floodlit to reveal the fountains and floral displays. The castle too was lit up. Built on a huge menacing rock, it glowers over the city. Our hotel was in the 'new' town of Edinburgh, built in the Georgian style of beauty, grace, and symmetry, and we were glad to reach its comfort.

MONDAY, JULY 30TH

We were up early and spent a rather frustrating morning getting our hair done, going to the bank, arranging for a car and other mundane matters, when we should have been exploring the wonderful city. The weather surprised us, for a heat wave arrived in this northern latitude and caught us unawares. Edinburgh certainly looked lovely, and it seemed as if every resident and tourist was out in Princes Street Gardens to enjoy the unusual weather. After lunch Margaret and I went shopping, buying gifts for people back home in the fine shops in Princes Street. We especially liked shopping in Jenners, the old and famous department store, and we enjoyed a proper Scottish tea in the restaurant there. We had to walk back to our hotel as we couldn't get a taxi and found the heat quite overpowering.

After a short rest we dressed for a Scottish evening at the George Hotel. The menu – cock-a-leekie soup, haggis, roast lamb or beef, a variety of vegetables, and sherry trifle – was accompanied by whisky (especially needed for the haggis) and a nice Beaujolais. A small ensemble opened with, of all things, 'Dixie' and a medley of other Southern songs. There was some dancing with a piper in full regalia followed by a display of Scottish country dancing. The women wore white with their plaids over one shoulder and the men wore kilts made of their clan tartans. Very lovely they were as they tripped lightly through the complicated steps, occasionally emitting shouts which sounded like the Southern rebel yell.

And so ended our very short stay in Edinburgh. David and I have been here several times, but I felt badly that the McKnights saw nothing of the Castle, the Royal Mile or Holyrood House, the palace of the ancient kings of Scotland still used by royalty today. I hope there will be a next time for them.

TUESDAY, JULY 31ST

The men went to collect our car, a mustard-coloured Ford station wagon, and we were on the road by 10 o'clock, destination Fort William. It looked a very short distance on the map, so we decided to take an alternate longer route. But in Scotland distances are deceptive and roads not very good, so we were driving all day and did not reach Fort William till 8 o'clock.

The countryside was beautiful, however, and there were many things to see. The weather steadily brightened after a cloudy start, though it remained much cooler than yesterday. The roads curved and twisted past rocky mountain streams, followed for a while 'the bonnie, bonnie banks of Loch Lomond,' and travelled in the lee of forbidding mountains rising steeply skyward. On all sides the landscape colours were the muted heathery tones that are typical of Scotland. We saw many roadside wildflowers, among them the Scotch bluebell, known as the harebell in England and not to be confused with the English bluebell. The harebell is a flower of pale lavender blue growing on moor or heath which quivers on its slender stem at the slightest breeze. The English bluebell, related to the hyacinth, grows in woods and is a deeper blue. Purple-red foxgloves grew in profusion and everywhere we saw the tall purple thistle which is Scotland's national flower.

Sheep roamed at will amidst the heather, which was not yet out in its purple glory. They posed a hazard, wandering unpredictably and often lying down in the road. Most of the cattle we saw were Black Angus, generally raised for beef, and Friesians seemed the preferred dairy cows. Only occasionally did we see the red shaggy Highland cattle with wide pointed horns. One fine specimen of this breed reminded me of a Landseer painting as he stood majestically on a rocky crag.

We stopped for lunch at a little restaurant in a crossroads town called Crianlarich. It was an unpretentious place, the linen spotted and the china smeared, but the food was delicious – steaming Scotch broth, steak and kidney pie, and hot apple pie and custard. It was a humble crofter's meal but welcome to hungry travellers. We then pushed on, seeing a castle here, a laird's house there, until we reached Oban, the ferry point for the Hebrides and Outer Isles. We drove along the edge of a deep inlet cutting far into the waist of Scotland. Sometimes the road led us up one side of a loch only to make a hairpin bend and come down the other side, resulting in many miles but little distance covered. One loch was crossed by a ferry, an antiquated, quaint little operation which quite fascinated Tom and David. While waiting we bought a sprig of white heather for luck from a gypsy and took a picture of her little daughter, a pretty 10-year-old dressed in tartan skirt and velvet tam-o'-shanter.

We reached Fort William at last. General Monk, 1st Earl of Albemarle, first built an earth-and-wattle fort here in 1655, but it was rebuilt in 1690 by William III, for whom the town was named. The town stands at the southern end of the Caledonian Canal, the waterway which extends diagonally across Scotland by linking a series of natural lakes with manmade canals. Engineered by Thomas Telford and opened in 1847, the waterway contains 29 locks and is considered a major feat of engineering.

Fort William grew rapidly with the advent of the railway. It played some part in the eighteenth-century Jacobite uprisings of the Scots hoping to restore the Stuarts as the kings of England. It is quite close to Ben Nevis, the highest mountain in Great Britain. Today, perhaps because we were exhausted, the town struck us as unattractive, crowded with trippers and tourists. We were rather disappointed in our hotel, our rooms small and dinner rushed because of our late arrival. An evening walk was spoiled by clouds of black midges which got in our eyes, noses, ears and hair. So we went back and to bed, uplifted by the glorious scenery but rather dashed by the irritations that sometimes arise, partly because we were all very tired.

WEDNESDAY, AUGUST 1ST

We all slept well and after an excellent Scottish breakfast of porridge, kippers and finnan haddie – smoked haddock – drove towards Strathpeffer, following a route that roughly paralleled the Caledonian Canal. It was raining – a thick Scotch mist interspersed with heavier showers. We drove across Spean Bridge to the Commando Memorial, built on a high point that commands a fine view of valley and peak. Ben Nevis loomed ahead, its summit shrouded in mist and cloud. Soon the skies cleared and we admired the profusion of wildflowers and fine trees abounding in the countryside. We saw many sheep, the source of wool for clothiers and mutton for butchers. We stopped at Fort Augustus, a town which controls a stretch of the canal. Though to us it seemed rather a dirty little town, crowded with tourists, it has an interesting history. The fort was built after the 1715 Jacobite Rising and was named for Augustus, Duke of Cumberland. In 1730 it was enlarged. In 1745 it was captured by Bonnie Prince Charlie and held by his forces until after his defeat at Culloden the following year.

We had lunch in Lewiston in a simple but delightful little inn. A low building of white stucco, it was set in a beautiful garden with manicured green lawns and herbaceous borders. The meal was simple but very good and was graciously served by a Scotswoman with an exquisitely chiselled face like a cameo. After lunch the traffic grew heavy as we went on, slowed by the narrow twisting roads. We were glad when we saw a signpost to Strathpeffer.

This is a spa town which was very popular with European royalty at the turn of the century, after which it went into a period of decline. It has now been developed into a resort for skiing in winter and mountain climbing and sightseeing in summer. It seems mostly to consist of hotels grouped around the spa rooms and concert hall, and there are some fine shops selling gifts of Scottish origin. Our hotel, the Highland, is one of the largest and oldest and is built in Victorian style on a hillside amidst green shrubs and flower gardens. One enters a vast lounge covered in deep luxurious carpet with a great curved staircase leading to the upper floors. At the bottom of the stairs are two enormous fuchsia plants heavy with blossom, and on the landings are red geraniums and feathery silver-green fir trees. Our rooms are large, airy, twin-bedded and elegantly furnished, the walls hung with watercolours of Highland scenes. After a Scottish tea in the lounge, Margaret and I explored the shops in the hilly, pretty little town. We much admired the Ben Wyvis Hotel set among green lawns and gardens nestling at the foot of the mountains.

We changed for dinner, served in the dining room where we sat at a table in the window. A pretty lassie in a blue plaid kilt waited on us. Dinner was followed by a Highland Cabaret in the Assembly Hall. It was very enjoyable – just the simple entertainment we needed. There were dancers, a piper, a comedian, an emcee and a band playing Scottish tunes. A soprano sang 'The Road to the Isles,' its minor-key melody hauntingly eloquent of lost cause and struggle. The comedian, we were told, was a fairly well-known Scottish television star. A 4-year-old named Michael Urquhart performed some Highland dances with great skill. He was blond and beautiful in his clan kilt, black velvet jacket, and white shirt with lace stock, and we dubbed him Bonnie Prince Charlie. There was also a quite sensational mind-reading act. David was identified by a blindfolded woman as being named David, from the U.S. with North Carolina as his place of birth, and with June 14th 1916, as his birthdate. All correct! Of course she may have seen the hotel records!

THURSDAY, AUGUST 2ND

This is our last day in Scotland and virtually the end of our holiday, for we will spend tonight on the train to London and leave for New York tomorrow. We were up early to pack and started with a good breakfast of oatmeal, finnan haddie, and toast and bitter marmalade. It would be sacrilegious to eat anything else in Scotland. The weather, bad news – very persistent bone-chilling rain.

We started out towards Ullapool going north and west. For much of the way the road was single lane with wider places every so often for passing, and it was slow going as the oncoming traffic was quite heavy. We crossed over a bridge and for several miles the road paralleled a lovely stream called the Blackwater. The water was clear, the river bed rocky, and the stream gurgled along at a fast pace while all kinds of lush plants and trees grew on the banks. It was very beautiful with the pure untouched loveliness of the Highlands. If anything, the rain made it lovelier, muting the colours though obscuring distant views. Later the road ran through some of the most desolate, barren country that I have ever seen in the British Isles, but even that had a rough bleak majesty. The ground was covered in short scrubby heather with just a gleam of purple showing here and there, and the very sparse grass looked tough and brown. Sheep roamed at will, a few inevitably getting on the road and bringing the car to a halt. We saw only an occasional crofter's cottage clinging to a hillside, so that I recalled a similar dwelling, known in Gaelic as a 'shieling,' brought from Scotland and placed on the Cabot Trail in Nova Scotia in Canada. Outside it stands a granite boulder supporting a plaque engraved with John Galt's lines:

> From the lone shieling of the misty island
> Mountains divide us and the waste of seas.
> Yet still the blood is strong, the heart is Highland,
> And we in dreams behold the Hebrides.

Scots wherever they may be remember their wild land with love and longing.

We passed an isolated hotel and gas station. It bore a sign: 'Last petrol for 30 miles.' We went past a reservoir and a hydroelectric plant, both of which were quite deserted with not a soul in sight, so that despite the plant there seemed no modern intrusions. We drove along the shore of a small narrow loch, its still water pocked by the falling raindrops, its banks lined with pine trees. Then we came to the river again, which soon entered a gorge of such spectacular beauty it has been acquired by the National Trust.

At last we reached Ullapool, a pretty little port on the western shore. Here the weather is unusually warm due to the waters of the Gulf Stream, warm enough in fact for palm trees to grow in sheltered spots. But today we could see nothing, with the rain, mist and fog predominating over the effects of the Gulf Stream. The little town was packed with holidaymakers milling around wondering what to do with themselves. We stopped in the Caledonian Hotel for a drink of whisky to warm us up. The barman was horrified when we asked for ice, and none was forthcoming. And then we headed back towards Inverness and the night train for London.

Back we went along the same road. It was very foggy near the town but cleared a little as we went on. We stopped at the only inn for miles, the Althuish, where we had a delicious lunch – asparagus soup followed by local salmon and raspberries, cream, and pastries. The inn has been here for many years, a landmark and oasis for travellers. It was a stage stop for the coach that in olden days made regular journeys across the moors of Wester Ross. Old photographs hanging in the lounge showed the inn deep in snow and herds of deer foraging nearby. Now the inn is a haven for fishermen, hunters and others who want isolation and peace, and today we felt indeed grateful for its good food and warm welcome.

As we drew nearer to Inverness the country looked more civilized, but it rained harder than ever. Inverness is a very beautiful and important town, often called the Capital of the Highlands. It is built on both banks of the River Ness and mountains rise on either side. Loch Ness of monster fame and the Caledonian Canal are to the south. It is a cultural centre and Highland Games are held here every August. There are fine buildings, among them St Andrew's Cathedral. Some buildings are of Georgian design. There is a statue of Flora MacDonald, in which we as North Carolinians had a special interest, for, after being imprisoned in the Tower of London for aiding Bonnie Prince Charlie's escape after Culloden, Flora and her husband emigrated to North Carolina and remained there for several years.

After checking in our luggage at the railway station, we drove the few miles out to Culloden Field. The defeat here marked the end of the Jacobite Rebellion of 1745 (commonly known as the '45) led by Bonnie Prince Charlie. The Scots remember it as the last heroic stand of the Stuarts and as a hideous massacre perpetrated by the Duke of Cumberland. The battlefield is undeniably impressive. The fallen Scots lie in communal graves according to their clans, and signs tell us we walk on ground hallowed by the blood of martyrs. The English dead are buried together in what has come to be known as the English Field. One of the original cottages has been restored and made into a museum, and there is a modern building operated by the National Trust of Scotland with a chronological chart of Scottish history.

We left Culloden sated with Scottish history and returned the car to the rental company. We were glad to board the train at last, for a journey south that was comfortable and uneventful. After a good dinner we went to our compartments where we were lulled to sleep by fatigue and the rocking motion of the train hurtling through the night.

1983

with the West Side Presbyterian Church Choir of Ridgewood N.J.

EDINBURGH – BORDER ABBEYS – SCOTT AND LIVINGSTONE HOMES

MONDAY, JULY 4TH

Our first stop in Scotland was Jedburgh, and on the way there we passed through some very beautiful countryside. The Redesdale Forest gave way to the Cheviot Hills forming the boundary between England and Scotland. We saw many rhododendron bushes in full bloom, the colours of their flowers running the gamut from palest pink and lavender to deepest red and purple. We saw also many laburnum trees, once a whole avenue of them, their deep yellow pendulous blossoms hanging down to give the tree its common name of golden chain. It is interesting to note that this far north these trees are still in bloom, while in southern England their flowering season is long past. Here RAF planes fly low to practise going under enemy radar in case of war, and several of them gave us a nasty scare. Their unexpected sorties right above our head were quite unnerving.

We stopped only briefly at Jedburgh. It has one of the Border abbeys ruined not by Henry VIII's closure of the monasteries but by the constant warfare that went on for centuries between the English and the Scots in this region. Despite lacking a roof, Jedburgh Abbey is very beautiful – very graceful in the Early English style, its glassless windows delicately traced in stone. Its semi-ruined state seems to make it more romantically appealing, and I think it would be particularly attractive by moonlight. Nearby is a house where Mary Queen of Scots stayed. It is now a museum and contains relics of the unfortunate lady, including her thimble and watch.

Proceeding through spectacular Scottish scenery the road wound through green forests and followed crystal streams bubbling over rocky beds. Then again it rose over rocky barren moors where woolly sheep as yet unshorn grazed perilously on the steep slopes.

And then Edinburgh at last. How glad we were to see the spires, towers and chimney pots of 'Auld Reekie' appear on the horizon. It had been a very long day, and we piled into the North British Hotel, a nice large hotel of the old-fashioned type. Built as a railway hotel over the station, it enjoyed great popularity and prestige in the heyday of train travel. After finding our rooms we enjoyed an excellent dinner where we were toasted as a honeymoon couple of almost forty years ago, for it was in Edinburgh in this very hotel where we had begun our married life.

TUESDAY, JULY 5TH

The morning passed quietly and pleasantly with a good choir practice in the Forth Room, a much-needed visit to the hairdresser in the hotel, and lunch in the Palm Court. In the afternoon we took a guided tour of the city. Our guide was named Angus Davidson, a middle-aged Scot with a strong but understandable accent and a great fund of knowledge. To this he added a wry sense of humour and a supply of funny stories about Scotsmen and their well-known propensities for saving money and drinking whisky.

In contrast to other large cities, most of which are found along river valleys, Edinburgh is ringed by hills and built on rock near an extinct volcano named Arthur's Seat. In the Middle Ages the city grew along a ridge that runs from the castle to Holyrood House. This ridge today is the street called the Royal Mile, from which branch off other streets, alleys, and courts lined by the high tenements of the old city. After the Scots were defeated by the English at the Battle of Flodden in 1513, a strong fortification known as the Flodden Wall was built around the city, and for many years the citizens were afraid to build beyond its shelter. This caused the city to grow upward in many-storeyed tenements and to crowd all classes of people together in narrow courts and closes. At the same time the city was torn by religious strife, often under attack, and suffered periodic epidemics of bubonic plague and smallpox.

With the passage in 1707 of the Act of Union uniting England and Scotland, Edinburgh was free from the fear of invasion. Although there was some bitter resentment in Edinburgh at the union, it finally worked to the city's advantage as trade flourished and building outside the wall became possible. The great lake at the foot of the rock was drained, and the building of New Town began. Princes Street was laid out with gardens in the old lake bed on one side and fine shops on the other. An elegant Georgian area was created and Edinburgh developed as a cultural and intellectual centre. With many towers and pillared public buildings designed in Greek Revival style by Robert Adam, the city came to be known as the Athens of the North.

We started our tour today on Princes Street (not Princess, as it is often wrongly called), with its shops on one side and gardens on the other. It was named for two princes, the Prince of Wales nicknamed Prinny, who later became George IV, and his brother the Duke of York. We drove past the university, most famous for schools of medicine and theology. The university and the Royal Infirmary have been the site of much medical research. Famous Scottish doctors include Sir James Young Simpson, the first to use chloroform as an anaesthetic; Joseph Lister, whose use of antiseptics saved countless lives; and Hubert Phillips, pioneer in the treatment of tuberculosis. The university has likewise produced outstanding theologians, and many famous preachers have studied at Edinburgh.

Our first stop was the castle. As we approached we noted how the brilliantly green close-mown grass dotted with fresh white daisies sparkled against the grey soot-begrimed granite of the buildings. We parked the bus in the Esplanade, or outer courtyard, that leads up to the castle buildings. Here the famous Edinburgh Tattoo is held every year in late summer. It is a stirring display of British military pageantry and colour and is performed at night with the floodlit castle as a backdrop. Several years ago we were fortunate enough to attend one. Today workmen were erecting the viewing stands for this year's performance, using, we were told, Buckminster Fuller's geodesic system.

The castle was begun very early in Scotland's history. Strongly guarded with seven gates, a drawbridge and portcullis, the castle has never been taken by frontal attack. In 1313, however, amidst one of the constant wars between Scotland and England, a band of 30 men entered by stealth and razed the castle to the ground. Only the tiny Queen Margaret's Chapel was left standing. This queen died here in 1093 after being brought from a nearby nunnery. She is credited with making Scotland Christian and was canonized for this achievement. Today a guild of 52 ladies named Margaret are each responsible for the flowers in the chapel for one week out of the year. The best-known member of this guild is Princess Margaret, younger sister of Queen Elizabeth II. At the door to the tiny chapel stands a massive cannon known as the 'Mons Meg', though it was inoperative long before the famous battle of 1914.

The most famous castle buildings are grouped around the Square. We saw the room where Mary, Queen of Scots, gave birth to her only child, a son named James who was fathered by her second husband Lord Darnley. Shortly after his birth and hasty baptism in the Catholic faith he was lowered from a window in a wicker basket and spirited away to Stirling Castle some miles to the north. He was raised a Protestant, though he always had strong Catholic leanings. On his mother's execution he became James VI of Scotland, and on his cousin Queen Elizabeth I's death in 1603 he became James I of England and the first of the Stuart line. Today we chiefly remember him for the beautiful translation of the Bible completed in his reign and known to us as the King James Version.

We saw the Honours of Scotland, the ceremonial regalia of the country, and the crown of Scotland with its bejewelled gold headband and ermine trim. A ceremonial chain was surprisingly engraved with the motto of the Order of the Garter and hung with a diamond pendant depicting St George, England's patron saint, and the dragon. Once during troubled times these jewels of symbolic significance were hidden and remained lost for many years before being discovered in an old black coffer. Today they are displayed for public view arranged on the same old chest.

One of the most impressive sights in the castle is the War Memorial. It lists in commemorative books the names of Scots who gave their lives in the two world wars. The missing are memorialized in a separate chamber. The walls are covered in plaques and memorials to individual Scottish regiments and heroes. It is like an open history book of the two horrendous conflicts.

The castle is guarded by soldiers of the Royal Scots Regiment. With its motto 'Nobody Insults Me With Impunity', it is the oldest foot regiment in the British army. The soldiers were clad in uniform with trousers of Royal Stuart tartan – only for dress do they wear the kilt. In World War I some Scottish regiments fought wearing their kilts and came to be called 'the Ladies from Hell' by the Germans.

Leaving the castle we drove along the Royal Mile. There was history on every side requiring a nimble mind and good historical background to take in even a fraction of all we were told. We stopped first at Greyfriars to see the ancient church and the nearby statue of Greyfriars Bobby. Bobby was a terrier owned by a Border shepherd who died in 1858 and was buried in the churchyard. Bobby watched over the grave for the rest of his life, with the local people bringing him food. When Bobby died he was buried with his master and a statue was erected to him.

We passed Deacon Brodie's house. Pillar of the church by day, thief and reprobate by night, he is thought to be the prototype for Robert Louis Stevenson's Dr Jekyll and Mr Hyde. Perhaps of most interest to us as Presbyterians was the house of John Knox, great Protestant leader of the Reformation, disciple of John Calvin, and bitter enemy of the Catholic Mary, Queen of Scots.

The Royal Mile ends at Holyrood House, the official royal residence in the Queen's Scottish capital. Queen Elizabeth left Edinburgh just this morning, and the Prince of Wales was due to arrive later in the day, so the palace was closed to the public. While David and I have been through it before, today we could only look through the gates and listen to our guide tell us something of its long turbulent history. For its backdrop it has the brooding rocks of Arthur's Seat, the great rocky protuberance that is an extinct volcano. The palace was begun about 1500 by James IV and was subsequently the scene of many of the dark tragedies that dogged the Stuart dynasty. Mary, Queen of Scots, lived here from 1561–1567. In 1566 David Rizzio, her secretary and favourite, was murdered in her private apartments by a gang led by her jealous husband Darnley. In 1603, several years after her execution by her cousin Elizabeth, her son James VI of Scotland was at Holyrood when he received the news that he had inherited the throne of England. Bonnie Prince Charlie held court here briefly in 1745 while vainly planning to restore the throne to the Stuarts.

In the grounds stand the picturesque ruins of Holyrood Abbey. In 1128, so the story goes, David I was out hunting deer on a holy day, thus breaking church law. He was attacked fiercely by a maddened stag and was in danger of losing his life when, with a prayer of penitence on his lips, he seized the beast by the horns. The animal miraculously vanished, leaving the king grasping not antlers but a cross, or rood, into which they had been changed. In gratitude David built an abbey on the spot where the miracle took place. Some of Scotland's kings are buried here and Mary, Queen of Scots, was married both to Darnley and Bothwell in the abbey.

From Holyrood we went to St Giles' Cathedral for positioning and a short rehearsal. This 'high kirk' of Scotland stands in the High Street. It is dark and forbidding, more so even than Durham, although it cannot compare with the latter for size or grandeur. Built of red sandstone in the fourteenth and fifteenth centuries, it underwent considerable alteration during the Reformation years and was restored in the nineteenth century. Its most striking feature is the crown-shaped steeple that tops it. It is named for St Giles, a crippled monk who came from France and endeared himself to the Scots.

St Giles' is the mother church of Presbyterianism and is full of relics of its bloodthirsty struggle for survival. John Knox was minister here till his death in 1572. He thundered forth fiery sermons from the pulpit. It was in this church in 1637 that Jenny Geddes hurled her stool at the head of the preacher as he read from the Anglican Book of Common Prayer, thus setting off a long period of schism among the churches known as the Covenant Wars. A huge statue of the dour-faced Knox stands in the Cathedral. Later, in that grim place of worship, it was to give me a perverse satisfaction to sing the words of Isaac Watts,

> Religion never was designed
> to make our pleasure less,

a sentiment quite contrary to Knox's views. We were told that Cromwell stabled his horses in the nave and tore the lead off the roof to make bullets. The stained glass windows replacing those destroyed by the Puritans, though beautiful, are dark and contribute to the prevailing gloom. When I was here before, the interior was hung with the tattered and dusty flags and colours of famous Scottish regiments that have fought in wars and engagements all over the world. Today they are no longer present and I missed them, for they added to the dark atmosphere of the great church and told more of Scotland's long turbulent history. We went into the Chapel of the Thistle, a beautifully decorated room of lavish designs and heraldic symbols. This is the home of the highest order of chivalry in Scotland, equivalent to the Order of the Garter in England. Its workmanship represents the best of artistic accomplishment in Scotland, and its membership of only 50 the best in service.

After a dinner of Scotch salmon in the hotel we were taken by bus back to St Giles' for our concert. We were in place in good time and, after rising for the attending dignitaries, performed well, helped by the solemnity of the setting and its echoing acoustics. Jack's organ playing was magnificent and the congregation enthusiastic. We strolled home afterwards, the evening pleasantly warm and clear, and went to the wine and cheese party attended by Councillor Harry Taylor representing the Lord Provost of the city. Mr Taylor and his wife were charming and we enjoyed a brief chat with them.

WEDNESDAY, JULY 6TH

Most of us spent the morning exploring the beautiful shops of Princes Street and making modest purchases. In the afternoon some of us took advantage of an optional tour to Abbotsford. It was a beautiful day, sunny and warm, and the countryside looked its best with the stone walls crossing the green fields, haymaking in full swing, and huge leafy trees beneath which heavily fleeced sheep sought every bit of shade.

The wayside flowers amazed and delighted me – the dog roses in the hedgerows (deeper pink than their counterparts in England), the prickly yellow gorse, and the golden Scotch broom. Foxgloves grew tall and wild, and pink flowers known to me as ragged robins bloomed profusely. And then there were the tall prickly purple thistles, national flower of Scotland. In places we saw rhododendron bushes in bloom and also the hanging golden flowers of the laburnum trees.

Winding roads, blue sky, babbling brooks, children paddling, men fishing for salmon in the River Tweed – all contributed to the perfection of a rare summer day in Scotland. In one large farm we noticed an unusual sight, a stream being straightened possibly to make a more accessible drinking place for cattle. The road followed a stream named Gala for many miles, bringing us at last to a large town called Galashiels, a prosperous centre of tweed manufacture. We crossed and recrossed the River Tweed, spanned in two places by high, graceful many-arched aqueducts. Close to Abbotsford we stopped to take in a view stretching for miles across the valley of the Tweed to the hills beyond. It was one of Sir Walter Scott's favourite spots, and he would visit it often to seek comfort and draw inspiration. It is known locally as Scott's View.

Abbotsford was a delightful surprise – a grey stone-turreted mansion set among manicured lawns and walled gardens, a pleasant spot where Scott experienced both great joy and deep sadness. His family was brought up here, and in this house his beloved French wife Charlotte died. And here too he faced the financial disaster that plagued his last years, causing him to literally work himself to death. We visited his study, kept as he left it, and saw the desk where he wrote many novels under the pseudonym Waverley in a vain attempt to pay off the enormous debt into which a publisher's failure had plunged him. His descendants still live in the house, a shrine for Scott lovers.

Scott's works, both poetry and prose, were immensely popular during his lifetime and for many years afterwards. Queen Victoria read them avidly, and they became required reading in every British school syllabus. Copies of his works were often awarded in schools as prizes, and I have several nicely bound volumes of his novels obtained in this way. But few people read them now – they are too long and wordy and, alas!, not always historically accurate. Fashions change in literature, and radio and television have done much to spell the demise of long narrative and descriptive novels such as Dickens and Scott wrote so prolifically. In Scotland Scott remains second only to Burns in the country's literary pantheon, as evidenced by the beautiful landmark monument to the lame writer and his dog on Princes Street in Edinburgh.

Leaving Abbotsford, our next stop was Melrose Abbey, a Cistercian house built by David I in 1136 and then repeatedly ruined and rebuilt until it was finally destroyed for good by the English in 1543 and 1544. The heart of Robert the Bruce, Scottish hero of the fourteenth-century wars with England, is buried here. The sandstone ruins are beautiful, mysterious and otherworldly, touching in my heart a chord of regret that Englishmen could destroy anything so lovely.

Five miles south of Melrose we came to Dryburgh, my favourite among the ruined Border abbeys so important in Scottish lore and tradition. Here the grey stone ruins are set off by emerald turf and shaded by great silver-trunked beeches, spreading chestnuts and Lebanon cedars. Scott and some members of his family are buried here, as is Lord Haig, commander-in-chief of British forces in World War I. The Haig ancestral home is not far away.

We were back in Edinburgh with just enough time to get ready for the Scottish dinner and entertainment that was to conclude our visit to the Scottish capital. Strictly a tourist attraction, the menu consisted of cock-a-leekie soup, haggis ceremonially piped in and prayed over – everyone ate a very small amount quite tentatively, washing it down with sips of whisky – roast beef, shortbread and coffee. The food was followed by Scottish songs, dances and selections from *Brigadoon* with a kilted piper, and two fine singers.

It was still light when we left the hotel for a short stroll in the balmy evening air before packing up for the morrow's long ride to Chester.

THURSDAY, JULY 7TH

We were away early after a rather hectic breakfast. Most were sorry to leave Edinburgh, especially those of Scottish ancestry, for it is a fascinating city with much to see and fine shopping. It was a grey overcast morning, so the city was wearing its most familiar face. We took a westward route out of the city, going through a lower-middle class section before reaching open country. The way was unattractive compared with the rustic beauty we had seen yesterday. We were going towards Glasgow, centre of one of the greatest industrial complexes in the British Isles.

Our immediate destination was Blantyre, birthplace and boyhood home of David Livingstone, doctor, missionary, explorer and writer. He came of sturdy Scottish Lowland stock, strict Presbyterians who left their poor farmland for Blantyre to seek a better life in the mills which were just opening and needing workers. Blantyre Mill town was something of a social experiment, a planned community providing living quarters for the employees but exercising considerable control over their lives. The accommodations were anything but princely, however, for every family regardless of size was assigned just one room in a large dormitory-type building. It was not uncommon to find families of 10 or 12 living in such cramped quarters. There were communal arrangements for laundry, cooking and schooling. The work day was very long, at least 14 hours. Since most children were working in the mill by the time they were 8 or 10 years old, school was held at night.

Blantyre has been made into a museum, and the Livingstones' room is displayed exactly as it was in their day. The Livingstones were fortunate to have only four children. Two beds were curtained off in alcoves – in one of them all four children had been born. The room was furnished surprisingly well with solid furniture and family possessions including a highly prized wall clock. On the mantel was the teacaddy, made of shining wood containing the precious and costly tea, a caddy which was kept locked so that the tea was safe from prying hands. We saw the family Bible, well-thumbed and much worn from daily readings to the children.

Like other children, David worked from an early age in the factory piecing broken threads and went to school in the evening. As a student he showed exceptional promise, learning anything and everything rapidly and avidly. Later he went to Anderson's College in Glasgow and thence to the London Missionary Society, which helped him train as a doctor and sent him to Africa to begin his work as doctor, teacher and explorer. In Africa he married Mary Moffatt, daughter of a leading missionary, and she helped him in his life's work until her death from a tropical fever, to which he also lost a son. Another of his sons was something of a black sheep, disappearing for several years before surfacing in Richmond, Virginia, where he died fighting for the North in the American Civil War.

Livingstone's most famous discovery was the great falls on the Zambezi River that he named Victoria Falls for his queen. For several years he was thought to be lost until a search party led by the American newspaperman Henry Stanley found him. Stanley, of course, formally greeted Livingstone with a handshake and the now famous words, 'Dr Livingstone, I presume?'

Livingstone died in Africa in 1873, and his name became a household word synonymous with goodness and Christian love and service. The collection of material in the museum at Blantyre has been assembled by missionary societies, and it is a comprehensive collection of pictures, maps, charts and the doctor's possessions. Lighted dioramas tell much of Livingstone's story, with the scene of a lion attack which left him with a crippled arm and his deathbed scene particularly dramatic. As a child I learned much about Livingstone at St Mary's Girls School, a Church of England elementary school in Marlborough. Livingstone was extolled by our teachers as a missionary and explorer and extender of British influence and territory in Africa.

En route to and from Blantyre we passed through unprepossessing areas of industry, factories, small houses, and unattractive concrete high-rise apartments. These are the outgrowths of the huge city of Glasgow, where the chief industries are shipbuilding on the banks of the Clyde and textile and chemical manufacture. Much of the building is of postwar vintage put up to replace bomb damage to the area, which suffered much during the Blitz. Today it is the scene of high unemployment and economic stagnation, though the city itself is rebuilt and has become a cultural centre with many fine museums and art galleries.

Chapter Five

THE NORTH

'I have looked o'er the hills of the stormy North'
Felicia Dorothea Hemans 1793–1835

Geographically, the North is considered the land north of the Humber in
the east and the Dee estuary in the west, ending at the Scottish border
marked by the Solway Firth and the Cheviot Hills. The North is bisected
by the mountains of the Pennine Chain.

Road signs 'To the North' and names such as 'The Great North Road'
always sounded very important and romantic to me when I was growing up
in the South. In our geography lessons in school, the importance of the
North as the source of Britain's industry and wealth was stressed and so I
got the impression that the agricultural South (with the exception of
London) was a vastly inferior place to live. I longed to go north! It is hard
to believe but nevertheless true that I never got further north than midland
Birmingham during my childhood, and not much beyond to Leicester and
Nottingham during my young adulthood. My first view of the northland
was from a train speeding north in 1944 en route to Edinburgh for our
honeymoon. I got brief glimpses of York Minster, Durham Cathedral and
the Holy Isle of Lindisfarne.

Since then we have made several brief forays into the North. I have
found it most interesting, though I no longer think it superior to the
gentler South. Nevertheless we have enjoyed the wild mountain scenery of
the Pennines, the lakeland beauty of Cumberland and Westmorland, the
cathedrals of York and Durham, the stately homes and many ruined abbeys.
My school fantasies are brought to life in the Border country of romantic
ballads and the moors of the Brontës. Whitby Abbey reminds me of the
important synod held there in AD 663, while Hadrian's Wall conjures up
the olden times when Roman soldiers built the great fortification to keep
the land free from marauding Scots. The North still holds romance for me,
and I hope I have been able to communicate some of that romance to my
readers.

1975

YORK – AROUND YORKSHIRE TO HAWORTH, HOME OF THE BRONTËS

TUESDAY, JULY 22ND

Leaving Sleaford in Lincolnshire we took the road to Bawtrey, a pleasant little town on the Yorkshire border, where we had a good lunch in the Bull Inn in the wide main street. Bawtrey is quite prosperous due in part to a large air force base nearby. There were many uniformed men on the streets, though most of the customers in the inn appeared to be farmers. The main street was very wide, rather like Marlborough's, with double parking on one side.

From here we took a desolate road across moorland to an attractive little town called Thorne and thence drove north to Selby and York. At the former we regretfully got but a passing glimpse of the great abbey, a very splendid monastic church. Selby is thought to be the birthplace of Henry I, third son of William the Conqueror and the only one born in England. The town is on the River Ouse and is an inland port, though with the decline of canal traffic it is not as important today as it once was.

On then to York, our day's destination. Our first encounter upon arriving in the late afternoon was a total confusion of traffic, which was unfortunate as York is a compact well-ordered city of great beauty and historical importance. It is built on the River Ouse and stands at the junction of the three 'Ridings', the term for Yorkshire's administrative districts. It is completely walled, and from all points one can see the incomparable Minster, England's most important cathedral after Canterbury. After driving around the walls twice trying to get our bearings we found a parking place and set out on foot to look for a hotel, not realizing that reservations are a must in a city as popular as York. Eventually through the Tourist Bureau we found a room for one night only in the Elm Bank Hotel, a vast old mansion in a sadly deteriorating state. It is a mystery how we obtained the room, since the hotel is jammed with tour groups to the extent of having beds in the halls and lounge. Service is poor and the room is small, but it is comfortable and clean with a private shower and toilet.

After a quick wash we returned to the city and had dinner at the Dean Court Hotel. There were then still a few hours of daylight left for looking around, so we went to the Minster, the largest cathedral in England and seat of the Archbishop of York, the deputy head of the Church of England. The present cathedral is the fifth church on the site. The first was founded upon the conversion of King Edwin of Northumbria to Christianity by the Roman Christian Paulinus in AD 627, 30 years after Augustine founded

THE NORTH

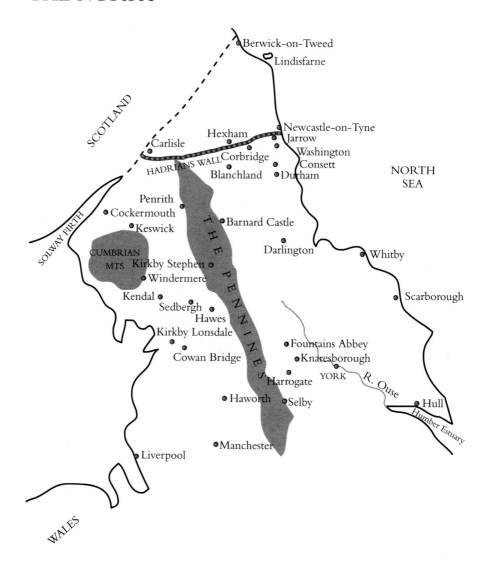

Canterbury. The crypt of the present building contains Roman, Saxon and Norman remains.

The present structure – an enormous three-towered edifice built of local limestone of a mellow yellowish hue – was begun in 1220 and completed about 1500, so that architecturally it combines the best of the Early English, Decorated and Perpendicular styles. It is highly decorated both inside and out. By special orders of Sir Thomas Fairfax, it escaped the destruction that befell so many churches in the seventeenth-century Civil War.

The cathedral has recently been refurbished and cleaned. The ceiling is painted very white, ornamented with gold, and its roof is decorated with bosses of the brightest colours. But the greatest glory of the Minster is its mediaeval glass. It is second only to Chartres in number of windows and vibrant colour. The old stained glass bathes the interior in a soft radiance of subdued colour hardly to be equalled elsewhere. The great rose window commemorates the Wars of the Roses with a border of entwined red and white roses emblematic of the Houses of Lancaster and York, the antagonists in that civil war of the fourteenth and fifteenth centuries. The justly famous Five Sisters window has five lancet windows executed in 'grisaille' – muted shades of grey brightened here and there with dots of brilliant colour. It was restored in 1925 and dedicated as a memorial to the women who died in World War I.

There are endless chapels and monuments to admire, including the tomb of Prince William of York, brother of the Black Prince and second son of Edward III. He died at a young age in 1348, possibly from the plague since that was the year of the Black Death. There is a very fine rood screen with statues of English kings from Henry I to Henry VI. In the chapter house we saw gospels dating from Saxon times, an ivory horn of great antiquity, and illuminated manuscripts. As I was standing in an aisle trying to comprehend the beauty and history before us, I happened to glance down and saw that I was standing on the grave of one MARGARET WHARTON. I experienced a macabre feeling that sent shivers up my spine. As we left, it was quite dark and beginning to rain, so we returned quickly to our hotel.

WEDNESDAY, JULY 23RD

Breakfast was served in a beautiful square room with a marble mantelpiece under a fine mosaic. A huge bay window looked out on a garden run wild. Immediately after the meal we were told by the manager we could not stay longer, so our first task was to find accommodation for the next two nights. We were lucky to find a modest bed-and-breakfast establishment in a rather rundown street. The room was adequate, however, and we were given a warm welcome by our hosts, a genial Yorkshire couple who were quite talkative and full of information. It was a delight to listen to their accents.

After an early morning rain the weather had cleared and turned bright and sunny, and we went to Exhibition Square to meet our guide for a walking tour of the city. He was an elderly retired glassblower, smartly and conservatively dressed, and very proud to be a Yorkshireman born and bred. He made it clear in his opening address that his services were voluntary and that tips were not expected nor to be offered.

We went first to St Mary's Abbey and then to the ancient walls girdling the city. Our guide showed us the walls' four levels – Roman, Saxon, Danish and Norman. He was a veritable mine of information, and his lectures were larded with down-to-earth Yorkshire humour spoken in the local dialect. He walked with us along the city walls as we circled the Minster and admired the lush gardens of the houses below, which are still occupied by canons, deans and rectors. Some of the older houses are built right into the walls. The great gates are known as bars and are in a remarkable state of preservation, though only one retains its barbican, an outer fort that gave initial protection to the gates. We ended our walk at the Shambles, a narrow thoroughfare virtually unchanged from mediaeval times, with the upper storeys of the houses projecting far enough almost to touch those across the way. Here the butchers of the town lived, and all the houses had wide sills or 'shambles' where the meat for sale was displayed.

Our guide next took us to one of the old churches named for the Danish leader Guthrum. York was the most important town in Danish England and is an excellent place to study the history of that time. Largely because of its strategic position on the Ouse, it has in fact been important in every phase of Britain's historical development. Called Eboracum in Roman days, it was the great crossroads and fortress that held down the North for the Romans, a centre of both civil and military functions and the training ground for troops to be sent to Hadrian's Wall on the Scottish border. Later both Saxons and Danes recognized the city's importance, and York became the capital of the Danelaw when England was divided between its Saxon inhabitants and Danish invaders. Still later, the Normans made it their headquarters and garrison for holding down northern England.

Our guide spoke of the Wars of the Roses between the rival royal houses of Lancaster and York, their respective heraldic symbols the red rose and the white rose. York was of singular importance during the wars, which were a factional fight between the Lancaster and York families that started over the 1377 succession of and later dissatisfaction with the boy king Richard II, son of the Black Prince and grandson of Edward III. Each faction was descended from the royal house and contended for the crown. While the Lancastrians finally won, York gave England several kings during this period of internecine strife. The last of the York kings was the hunchback Richard III, defeated and killed at the Battle of Bosworth Field in 1485 by the

Lancastrian Henry Tudor, who is said to have found the gold crown of England hanging in a thornbush on the field of battle. Henry later united the rival houses by marrying Elizabeth of York, thus firmly establishing the Tudor dynasty and ending the long period of civil war.

York also played an important role in the great Civil War of the mid seventeenth century between Parliamentary and Royalist forces. The decisive battle of that war was fought at Marston Moor to the north of the city in July 1644. The forces of Charles I were defeated and though York remained loyal to the king, the Royalist cause was lost from that time on.

In more modern times York developed industrially and became a great railway, administrative and ecclesiastical centre. It is the site of several important factories, in particular Rowntree's and Terry's, makers of fine confectionery. It also has an important and ever-growing tourist industry.

Our guide left us after providing us with a great deal of information to digest and many historical facts to sort out. Before leaving he asked us to identify ourselves, and we found that our small group was quite cosmopolitan, with Australia, New Zealand, France and the U.S.A. represented. He was a man of very definite standards – he would not talk as long as anyone else was talking, and inside a church he asked one of the Australians to remove his hat.

We had lunch at a delightful pub near the Shambles and then went back to the Minster for a more thorough look. We rented a cassette programme and learned much from it. David took some pictures, but I was glad to sit in the peace and quiet of the cathedral, as I have developed what I fear is tendinitis in my foot. Later we had a good tea and then returned to the room for a rest and some packing. We had dinner in a restaurant in Stonegate, a straight Roman street and one of the few in England that has retained its original paving stones. If you could block out the shops lining the street, it would not be hard to hear the tramp of Roman legions on their way to Hadrian's Wall. We later took a stroll beside the Ouse, but it was cold and windy so David walked and I limped back to our room.

THURSDAY, JULY 24TH

We decided to spend this day touring the environs of York and to end up at Haworth, home of the Brontës which I have long wanted to visit. We travelled west in the direction of Harrogate, passing through some lovely villages and towns. The weather was unsettled, with a brisk wind blowing and bright sun one minute and hard rain the next. Just before reaching Knaresborough we saw the ruins of a castle that once belonged to John of Gaunt. Richard II was kept captive in the keep in 1399. Knaresborough is a lovely old town built on high banks above the River Nidd, with steps connecting street and stream. We made a brief stop at the damp and eerie

Dropping Well, a petrifying spring where for good luck visitors hang objects of clothing and other such articles which are slowly solidified by the lime. In a cave nearby Mother Shipton, a prophetess remarkable for the accuracy of her prognostications, is said to have been born in 1488. We are waiting to see if her prediction comes true that:

> World then to an end will come
> In nineteen hundred and eighty one.

We next followed signs to Fountains Abbey, so called because it was built on seven streams that unite to form the River Skell. The spot was chosen by 12 Benedictine monks who left York in 1132 in search of solitude and isolation to embrace the stricter Cistercian rule of monastic life. The abbey prospered in subsequent centuries, as the monks gradually abandoned their vows of poverty, raised sheep, spun the lucrative wool, and exported it both as raw wool and finished cloth. With Henry VIII's dissolution of the monasteries, Fountains and other religious houses fell into decay. The roof was torn off for the valuable lead, and the vast buildings crumbled. The great central tower still stands tall and erect, though today it was covered by scaffolding as part of an extensive restoration.

The whole grey ruin is surrounded by the greenest grass, and while we were there the sun came out and shone brilliantly. At night the ruin is floodlit, and it must then be very beautiful with the darkness hiding imperfections and the shadows from the great lights throwing into relief the delicate carvings and tracery. I thought of Glastonbury, with which I am very familiar, and think Fountains more beautiful, though it is less important in legend and story. In all such places, I think of the lines of Shakespeare's contemporary John Webster:

> I do love these ancient ruins:
> We never tread upon them, but we set
> Our foot upon some reverend history.

As we left we saw a 'broken chancel with a broken cross' standing beside a stream in a field belonging to the abbey farm. It then began to rain, a sudden wild lashing storm that blotted out the sun that had shone so brightly just a few minutes earlier. We took a quiet untravelled road winding narrowly through fell and dale country that seemed to grow wilder and more desolate with every mile. Once we were stopped by a herd of cows, thin rangy animals unperturbed by our efforts to get by, and twice we were held up by flocks of sheep. It was fun to watch them marshalled and kept in order by the black and white border collies which seemed to be everywhere at once while the shepherds merely looked on. We were relieved to reach the small town of

Pateley Bridge for we were getting low on gas. The road climbed as we left the town, and we passed some very poor and depressed coal mining settlements. Small groups of dust-encrusted houses huddled close to the ground, and the few people we saw had the dull look of chronic hopelessness. It was a very different sight from the prosperous England seen by most tourists. Around these sad little habitations the lonely moorland stretches for miles, offering no escape from the desolate isolation.

At last we came to more agreeable farming country and crossed a mediaeval humpbacked bridge across the River Wharfe into Grassington, where we had lunch in a delightful pub. We drove on to Haworth, the birthplace of Charlotte, Emily and Anne Brontë and the setting for much of their writing. We found the little textile town just as dark and drab and depressing as they described it. To use Matthew Arnold's words:

> Where, behind Keighley, the road
> Up to the heart of the moors
> Between heath-clad showery hills
> Runs, and the colliers' carts
> Poach the deep ways coming down,
> And a rough-grimed race have their homes –
> There on its slope is built
> The moorland town. But the church
> Stands on the crest of the hill,
> Lonely and bleak; – at its side
> The parsonage house and the graves.

Leaving the 'dark Satanic mills' in the valley below, we climbed the steep road to the church where the writers' father was rector and to the parsonage where the family, most of them doomed to an early death from consumption, lived, loved, suffered, wrote and died. We passed the Black Bull, where the only son Branwell drank himself to death, his creativity stifled by the harsh living conditions and an overbearing father. It seemed right that the rain was hard and the wind fierce as we trudged on. The church is now almost entirely rebuilt, but inside are Brontë family memorials and a chapel dedicated to them. Except for Anne, who died and was buried in Scarborough near the cliffs she loved, all the family are interred in the churchyard here. Wild and overgrown and full of old tombstones leaning crazily at odd angles, it fosters the feeling of sad desolation evoked so faithfully and yet so lovingly by the gifted women. All, and especially Emily, loved the bleak town and the wild moors, and in their writings described their surroundings with a passion and intensity never before or since conveyed so vividly.

The parsonage is now a museum, preserved as it was in the Brontës' lifetime by the Brontë Society. The solid stone house is entered through a wide flagstone hall with a fine staircase leading to the upper rooms. The sisters spent most of their time as aspiring young writers in the dining room, and here is the horsehair sofa on which Emily died. Opposite is the parlour that served as Mr Brontë's study, where he wrote his interminable sermons and from which he ruled his family with an iron hand. Upstairs we saw the small room where as children the girls and Branwell wrote miniature books. Occasionally the grown-up girls left Haworth to work as governesses, Charlotte going as far afield as Belgium. It was she who bravely contacted a publisher and submitted the work of all three sisters under the names of Currer, Ellis and Acton Bell, a concession to the male-dominated world of their day.

But the moorland inspired them and always drew them back. For Emily especially, the heathered hills were her very reason for being, to the extent she would become physically ill upon leaving them. Place was more important to her than people, and she developed her characters from the scenery. All her work, prose and poetry alike, is imbued with the hazards and rare delights of the Yorkshire moors, the bleak discomforts of the parsonage, and the strange solace she drew from the churchyard graves. Though the harsh conditions of climate and lack of comfort in the parsonage probably killed her, the moors were an integral part of her writing and short life. I would have liked to walk the two miles across the moors to the bleak ruin of High Withins, the setting for *Wuthering Heights*, generally considered the masterpiece among the works of all three sisters. But it was raining hard and my foot was painful, so I could not say with Emily, 'No coward soul is mine ...'.

I left knowing that the visit to Haworth would be the high spot of this trip. I remembered how as a schoolgirl I revelled in the Brontë books, how I had lain in bed terrified with Jane Eyre as the mad woman rent her bridal veil, how I had tried to fathom Cathy's love for Heathcliff, and how horrified I was at the conditions in the boarding schools of the day. Now at long last, in middle age and by way of America, I have seen the place that gave birth to these rare geniuses.

1976

BLANCHLAND IN NORTHUMBERLAND – HADRIAN'S WALL – DURHAM – WASHINGTON OLD HALL – ACROSS THE MOORS TO WHITBY

TUESDAY, JULY 13TH

Leaving Coventry we drove to the M1 motorway which would take us north to Blanchland in Northumberland, where we had a reservation at the Lord Crewe Hotel. It was a long way – about 200 miles – but we were able to travel fast on the motorway. There was a great deal of traffic on the road, as it is the main artery linking London to the North. We stopped for a pub lunch at a place in Yorkshire called Darrington and arrived at the Lord Crewe in time for tea.

Blanchland is a small stone village in a moorland valley, reminding me of the Cotswold villages and Castle Combe, only much smaller. Set on the River Derwent, which is crossed by an old stone bridge, it was built in the eighteenth century as an industrial estate by the Earl of Crewe, also Bishop of Durham, for workers in the lead mines. Its construction followed the general plan of a twelfth-century monastery built by the White Friars, a monastic order that wore white robes – hence the name 'Blanchland.' After the Dissolution – the closing of all monasteries by Henry VIII in 1536 – the monastery and the small village nearby fell into disrepair and decline. John Wesley preached here in 1747 and pronounced it a heap of ruins, but shortly thereafter Lord Crewe began his rebuilding. The church, gatehouse and inn enclose a broad square lined with shops and brown tile-roofed sandstone houses, a square that seems to have retained something of the peace and serenity of mediaeval cloisters. The inn is built on the foundation of the monastery's storehouse, and the bar is in the crypt, the oldest remaining part of the religious house.

After tea we walked around the village square and found the air very cool in spite of bright sun. Cottage gardens were gay with flowers, asters and dahlias predominating, and mother swallows were feeding their young in mud nests plastered under the eaves. The birds were so numerous that cottagers had hung paper bags beneath to catch their droppings.

Back at the inn we had dinner in a gracious room hung with oil portraits, among them one of the forbidding-looking Lord Crewe, the peer and bishop who was the developer of Blanchland as it appears today. Afterwards we drove around the Derwent Reservoir, which looked very beautiful and tranquil in the still cool evening. We watched a hawk hovering motionless above two unsuspecting hares but did not wait to see the kill. We explored a narrow lonely road but it petered out to a rutted track, so we turned back across the dam and returned to the warm welcome of the hotel.

WEDNESDAY, JULY 14TH

We left Blanchland early to see as much as we could of this northeastern corner of England. It is a land of mountains and huge expanses of moorland where grass and heather grow, and grouse, curlew and plover wheel above. It is land once rich in coal, iron, and people endowed with the engineering skills to create from these elements great centres of shipbuilding and heavy industry such as Newcastle and Middlesbrough. Unfortunately today many of the mines are worked out and consequently the area has fallen on harsh economic times. The countryside just outside the industrial cities, however, remains beautiful, unspoilt, and dotted with half-ruined abbeys and fine castles and country houses.

Our destination today was Corbridge, from where we hoped to see something of Hadrian's Wall, the most spectacular relic of the Romans in Britain. The wall was built in the reign of the emperor Hadrian between AD 122 and AD 126 and marked the northernmost boundary of the Roman Empire. It stretched across the narrow waist of England from Carlisle in the west near the Solway Firth to a section of Newcastle in the east known as Wallsend.

Corbridge was the first fort on the Stanegate, the supply and communications road that paralleled the wall. There are some Roman remains at Corbridge, but the town's building of greatest note is the church, which has a Saxon tower and an interesting Roman arch inside. Our first view of the wall came at Housesteads, a garrison under excavation and restoration by the National Trust. We took our first walk along the wall and were surprised to find it neither as high nor as wide as we had expected. Some 73 miles long when built, the wall was then a threefold structure consisting of a stone wall more than 12 feet high and about nine feet thick; a deep wide ditch (or fosse) reinforcing the wall in front; and three earth walls, also ditched, reinforcing it behind. Castles and forts were built at frequent intervals. Only occasionally were the wall's defences pierced. It was constantly patrolled by sentries and was wide enough for horse-drawn chariots and supply wagons to drive atop it.

The wall was abandoned in AD 383, and by AD 410 the Romans had left Britain. Today its height is not impressive, as much of it has disappeared, the stones taken for other construction. What remains is thus considerably lower than that which the Romans built. It is nonetheless still possible in places to grasp the wall's immensity as it follows the crest of hills over the moors.

It was very cold and windy up on the wall, and we realized what a dreaded assignment it must have been for soldiers from sunny Italy. While many of the troops were drawn from subject peoples such as Gauls and Britons, the centurions and other officers were Romans. These lived in considerable style, and it is thought there was some intermarriage with British women. The stones they used in building the wall were squared and remarkably even, and the wall shows the care, precision and thoroughness that marked the Romans as an able people superior to their contemporaries in organization and engineering.

We drove along the Stanegate to Thirlwall, a spot where the Picts and

Scots 'thirled', or pierced, the wall several times. We stopped in a small pub called the Milecastle, so named for the defences which appear at intervals along the wall. It was quite small but full of interesting pictures and brasses and presented us with a very impressive menu lived up to by the excellent fare that was provided.

We stopped again at Housesteads, one of 17 major forts along the wall. It was crowded with sightseers, among them schoolchildren on field trips and a large detachment of soldiers perhaps studying the military science of ancient times. It is a very impressive fort with ramparts, gateways, granaries, latrines and barracks. There is a milecastle nearby which is well-preserved. The Housesteads headquarters building included a place of worship to the Roman gods. Several soldiers were assigned to two rooms serving as bedroom and living room, and cooking was done on a verandah. Officers had separate quarters. Outside the ramparts were huts built for British traders and camp followers. We had a long cold uphill walk to the fort and found much to interest us in the museum.

We returned to Blanchland, with brief stops along the way at Langley Castle and the beautiful town of Hexham – so much history and so little time! After dinner in the Lord Crewe we took another ride around the Derwent Reservoir. There are many reservoirs in this country that supply water for the great manufacturing cities near the coast.

THURSDAY, JULY 15TH

St Swithin's Day and we awoke to rain. We drove east towards Durham, going past the mighty iron works at Consett. For miles around the iron-rich earth has a reddish cast from the ferrous oxide. Though very prosperous for many years, the area is now depressed, with the iron mines exhausted and the steel industry at a low ebb.

We found our way into Durham, a very ancient city on the bluffs above the River Wear. It lies in an almost circular bend in the river. With its cathedral and castle – now the home of the university – Durham is one of the great sights of England. It is also a pocket of culture in the heavily industrialized area of shipbuilding around Newcastle, Jarrow, Gateshead and South Shields, a district severely hurt by today's depressed economy just as it was devastated by depression in the 1930s.

After parking with some difficulty, we climbed a very steep hillside through a harsh wind into the cathedral close. The great church is built on a rocky peninsula sticking out into the river with the castle positioned to defend it. The nave is supported by great heavy pillars decorated in simple almost crude geometrics, and the rounded arches are ornamented with the dogtooth design so popular with the Normans. A great lion's head doorknocker is on the massive main door – it is known as the sanctuary knocker, for any fugitive who could gain entrance to the cathedral could not be harmed by his pursuers. Criminals of the past have been known to seek refuge in the church and remain free from prosecution as long as they stayed within its sacred confines.

The cathedral as we know it was begun in 1093 by Bishop William of Calais on the site of the final resting place of St Cuthbert. Cuthbert was an early saint who died in AD 687 on the Holy Isle of Lindisfarne, where he was the bishop. Afraid that heathen raiders would disturb his grave, his faithful disciples carried his body for many years until at last they reached Durham, where they buried him. His body was said to be still undecayed at the time of interment. Cuthbert's remains were not discovered till 1827 in the Chapel of the Nine Altars.

The Venerable Bede, another holy and learned man, is buried in the cathedral's Galilee Chapel. A monk, scholar and historian, Bede spent his life in the monastery at nearby Jarrow, writing *An Ecclesiastical History of the English Nation* and beginning a translation of the Bible into the vernacular. He was called 'Venerable' both because of his scholarship and knowledge and the advanced years he had attained – for that era – when he died in AD 753 at the age of 63. In addition to the graves of these two early Christians, Durham Cathedral possesses a great throne of stone built by the fourteenth-century Bishop Hatfield above the tomb he had prepared for himself.

Sir Walter Scott described Durham Cathedral as 'half Church of God, half castle 'gainst the Scot.' Right he was, for the cathedral, along with its defending castle, was subjected to many attacks from wild Scottish tribes. It was well-protected, however, by its position and the bravery of its inhabitants. During the Civil War the Puritans held Scottish prisoners in the cathedral.

We spent about an hour in the cathedral seeing the tombs and chapels; those of the Durham Light Infantry were especially moving. We went briefly into the museum in a hall with a marvellous hammer-beam roof and saw vestments, seals and illustrated manuscripts of great antiquity.

We had a quick lunch in a pub and then drove on through a heavily built-up area to Washington Old Hall in a town recently created and named Washington. Ancestors of George Washington – the family was originally named 'de Wessington' – lived in this seventeenth-century house built of red sandstone. Eventually it fell into disrepair, its grounds encroached on by the growing industry of the area. Some time before this bicentennial year, restoration began with largely American funds, and when we saw the house its ground floor had been completed and furnished with appropriate antiques. The village in which it is situated is now incorporated in the new town of Washington, which is projected to grow to a population of some 80,000. Washington himself had no personal connection with the old hall, but it seemed right and proper to visit the house of his ancestors in this special year of 1976.

Later in the evening we took a ride over the moors. Dusk had gathered and the moon had risen, and the white road rose and fell over the undulating land with no human habitation in sight. I was reminded of Alfred Noyes' line in 'The Highwayman':

> The road was a ribbon of moonlight over the purple moor...

The moor was not yet purple, however, for the heather is not out till August, and no highwayman came riding – in fact it was a scene of utter and complete loneliness. Job's comforter that I am, the thought crossed my mind that we might have a flat tyre, or worse, a breakdown, but no such mishap occurred. We got back to the inn safely, somewhat overawed by the lonely immensity of nature that still exists in this heavily populated island.

FRIDAY, JULY 16TH

We departed Blanchland with some regret, realizing we had seen only a fraction of all there is to see in this northeastern corner of our land. We left along the moorland road of our ride last night, the moors looking less terrifying in bright sunshine but still bleak and lonely. In some places we could see nothing but the undulating moorland, inhabited only with pairs of shaggy ewes and their spring lambs, now almost full-grown. Because of the depleted coal and iron mines, many of the small settlements we saw appeared to belong to a dead past, though some farms and villages showed some prosperity. Here and there we saw an old abandoned mine and more often the circular stone animal shelters known in the South as pounds. We saw only a few cars on the road and were disappointed at not seeing more wildlife – just two hares, though curlews were wheeling and dipping overhead while uttering their mournful cries.

The moors are on a high tableland rising in the west to more than 2,000 feet. The comparative flatness of the terrain and the high rainfall produce huge areas of peaty ill-drained land ideally suited for water supply. There are thus many reservoirs here and, on the edge of the moors, high dramatic waterfalls. When we began the steep descent to the valleys below, we could see from the road tiny villages clinging precariously to hillsides, the houses built with their front doors opening on to narrow twisting streets overlooking the valleys. Other villages built on the slopes of sheltered dales or on river banks looked neat and prosperous. We followed the River Tees for some miles, and, when we saw a sign for High Force Falls, stopped and took the 600-yard walk through the woods to view them. Going through sun-dappled woods beside the river rushing along its rocky bed, we came to the falls tumbling over a ledge some 60 feet high. We climbed the steps above the falls and had a wide view of the moorland. Because of the unusually dry summer, the falls were less spectacular than usual, and we were told that they are best viewed after a heavy rain.

We passed through the lovely old town of Barnard Castle and the industrial town of Darlington, the birthplace of George Stephenson's steam engine, and came to the pretty little town of Guisborough, where we stopped for lunch. We then drove along the side of the North York Moors and decided to digress to Whitby, a diversion that proved most enjoyable and worthwhile.

We could see the jagged ruins of Whitby Abbey crowning the cliffs looking out to the North Sea long before we reached the town. They tower over the mouth of the River Esk. There has been an abbey on this site since AD 657, when the first one was founded by St Hilda. In AD 663 a very important convocation known as the Synod of Whitby was held between the Roman and Celtic branches of the church. Here it was decided that the future church would accept Roman authority and practices. The date of Easter was determined and other points of dogma and procedure set. Most importantly, England, through the decision to follow the Roman church, developed closer ties to and was influenced more by the culture of continental Europe. Had she stayed with the Celtic Christians based in the remote islands of Iona and Lindisfarne, she would have become increasingly isolated.

In the seventh century the abbey was home to Caedmon, a stableman who became one of the earliest English poets, and a cross in St Mary's churchyard commemorates him. The abbey was later destroyed completely by the Danes and then rebuilt by the Normans. The present ruins are thirteenth-century.

The old town, its roofs red and higgledy-piggledy, clusters around the mouth of the river. The Norman tower of St Mary's Church looks down upon it, and town and church are connected by a walk of 199 steps. In 1914 the town's west end was shelled by the German fleet, and the old abbey sustained some damage.

The sea has always figured prominently in the life of Whitby. Captain Cook sailed from here for Tahiti in the *Endeavour* in 1768 and as a young man lived for awhile in the town. The town's chief industry has always been fishing and it was an important whaling port. Another profitable industry once found its raw material in jet, a kind of fossilized wood found in the cliffs. In the days of Queen Victoria's widowhood its black colour made it suitable for jewellery for women in mourning. Today the cliffs here – as elsewhere along the east coast – are badly eroded. The sea has eaten away at their base, leaving them top heavy, and it is sad to see the church graveyard covered in rank grass while gravestones tilt at crazy angles ready to tumble into the sea below.

Leaving Whitby we retraced the road we arrived by for a few miles and then cut across the moors through a lovely heathered landscape rather gentler than the Durham moors. We went through Castleton and Hutton-in-the-Hole, the latter a show village a little like Gloucestershire's Bourton-on-the-Water. As we approached York we thought we should try for a hotel there and were lucky enough to secure a room in the old but opulent Royal Station Hotel. After a good meal in the restaurant we took an evening walk on the old city walls, the Minster glowing golden in the setting sun. The wall seemed deserted, and we had not gone far when a man approached and asked us to descend to the street at the next bar, or gate, as the wall is closed at dusk.

1983

with the West Side Presbyterian Church Choir of Ridgewood N.J.

YORK – PAST HULL – DURHAM – HADRIAN'S WALL – LAKE DISTRICT – WHARTON ROOTS IN WESTMORLAND

SUNDAY, JULY 3RD

The day began in a relaxed fashion with a lessening of tension, which most of us needed. We were to spend the day in York and buses were not to leave Scunthorpe, where we spent the night, until 10. I skipped breakfast, making do with tea and biscuits in our room and enjoying the extra rest. The weather appeared unsettled, dry but with dark rain-threatening clouds scudding across the sky and a brisk wind blowing. We piled on the buses, collected the other half of our party from the Royal Hotel and set out for York. The countryside continued flat, and, though obviously fertile, it was not very attractive. I volunteered my services as a commentator and had a lot of fun dispensing titbits of English lore not generally found in guidebooks.

We drove for about an hour and a half before we saw the three towers of York Minster on the horizon. We crossed the River Ouse and drove along a road paralleling the wall encircling the city. We parked the bus and split into three groups each with a guide for a short walking tour. We walked a short distance to the wall and moat, now dry.

As we had done several years ago we walked along the wide city walls, and strolled through the grounds of the King's Manor, a lovely old house surrounded by beautiful grounds where strutting peacocks occasionally emitted their raucous cries and spread their gorgeous tails. From there we went to Stonegate, a shopping street that was once a Roman way where we were happy to find the Raffles Tearoom open for lunch, and we had a good meal served by a pleasant and efficient waitress.

After lunch we walked to the Minster and admired its splendour both outside and in. After spending some time in the cathedral it was late afternoon and time to assemble to hear Joanne Rodland's organ recital before evensong. The service was beautifully intoned and sung, yet seemed remote, austere and otherworldly. The music seemed to hang and hover in the air. The choir was composed of boys and men, the boys pupils at the choir school and chosen for their treble voices with the timbre of birdsong or flute. The service was a wonderful, ethereal and uplifting experience.

We then gathered at the buses and set off for Scunthorpe by a different road. This took us farther east where the countryside became hillier and more wooded. We saw a lot of sheep grazing on the low chalk hills known as wolds. We passed some lovely little streams, their banks abounding with masses of tiny wild iris of a lovely shade of yellow.

Our drivers were able to maintain a steady speed on the new road, which leads to a suspension bridge over the Humber estuary. Just opened last year by the Queen, it is the longest suspension bridge in the world and a fine sight it is as it spans the murky muddy waters of the estuary with pillars of concrete and graceful curves of steel. On the left as we approached the bridge we passed what once was a huge private park full of great trees. In its midst stood a once elegant house now sad and lonely in a derelict state, a victim, I suppose, of progress.

The Humber estuary is formed by the waters of the Ouse and the Trent. With the great port of Hull at its head it is a very important commercial waterway. As with the rest of the east coast, silting is a problem and constant dredging is necessary. The town of Hull — its full name actually Kingston-upon-Hull, the Hull being another river that here joins the Humber — lay to our east. Until the opening of the new bridge, Hull was somewhat inaccessible and off the usual tourist track, so that it was twice damned in literature, first by Daniel Defoe, who wrote:

> . . . from Hull, Halifax and Hell, Good Lord
> deliver us,

and later by Noel Coward's famous couplet,

> If some of you think Monte Carlo is dull
> Come over and try a wet Sunday in Hull.

Things have now changed, however, and Hull is being discovered not only by overland visitors but also by many coming by sea from Europe. It is of special interest to visitors like David and myself from North Carolina, for the state capital Raleigh is Hull's sister city.

In and around Hull are artifacts from the Bronze and Iron ages as well as some very fine Roman remains. Hull was the first Viking settlement in England. During the Middle Ages the abbots of Meaux maintained it as a port for the export of the fine wool produced by their sheep. In 1296 Edward I made the town a base for his Scottish campaigns and later conferred a royal charter upon the town so that it henceforth became known as King's Town-upon-Hull. In the seventeenth-century civil war the city was a Parliamentary stronghold. It was the birthplace of Andrew Marvell, poet, scholar and sometime secretary to Oliver Cromwell. Robinson Crusoe sailed from Hull on his fictional voyage. William Wilberforce, the lifelong abolitionist, was born here in 1759, and a fine statue of this most important citizen stands in the centre of the town. Amy Johnson, the British aviatrix who in 1930 flew solo from Britain to Australia, was likewise born in Hull.

The city at one time was a whaling port and is today a great fishing port. For many years it ranked only behind London and Liverpool in shipping tonnage. Although it suffered dreadfully from Zeppelin raids in World War I and from blitz attacks in World War II, the damage has been corrected by tasteful and thoughtful rebuilding. Docks have been redesigned and reconstructed to accommodate the containerization of land and sea shipping, and, with the completion of the new bridge, Hull today seems about to regain her former prosperity.

We were unfortunately unable to stop in Hull and drove past it on to Scunthorpe, passing great steel mills on our left. Scunthorpe is hardly an elegant town and an unlikely place for an American tour group, but we were heartily welcomed at our hotels with food and drink and rest.

MONDAY, JULY 4TH

Happy Birthday, America! It is strange to be celebrating Independence Day in the country from which we declared our independence some 207 years ago. Three years ago with this same group of people we began the day on a very solemn note – a visit to the concentration camp at Dachau near Munich. That was a sobering experience, perhaps serving to make us all the more thankful for our life of free choice.

But today a holiday air prevailed in our buses as we set out on the long ride north to Edinburgh. We said goodbye to Scunthorpe with mixed feelings. The hotel had given us a warm welcome, excellent food and good accommodation, but the town could not be classed as a scenic spot, and there was an air of economic distress about it that made us slightly uncomfortable. It was disturbing to see young people in bars drinking beer with a look of hopelessness in their eyes, for to them the future must look bleak indeed.

I was lucky enough to get a front seat on the bus, and we made good time staying on motorways and main roads through the flat fields of Lincolnshire and southern Yorkshire. Sights of heavy industry intruded upon the pastoral scene in some areas, for this part of the country is rich in coal and iron, still the basis for modern manufacturing. As we went north, more cattle and large flocks of sheep appeared in the fields. The sheep had recently been sheared, their wool the raw material for the huge Yorkshire woollen industry. A combination of sheep farming, good water for dyeing the wool, iron for machinery, and coal to power it led to the rise of this industry at the beginning of the Industrial Revolution.

After one stop for refreshments and petrol we reached Durham about lunchtime. Before attempting the formidable climb to the cathedral and castle, David and I popped into a convenient pub to fortify ourselves. We had a most enjoyable ploughman's lunch. The pub was patronized largely by local people, and we drew some curious glances.

Outside the weather was glorious, adding to and softening the stark grandeur of the mighty church. It was very different from our previous visit when the weather was cold with storm clouds racing across the sky whipped by a fierce wind. Then cathedral and castle looked grim and forbidding indeed. Inside, as David and I looked about, a verger spotted us as Americans and took us to see a plaque on the cloister wall erected to a John Washington, prior of the cathedral from 1416 to 1446. Undoubtedly he was of the same family as the famous George.

Durham remains one of my favourite cathedrals – it seems to be the safe stronghold that God still offers. In World War II part of the student body of Whitelands College from which I had graduated in 1938 was evacuated from London to Durham. I feel I would have liked the experience of living here and am sorry that today's visit was of necessity cursory. Before leaving, David and I had our pictures taken grasping the mighty twelfth-century sanctuary knocker that traditionally has opened the church as refuge to those fleeing pursuit or persecution.

Once more in the bus we went on through high moor-like country which flashed by at motorway speeds. I felt a deep sadness as we came to the town of Consett. Once the home of the largest iron and steel mill in the country, the works are now closed and being razed. Today the town is a blot on the landscape and a deep well of human misery. As we rode through we noticed large numbers of able-bodied men gardening in lacklustre fashion, doing odd jobs, or just sitting with the air of hopelessness that irremediable unemployment breeds. I think though it is just as well for foreign visitors to see a side of life in England that is quite different from the historic sites and picturebook countryside they usually see.

We came to Corbridge, a famous Roman garrison town and provisioning station for Hadrian's Wall. Here we left the main road, getting slightly lost trying to locate the spot where we were scheduled to view the wall. Our admiration went out to our drivers for getting their huge buses around impossible corners and through the narrowest of streets, much like the Biblical camel going through the eye of the needle. Arriving at the appointed place, we took a pleasant walk through a field of grazing sheep where we saw the recently reconstructed Roman stables and barracks. We saw only a small section of the wall itself, and even that was some distance away. Further west there is a section of wall which rises and falls over hill and dale and can be viewed for miles. At the very nice tourist stop we were able to get some refreshment at a little shop bearing the name Lucullus, a nice Latin touch.

THURSDAY, JULY 7TH

Our next stop was Carlisle, a large and important fortress town on the English side of the Border. Walled and built of red sandstone, it is the western end of Hadrian's Wall. We saw the threatening castle as we drove into the town, and I remembered that Carlisle had withstood every attack but one, when it was captured by 'a hundred pipers, an'a an'a' in Bonnie Prince Charlie's 1745 rebellion. Here in the cathedral, red sandstone like the rest of the town, a papal legate had solemnly cursed Robert the Bruce 'with candel's light and causing the bells to be roong' during the thirteenth- and fourteenth-century wars between Scotland and England. An excellent lunch awaited us in the Sword and Mitre Hotel, after which we were on our way southwards once more.

We now entered the Lake District, thought by many to be the most scenic area in all of Britain. There are 16 lakes, clear and blue, surrounded by high and craggy mountains. Windermere, name both of the largest lake and a town on its shores, is full of tourists and heavily commercialized, but the rest of the district is carefully preserved by the National Trust in natural unspoiled beauty. We saw it under almost perfect conditions – the sky slightly overcast but blue, the water glistening and rippling and reflecting the sky, the trees in full summer leaf, the flowery gardens brightening little stone villages, and isolated white farmhouses standing alone in the fields. The bus detoured through the market town of Penrith and then crossed the mountains by the Kirkstone Pass. Here were wild, steep, rocky hillsides crisscrossed with stonewalls and inhabited only by sheep that roamed at will to nibble the sparse grass.

As we enjoyed the scenery we regretted that by taking this route we had missed Grasmere and Rydal Water, both dear to all lovers of the poetry of Wordsworth. The Lakes are associated with many poets, Wordsworth, Southey and Coleridge chief among them, all of whom expressed their feelings for its beauty in immortal language. Wordsworth was born at Cockermouth and lived in several houses in the Lake District with his sister Dorothy, also a writer and journalist of considerable skill and fame. Dove Cottage at Grasmere is the best known of his houses and is a museum and shrine for all his admirers.

We passed very close to Troutbeck, where John Peel lived 'once on a day'. Peel was a local farmer and hunter about whom a popular song was written:

> D'ye ken John Peel with his coat so gray,
> He lived at Troutbeck once on a day.
> Peel's view halloo would awaken the dead
> Or a fox from his lair in the morning.

The first line is often misquoted 'gay' instead of 'gray' since most huntsmen wear red. The Cumberland Hunt wore gray, however – good hard-wearing tweed woven in nearby Kendal from the coarse harsh wool of mountain sheep. These huntsmen did not ride horses; instead they pursued the fox on foot behind their hounds.

LATER IN JULY

Our one long trip from Marlborough was to Kirkby Stephen in Westmorland to see the church there and find a house called Wharton Hall. According to research done by David's uncle the Reverend Samuel Rankin, a Presbyterian minister in Greensboro, North Carolina, this should be the ancestral home of the Wharton family. We left Marlborough very early for the day-long ride north. We took the motorways and had no time to deviate from them, though the prospect was tempting, for Cobbett's words from his nineteenth-century *Rural Rides* still ring true: 'Those that travel by turnpike roads know nothing of England.'

We found Kirkby Stephen to be a pleasant wide-streeted market town noted for its regular horse auctions. Parking in the centre of the town, I went into a wool shop to buy yarn. When I told the assistant my name was

Wharton, she said it was a common name in the locality and that the town was often visited by Whartons from America. We went first to the church, quite large and Saxon in origin though added to by the Normans. It is dedicated to St Stephen. We entered it through an impressive stone portico built in 1810 with money given by one John Waller, a sailor who once lived in the town. The red sandstone church is surrounded by green lawns and neat hedges. Off to the side of the spacious nave is the Wharton Chapel, full of facsimiles of Wharton tombs – the originals are in Tadcaster, Yorkshire, where the family had sizeable estates in addition to those in this area of Westmorland. There was little information about the church except for an account in French, presumably written for the benefit of visitors from the French town with which Kirkby Stephen is twinned. Fortunately I remembered enough of my schoolgirl French to be able to translate fairly thoroughly. Returning to the town we made some enquiries at a book shop and made a futile attempt to run to earth an old man who is the local historian. We then asked for directions to Wharton Hall and found our way thither.

The old house is a partial ruin, an enormous stark stone construction, half castle, half dwelling. It has recently been acquired by a dairy farmer and to reach it we drove through a field of poor pasture land full of cows and one enormous bull of terrifying aspect. The road was nothing but a narrow single track of concrete raised inches above the turf, and I was nervous that somehow we would be 'derailed' and left to the mercy of the bull. But David's driving skill prevailed and we reached the 'farmyard,' full of derelict machinery and surrounded by sheds in which we saw a few sheep and some cows. The place was deserted and surrounded by great grey ruins, on one wall of which we could make out a half-eroded carving of the Wharton coat-of-arms. We caught a glimpse of an interior courtyard, a grassy square ringed with buildings that indicated human occupancy, but we saw no one. We left feeling rather deflated yet somehow overawed by the desolation and dereliction of a once important manor.

We drove fast to the old grey stone town of Kendal where we spent the night in a modest hotel. Kendal was at one time home to a clothing industry begun by Flemish weavers in 1331. These weavers taught local workers to make a strong hard wearing material that came to be known as Kendal Green. From this was made the clothing worn by the famous longbowmen of the Hundred Years' War. The ruined castle was once the home of Catherine Parr, sixth wife of Henry VIII. The town was the birthplace of eighteenth century portrait painter George Romney. Today its main industry is the manufacture of shoes.

The next day en route to Marlborough we detoured through Kirkby Lonsdale. It is another town with Wharton family connections, but I was more interested in the fact that we passed through Cowan Bridge, once site of a girls boarding school now moved to the nearby village of Casterton. The Bronte sisters attended the school at Cowan Bridge, and it served as the model for the infamous Lowood Institution in Charlotte's *Jane Eyre*.

1986

with Jane Sockwell & Betsy Newland

THE LAKE DISTRICT – KIRKBY STEPHEN – YORKSHIRE DALES

SATURDAY, SEPTEMBER 20TH

Bypassing Lancaster, an old city full of history, we entered Cumbria, a new nomenclature for the former counties of Cumberland and Westmorland. Here is the Lake District, the most famous and extensive beauty spot in the country and now almost entirely under the control of the National Trust. The lakes and mountains were formed eons ago by successive geological upheavals and ice-age changes. We missed the turn off the motorway for Kendal and continued on to Penrith, but did not go into the pretty little market town where 17 years ago we had stopped for tea and Chris had bought an antique candlestick as a wedding present for our older son David and his wife Marianne. We drove along the shores of Ullswater on the way to Keswick. The surface of the lake was rippled by waves caused by a strong breeze, but the water was azure blue from the reflection of the sky and bordered by woods and high mountains. Many little boats were taking advantage of the good weather and with spread sails of brightest colours were tacking along in fine fettle. The narrow winding road was lined with trees, big oaks and mountain ash laden with bunches of red berries.

Leaving the lake we climbed a steep hillside where many sheep were grazing. The breed seemed more leggy than usual, and their wool a darker grey. One field we passed had white sheep, black sheep, and heavily spotted sheep, so that I was reminded of biblical Jacob's experiments in stock breeding.

At last we came to a good road leading to Keswick, a bustling market town and centre of tourism. In keeping with the literary associations of the Lake District, the poet Robert Southey lived at Greta Hall in the town and is buried in a churchyard nearby. Today the town was bursting at the seams with people and traffic, and it was with difficulty that we finally reached our hotel. David and I had stayed here with Chris those many years ago, and we saw many changes today, not all for the better. It was originally built as a railway hotel connected to the station by a covered walkway that is now a conservatory. It is a large grey stone Victorian building with big bay windows and the towers and turrets typical of Victorian architecture. It is approached by an impressive driveway and surrounded with green lawns, but the hotel's former elegance seems somewhat faded. In 1894 the grandson of Queen Victoria who later became the German Kaiser was entertained here, and Queen Elizabeth visited in 1954. The hotel has recently become a member of the Trust House Forte group, so it will undoubtedly undergo a restoration.

A tour bus full of American tourists had preceded us by a few minutes, so the hotel staff was very busy with them. We eventually reached our rooms via the lift. After unpacking and freshening up, we took a stroll in the gardens but were saddened at the state of neglect they were in. We did find a fine display of sweet peas, though, their delicate hues ranging from white to pink to red to lavender, and enjoyed their fragrance.

After drinks in the bar we had an excellent dinner in the dining room, which has a big bay window overlooking the garden. Our waiter was a young man who charmed us with his North Country accent.

SUNDAY, SEPTEMBER 21ST

We woke to cloudy skies and a heavy mist, but after breakfast we set out for Kirkby Stephen hoping the weather would improve as the day wore on. We wanted David's sisters to see the church, the Wharton memorials and Wharton Hall.

En route we went to Grasmere to see Dove Cottage, where Wordsworth lived for some years and where he wrote some of his finest poetry. Being Sunday the house was closed, which was something of a disappointment. Our next stop was Windermere, and drove on to Kendal.

Leaving the environs of the lakes, the countryside became dull and uninteresting, rendered so partly by the fog that partially obscured the mountaintops and partly by large tracts of infertile and unproductive land that appeared barely able to support a few scattered sheep. We reached Kirkby Stephen about noon and found the wide main street almost deserted, quiet in the way of country Sundays in small towns when church is out.

Parking near the church we found the outside air cold and bone-chilling even though no rain was yet falling. It was in 1543 that a member of the landowning Wharton family was raised to the peerage. Years later, a descendant named Philip was created the Duke of Wharton, but he lost the title and the family fortunes in a life of profligacy and espousal of lost causes. There is no established link between the English Whartons and the family of the same name that arrived in Delaware about the time of the

American Revolution, a branch of which later migrated to and settled in North Carolina, but there is some evidence that a connection may exist. Certainly one of the Whartons in Kirkby Stephen set up charities for local people and Bibles are still distributed to local children under the terms of an old Wharton will, an act that seems in keeping with many members of the American family. There was a lot of family and historical information in the chapel, and Betsy seemed especially interested and regretful that the time was so short and the light so bad.

We left the church and went into a pub for lunch. We sat in a bow window that commanded a good view of the street. Hanging on the wall was a photograph of a farmer named Wharton. He was at a horse show with one of his hunters, and we learned that this is good horse country. The landlord told us that very morning Prince Charles had attended services at the local Catholic church. This raised quite a few eyebrows, and subsequently articles appeared in the newspapers questioning his wisdom in worshipping in a Roman church.

We then drove the few miles out of town to Wharton Hall. Still a dairy farm it seemed unchanged since our last visit. David spoke briefly to a girl farmworker, and she said that occasionally American tourists visit, perhaps other Whartons like us in search of their roots.

On our return journey we drove through the charming little town of Cockermouth, going through the mountains by the Whinlatter Pass. In addition to being the birthplace of Wordsworth, it is also the town where Fletcher Christian, leader of the Bounty mutiny, was born. Another famous son was John Dalton, the chemist who formulated Dalton's law and the atomic theory of chemistry.

MONDAY, SEPTEMBER 22ND

Leaving the Lake District we drove from Keswick to Penrith, where we took the M6 south to Sedbergh, the westernmost town in Yorkshire and a local market town of some importance. Stopping at a country gas station on the outskirts of the town, we became objects of great interest to a solemn rosy-cheeked toddler who, thumb in mouth, and nose pressed against the window of an adjacent cottage, watched our every move. Sedbergh is the site of a very famous public school founded in the sixteenth century by Roger Lupton, Provost of Eton. The town has Quaker connections, and there is a meeting house where George Fox, founder of the Society of Friends is said to have preached. The streets in the town are very narrow and winding, and we were held up for a short time by a truck blocking the road between two large old hotels. The main street was once part of the turnpike between Kendal and Kirkby Stephen.

Sedbergh is the gateway to the beautiful wild dale country of northwest Yorkshire, locale of the books of veterinarian James Herriott and made familiar to thousands through the television show based on them. The upland moors sweep to high summits in the Yorkshire Dales National Park. They are wild, windswept and solitary, the stillness only broken by the plaintive cries of curlews, plovers, and grouse, and the baaing of wide-ranging sheep that for their very survival continually nibble the short turf. The high hills and fells descend sharply to clear, fast-running streams, and the emerald green fields are divided into odd shapes by stone walls built by the labour of countless thousands as they cleared the land for pasture and tillage. The few houses we saw were built of stone clinging to hillsides or huddling in farmyards. They were old and weatherbeaten and appeared comfortless, residences of men and women wresting a bare livelihood from the rugged land. As we drove along, the sun occasionally peeked out from behind the clouds but did little to brighten the sombre scene. Few of the houses had flower gardens, and the animals often seemed to be housed in stone barns bigger than the houses. There were a few rough-looking cows, but little land seemed to be under the plough, and the main crop seemed to be hay. Each farm seemed to have sheep and more sheep – their wool the raw material for Yorkshire's woollen industry. Today the woollen industry is less prosperous, as it is faced with foreign competition, outmoded machinery, and the popularity of synthetic fabrics.

We crossed and recrossed streams and rivers going over little humpbacked bridges and came at last to a small town called Hawes, set in some of the wildest and most rugged country in the area. Hawes is the site of a famous annual sheep and horse fair, and we stopped briefly in the town to visit a dale country museum run by the National Park Association.

Going on we saw a group of locals dressed in tweeds, leggings and deerstalker caps scanning the hillsides with binoculars. We learned from a bystander that the hounds were out after the foxes, but the accent of our informant was so broad that we could not figure out whether it was an organized hunt or just a method of exterminating foxes. Later on we saw a group of men with guns and dogs, mostly Labradors, stalking and beating the hillsides after grouse, partridge, and pheasant. Shortly afterwards we saw two pheasants, a cock and a hen, half concealed in the grass on the verge of the road.

We stopped for a pub lunch at the Black Swan in the marketplace of the pleasant little town of Leyburn. Then, going south, we left the dale country and entered the flat uninteresting – though very fertile – Vale of York. We joined the A1 on what used to be known as the Great North Road. Sounding very romantic to me when I was a child, today I found it dirty, noisy and lined with petrol stations, eating places, small factories, and agricultural stores, all of which looked dusty, grimy, and depressed. The road was heavily travelled with trucks and lorries, and traffic was held up at intervals by road repairs. We joined the M62 eventually, going west until it linked up with the M1, which took us through the mining and manufacturing of the North Midlands.

York Minster

Sanctuary Knocker on the door of
Durham Cathedral

Fountains Abbey

Whitby Abbey

Haworth, home of the Brontë Family

Wharton Hall, Westmorland. Half eroded Coat-of-Arms

Wharton Effigies in the church at Kirkby Stephen

Sheep on the road – a hazard in rural Yorkshire

Chapter Six

THE MIDLANDS

'. . . those dark Satanic mills'
William Blake 1757–1827

The large area in the centre of England is known as the Midlands. It is generally divided into the South Midlands – the counties of Gloucestershire, Herefordshire, Leicestershire, Northamptonshire, Rutland, Warwickshire and Worcestershire – and the North Midlands, consisting of Derbyshire, Lincolnshire, Nottinghamshire, Shropshire and Staffordshire.

The South Midlands area – roughly the old Saxon kingdom of Mercia – is the very heart of England. An ancient cross near the village of Meriden near Coventry is said by many to mark the exact centre of the country. The area is sometimes also called the Cockpit of England because of the many important battles fought within its boundaries. These include battles at Worcester, Naseby and Edgehill during the Civil War; at Evesham, where Simon de Montfort was defeated and killed by Henry III's army in 1253; and, perhaps most important of all, at Bosworth Field, ending the Wars of the Roses and establishing the Tudor dynasty in 1485.

There are many beautiful towns and villages in the South Midlands, including Shakespeare's Stratford-on-Avon, and much lovely pastoral landscape. Industry now encroaches upon much of the area, however. The great city of Birmingham is the hub, its tentacles stretching far out to link surrounding towns into a vast megalopolis of factories in the fashion of 'the great wen,' as Cobbett described London 200 years ago.

The North Midlands stretch from the border of Wales and the River Severn to Lincolnshire's North Sea coast. They encompass the southern mountains of the Pennine chain in Derbyshire's Peak District and the marshy fenland of Lincolnshire. Shropshire and Lincolnshire are largely agricultural, but there is much industry here also. Nottingham is the home of lace curtain-making, Derby is the site of the Rolls Royce aero division, and Staffordshire is known for its pottery and china manufacture. This part of England has produced many literary giants, among them D. H. Lawrence

THE MIDLANDS AND EAST

and Arnold Bennett of the factory towns of Nottingham and the Potteries, Tennyson from Lincolnshire, and A. E. Housman from Shropshire.

I am afraid I have given the Midlands short shrift in my journals. My knowledge of this part of the country was acquired early in my life. As a child we often visited an aunt who lived at Sutton Coldfield near Birmingham, and our parents took us to visit Stratford, Warwick Castle, Southwell Minster, and Lichfield Cathedral. In 1938 I began teaching in Birmingham and spent some time during the war on school evacuation duty in Leicestershire villages and in Loughborough, a pleasant market town situated midway between Nottingham and Leicester. In our visits from America it seems we have passed through the Midlands en route to the North but have seldom lingered, though rebuilt Coventry and its new cathedral as well as visits to Lincoln and the Peak District have been memorable experiences.

1975

THROUGH LINCOLNSHIRE TO YORK – FROM YORK TO MARLBOROUGH

TUESDAY, JULY 22ND

We were up in good time and after a good breakfast drove towards Sleaford from King's Lynn through the flat seemingly endless fields of Lincolnshire. This is the largest county in England after Yorkshire and is divided into three administrative districts: Lindsey, Kesteven and Holland. The name of the last has nothing to do with the Netherlands but means 'overlooked by high ground,' for though very flat near the Wash it is overlooked by the higher chalk 'wolds.' From the elevated road the black earth stretches as far as one can see, unbroken by hedges or fences though scored with drainage ditches. Most of the houses are small and low to the ground with few windows. Though this is July and today was sunny, it was a bleak and cheerless scene, and I imagined how bare and desolate it must look in winter. This land is nonetheless the breadbasket of England. Many crops are almost ready for harvest, and today men and women were in the fields picking and packing potatoes, strawberries, beets, onions and cabbages. There were more potatoes than anything else for they are a staple of the British diet.

We stopped in the town of Sleaford to go to a bank and pick up a map. The town is a market centre and a hub of road and rail connections. It is also the district seat of Kesteven. There are some nice old houses here, and the beautiful church of St Denis is cathedral-like and has fine window tracery and a chained Bible.

FRIDAY, JULY 25TH

Over breakfast we talked to a pleasant couple from Bath and then said goodbye to our gracious hosts and left York. We followed a road southwest through Tadcaster, where the Romans and succeeding builders quarried the honey-coloured stone from which York is built. We went close to Leeds but turned onto the A1 just before reaching it. The morning was heavenly, one of those rare and perfect summer morns. But the road, at first scenic and rural, soon brought us to the industrial spine of England, with its unbroken lines of factories, mines, and smokestacks belching forth acrid fumes, all the ugliness of modern mass production. Here and there were row upon row of small identical terrace houses where the workers live. Occasionally the monotony would be relieved by a group of houses retaining their village characteristics, a few cows in a field, or a stately house in a fraction of its original parkland – just hints of what the land was like before the social upheaval of the Industrial Revolution.

We picked up the M1 near the large industrial town of Doncaster. A town whose charter was granted by Richard the Lionheart at the end of the twelfth century, it is hard to reconcile its present factories with its gracious past. We continued south through the Midlands, an area containing many towns which have well-nigh merged together in massive urban sprawl. Here we saw many coal mines with their cages, machinery and black tipples. We passed through the remains of Sherwood Forest, its green wood in Robin Hood's day covering many square miles. It seemed strange to see warnings of deer crossings among the factories. We came close to Leicester and saw signs to Loughborough, where I had taught school for several years during the war. We did not go into any of the towns, however, as the major roads and motorways bypass them.

We left the motorway near Northampton, following signs for Oxford. We stopped in the pretty village of Pattishall for lunch at an old inn called the Red Lion, a popular inn sign and the heraldic insignia of many noble families. There were many customers, and we shared a table and enjoyed a ploughman's lunch featuring the local cheese with a pleasant couple who were returning to Sheffield after a summer holiday in Bournemouth. While David made a phone call after the meal, I sat outside on a low stone wall and basked in the perfection of an English summer's day with English flowers all around me.

On then through Towcester, pronounced 'Toaster', an important town, road junction and military camp in Roman days. A mediaeval inn there called the Saracen's Head is mentioned in Dickens' *Pickwick Papers*. We bypassed Oxford off to our left, remembering the lines by Winifred Letts:

> I saw the spires of Oxford
> As I was passing by,
> The gray spires of Oxford
> Against a clear blue sky.

We took a country road which led us through the rich fertile farmland of the Vale of the White Horse and to the town of Uffington in Berkshire, site of the ancient white horse immortalized in *Tom Brown's Schooldays*. At the old grey stone town of Faringdon we took a road to Wantage. The town was very busy, and we had trouble finding a parking place and even more trouble finding a sorely needed cup of tea. In the birthplace of King Alfred not so much as a burnt cake was to be had!

We reached Axford and its Red Lion about five. Joan and Oscar were busy and without help, so we went into Marlborough for dinner at the Ailesbury Arms. Our friend Chappie set up a table for us in the bar and served us a delicious meal. We got back to Axford in time to meet some of our friends for a little farewell party, for we leave tomorrow.

1976

NORTH FROM MARLBOROUGH – A CATHEDRAL REBORN IN COVENTRY – FROM YORK TO NORFOLK

MONDAY, JULY 12TH

We left Marlborough in the middle of the morning on the first leg of our trip to the far north of England. Our first destination was a hotel at Princethorpe near Coventry, for tomorrow we plan to visit the cathedral in that city. We went by way of Chippenham to have lunch with a cousin of mine, taking the familiar road past the College, Preshute Church and Silbury Hill, where we saw television crews taking pictures. As we usually do we stopped just past Beckhampton to watch the racehorses from the stables there exercising.

After lunch we drove through the famed Cotswold country, stopping briefly in two charming towns, Stow-on-the-Wold and Bourton-on-the-Water. Both were crowded with tourists. The latter is especially attractive with its old golden-stone houses and shops on one side of the street and the babbling gurgling River Windrush on the other. For much of the journey we were on the Fosse Way, one of the major Roman roads, which originally pursued its straight course from Cornwall to Lincoln.

We found our country-house hotel, set in park-like grounds, comfortable but slightly shabby. We had an excellent dinner there and afterwards drove into Rugby where we caught a glimpse of the famous school. As a schoolgirl I read *Tom Brown's Schooldays* and have recently enjoyed the Masterpiece Theatre presentation of it on television. It is not widely known that Thomas Hughes, its author and idealist, reformer, and Member of Parliament, visited America in 1879 in order to found a utopian community in the Cumberland hills of East Tennessee. The community, which he named 'Rugby', was modelled on an English village. Hughes had long been concerned over the limited prospects for the younger sons of England's landed gentry, who, because of the law of primogeniture, often went into the church, army or navy regardless of their real aptitude for such careers. Hughes felt that immigration to a community in America where they might pursue a life similar to that found in England might provide a satisfactory alternative for some of them. In his opening speech in October of 1880, he said, 'We are about to open a new town here ... a new centre of human life, of human interests and human activities in this strangely beautiful solitude, a centre in which a healthy, hopeful, reverent life shall grow.' After a flourishing start, the project failed, however, due to business mismanagement in which Hughes himself suffered considerable loss, a typhoid epidemic, and an emphasis on cultural and pleasurable activities at the expense of hard work. It remains today an interesting anachronism and is becoming a tourist attraction under the name of 'Historic Rugby'.

TUESDAY, JULY 13TH

Breakfast was as good as dinner had been and we left the hotel reluctantly. The early morning sun was very bright but the sky clouded over as we neared Coventry.

We found the modern town of Coventry pleasant and well-planned, risen like the legendary phoenix from the ashes of the old mediaeval town virtually destroyed in the blitzkrieg of November 14th 1940. That was the first night that heavy German bombing concentrated on a particular town, and so great was the ruin and destruction that a new word, 'to coventrate', was born. I thought back to that night when, huddled in an Anderson shelter in Birmingham some 20 miles away, I listened all night to the throb of German engines overhead, heard the muffled explosions of bombs, peeked out at the red glow from the burning city and the night sky pierced by the beams of roving searchlights, and heard the sharp 'ack-ack' of anti-aircraft fire, a mere symbol of helpless defence. The next day we learned that the centre of the city was virtually destroyed and that the spired mediaeval cathedral dedicated to St Michael, Coventry's patron saint, was completely gutted.

After the war a vast reconstruction programme was undertaken and a new city arose from the ruins. A new cathedral, with the shell of the old an integral part, was designed by Sir Basil Spence. Built from pinkish grey sandstone, it was consecrated on May 25th 1962. Though praised by many, it proved too radical for some, so it must be considered controversial. The design relies heavily on symbolism of the linkage of old and new – in fact fragments of charred wood and nails twisted by the heat of fire are used throughout the old and new cathedrals to stress the connection. In the ruined nave of the old cathedral, open to the sky, stands Jacob Epstein's statue of Christ 'Ecce Homo', upsetting to some, praised by others, and understood by few. Perhaps the ruined church represents death and the new one resurrection.

The new cathedral is entered through the old. Its entrance is marked by a transparent glass screen etched with random representations of the Twelve Apostles. Hung against the rose-pink wall to the right of the entrance is another Epstein work, a bronze grouping representing St Michael vanquishing Lucifer. A great green tapestry designed by Graham Sutherland, its central theme 'Christ in Glory', is the backdrop for the altar. It was made in France, is the world's largest tapestry, and took 10 men three years to weave. The grand organ stands with ranks of pipes exposed, while the choir stalls are canopied with three-pointed stars that look like birds in flight. The clean uncluttered lines and the slanted banks of jewel-toned glass illuminating the nave give an impression of strength and light contrasting with the Gothic mystery of the ruins. Tall thin fan-like windows of stained glass are set in the wall of the nave, but the outstanding window is in the Baptistry, where it takes up an entire wall. Made of blocks of coloured glass alternating with blocks of stone, the sun shining through it bathes the nave floor in multicoloured light. Beneath stands a great rock, shaped like a cup, which came from a Bethlehem hillside. Filled with water from the River Jordan, it serves as the font. A multitude of gifts came to the cathedral from many nations. Germany gave much of the stained glass, a mosaic floor came from Sweden, Russia sent a jewelled icon, and vestments were given by Hong Kong. The cost of the organ was underwritten by Canada. Perhaps one of the most moving objects is the crooked cross of blackened timber, salvaged on the night of the raid and now placed on the original altar of the old church in front of the gold-lettered phrase 'Father Forgive'. I left feeling that the union of the cathedrals old and new had made a resounding statement that ultimately good triumphs over evil.

We spent the next hour or so looking around the town, clean and modern today with some of the ancient buildings restored and rescued. The town was a place of some note in the ancient Saxon kingdom of Mercia. Its most enduring legend has been that of Lady Godiva. Married to Leofric, Godiva protested against the heavy and unfair taxes he levied on Coventry's citizens. Joking, he told her he would repeal them if she rode naked through the streets of Coventry at noon. She took him at his word, appealing to the townspeople to stay within their closely shuttered houses. All did so except one, earning for himself the opprobrious epithet of Peeping Tom. Godiva is commemorated by a fine statue and there are three representations of Peeping Tom. We saw the clock in Broadgate across whose face Godiva rides every noon while the voyeur's head pops up to watch her. Later Leofric, perhaps in a spirit of penitence, founded a Benedictine monastery, around which the town developed. The town's importance grew rapidly in the fourteenth century, its economy based on wool. After the Industrial Revolution Coventry became the centre for the manufacture of small machinery. In the early twentieth century it made bicycles, cars and small arms, which may have made it a target for the vicious German raid of 1940.

SATURDAY, JULY 17TH

We were up betimes for the long ride to Diss in Norfolk. The country became flat and less interesting as we drove along, but at last the towers of Lincoln Cathedral, built on a hill in flat land, came into view. Though we had very little time we followed signs to the centre of the city, parked the car, and climbed the 59 steps to take some pictures. An orchestra and choir were rehearsing, so strains of beautiful music accompanied our hurried visit. Then we pressed on through Lincolnshire's flat fields, stopping at a pleasant little pub in Leasingham called the Duke of Wellington for a bite to eat. Outside the pub there was a swarm of ladybirds – or ladybugs as they are called in the States – and we found them in the car for the rest of our trip. We drove hard through Thetford where we saw a statue of native son Thomas Paine, and on through Diss, and at last about 5 we reached our destination, Ripley Cottage in the tiny Norfolk village of Upper Oakley. Here we found two very old friends from my college days, Betty Glover from Ipswich and our hostess Winnie Bourne, who with her husband Reg is newly retired from teaching in the area. After tea in the garden and dinner in a lovely restaurant, Betty returned to Ipswich while we spent the night in the old cottage – so English! Winnie and I talked of old times into the wee hours, and then we went to bed up the crooked narrow stairs, ducking through the very low doorway into a room tucked up under the eaves.

1983

with the West Side Presbyterian Church Choir of Ridgewood N.J.

LINCOLNSHIRE – PILGRIM COUNTRY – GAINSBOROUGH OLD HALL – LAKE DISTRICT – CHESTER

SATURDAY, JULY 2ND

Continuing north from Cambridge through flat land, our guide pointed out an outcropping of higher land in the large county of Lincolnshire. Such a hill in flat land is an ideal position for command and defence, and thus the site for the important town of Lincoln was chosen. Before the Romans came there was an ancient British settlement here called Lindum. The Romans conquered it and held down the surrounding country with a large garrison. The name Lincoln is an unusual combination of the Celtic name 'Lindum' and the Latin 'colonia'.

We could see the three towers of the majestic cathedral, the Church of St Mary, for many miles before we reached it. We drove up the steep hill to the cathedral, its mellow limestone glowing golden in the bright sun. It is the third largest cathedral in England, originally of Norman architecture but with many later additions and restorations. Some of these were necessitated by damage from an earthquake, an unusual occurrence in England. The castle of the same warm stone is nearby, standing ready to guard church and hill from any who might dare to attack. The cathedral is vast beyond description, but none can fail to be moved by the skill, faith, devotion and sheer labour of the thousands who built it to the glory of God.

In typically American fashion we were in and out very quickly, for our time was short and our human needs of food and drink had to be met. The inns abounding on Castle Hill took care of those very adequately. Returning to the bus we went on to a part of Lincolnshire very special to Americans – the heart of Pilgrim country. As we went we passed Saturday cricket matches and school sports days. We were briefly held up while a pageant of school children in mediaeval costume crossed the road in front of us. What a lovely way to see history being taught as we were in search of our own history! For the Separatist movement away from the Church of England began in towns and villages near here such as Stourton-le-Steeple, Babworth, and Scrooby, when, at the beginning of the seventeenth century, a handful of God-fearing men were determined to shake off the tyranny of the Stuart kings and their bishops. Among them were the Reverend Richard Clifton, in whose rectory at Babworth the group customarily met;

William Brewster, postmaster of Scrooby; the Reverend John Robinson of Nottingham; and the Reverend John Smith of Gainsborough. All were educated men from Cambridge whose desire it was to worship God as they felt was right, even if it meant emigrating to the New World. Brewster, as a postmaster, was an important official and also a landowner with enough wealth to finance the group's plans.

As their movement grew so did opposition to it, and eventually the group found itself in the paradoxical position of facing deportation but not being allowed to leave the country of their own free will. After an initial attempt failed escape became imperative, so in 1608 they enlisted the help of a Dutchman to take them and their families to Holland for temporary asylum. Boarding small boats near Brewster's home in Scrooby, they sailed down the small river called the Idle to rendezvous with the Dutchman's ship in the Humber estuary. But again plans went wrong. The boats arrived early, and the women and children disembarked to wait on land. Soldiers arrived and the families scattered, while the men finally met their guide and sailed on their way to Amsterdam.

The women and children left behind lost their homes and possessions as well as their husbands and fathers. How they survived is a mystery – perhaps their survival was due to faith in God and the rightness of their cause. At last most of the families were somehow reunited, as described by a contemporary: 'some at one time, some at another; and some in one place and some in another; and met together again according to their desires, with no small rejoicing.' Eventually, after many vicissitudes, personal tragedies and exile in Holland, the Pilgrims' departure for America aboard the Mayflower took place in 1620.

At Babworth we heard the story of the Pilgrims' flight on the first leg of their long journey to America. We met there in the church and sang some early American hymns and then went on to Scrooby, a large village on the small River Idle, whence was launched the Pilgrims' ill-fated expedition of 1608. A well-informed guide took us to the church and manor house, once the home of William Brewster, the most prominent Pilgrim and one of the founders and early leaders of Plymouth Colony. In his time he was a rich man, but the present state of the manor is in no way indicative of its one-time prosperity. Today it is a rundown farm, with only three plaques describing its illustrious past. Our guide was indeed an interesting man – an M.A. (Cantab.), archaeologist and antiquarian who had worked at Avebury and Devizes in my home county of Wiltshire – but most of our group seemed more interested in a newborn calf than the history he tried to impart. After enjoying a strawberry cream tea served under great trees in a wide lawn near the church, I left Scrooby with some feeling of sadness at the state of the manor and general aura of depression in the village.

We then proceeded through undistinguished country to the town of Scunthorpe. At one spot we passed great bins of harvested potatoes, guarded from predatory birds by men with guns who shot to kill. We saw two fall to their aim. The potato crop is valuable, and a few pecks from birds could cause widespread rot. According to the morning news on the BBC, the crop this year is well below standard, and there may be a potato famine that will cause a drastic price rise.

At last, hot and tired from cumulative small delays, we reached Scunthorpe with little time to prepare for the gala evening planned at Gainsborough Old Hall nearby. Scunthorpe is a town of heavy industry with iron and steel mills. Ironstone is also mined nearby. At present the town is suffering from severe unemployment. Our large group had to be housed in two hotels, both comfortable but lacking in charm.

After a quick wash and change of clothes we assembled at the buses for the 25-mile drive to Gainsborough Old Hall. This mediaeval building was saved from demolition by a band of devoted volunteers who worked long and hard to restore it and obtain government money for its salvage. It is a rare example of the great hall which, with a few auxiliary rooms, composed the household of a mediaeval lord. The original building was destroyed by fire in 1470 but was rebuilt in 10 years. Richard III stayed here just before the Battle of Bosworth Field in 1485, and Henry VIII visited here with his fifth wife Catharine Howard.

On this night it was set for a banquet, the long tables sparkling with crystal and silver and decorated with bowls of fresh fruit and delicate flower arrangements. Henchmen and serving maids in Elizabethan costume waited on the guests, and entertainment was provided by madrigal singers clad in red velvet and accompanied by lute and harpsichord. Margaret Peckham, one of our guides, sang old English ballads from the musicians' gallery. The authentic Elizabethan food was cooked to perfection, though it was not entirely to our American tastes – the dishes served included chicken in orange jelly, spinach tart, and eel pie. At the sight of the latter many of us probably thought of Ogden Nash's lines:

> I like eels,
> Except as meals
> And the way they feels.

All the dishes were highly spiced, since spices were in much demand in olden days. Columbus of course set out to find a shorter route to the Spice Islands of the Orient and only incidentally discovered a new world. Spices were desired not only to add flavour but also to disguise tainted meat and offset the heavy use of salt used to preserve meat from animals killed before each winter. For dessert we had crystallized flowers – flowers preserved in clear hard sugar – marchpain (or marzipan), cherries and ginger. The Elizabethans craved sweetness as well as spice, since sugar was almost unknown and highly prized. Honey was the common form of sweetening, and we could certainly taste it in the mead which concluded our meal.

THURSDAY, JULY 7TH

After several days in Scotland we drove to the Lake District where we got on to the motorway going south through flat drab land leading into the industrial area of Lancashire, home of England's cotton industry. Raw cotton was brought in from India, Egypt and America through ports on the Mersey. There was plenty of local iron and coal for machinery and power, and a damp humid climate that was ideal for the spinning of cotton thread with a minimum of breakage. Today modern air-conditioning serves better than natural humidity, and, with old machines outworn, the area is in something of an economic slump. We crossed the Manchester Ship Canal, the waterway that made an inland city into a great port for it connected the city of Manchester with the Mersey estuary. It was opened in 1894 and was considered one of the engineering marvels of the Victorian Age.

We came upon the Abbot's Well Hotel on the northern outskirts of the city of Chester rather suddenly. It is a modern low-lying building, very comfortable in American style. It is built on the site of an ancient monastery. Water from the well from which the hotel takes its name was piped into the cathedral for the clergy's ablutions, and the pipe which brought it in is still visible. Tired, hot and dirty, we washed, changed and enjoyed a good dinner, after which we were able to take a brief stroll in the pleasant garden.

FRIDAY, JULY 8TH

Shortly after 9 we were at the bus for the short ride to Chester where we were to meet our guides for a tour of this ancient and important city. We got off at the town hall, a large Victorian building where our guides were waiting, each taking a party of about 20.

Under the Romans, Chester (or Deva, as they called it), was a most important garrison and fort. It controlled the ford across the River Dee and access to the wild country of Wales, where many ancient Britons under the Druids sought refuge from the Romans. With the departure of the Romans Chester declined in importance, but the Danes refortified it, and it was the last town of any size to hold out against the Normans. For many years it was ruled by an earl in the fashion of a kingdom within a kingdom. When it was incorporated into England, the king took 'the Earl of Chester' as an additional title, and today it remains one of the titles of the Prince of Wales.

Chester's city walls are the most complete of any in England and we walked around atop them. We saw a great deal of the half-timbered black and white architecture for which Chester is noted. Some of it is authentic, but, according to our guide, much is clever reproduction. Whichever, it is most attractive.

Walking the walls, we listened to our guide tell us old legends of the city and admired the Roman remains – baths, heating systems and amphitheatre – all remarkably well-preserved. The amphitheatre was a vast, partially excavated stadium where gladiatorial shows were held. It had 7,000 seats, indicating that the spectacles played to the local populace as well as to the Roman soldiers, for the full complement of each Roman legion was 5,500. In the corner was a small shrine to Nemesis, a vengeful goddess whom the gladiators wished to propitiate before their encounters, a sadly human touch, I thought.

The 'Rows' are another distinctive feature of Chester. In fact the arrangement of shops in two levels one above the other is unique. The origin of the Rows is uncertain though it is thought they were built beside and atop Roman fortifications.

Close by the Norman church of St John we saw a partially finished cathedral, abandoned when a later bishop preferred the site of the present one. Near the gaunt shell we saw a great hollow slab of stone where an anchorite once walled himself in. Workmen found his bones along with those of a servant and out of superstition refused to move the stone.

In the town itself we saw a leech's house, a mediaeval doctor's residence so called because leeches were used to suck blood in the belief that illness was caused by an excess of blood. Our guide pointed out one house as the only one on the street whose inhabitants escaped the plague one summer. They thought their immunity came from the fumes from a wine cellar next door.

Cut in the thickness of the city walls we saw a little entry gate to the 'kaleyard' or vegetable garden of the monks. The gate was just wide enough for a horse and handcart. It was closed at the stroke of the curfew at 8 o'clock every night. Curfew is still rung at 9 every night but simply as a token of the past and no longer requires people to be safe at home with the fire out. We saw the modern bell tower built to remove the bells from the cathedral tower because of their weight. Its design seems incongruous and our guide termed it 'ghastly'.

Chester was besieged by Cromwell's army during the Civil War, and Charles watched the defeat of his army at Rowton Heath in 1645 from the walls of the city. A tower marks the spot where he stood. The siege of the city lasted six months after Charles asked Chester to hold out long enough to cover his army's retreat into Wales. From the walls we saw some beautiful black and white cottages built to house widows of that war.

Chester also has an interesting link with New Haven and Yale University in Connecticut – the daughter of a fifteenth-century Chester merchant married Thomas of Yale, whose grandson Elihu was founder of the university. A second husband was the first governor of New Haven.

We were at the cathedral by noon for Jack's organ recital. It was preceded by a short tour conducted by one of the vergers, a short grey-haired man named Mr Jones who was well-informed and a good guide. He pointed out the beautiful modern stained-glass window replacing the one shattered by bombs in World War II. It depicts and is dedicated to eight famous saints from the north of England. We saw a carving of the Chester 'imp' hiding in the ceiling vaulting and the mosaics along the chancel wall representing Old Testament stories and looking from a distance like tapestry. The dark oak choir stalls are decorated with incomparable carving, and the mosaic of the Last Supper over the altar appeared to be three-dimensional from where we were standing. We saw the grave of William Makepeace Thackeray, author of *Vanity Fair* and *Henry Esmond*. In one of the chapels hangs the flag in which the body of General Wolfe was wrapped after the Battle of Quebec, a flag that was later carried at the Battle of Bunker Hill. And we saw the shrine of the local saint Werburga behind the high altar and learned that pilgrims came to pray to her especially for the restoration of hearing to the deaf. In the cathedral garden is a cutting from the Glastonbury thorn – I wonder if it blooms at Christmas.

We sat in the nave for the recital, listening as the music swelled to fill the great church and sometimes hovered delicately, the notes seemingly suspended in midair. Jack played the Bach piece dedicated to Saint Anne on which the hymn 'O God, Our Help in Ages Past' is based.

Afterwards we enjoyed a pub lunch with Jim and Betty Caldwell, window shopping in the Rows, and then a quiet rest in a beautifully landscaped park. The heat had become intense by this time, and we were glad to sit awhile before making our way to the cross in the town square to hear the town crier. In the Middle Ages, pillory and stocks stood in the area by the cross, and bull and bearbaitings were held in the vicinity. A weekly market and twice yearly fairs were held here. Forestalling was forbidden, thus ensuring that no advance sales could be made – the word 'forestall' remains in our language.

The cross itself was damaged in the Civil War, but pieces of it were salvaged and it stands today partially restored. The town crier appeared in full regalia, ringing his bell for attention and clowned his way through an obviously commercial pitch, striking to me a discordant note. He introduced the West Side Choir and we obliged with an anthem, though it seemed to me neither the time nor the place.

1986

with Jane Sockwell & Betsy Newland

Through Worcestershire and Herefordshire to Wales – From Wales to the Lake District – The Peak District – En Route to Great Fosters Hotel, Egham, Surrey

Thursday, September 18th

We drove from East Harptree to Worcester where we left the motorway but the road remained good. We passed the cathedral and caught a glimpse of the great china factories. We three ladies would have liked to stop to see them, but David was adamant that we did not have enough time. We drove towards Leominster (pronounced 'Lemster'), one of the market towns my mother used to visit in her childhood. The countryside of these border counties of Worcester and Herefordshire is lush and rich and green. This is fruit country, and we passed orchards of apple trees loaded with rich ripe fruit waiting to be picked. In some places picking was already in full swing.

The green fields were the grazing grounds for many white-faced hornless sheep with thick white fleeces and also many Hereford cattle red with white faces, good beef stock. The breed originated here and has been introduced into cattle country all over the world. The famous Rylands breed of sheep, bred for their wool by monks over 600 years ago, has also been exported to Australia, New Zealand and South Africa for the production in those countries of both wool and mutton.

We passed through lovely villages with black and white half-timbered houses clustering around churches and greens and ponds, their gardens bright with the flowers of early fall – begonias, asters, dahlias and tall purple Michaelmas daisies. We passed by walled estates, sometimes catching a glimpse of the big houses in park-like settings. A few of these manors have remained private homes; some have been taken over by the National Trust; and others have been turned into group homes, hospitals, or hotels in line with the changing face of British society. This was the countryside my mother roamed as a child, and I thought back to her romantic descriptions of the leafy lanes and wildflowers such as foxgloves and daffodils that did not grow in Wiltshire where I grew up.

The town of Leominster grew rich on the manufacture of a type of woollen cloth that came to be known as 'lemster ore,' so lucrative was its production. When the woollen industry moved to Yorkshire, the town declined economically, though it has remained an important local farming centre. We stopped at an old half-timbered inn on the outskirts of the town for lunch. The interior was seedy and run-down, not fulfilling the promise of the exterior, but the welcome was warm, the barmaid attentive, and the food and drink good. There was a young mother there with a lovely rosy-cheeked baby.

SATURDAY, SEPTEMBER 20TH

We spent the night in Machynlleth. I slept well until 4 a.m. and then stayed awake until it was time to get up. We faced a long journey but made good time going through beautiful country by way of Welshpool, leaving Wales and re-entering England at the important border town of Shrewsbury (pronounced 'Shrowsbury'), the county town of Shropshire. For a while the road ran beside the River Severn, quite a small stream at this point. The Severn is the longest river in England and is second only to the Thames in importance. It flows southwards into the Irish Sea in a deep wide estuary where it is joined by the Avon, and Bristol is the great seaport at its mouth.

At Shrewsbury we got on to M54 motorway leading to the M6. The well-engineered network of motorways all over England never ceases to amaze me. The highways have for the most part been developed since the war, and new stretches and connecting links are still being added. The speed limit of 70 mph I think is honoured more in the breach than in the observance, and beauty regrettably has been sacrificed on the altar of speed. In places the motorways follow the straight highways laid down nearly 2000 years ago by the Romans.

We stopped at a tremendous service complex at Knutsford, though we saw nothing of the charming Cheshire town immortalized as Cranford in Mrs Gaskell's widely read Victorian novel of the same name. The service area and the large serve-yourself restaurant were teeming with people, but once we figured out the system we were able to eat quickly and well. For myself I found a most enjoyable pork pie, a famous English delicacy that seems to be disappearing from stores and restaurants.

This leg of our journey took us through the industrial heart of England, going from just north of Birmingham through the Potteries around Stoke-on-Trent, where most of the well-known brands of china and earthenware are made. Towns that when I lived in England were separated from each other by green spaces now run together in a vast mass of manufacturing.

We passed into Lancashire where cotton has been manufactured since the Industrial Revolution and crossed the Manchester Ship Canal. There is much economic depression in this northern part of England, and, except for driving through it as we were, it is a part not often visited by the American tourists. Nonetheless there is still much beautiful country away from the industrial areas.

MONDAY, SEPTEMBER 22ND

We left the motorway in the vicinity of Derby and found our way by country roads to Ashbourne and thence through beautiful and hilly pastoral country to the village of Thorpe and our hotel, named Peveril of the Peak. Modern and well-equipped under the management of the Trust House Forte chain, it has grown from an old rectory into a complex of buildings suitable for conferences and parties as well as hotel guests. It is approached by an avenue of horse chestnut trees and is surrounded by lovely flower gardens. Mountains tower high above, and cattle and sheep graze on the slopes.

TUESDAY, SEPTEMBER 23RD

We were up early enough to make a 9 o'clock start for Chatsworth. We drove first over hill and dale to the quaint old village of Ilam, passing on the way a farm where a black and white sheepdog was busily and effectively herding cows. Ilam is in the lovely valley of the Manifold River. Its church is part Saxon and there are two very old Saxon crosses in the churchyard. The Restoration dramatist William Congreve wrote *The Old Bachelor* here, and Samuel Johnson visited.

In Ashbourne the centre of the town is undergoing extensive renovation. We stopped at St Oswald's Church, a very large and fine parish church with a spire pointing 212 feet into the air. The interior contains many fine tombs and memorials of Boothbys and Cockaynes, the local landed gentry. The most famous memorial is the eighteenth-century white marble sculpture of Penelope Boothby carved by Thomas Banks. She died at the age of 5 in 1791, the beloved only child of elderly parents. Penelope was said to be the model for Sir Joshua Reynolds' portrait of a child entitled *The Age of Innocence*. The Grammar School is very old, and opposite it we saw the red brick mansion where Dr Johnson and Boswell stayed several times with Dr John Taylor.

We went through the towns of Wirksworth, Matlock and Bakewell. Today Wirksworth is a little narrow-streeted town of grey stone houses, but in the past it was a prosperous lead mining centre and the setting for much of George Eliot's novel *Adam Bede*. Matlock was a famous spa in Victorian days and was busy with tourists today. Built on the Derwent it crouches beneath craggy limestone cliffs called the Heights of Abraham, so named by an officer who had fought under Wolfe and thought they looked like the heights scaled in stealth and secrecy at the capture of Quebec in 1756. Bakewell, a pretty town on the River Wye, is considered the centre of the Peak District and was once a spa town. A fine arched and buttressed bridge crosses the river. A famous English dessert called Bakewell tart originated here and is still made and sold in the town. The story goes that it was originally made accidentally when beaten egg was spread on top of a jam filling instead of the other way round.

Before reaching Chatsworth we got a distant view of Haddon Hall, the seat of the dukes of Rutland. There are many fine and famous houses in this part of England, but Chatsworth is the prime attraction of them all. We drove for several miles through woods and farmland before coming to the great classical mansion set in an immense wooded park. In the distance we could see deer grazing. The splendid gardens were planned by Sir Joseph Paxton, later designer of the Crystal Palace. They are planted with rare trees and shrubs and are famous for fountains and water cascades.

The house assumed its present form in 1707 through additions to a much earlier house built by Bess of Hardwick, an ancestress of the duke of Devonshire. It is enormous, magnificent, and full of the treasures of a world-famous collection of paintings, sculpture, manuscripts, and furniture.

We took the house tour following a guide book written by the present duchess, who, before her marriage, was Deborah Mitford, daughter of Lord Redesdale and one of the famous Mitford girls. Out of one window we caught a glimpse of her in a private section of the gardens, an elegant grey-haired lady with a black Labrador retriever on a leash. Of the Mitford daughters, she has led the most conventional life. She married Lord Andrew Cavendish, younger son of the then Duke of Devonshire, who became heir to the dukedom when his older brother the Marquess of Hartington was killed in the war in 1944. The latter's widow was the former Kathleen (Kick) Kennedy, sister of the later American president, who herself died in an air crash some years later. In the family portrait gallery there was an oil painting of the handsome marquess in his major's uniform and a photograph of Kathleen beside him in the uniform of the American Red Cross, a lovely fresh-faced girl full of life and vitality. The marriage was very unpopular with both families, mostly because of religion, and they did indeed seem a pair of star-crossed lovers.

We had an excellent lunch in the tearoom housed in the former stables, then toured the greenhouses full of fuchsias, grapes, begonias, geraniums and other plants unknown to me. We then left Chatsworth about 4 p.m. and took a different road back. We went through some very beautiful country, though the distant hills were misty and partially obscured by late afternoon fog. This Derbyshire country, the Peak District, is excellent country for hikers, and we saw many walkers. The area is sometimes called the lungs of the industrial North as people from the factory towns flock to it in search of fresh air and beauty.

We made a detour through a village called Tissington. It was a joy and delight on a par with Castle Combe and Lacock. We left the main road and entered an avenue of trees that I believe were limes. The trunks were thick and silvery and the leaves were just beginning to yellow with the coming of autumn. On either side were fields ridged with lynchets, relics of the three-field system of feudal times. Then the land that belonged to the lord of the manor was divided into strips that were portioned out to the villeins or serfs. The lord continued to own many of these strips, which were tilled by the serfs as part of their obligation to their lord. The strips that belonged to individuals were widely separated to avoid any buildup of land in the hands of enterprising men. The use of woods, pastureland and mill were common to all, though each serf owed a portion of his harvest to the lord in payment.

Here at Tissington we could clearly see the marks in the fields left by the strips, and entering the village seemed like stepping back into the Middle Ages. The church of warm brown stone set in its green churchyard full of old headstones had the strong squat tower of the Normans. Just down the street stood the manor house, its ancient stone walls clothed in the fall scarlet of Virginia creeper. Little grey stone cottages line the street, their windows deeply embrasured in the thick walls and their tiny flower gardens ablaze with colour. A watering trough stood in the middle of the village, and a stream of clear water bubbled merrily along beside the street.

We drove next to Dovedale where we took the walk through the gorge beside the limpid waters of this famous river. The Dove was one of the favourite fishing streams of famed angler Izaak Walton, who came here whenever he visited his friend, local resident Charles Cotton. The gorge cuts through limestone, its sides heavily wooded. Today one bank is bordered by a wide paved path for easy walking, but the other side remains rough and rocky. We walked to the famous stepping stones where David crossed the river while we three ladies kept to the easier side. I was reminded of Treacle Bolly by the Kennet – of course hardly known except to Marlborough people – where I used to play when I was a child.

I enjoyed our stay in the Peak District and hope I can return to see more of it. It is an area of England that is unfamiliar to me. I would like to visit more of Derbyshire's stately homes, see the famous spa town of Buxton and also Eyam, the 'plague' village. This remote village was infected with the dread disease from germ-laden clothes sent from London in 1665. The heroic rector William Mompesson sealed the village off to prevent the spread of infection. Five out of every six people died. The whole area played an important part in the Civil War. In the village of Castleton stand the remains of a Norman castle belonging to the Peveril family. During the war Sir Geoffrey Peveril was a leading supporter of the king, and his deeds of bravery, though they led to ultimate defeat, gave him fame as Peveril of the Peak. Sir Walter Scott wrote a novel about his exploits, and it is from him that our hotel takes its name.

WEDNESDAY, SEPTEMBER 24TH

Our holiday is drawing to a close, and we were up early for the long drive to a hotel in Surrey that is within easy reach of Heathrow for our flight back to the States tomorrow.

We drove through Derby en route to the M1. The weather was cloudy and cool but held a promise of sun later on. Derby is a large, heavily industrialized town, the Rolls Royce works prominent among its factories. The route to the motorway took us circuitously through the outskirts of the city, through poor mean streets, and suburbs of identical bay-windowed semidetached houses that went on mile after mile.

Shortly after leaving the Derby area we joined the M1, perhaps the most important and heavily travelled of all the motorways in England, as it connects London with the North. We bypassed the great industrial complex around Nottingham – it seemed dominated by great round cooling towers. And where was the Sherwood Forest of Robin Hood?

On our left we passed Loughborough, my home for two years and a place still dear to my heart. At the time I lived there it was a pleasant market town, home of a famous engineering college, and known worldwide for its bell-casting foundry. The place names on the signposts brought back memories of my teaching years there. I lived in several villages in the vicinity working with schoolchildren evacuated from Birmingham during the war.

The outgrowth of Derby, Nottingham and Leicester seems to run together along the main artery of the motorway. The road was very heavily travelled with many lorries. Most of them were flatbeds with their loads shrouded in tarpaulins, a haulage method rarely seen in the United States. The traffic moves at very high speed, but accidents are comparatively rare. We passed a host of radio masts and antennae that marked Daventry, the pioneer radio station of England. As a child in the early days of wireless I heard much talk of Marconi, Radio Luxembourg and Daventry from my father. We used to drive through Daventry on the way to see an aunt, and it always elicited a lecture from my father on the marvels and intricacies of radio, as incomprehensible to me then as it is now. About 30 miles from Stratford we crossed Shakespeare's famous Avon.

1989

WASHINGTON ANCESTRAL HOME IN SULGRAVE, NORTHAMPTONSHIRE
SUNDAY, SEPTEMBER 24TH

Today we visited Sulgrave Manor in Northamptonshire, which we have long felt we should, for it is George Washington's ancestral home and so is something of a shrine for Americans.

It was a glorious day, one of those rare and perfect days that England occasionally experiences. We left early taking the Roman road across the downs to Swindon and going around its urban sprawl to the old town of Highworth built high on the crest of a hill. Leaving Wiltshire for Gloucestershire we passed very close to the source of the Thames and came to Lechlade, a town at a spot on the river where it has already widened considerably, as it is fed close to its source by several important tributaries. Lechlade, its narrow streets lined with gracious stone houses, is very old and had a mediaeval economy based on wool. The river is wide and fast-flowing here, there is a thriving trout farm and fish hatchery, and the area draws many visitors bent on recreation. When I was a child the river was crossed by a bridge with three 'humps' and my sister and I always enjoyed the switchback effect we got. But as traffic and speed increased so did accidents and two of the 'humps' were eliminated in a new bridge. It is still narrow and so traffic is controlled by lights and a one-way system. On busy days traffic jams develop. At one time a halfpenny toll was exacted for crossing the Thames here.

Continuing on we passed through many pretty villages, among them Inglesham where the mediaeval church was restored by William Morris. We came next to Burford, gateway to the Cotswold country. Like Marlborough, Burford is a one-street town. We entered from the south through an extremely beautiful tree-lined avenue with the sun shining through leaves tinged with the colours of early autumn. The long street slopes down to the winding Windrush, its crystal clear waters crossed by a picturesque one-way bridge beside which rises the tall spire of the parish church. Stone buildings, among them the gabled town hall with its clock tower, lined both sides of the street and glowed warmly and richly in the sun. Altogether a beautiful town quite unspoiled.

Chipping Norton, built on high ground at the junction of several roads a few miles further on, is another old stone town. For centuries it has been the site of an important market, as the old Saxon word 'chipping' indicates. Past Chipping Norton we came to Banbury, once as beautiful as Burford but spoiled first by the Puritan zeal for plainness, which caused the destruction of many beautiful buildings, and later by industrialization and development. The original cross of the nursery rhyme was removed in the eighteenth century but a late Victorian version replaced it. The fine lady on the cock-horse is thought to be a member of the local Fiennes family, and riding to the cross may have been part of May Day celebrations. After Banbury we left the main road near the construction of a new section of motorway and got somewhat lost in a maze of country roads through flat farming land.

Eventually we found the pretty and prosperous-looking village of Sulgrave. The house there is a small manor built of the warm honey-coloured stone of the Cotswolds. It has been rebuilt and restored in authentic fashion but lacks the wings of the original house. Sponsored and partially funded by the Colonial Dames of America, the house is appropriately furnished and has a collection of Washington memorabilia. The garden and grounds are maintained in the fashion of a prosperous sixteenth- and seventeenth-century country squiredom. Over the entrance two coats of arms are carved in the stone. One is the royal arms of England while the other is that of the Washington family. The latter features both stars and bars and may have been the inspiration and prototype for Betsy Ross' later design for the American flag. To us as Americans it was quite a thrill to see the 13 stripes and 50 stars of today's flag fluttering in the breeze in the heart of the English countryside.

We were fortunate to arrive just in time to join a small group of visitors led by a knowledgeable guide. We were, surprisingly, the only Americans. We went first to the great hall, a large bare room furnished in seventeenth-century fashion with a minimum of heavy dark oak furniture. At one end there was a tremendous fireplace over which hung an extremely valuable original portrait of George Washington by Gilbert Stuart. On another wall was a copy of a large picture of Washington by Peale, the original of which is in Lexington, Virginia. It shows Washington as a younger man in the British redcoat uniform he wore as a colonel during the French and Indian wars. The mullioned windows are centred around a stained glass reproduction of the Washington arms, and the sunlight filtering through cast coloured bars of light on walls and floor. Other rooms in the house are furnished in a later period as they were used by families who succeeded the Washingtons after they left for Virginia. Upstairs several rooms furnished as bedchambers were open, and there was a small secret room hidden behind the chamber over the front porch. There is a legend that Elizabeth I was once hidden in this room during the stormy years leading up to her accession.

The first Washington owner of Sulgrave was Lawrence, who was born in

Warton in Lancashire after his family had moved there from Washington Old Hall in Durham. He was looking for a small manor property to farm and was able to buy Sulgrave at the time of the dissolution of the monasteries, for it had been part of land belonging to a priory. He married the wealthy widow of a wool merchant but achieved riches himself as a sheep farmer and wool manufacturer. He had a family of 11 children, and the prosperity of the family continued until the Civil War in which they were loyal supporters of the king. In the Cromwellian period after the war they lost much money, became suspect, and left England for Virginia in America, as did many others in similar circumstances. They acquired a large tract of land on the banks of the Potomac and became wealthy and influential, leading lives not very different from those of English landowners. Some members of the family returned to England to Appleby, Warton and Tring for schooling. Some remained in the country, but Sulgrave had passed out of the family and no Washington ever lived there again. It is unlikely that George, several generations removed from Sulgrave, ever heard much about it and, unlike his brother Lawrence, he never went to England at all.

We walked around the formal gardens, enjoying the herbaceous gardens against old brick walls and the parterre plantings edged with box, the air redolent with scent. We went into the vegetable garden and through the orchard, where the trees were laden with fruit and the ground beneath them scattered with windfalls. After lunch in a country pub not far away we returned to the manor to see the movie and browse in the museum. At Sulgrave it is not hard to imagine ourselves back in the days when the ancestors of our first president were living the lives of English gentry. It was a memorable day that seemed to bring together the best in England and America. At Sulgrave it seems that the bonds between our two countries are strengthened and the ocean bridged between the two great English-speaking countries of the world.

Chapter Seven

THE EAST

'. . . these scenes made me a painter'
John Constable 1776–1837

The eastern counties of Kent, Essex, Huntingdon, Cambridge, Norfolk and Suffolk are often called the breadbasket of England because of the grain, fruit and vegetables produced by the fertile soil and climate, which is drier, sunnier and hotter than elsewhere in Britain. Much of the land is flat, though there are gentle undulating hills and rolling heathland.

There are two areas of very flat land, the Fens and the Norfolk Broads. The Fens, waterlogged for centuries, have been drained, reclaimed and turned into very productive farmland. The marshes of the Fens were the refuge of Queen Boadicea of the Iceni during her rebellion against the Romans, and 1000 years later Hereward the Wake held out there for many months during his last ditch resistance to the Norman conquerors of 1066. The Norfolk Broads, long stretches of flat land and open expanses of water, form a vacation land for sailing, fishing and birdwatching. The tall reeds that grow here are harvested for thatch, the use of which is enjoying a revival today.

The shore line beginning at the Wash between Lincolnshire and Norfolk and extending to the Thames estuary and so to the English Channel has sandy beaches and fine harbours, though erosion has taken its toll. Fishing is very important, as is trade with northern Europe, and there are many coastal vacation resorts. Inland are many charming old market towns, some founded in the flourishing times of wool trade and manufacture. Cities such as Peterborough, Ely and Norwich boast fine cathedrals, while Cambridge is the site of one of the world's oldest and most prestigious universities.

The Romans conquered and settled this part of Britain early on. Upon their departure in the fifth century, Angles, Saxons and Jutes from Germany took their place. The Romanized Britons were driven west, so that racially the people of eastern England are of purer Germanic stock than elsewhere in the island. In later centuries, easy maritime access gave rise to flourishing trade with northern Europe, and thus new ideas, skills and craftsmen came in from the Continent. The region progressed accordingly, while the Saxon character of the people was reinforced.

Many of England's great men have been born and bred in the East – Thomas Paine, John Constable, Thomas Gainsborough and Oliver Cromwell among them. Diverse and great writers such as Rupert Brooke, Rider Haggard, Samuel Pepys, George Borrow and William Cowper learned and refined their talents at Cambridge. Musical composer Benjamin Britten was a native of the area, and important musical festivals are held at Aldeburgh, Norwich and King's Lynn.

I first visited the eastern part of England during my college days when I stayed with my friend Betty Glover in Ipswich. We have been to see her many times since, and she and her friends have shown us much of the area, so it is probably the section of England I know best after Wiltshire and the West.

In this section on the East, I include the environs of London and some of our travels in Berkshire and other counties east of Wiltshire.

1973

with Thomas & Margaret McKnight

A BOAT RIDE ON THE THAMES – WINDSOR CASTLE – BLENHEIM AND WOODSTOCK IN OXFORDSHIRE – ARRIVING AT DOVER FROM FRANCE

SATURDAY, JULY 14TH

We awoke in our hotel – the Londoner in Welbeck Street – to find the sun shining. We spent the morning shopping in the West End and in the afternoon took an Evans-Evans tour by bus to Windsor, where we boarded a boat for the return trip.

At Windsor we got a fine view of Windsor Castle and Windsor Great Park, noticing the postings 'CROWN LAND'. Nearby was Eton, the famous school dominated by its chapel and surrounded by the playing fields where it is said Waterloo was won. We passed the green fields of Runnymede where in 1215 King John was forced by his barons to sign Magna Carta. The American Bar Association has erected a domed classical monument topped by a cupola to commemorate the event. On a nearby hill is a memorial to John Fitzgerald Kennedy, its marble slab recording the tragedy of his assassination and praising the contributions he made to freedom. Though the treed meadow could not look more English, the land was given to the United States, and so it stands an acre of America in the heart of England. At the very summit of the hill stands the Air Force Memorial, a tribute to the Allied airmen who lost their lives in World War II and have no known graves. Runnymede is indeed hallowed ground for all English-speaking peoples.

Past Windsor the river narrowed and the banks became wider and more overgrown. Towering horse chestnuts, their blooms over, and graceful silver-trunked beech trees graced the woods, while velvet green grass and bright flower gardens surrounded houses and cottages. On the water and in the reeds we saw a variety of ducks and their families, graceful white swans belonging to the Crown, white-faced moorhens, and brown bewhiskered water rats. This is the country of *The Wind in the Willows*, which I have read aloud to so many classes of both English and American children. Sometimes we had to wait outside locks, their grounds veritable garden spots. Judging by the manicured grass and brimming, blossoming flower beds, every lockkeeper must surely have a green thumb.

We sailed past Egham and Staines, thriving river resorts and bedroom communities for many London workers, though at Staines a trailer camp rather spoiled the Thames' idyllic serenity. All kinds of craft were on the river, and it would appear that for many Englishmen, as for Kenneth Grahame's Water Rat, 'there is nothing – absolutely nothing – half so much worth doing as simply messing about in boats.' We saw cabin cruisers, skiffs, canoes, racing shells, tour boats – every conceivable kind of pleasure craft was there. Margaret and I were huddled in pant suits and coats, but the hardy British were in sun suits and bathing costumes catching every ray of the intermittent sun.

We glided down the river to Chertsey, looking anxiously skyward where ominous black clouds were gathering. Though we only got a passing glimpse at the old riverside town, we went under a graceful seven-arched bridge. In the distance we saw the church tower that Blanche Heriot climbed to stop the bell from ringing curfew and so save her lover from death during the Wars of the Roses. The brave deed is immortalized in a poem called 'Curfew Must Not Ring Tonight,' the work of Rose Hartwick Thorpe, an American poet.

And then we reached the spot for disembarking and walked about a quarter of a mile through damp green woods to our waiting bus. The first drops fell as we reached it and we drove back in a heavy downpour, grateful that the rain had held off for our boat ride.

SUNDAY, JULY 15TH

En route to Wiltshire we stopped at Windsor to tour the castle and State Apartments, renting cassette tapes to guide us as David and I had done twice before. What a wealth of art and historical objects the kings and queens of England have amassed, and with what superb taste it is displayed in the gorgeous apartments of 'Prinny', the gross libertine who later became George IV. Despite his excesses, he certainly contributed much of beauty to his country.

The sweep of history confronted us as we toured the castle chambers, while outside we can see the wide green stretches of Windsor Great Park. Begun as a fortification by Henry I on a site chosen by his father William the Conqueror, the early castle evolved into a military headquarters and royal residence. It also became the site of a chapel, which today rivals a cathedral, dedicated to St George, England's patron saint. In this chapel every June is held the Garter Investiture, a ceremony unequalled in colour, pomp and circumstance. The ceremony inducts new members into the Order of the Garter, the most exclusive honour that can be bestowed on an Englishman. Several of England's monarchs are buried in the chapel. Jane Seymour, third wife of Henry VIII, was buried there after dying in childbirth in 1537, and 10 years later Henry himself was buried beside her, the queen he loved most. On March 10th 1863, Edward, Prince of Wales, and later Edward VII, married Alexandra of Denmark in a glittering ceremony here, and I remember George V being buried here in 1936 in a ceremony that was carried by the wireless.

We had tea in a hotel in the town of Windsor, itself quite Victorian. It owes its prosperity to the castle towering over it. After tea we continued on the M4 past Reading and Newbury as far as Hungerford, leaving the highway there for Axford.

TUESDAY, JULY 17TH

We were up early and had breakfast in the Castle and Ball in Marlborough. It was raining hard, but since it had started very early I had hopes that the adage, 'Rain before seven, shine before eleven' would prove true, which it did. We dropped in to see David Chandler, one of the town's up-and-coming young businessmen, whose parents are very old friends. He is a Cambridge graduate, a former mayor of Marlborough, and now heads the saddlery business that has been in his family for generations.

We then set out for Woodstock in Oxfordshire, site of Blenheim Palace, seat of the dukes of Marlborough (no connection with my Wiltshire hometown). Blenheim is always high on the list of 'must-sees' for Americans because of the birth there of Winston Churchill to his American mother. We passed through Hungerford, then through the lush White Horse Vale to Wantage, which is just across the Wiltshire border in

Berkshire. Wantage has historical associations with King Alfred, the greatest of the Saxon kings, and is reputed to be his birthplace. He defeated the Danish invaders in the ninth century and much of the fighting took place in the area. A fine statue of Alfred stands in the marketplace, and we stopped long enough for me to buy a postcard of it for my son's pupils in Thailand who study King Alfred's story in their English lessons. As we drove on we could see in the distance the many towers of Oxford. Unfortunately we had no time for 'that sweet city with her dreaming spires', one of the greatest and oldest centres of learning in the country.

We reached Woodstock about noon, just in time for lunch before a 1 o'clock tour of the palace. We ate in an inn called the Star and had a most delicious meal – steak and kidney pie, marrow, cabbage, new potatoes, broad beans, pickled onions, strawberries and cream, and apple pie. Food that was a great treat for me and a new experience for the others!

Built in 1705, Blenheim Palace was the gift of a grateful nation to the first Duke of Marlborough for his victories in the War of the Spanish Succession during the reign of Queen Anne. This war was an attempt to preserve the balance of power in Europe and to limit the growing influence of the French king Louis XIV. Of the several major battles, Blenheim, fought on the banks of the Danube in Bavaria in 1704, was decisive. John Churchill, the commanding British general, was created Duke of Marlborough and granted the manor of Woodstock in Oxfordshire for the victory. He remains today one of history's military geniuses and was also an ancestor of Winston Churchill, who was born unexpectedly in a cloakroom of the palace where his American mother, the former Jennie Jerome, was attending a party.

Sir John Vanbrugh, famous as a dramatist as well as an architect, was commissioned to design and build Blenheim Palace at Woodstock. It is one of the largest private houses in England and a fine example of English baroque architecture. The massive bulk of the building, balanced and symmetrical in design, is built of the yellowish stone found in this part of the country. Entered through an impressive courtyard, it is set amidst beautiful grounds and gardens covering 2,500 acres and containing a lake created out of marshland by damming the small river Glyme. The grounds were designed by Lancelot 'Capability' Brown. Most of the beautiful trees abounding in the park were planted by a later duke.

The palace interior is magnificently furnished in the grand manner. We saw the small ground floor room where Winston was born and were guided through the main reception and dining rooms to the library and chapel. The walls are hung with priceless art and many family portraits. One of the loveliest is that of Consuelo Vanderbilt, whose marriage to a former duke brought an infusion of American money into the Marlboroughs' declining fortunes, though the marriage was not happy and ended in divorce. We saw many of the works of the master woodcarver Grinling Gibbons, and in the chapel we saw marble effigies of the first duke and his wife Sarah, a powerful figure at the court of Queen Anne.

We then drove the few miles to the little country church of Bladon to see the grave of Winston Churchill. It is marked by a simple marble slab engraved only with his name and the dates 1874–1965. He lies flanked by the graves of his parents and only son Randolph. The churchyard is difficult to reach and no special attention is called to the grave of the man who was the architect of victory in 1945. He himself chose Bladon to be his final resting place rather than Westminster Abbey, where many of England's great men are buried.

We returned to Woodstock for a cream tea. It is a lovely pleasant little town with fine seventeenth- and eighteenth-century houses built of the creamy Cotswold stone which makes such a lovely foil for the flowers that abound everywhere. There was once a royal palace here in which Edward III's son the Black Prince was born, but the building was demolished when construction started on Blenheim. Old village stocks stand on the village green, a reminder of the grim punishments of the past, often for very trivial offences. These stocks are unusual because they have five holes for the legs of those being punished. No one knows why they were made this way, unless at one time a one-legged man or woman needed correction!

We drove back by a different route, going through the old stone town of Faringdon and seeing in the distance the White Horse of Uffington, the oldest and least realistic of the White Horse figures that appear all over the chalk country.

SATURDAY, JULY 28TH

Four days later we were at Calais for the return trip to England. Calais is the town in France closest to England, for the Channel is only 20 miles wide between Calais and Dover. Calais was the last bit of France to be ruled by England. After the end of the Hundred Years' War the huge English possessions in France gradually shrank to nothing but Calais, which England finally lost in 1558 during the reign of Mary Tudor. It is said that on her deathbed she whispered that two words would be found graven on her heart, Philip, name of her Spanish husband, and Calais. The city, built on an island though now with modern suburbs spreading on the mainland, has always been an important port, especially in the Middle Ages for wool and wine. It was besieged by Edward III in the Hundred Years' War and was finally starved into submission.

The Channel was quite choppy but the weather clear and we got a good view of the White Cliffs of Dover, the view that has welcomed so many travellers back to England. Over the port of Dover sits the brooding castle built by the Normans on foundations laid by the Romans. The Romans also built the lighthouse, which for centuries steered ships to safety. Near the castle is a splendid park.

Much of Dover has been rebuilt since World War II. It is today an efficient port with fine modern passenger terminals. We got through all formalities quickly and were soon settled in our hotel. I looked from my window towards France and thought of Matthew Arnold's lines:

> The sea is calm tonight.
> The tide is full, the moon lies fair
> Upon the straits - on the French coast the light
> Gleams and is gone; the cliffs of England stand,
> Glimmering and vast, out in the tranquil bay.

SUNDAY, JULY 29TH

After a good night and a full English breakfast (as opposed to the continental ones provided in France), Tom, Margaret and David went to Dover Castle while I stayed on the hotel verandah to rest and catch up with writing my journal. The morning was misty but quite mild and I had a good view of the busy harbour. I could see Sunday strollers on their way to church and other destinations. Caravans filled with weekend travellers were crowding the roads leading down to the water. Over all the Union Jack was flying fully extended in a stiff sea breeze.

By 11 we taxied to the railway station where we got a train to Charing Cross by way of Folkestone and Ashford. The train followed the line of white cliffs to Folkestone, where a ferry boat was pulling in from Boulogne. Leaving the coast we went through some rather poor country which soon changed to the lush land of orchards and hopfields associated with Kent. Alongside the hopfields were the conical oast houses where the hops are dried, a distinctive feature of this part of the country. We ran through several tunnels under sections of the high ground of the Weald plateau in Kent before we approached London. We got a fine view of Tower Bridge and after crossing Hungerford Railway Bridge a glorious panoramic sighting of the Thames, the Houses of Parliament and Somerset House, where all government records are kept.

1975

Hastings – Kent – Northeast to the Suffolk Wool Country – Ipswich and the Felixstowe Seaside – Cambridge and Ely – King's Lynn

Thursday, July 17th

We drove east from Winchester, stopping first at Petersfield and then at Petworth hoping to see the great house there built by the 6th Duke of Somerset in 1696, but it was closed. The tiny town of Petworth is almost unchanged since mediaeval times. Its narrow houses and crooked streets crowd right up to the walls encircling the grounds of the Palladian mansion. The house stands by a lake in an enormous green park where deer were grazing. There is a very fine collection of Turner's watercolours there and also many carvings by Grinling Gibbons which I would like to have seen, but all we got was a distant glimpse of the house.

After lunch in the pleasant garden of a small pub outside Petworth, we began to approach the coastal areas and saw signs pointing south to Brighton, Worthing, Eastbourne, and Hastings. We stayed on our course, however, for the battle site of 1066 is several miles from the town of Hastings, for which the battle is named. We made a brief stop at Pevensey where William the Conqueror landed. The story goes that as he stepped ashore he stumbled and fell, a bad omen in the eyes of his followers. But quick-thinking William rose with both hands full of good English soil, saying that in this way he would conquer and subdue England. We saw the ruins of the great castle at Pevensey built by the Normans on Roman foundations, but because the sea has retreated they are now over two miles inland.

We followed signs for Battle, which proved to be a very pleasing old town with beautiful abbey gates at one end of the long High Street. We parked the car near a jam factory, the sweet smell of the preserves permeating the air. Much of the town is built on the low rise of Senlac Field, where Harold drew up his housecarls on that fateful day in October in 1066. Despite the Saxons' exhaustion after their 250-mile march from victory against Harald Hardrada at Stamford Bridge in the far north, their shield wall proved impregnable until wily William ordered his knights to stage a mock retreat. Seeing this, the Saxons left the hill, the Norman horsemen turned in pursuit, and William ordered his archers to shoot their arrows into the air. The Saxon shields perforce were raised, an arrow pierced the eye of Harold, and the battle was over. The Normans were victorious and the course of English history was changed.

At prayer on the eve of the battle, William had made a vow to build an abbey on the spot if victory was his. True to his word, he did so, the resulting Battle Abbey large and beautiful. It was partially destroyed when the monasteries were dissolved by Henry VIII in the sixteenth century, but some of it was rebuilt to house the young Elizabeth before she came to the throne. This very lovely Tudor mansion is now an exclusive girls school. We took a tour around the abbey and were fortunate in having a guide who supplied many fascinating historical facts.

Back in the car we headed next for Kent and Sissinghurst, the home of Harold Nicolson and his wife Victoria (Vita) Sackville-West. Harold was a politician and diplomat who was prominent in the pre-World War II era, while Vita was of noble birth and brought up at Knole, the great mansion we will visit tomorrow. She was a distinguished writer, scholar and member of the Bloomsbury group, the avant-garde literary coterie which flourished in the 1920s and 1930s.

We drove into Kent down a narrow one-way road, watching the time anxiously as the house was due to close at 6.30. Years ago the Nicolsons acquired the ruins of a Tudor mansion and through their own efforts and designs transformed them into living quarters of distinction. The gardens, their creation catalogued in the Nicolsons' diaries, are however Sissinghurst's principal attraction.

The rosy brick of the one long row of rooms and the tall towered gatehouse glowed in the late afternoon sunlight as we approached. The individual gardens, connected one after another by brick paths, spilled their blossoms in cascades of colour. We climbed the tower staircase to Vita's room where she did her writing and where she often withdrew to be alone. She died here in 1962, virtually a recluse, and all is kept as it was in her lifetime.

Descending thoughtfully we went into the great living room of the home they created by building on to one wall of the old house. It looks out on to what was once the central courtyard and beyond to the magnificent gardens. Some beds are planted in monochromatic shades, others are mixed herbaceous borders in front of old brick walls. Perhaps my favourite was the all-white garden. In the orchard roses are planted so that their blooms hang down from the branches of the fruit trees. Part of the old moat remains, and the surface of the still water is covered with waterlilies. In the herb garden we watched a baby thrush, still tailless, take its first tentative flutters. I tried to determine what it was that made these gardens so beautiful and decided it was clever use of colour and, through the way the gardens are separate but linked, an effect at once abandoned and controlled.

We walked back past the oast house, which now serves as a restaurant, to look for lodgings for the night. After some disappointments we found a room in an inn in Goudhurst. It was small, modern and tastelessly furnished, but it was also clean, comfortable and cheap with good food. As for ambience, our window looked out onto a hopfield, a mill and an oast house. What more could we ask for?

FRIDAY, JULY 18TH

After a good breakfast we set off for Sevenoaks to see Knole, the ancestral home of the Sackville family. We wanted to be there by 10 to take the first guided tour. We missed the turning for the mansion and continued into the town where we were directed to a narrow opening off the main road. This led us to the gatehouse and into a wooded park dotted with great oaks and grey-trunked beeches. As we entered the park we saw a large herd of what we thought were fallow deer but later learned were a Japanese species. They were small animals with creamy white underparts and backs of light reddish brown with lighter spots. The stags carried their velvet antlers proudly, and most of the does had fawns alongside. The park is home to many of these deer, and they seem quite tame and friendly.

The enormous house came into view, and we could see its battlemented towers, gabled roofs and the brick chimneys of Tudor design. The house is named, but purposely misspelled, for the knoll on which it is built. Some claim it to be the largest private house in England, though others maintain that Blenheim and Castle Howard are larger. Begun in 1456 for an archbishop of Canterbury, it came into the possession of the Sackville family in 1566 when it was granted to Thomas Sackville by Queen Elizabeth. Additions were made over the next 200 years so that the architecture is considered Jacobean rather than Tudor. Though Lord Sackville still resides here, it is now National Trust property.

The house is built of grey stone and brick. Like the church of Boston Stump in Lincolnshire, some of its features reflect the numerology of the calendar – there are 365 rooms, 52 staircases, seven courtyards, and so on – making it a house for all the year. We were fortunate to have a guide of rare quality, an old man who loved Knole with a passion. He transmitted his love and knowledge to us with a dry, delicious, understated humour which was most enjoyable.

We went first into one of the courtyards where he gave us some general facts about the house and family, then into the great hall, and then through several galleries and rooms hung with portraits and pictures of great antiquity and value. Among them was a portrait of Nell Gwynn, mistress of Charles II, an odd gift from the king to a Sackville lady with whom he also had an affair. We saw the tiny room with stained glass windows which Vita called her jewel box. In the Kings' bedroom where visiting kings always stayed, we admired the priceless silver furniture but wondered about its comfort and practicality. Knole has many interesting beds for it has been the custom of kings to present beds to their hosts, and the Sackvilles have had many kings as guests. We saw the prim apartments decorated with the embroidery of Lady Betty Germain, who lived at Knole as companion to the lady of the house for almost 50 years in the seventeenth century. There is a musicians gallery overlooking the great hall. The great firedogs there were made to mark the wedding of Henry VIII and Anne Boleyn. All drapes and shades were tightly drawn to protect the priceless furniture, paintings and hangings from the sun, but occasionally we could glimpse the beautiful gardens outside. The gardens are not open to the public in an effort to preserve the privacy of Lord Sackville and his family.

Seeing such stately homes is perhaps my favourite form of sightseeing. As Nigel Nicolson, son of Harold and Vita, wrote about the English country house, 'Except in literature we have produced nothing of so high a standard, so varied, so audacious, so beautifully executed.' We walked slowly to our car savouring the glory of a perfect summer day. Deer were grazing close to the car and one came near enough to me for David to take a picture. We left along a magnificent drive lined with chestnut trees – if only they had been in bloom!

We followed signs for the Dartford tunnel, stopping on the way for lunch at a charming little pub where, although in Kent, I had a Cornish pasty. Now the character of the countryside began to change. The fields, orchards, and black and white houses of rural Kent were replaced by factories belching forth black smoke and noxious fumes, and the wide multi-lane roads were full of trucks and other commercial vehicles. The tunnel under the Thames saves many miles around London. Traffic was not excessive, and we got through quickly and headed north and east through Essex, leaving Tilbury Docks on our right. We followed signs to Ipswich, and by 3 o'clock we were near Dedham and Flatford. As we were not to meet my friend Betty Glover till 6, we took a detour through Constable's heavenly corner of England which he painted so often.

We found a narrow one-way road leading to Flatford Mill and Willy Lott's cottage. Flatford Mill belonged to the Constable family, who were relatively prosperous farmers, and John spent much of his boyhood there. Today it is a very popular spot for tourists, and there are cafes and souvenir shops catering to them as well as boats for hire on the River Stour. But it is easy enough to cross a wooden bridge to a towpath and find oneself in Constable's unspoiled countryside of winding river, shining meadows, and thickets of ash, willow and alder. Willy Lott's cottage, home of Constable's childhood friend and subject of some of his most famous paintings, has been meticulously preserved.

We drove then to the nearby town of Dedham where we walked up the sunny High Street lined with quaint shops with bow windows paned with wavy glass. Their upper storeys project with irregular rooflines. We admired the rosy brickwork of the Elizabethan Free Grammar School. We went into the great parish church, the tower of which appears in many of Constable's landscapes. The church was richly endowed by the weaver guilds, for the prosperity of towns such as Dedham was based greatly on the rise of the wool trade in the fourteenth century. Another great artist also lived in Dedham – Sir Alfred Munnings, known chiefly for his paintings of horses.

As we left the church we noticed dark clouds had gathered and a few drops of rain fell. Hastening to the car we drove to the Post House Hotel in Ipswich for our rendezvous with Betty. She led us through the streets of the city to her house. After catching up with news over sherry, we changed clothes and drove to Seckworth Hall, an old Tudor mansion of ivy-covered rosy brick set in a beautiful park. It is now a restaurant and hotel. We looked around the grounds very quickly – everything was dripping wet from a storm that had hit Ipswich while we were feeling a few drops in Dedham. We then entered a candle-lit hall. 'Lovely atmosphere!' we thought, until we realized from the receptionist peering at the reservation list that the storm had caused a blackout and that the candles were born of necessity rather than ambience. We had drinks at the bar, followed by an excellent dinner in the gracious dining room. Our waiter was one of Betty's old pupils and consequently took good care of us. He spoke in the slow speech of rural Suffolk, interpolating 'Miss' into the conversation with great frequency and making sure 'Miss' and her guests received extra special service.

SATURDAY, JULY 19TH

We rose early and after a proper English breakfast spent a restful hour in Betty's tiny but well-maintained garden. Betty's King Charles spaniel Roly, a nervous, highly excitable little dog, stayed with us. He is quite small, with the silky coat and feathery tail of a spaniel but with the snub nose and prominent eyes of the Pekinese. This is considered a royal breed as it was popularized by Henrietta Maria, French queen of Charles I, and by Charles II and other Stuarts. These dogs appear in many of the Stuart portraits and have remained a favourite breed of the English. Betty's mother breeds them, and Betty has had one for many years. Roly is black and white and is, I think, of the Blenheim variety.

About 11 a.m. we left with a picnic lunch for a tour of the area, planning to end up for tea and dinner in Norfolk with Winnie and Reg Bourne.

Ipswich is a big industrial town which was once an important port until

the estuary silted up. It is known historically for its connection with
Cardinal Wolsey, whose father was a butcher here. Leaving Ipswich along
the narrow lanes and byways of rural Suffolk, we passed through the little
town of Hadleigh, its High Street lined with many different styles of Suffolk
architecture. We came to Kersey, an old wool village with a ford and
weavers' houses tottering like drunken old men at the edge of the street.
We splashed our way merrily through the ford without disturbing its ducks
and geese. Kersey's huge church, built with wool money, stands on a slight
eminence and towers over the village. We stopped in the village inn for
some refreshment and inside saw some interesting wooden panels of rural
life done by local craftsmen. There was a wonderful collection of the corn
dollies for which Suffolk is famous.

Suffolk is primarily agricultural today and noted for its grain crops
known collectively in England as corn. Formerly, however, the area owed
its prosperity to wool. Most of its wool came from local sheep, but some
was imported from France and the Low Countries, which had easy
maritime access to England's east coast. With the imported wool came
skilled craftsmen and weavers to teach their trades. They also brought
some of their native cultures, and they certainly influenced the
architecture of the towns they settled in. Local wool merchants and
manufacturers became very wealthy and – partly to give thanks, partly to
escape heavy taxes, and partly to atone for their frequently unfair
commercial practices – built the enormous, richly decorated parish
churches which mark these towns and villages. With the coming of the
Industrial Revolution, however, wool manufacture moved to Yorkshire
where mass production powered by plentiful coal and iron became the
technology of the future. The wool country here closely resembles that of
the Cotswolds in southwest England, where similar churches and weavers'
houses are to be found.

Leaving Kersey, which gave its name to the fabric called 'jersey', we
drove out of the village and parked in a narrow road for our picnic lunch.
We were in sight of the church tower and beside a field of ripening barley
out of which an occasional meadowlark flew pouring out song in sweet
liquid notes. Planes flying overhead, towing and releasing gliders, did not
disturb our pastoral idyll, but a bus trying to pass on the narrow road
brought it to an abrupt halt. Gathering our things up, we moved to a wider
place in the road.

After lunch our next stop was Linsey, another cloth village which gave its
name to 'linsey-wolsey', a material made from wool mixed with linen from
local flax. This was the common fabric for the clothes of the labouring
classes. We then went on to Lavenham, the jewel of all the Suffolk wool
towns. It is a lovely old market town with an ancient inn named the Swan

and a Tudor guildhall now the property of the National Trust. The Swan has been added on to very much throughout the years, and the old Wool Hall is now incorporated in it. Inside at the bar a section of the counter is glassed over to preserve the signatures scratched into it by American airmen stationed in the vicinity during the war.

We spent a pleasant half hour in the guildhall learning something of its history and then went on to the church, very large and ornate with an impressive tower. The church was heavily endowed by John de Vere, 13th Earl of Oxford, and by Thomas Spring, a wealthy clothier who by so doing asked forgiveness for 'usurious covenants, illicit sales and deceptions in measuring cloth.' We saw the old grammar school, its most distinguished pupil John Constable. While at school here Constable liked to visit a family nearby named Taylor, whose daughter Jane was the author of 'Twinkle, Twinkle, Little Star'.

A few drops of rain fell and we decided to hurry on to Winnie's house near Diss. Passing through Bury St Edmunds, Betty insisted we stop to see the old cathedral and its new addition as well as the old monastery dedicated to the martyred St Edmund. He was the saintly king of East Anglia murdered by the invading Danes in AD 870. In the cathedral there is a fine display of ecclesiastical needlework and needlepoint. Every parish in the see had made a kneeler, each of the same two shades of blue but with a different motif. I also saw panels made by schoolchildren illustrating the story of Edmund's martyrdom. As we left the cathedral we walked through the lovely abbey gardens bounded by the ruins of the old monastery. Seeing some children playing bowls on the green, I thought, 'How English!'

We arrived at Upper Oakley a little late, for we had trouble following the directions down the narrow twisting lanes. I was so happy to see Winnie again. She and her husband live in an old cottage with a huge garden. Since my last visit about seven years ago they have uncovered an old fireplace hidden in one of the walls which has added a lot of charm. We were given a tour of the garden and were introduced to the resident geese who are not very hospitable but, like the legendary birds of ancient Rome, warn of intruders. We had a proper English tea in the garden – cucumber sandwiches, scones, jam, cream, meringues and chocolate cake.

Betty, Winnie and I then changed into long dresses, and we went to a modern restaurant in Diss. So many English people take American visitors to a new or modern place when we would vastly prefer genuine Old World charm. Nonetheless, the meal was excellent, though tea had taken the edge off my appetite. After dinner we drove back along the Norfolk lanes to pick up our car for the drive back to Ipswich.

SUNDAY, JULY 20TH

Everyone slept late after such a strenuous day. After breakfast Betty packed a picnic lunch – the good al fresco food of my childhood, potted tongue and chocolate biscuits included – for us to take to Felixstowe, a few miles away on the coast. She and two friends share there a 'chalet', actually a small structure for shelter and storage at the beach. Roly, her aged King Charles spaniel, came with us.

Before we reached Felixstowe the resort, we passed Felixstowe the modern container port, which has grown by leaps and bounds in recent years. David was interested because much of the cloth which he sells for Cone Mills to British customers is shipped through Felixstowe. Prior to the development of container shipping, Felixstowe was a small though busy resort for the middle classes. It knew a short-lived popularity among the upper classes after an 1891 visit by the German empress Augusta and her family. Close by is the great port of Harwich, which has always had a thriving trade with the North Sea ports of Europe. The weather unfortunately was grey and overcast with light sporadic rain, but Betty felt that since there was no wind we would be able to sit out at least part of the time.

Betty's friends Kate and Bar were waiting for us. Bar had her dog Simba along, a fox terrier whose advanced years in no way diminish his high spirits. A state of grudging co-existence and tolerance seems to exist between Roly and Simba. Bar is a teacher of very young children. Quiet and patient, firm and kind, she must be very good with them. Kate, big and athletic, is headmistress of a large secondary modern school. She is very dominant, forceful and lots of fun. She too is an old Whitelander, though several years behind Betty and myself. It was fun to talk shop with her. She is one of the old breed of English teachers, a leader and model for her school and community, and I could wish for more like her in the town where I teach. Just as American teachers do, Kate bemoans the deterioration in education and believes it due to family decline and other trends in modern society.

We had lunch in the chalet rather than outside, a concession to our thin American blood. It is one of a long row perched high on a cliff overlooking the North Sea. Each is exactly like its neighbour, except for being painted a different hue, a way for the British to express their individuality and indulge their love of strong colour. Each is a box with a pointed roof measuring I guess some eight by ten feet and designed mainly for storage of chairs, blankets, wireless and food. They also serve as a crowded shelter when the weather is too inclement for even the British to be outside. Although each hut is cheek by jowl with its neighbours, privacy is highly prized and greatly respected by one and all. Dogs roam freely and are generally more neighbourly than their owners. Nero, a yellow Labrador in the next chalet, was very sociable. The chalet experience was new to David and myself, but it is a way in which many British spend their leisure time in the summer, giving them a *pied à terre* at a beach.

With no sun the sea was grey and forbidding, though the surface was still like polished steel. A few brave souls were swimming, but many more were taking brisk walks along the pebbly beach while their dogs chased sticks and balls in and out of the water. Large vessels were coming and going with some frequency, an indication of the port's growth. The sun came out late in the afternoon and after taking a walk we basked in its rather uncertain rays. After tea, the usual and to me very welcome old-time English meal, we packed up and returned to Ipswich, making a brief stop at a very old inn called the Ship. For many years it was the haunt of smugglers – a great deal of contraband came in through this coast – and the dark, cold, dingy, mysterious old building seemed to have changed little from those times. We sat in the bar, or 'snug,' served by the dour sardonic innkeeper, who might have been a smuggler himself, so much he looked the part. He knew Betty, who said that as a young man her grandfather had courted his mother.

We made one more stop at Kate's house, a row house of the Victorian era which she inherited from her parents, to see some of her father's woodcarving. Two mantelpieces and a sideboard of dark oak were heavily and intricately carved. I was reminded of my own father's work.

When we reached Betty's house it was quite late. We had tea, biscuits and cheese and then went to bed tired and relaxed from the salt air of the North Sea.

MONDAY, JULY 21ST

We were up early and packed, breakfasted, and left only minutes after Betty had departed for her school in Woodbridge. We were on our way to Cambridge, going by way of Newmarket in western Suffolk. We caught a glimpse of a racehorse and the famous racecourse screened from the road by a high wooden fence. Notices along the road warned motorists that strings of horses often cross, and we saw that the heathland is dotted with stables and studs. James I began the tradition of horseracing here, and the first recorded race took place in 1619. The heath provides gallops much like the chalkland of the Wiltshire Downs whence I hail and where horseracing is also an important activity. In both places racehorses are bred, trained and raced on the short springy turf. In the High Street in Newmarket we saw the Georgian building housing the Jockey Club which controls British racing. We saw also the Rutland Arms, which brought back memories of

drinking sherry there with an old and dear friend Ian Taylor when he drove
me from Loughborough to Diss on a rare summer day many years ago.

The usual parking problem faced us in Cambridge. It was hot and sunny,
and we had to leave the car some distance from the centre of the town and
walk to King's College and its famous chapel. The town, the site of a
Roman settlement known as Granta, was built on the river called Cam to
the north and Granta to the south. The first college there was Peterhouse,
established in 1284 by a bishop of Ely and a dissident group of students
from Oxford, which had been founded 35 years earlier. Throughout the
Middle Ages Cambridge and its rival counterpart Oxford were the focal
points of higher education and intellectual life in England, and though
today many institutions emulate them, none surpass them. By the early
twentieth century, Cambridge had become the part of England of which
Rupert Brooke spoke for all the English when he wrote:

> God, I will pack and take a train
> And get me to England once again.

Apart from the university, Cambridge today is a busy industrial and
commercial centre. For many years there was strife between town and
gown, but most of that has now disappeared.

The beautiful college courtyards and the 'backs' – the grounds sloping
down to the river – are usually open to members of the public, who are free
to punt lazily along the river in rented craft in company with the students.
The best-known building, and generally considered the most beautiful as
well, is King's College Chapel. It is one of the finest examples of
Perpendicular architecture in England. This was not our first visit, but this
time the chapel looked more beautiful than ever as it has recently been
cleaned and renovated. The chapel was begun by and named for the saintly
Henry VI in 1446, but the Wars of the Roses caused so many delays in
construction that it was not finished till 1515. Its famed stained glass and
fan-vaulted roof inspired Wordsworth's description:

> Where light and shade repose, where music dwells
> Lingering - and wandering on as loth to die.

At the east above the altar hangs the famous Rubens painting 'Adoration of
the Magi', illuminating the nave with a special radiance. The jewel-toned
stained glass created by Flemish workmen in the early sixteenth century
adds to the beauty of the interior.

We walked back to the car and drove until we found a better parking
place, after which we set forth to take pictures of the colleges, the river and
the famous 'backs.' Clare College is noted for its beautiful gardens, while

Queens is named for two queens, Margaret of Anjou who founded it in 1448, and Elizabeth, wife of Edward IV, who enlarged and endowed it in 1465. It is famous for a wooden bridge built without a single nail, constructed solely on mathematical principles.

Trinity, which united several of the earlier colleges, is the largest college and numbers many famous men among its scholars, including Tennyson, McCaulay, Newton, Bacon and Byron. It was largely built by Thomas Nevile, master from 1593 to 1615. Trinity's famous library was designed by Sir Christopher Wren in 1676. Roger North wrote of the beautifully proportioned interior in 1695, 'it touches the very soul of anyone who first sees it.' Inside are woodcarvings by Grinling Gibbons.

At Pembroke College there is a chapel designed by Wren during his early years and looking much like some of his later churches in London. St John's College is the finest architecturally after King's and is noted for the Italianate Bridge of Sighs, an enclosed bridge with beautiful traced windows. Magdalene (pronounced 'maudlin') College was founded in 1542 and possesses the Samuel Pepys library, a collection of books and manuscripts willed by the writer to the college. The college also owns the famous Pepys diaries written in his famous shorthand. Milton was a scholar at Christ's College in the seventeenth century. In the garden there is a mulberry bush which he is said to have planted. Many mulberry trees were planted in England at this time as James I attempted to launch a silk industry, which required mulberry leaves as food for the silkworms. New Jerseyites might compare this introduction of silk manufacture with Paterson's once-thriving silk industry, which met disaster when disease attacked the mulberry trees.

The several colleges at Cambridge are independent self-governing institutions offering undergraduate degrees. Only students with the highest scholastic records are admitted to the college of their choice. The university is a separate body of men and women, mostly graduates of one of the colleges, in pursuit of graduate degrees. The university offers degrees in many disciplines, including medicine, law, and philosophy.

There are some fine museums in Cambridge and a beautiful church, St Mary's, overlooking the wide marketplace. There is a wonderful view of the city from its high tower. Today many young people were sunbathing on the green lawns, and some were punting on the Cam, poling along in leisurely, seemingly effortless fashion. It was the lovely pastoral and peaceful picture of England we expatriates carry in our hearts and memories.

We had lunch at a little pub called the Jolly Miller. Outside the city and en route to Ely we stopped at the very impressive American Military Cemetery located on a hillside overlooking the city. Circles of white crosses radiate in geometric precision among blooming American Beauty rose gardens and reflecting pools covered in waterlilies. Only a few people were there, most of them Americans come to mourn sons, husbands, fathers, brothers and lovers. I hoped they drew some comfort from the beauty of the place where their loved ones lie.

The Isle of Ely is the second of Cambridgeshire's two jurisdictions. In contrast to Cambridge, Ely stands in a plain of prehistoric marsh that has been embanked and drained repeatedly since Roman times. The most vigorous effort began under Dutch supervision in the seventeenth century and is ongoing even unto the present. Going on towards Ely we passed through flat fields, diked and ditched with drainage channels. The road was built up over fields black and heavy with fertile soil and producing vegetables, sugar beet and some grain. This is the fen country, called by Daniel Defoe 'the sink of no less than 13 counties.' The land was impenetrable marsh in the days of Hereward the Wake's last-ditch stand against the Normans, but it is now tamed by man's invention into productive farmland. Geographically the country is a continuation of the flat land of the Low Countries from which it is now separated by the North Sea. Both the people and their way of life are much like the Dutch and the Scandinavians. Though not pretty the area is most interesting in its context of history, geography, agriculture, ecology and reclamation.

The cathedral of Ely was visible for many miles before we reached it. The great west tower and octagonal lantern provide welcome relief from the miles of surrounding flatness. Ely itself seems rather a sad and depressed little town, the sort of place forgotten by all except the tourists drawn to the great church. It became an important ecclesiastical centre of learning in the early Middle Ages but gradually lost out to Cambridge because of its isolation and inaccessibility. The town was built on a slight eminence which remained dry and above water when the surrounding fen land was flooded and waterlogged. The dry higher land was called an isle and came to be known as the Isle of Ely from 'isle of eels,' which were an important part of the Saxon diet. The island disappeared when the fens were first drained, but the name remains as one of Cambridgeshire's administrative districts.

The cathedral, originally a monastery founded by St Ethelreda in AD 673, was begun in 1083 and completed in the next century. The nave is Norman and once led to a chancel beneath a central tower. When this tower collapsed in 1322 it was replaced by the great lantern built by Alan of Walsingham, who also designed the heavily carved choir stalls. Today the cathedral seems in a rather bad state of repair. The great lantern is the glory of the building, its light streaming down on the crossing of the transepts. The chapter house is said to have the finest acoustics of any in the country.

There are some fine buildings around the edge of the cathedral close, which is not quite large enough to set off the great church to its best advantage. The King's School is there, and some of its oldest buildings are part of the original monastery. The close is entered by the Ely Porta, a three-storey gate which was also part of the old monastery. I sat in the sunny close and enjoyed its peace while writing some postcards to friends in New Jersey.

We left Ely with some sad thoughts at its decline, passing as we did the timbered vicarage of St Mary's Church where Cromwell and his family lived from 1636 to 1647. We drove north and east for King's Lynn in Norfolk, going for many more miles through the marshy country of the fens. The large fields were mostly growing potatoes, which were in full bloom with white and purple flowers. This is desolate country indeed, though its drabness belies the fertility of the land and the prosperity of the farms. Most of the houses seem small and huddle close to the low land, but their summer flower gardens, bright with roses, petunias and daisies, relieve the flat ugliness around. The monotony is also broken by the enormous churches of the small villages, even though most of them appear decrepit and in need of repair and maintenance.

We got into King's Lynn, a town with a lingering air of old sailing ships, and drove to the fine main square in the centre of the town. With evening drawing on our first priority was to find a hotel. We went to several but found them full and were advised to look further out of town. Eventually we found a room in a hotel called the Victory in Clenchwarton. We went back to King's Lynn for dinner at the Globe Hotel, but it was a mediocre meal at best. Afterwards we drove down to the waterfront, for 'Lynn' is the port at the mouth of the Great Ouse which empties into the great inlet known as the Wash. Due to silting the town is further inland now than it was in its prosperous past. Nearby we saw the Hanseatic Warehouse and the Greenland Fishery House, reminders of the town's past as a trading port with the Baltic states of the mediaeval Hanseatic League and as a whaling centre later. We saw the ancient Custom House, built in 1683 by Henry Bell, architect and town mayor. Its size is an indication of Lynn's importance in European trade. We also saw the ancient Guildhall with its checkerboard facade. My maternal grandfather came from King's Lynn, but I know nothing of his antecedents and nowhere did I see the name Sharpe.

1976

TO GREENWICH BY BOAT
THURSDAY, JULY 22ND

On Wednesday, our last day, we took a boat trip down the river to Greenwich, an old town on the south bank of the Thames closely connected with British seapower. It was a hot sunny day and the cool breezes on the river were very pleasant. There were many craft on the water and as we approached the Pool of London a great deal of commercial shipping, though London is no longer the port it once was. We passed under Tower Bridge and saw the Tower of London on the north bank. Further on we passed the famous old inn The Prospect of Whitby and could see its sign, which pictures a fine sailing ship called the *Prospect* whose home port was Whitby in Yorkshire. Today the inn is proving a popular spot for young people to meet and dine. We travelled the great bend in the river enclosing a piece of land known as the Isle of Dogs, its banks a hodgepodge of docks, industry, slums and hasty postwar construction, for this part of London was heavily damaged in the Blitz. The river widens as it nears Greenwich. Here is anchored the Cutty Sark, the last of the great tea clippers, its delicate rigging outlined against the sky. Close by is berthed the Gypsy Moth IV, in which Sir Francis Chichester sailed solo around the world in 1966–67.

Greenwich first came to historical notice in the reign of the Saxon king Ethelred the Unready when the Danish fleet assembled in the river close to the town. Today the two most noteworthy buildings are the Royal Naval College and the Greenwich Observatory. The college was once the Greenwich Hospital, which was constructed on the site of Placentia, the palace built in 1433 for Humphrey, Duke of Gloucester. Here the Tudors lived and here were born Henry VIII and his daughters Mary and Elizabeth, while his son Edward VI died here. Many architects, including Christopher Wren, contributed to the restoration and extension of the buildings. In the reign of William and Mary the buildings became a hospital for disabled sailors and later in 1869 the Royal Naval College, an academy for the higher education of naval officers. The college buildings include the Painted Hall – the walls were painted by Sir James Thornhill with columns that give the illusion that they are supporting the ceiling. Hanging here are portraits of famous naval leaders and depictions of important naval engagements.

The Greenwich Museum, a treasure house of marine history and science, is located on the college grounds. It includes the Queen's House, erected by James I for his consort Anne of Denmark and also used extensively by Henrietta Maria, French queen of the luckless Charles I. Designed by Inigo Jones, it was the first house of Palladian style to be built in England.

We took the guided tour of the college which put the history of the place into perspective and brought much to our notice that otherwise would have escaped. Leaving the buildings we went through Greenwich Park, which was laid out by Charles II. We were quite shocked that its usually green lawns were yellow and burned, parched in the hot sun of a very dry summer. We ended up at the Royal Observatory, established in 1675 for the advancement of nautical science. Longitude is reckoned east or west of the 0 meridian, which runs through the observatory marked by a brass strip, and like all tourists we stood astride it, one foot in the Western Hemisphere, the other in the Eastern. By late afternoon we had spent several fascinating hours in Greenwich before returning to the city by boat as we had come.

1977

MAIDENHEAD – AN AFTERNOON AT CANTERBURY
MONDAY, OCTOBER 3RD

We got off the plane early in the morning to be confronted with the welter of confusion that Heathrow always presents. But we were fortunate to get through the formalities quickly, pick up our car, and head west on the M4. Tired and hungry we stopped in Maidenhead for a meal combining breakfast and lunch at a riverside restaurant that was once an elegant nightclub but is now down on its luck and seedy, suffering the ravages of time and changing lifestyles.

Maidenhead is a rather big town on the river Thames some 25 miles west of London. Today it is mainly a bedroom community and tourist centre for exploring the river country, but in the past it had some importance and historical interest. The name was originally Maidenhythe, meaning 'maidens' landing place', and the settlement grew up because it was a natural place to bridge the river. The first pontage grant was made in the reign of Edward I and was continued for many years to guarantee the upkeep and repair of the bridge. In 1451 Henry VI formed the guild of Brothers and Sisters of Maidenhythe to look after the bridge. Today the old bridge has been replaced by a fine balustraded one, and the river is also crossed by an impressive railway bridge designed by famed nineteenth-century engineer I. K. Brunel. Many think they are the finest bridges across the Thames outside of London.

Apart from being the home of countless commuters, Maidenhead today seems to be a town of the past, the home of once thriving nightclubs and speakeasies. Our restaurant experience confirmed this assessment. The town knew its heyday in Edwardian times. Then the river was fashionable and every young guardsman had his punt and every mother with a marriageable daughter hired a riverside house at Maidenhead for the season. The river is very beautiful here, and many fine houses remain. Though we caught no glimpse of it on this occasion, the mansion Cliveden is not far away on the Buckinghamshire side of the Thames. It was once the home of the Astors and figured prominently in the Profumo scandal of the 1960s.

Continuing on from Maidenhead we passed through an area devoted to light industry that extended through Reading and on to Newbury. The lorries serving these factories contributed to the heavy traffic. But thanks to the high speeds permitted on the M4, and to the fact that it bypasses the town centres, we soon reached the turn off for Hungerford and the quieter road to Marlborough.

THURSDAY, OCTOBER 20TH

The fine weather lasted for our bus trip today to Canterbury. The bus was less than half-filled, and we had a pleasant driver and a well-informed articulate guide. Going east from London along A20 we got a fine view of Leeds Castle, a majestic battlemented fortress surrounded by a wide moat. Privately owned now and seldom open to the public, it was once the home of Catherine of Aragon, and Elizabeth I was held prisoner there before her accession. The green countryside of Kent with its lush meadows, hopfields, half-timbered houses, and picturesque oast houses added to our enjoyment of the ride, especially David's, as today he was being driven instead of driving.

We reached Canterbury about noon and walked into town from the bus parking area. The streets were busy and crowded, and we stopped for lunch before beginning an afternoon of sightseeing. The great grey cathedral, with its square central tower called Bell Harry after the huge bell it houses, dominates the city, dwarfing all else. Through the ages, the great church has been built and rebuilt after fire, pillage and destruction, the latest of which occurred during the German bombing of World War II.

Canterbury was once the capital of the Saxon kingdom of Kent and is still the spiritual capital of England. The city grew out of a prehistoric settlement on the River Stour and developed through Roman, Saxon and Norman times into the modern city of today. Its Christian heritage began with the arrival of St Augustine from Rome in AD 597 to baptize King Ethelbert and his queen and to establish a monastery and build a cathedral. Though these events marked the conversion of England to Christianity, no trace of that cathedral remains today.

The present cathedral was begun in 1067, one year after the Battle of Hastings, with the naming of Stephen Lanfranc from Caen in Normandy as archbishop. His successor Anselm added much that was unfortunately destroyed by fire. Major reconstruction began in 1175 under a French architect named William of Sens, who rebuilt the choir and used black Purbeck marble to great effect for the columns in the nave.

In the years before this reconstruction, events that were to have a momentous effect on Canterbury took place in the cathedral. In 1162

Henry II, a strong and able ruler, named his friend Chancellor Thomas à Becket to be Archbishop of Canterbury. Henry had mistakenly believed that Thomas would be little more than a puppet and that the king would thus be more powerful than the church. But Thomas changed, turning away from the temporal affairs of king and state and wholeheartedly embraced the spiritual concerns of the church. Relations between Henry and Thomas rapidly deteriorated and reached an impasse. The thwarted king, in residence at his castle at Avranches in France, one day in 1170 burst out in anger with the thoughtless utterance, 'Who will rid me of this troublesome priest?' Whereupon four of his knights crossed the Channel, rode into Canterbury by stealth, and murdered the archbishop as he knelt at prayer on the altar steps of the cathedral. News of the murder spread, and Thomas was soon regarded as a martyr by all of Christendom, so that in 1173 he was canonized. One year later the proud Henry himself, barefoot and clad in a hair shirt, walked through the streets of Canterbury in penance for the evil deed, and in succeeding centuries pilgrims from all over the Christian world came to worship at Thomas' shrine.

As we walked the spacious aisles we felt the full impact of history's hallowed ground. The spot where Becket fell is marked and his tomb is behind the altar. Here too we saw the tombs of Henry IV, an unhappy ineffective king who died of leprosy, and of the Black Prince, the shining knight of chivalry who died before he could inherit the throne. As the cathedral's lovely stained glass shed its soft-hued radiance over all, the memory of the martyred Becket and the words of T. S. Eliot in *Murder in the Cathedral* came back to me:

We thank Thee for Thy mercies of blood, for Thy redemption by blood. For the blood of Thy martyrs and saints
Shall enrich the earth, shall create the holy places.
For wherever a saint has dwelt, wherever a martyr has given his blood for the blood of Christ,
There is holy ground, and the sanctity shall not depart from it
Though armies trample over it, though sightseers come with guidebooks looking over it;
From where the western seas gnaw at the coast of Iona,
To the death in the desert, the prayer in forgotten places by the broken imperial column,
From such ground springs that which forever renews the earth
Though it is forever denied.   Therefore, O God, we thank Thee
Who hast given such blessing to Canterbury.

The pilgrims of old most likely followed the ancient track now known as the Pilgrims' Way, which runs along the spine of Surrey's North Downs. No doubt the travellers whiled away the weary miles with jollity and mirth, singing and telling tales of the sort that inspired and are retold in Chaucer's *Canterbury Tales*. For most it was the adventure of a lifetime.

Today we spent so much time in the cathedral that there was none left to see anything else. But I was glad, for there was nothing to intrude upon the mood of exaltation I experienced from this most hallowed place.

1982

TO IPSWICH BY TRAIN – CONSTABLE COUNTRY IN SUFFOLK – FELIXSTOWE

WEDNESDAY, MAY 12TH

We both slept well and woke in our London hotel feeling quite restored. We went down to the dining room for the continental breakfast. It is an elegant room, well-proportioned with a plaster ceiling and walls with panels of blue moire wallpaper and decorated with a few well-chosen Oriental paintings. It is unfortunate that we came upon this place before it has been fully renovated, for one day it will be a very pleasing small hotel.

We took a taxi to the railway station in Liverpool Street. It is the classic dark, dingy, dirty London station, yet about it there is an atmosphere of excitement and hustle and bustle of people on the go. This impression, I think, comes from my childhood, when a rare ride on a train promised adventure unlimited. We had coffee and more food in the buffet and watched with fascination the crowds coming and going – proper English, turbaned and sari-clad Indians, lanky Australians, and big blond Europeans.

The train was comfortable, fast and uncrowded. We glided past factories, housing estates, and blocks of flats looking like enormous child's blocks. The flats have replaced much of the slum property which once lined the tracks, but some such areas unfortunately remain. The drabness of the city environs soon gave way to green fields and lovely woods decked out in all shades of spring green. The steep railway banks supported prickly gorse bushes and broom, both covered in yellow pea-like flowers, and the grass here and there was starred with primroses and cowslips. Now and then we would pass fields of mustard, the dense acid yellow a brilliant contrast to the soft greens and browns of the adjacent land. Many fruit trees and ornamental shrubs were in full bloom, often planted and flourishing in unlikely places along the tracks. Cows grazed in buttercup meadows around half-timbered manor houses and thatched farmhouses, and occasionally groups of houses around a steepled church denoted a village. The train stopped only once before Ipswich at the large town of Colchester in Essex. This has been an important town through the ages, especially in Roman times when it was a military base and cultural centre. It stands at the head of the estuary of the River Colne. With the tide out we could see the mud flats from the train. Oysters have always been abundant here, the Romans accordingly naming the town from the Latin for 'oyster'.

Betty was waiting for us at Ipswich in her 'mini' car and whisked us off to her house in Hillary Close. Here we met Brandy, her aristocratic King Charles spaniel who has replaced the deceased Roly. Brandy has a lovely silky coat of reddish brown indicating that he belongs to the Ruby variety of the breed. Betty's house is full of her lovely paintings and the treasures she has picked up in her world travels. Her small fenced garden is a private oasis of green grass, flowering shrubs, bulbs and a greenhouse.

After lunch Betty's friend Kate came along to take us all for a ride in her car, which is larger than Betty's. It was a lovely day and the Suffolk countryside, always beautiful, was in full spring glory. We went first to Flatford Mill, Valley Farm and Willy Lott's cottage, all boyhood haunts of Constable and subjects of much of his painting. In the River Stour at Flatford tiny ducklings were swimming in line behind their parents, apparently unawed by the larger swans and geese sharing the water. One big goose eyed Brandy menacingly, and he growled back but was careful to stay very close to his mistress.

We went on to East Bergholdt, the large village where Constable was born in 1776. The name comes from the Anglo-Saxon for 'wooded hill'. There are many fine houses and a large church which, however, lacks a tower. The church bells are instead mounted in an upright position in a specially constructed cage and are rung every Sunday as well as once during the week for practice. Legend has it that the devil threw the bells out of the belfry and then knocked the tower down, though a more historical explanation is that work on the tower was abandoned during the religious upheavals of Henry VIII's reign. In the churchyard we saw the graves of Constable's parents, and inside there is a memorial to his wife Maria, who was a daughter of the rector. Randolph Churchill, only son of Winston, also lived in East Bergholdt. His former house is now the Stour Garden Centre.

Continuing on through narrow winding lanes we passed tiny villages, enticing inns and grey stone churches. At Erwalton we saw a gated Elizabethan mansion associated with the ill-fated Anne Boleyn, queen of a thousand days. We digressed to Shotley at the estuary of the rivers Stour and Orwell. There we trespassed across the grounds of the Royal Hospital School, a private boys school, to get a fine view of a new bridge being built over the estuary. Then back to Hillary Close for a roast chicken dinner and a slide show of Betty and Kate's recent trip to the Holy Land – quite a change of pace from rural Suffolk.

THURSDAY, MAY 13TH

The day broke fine and promised to be warm. For breakfast we had tea, boiled eggs, toast and real English marmalade. It was fun to watch David struggling to eat egg out of the shell. Accident-prone Betty cut her thumb making sandwiches for lunch, but cold water and bandaids stopped the bleeding and we decided it did not need stitches.

We drove to Felixstowe with Betty and Brandy. Even built-up areas were brimming with flowering gardens and blossoming bushes, while outside the town we passed woods and heath. One bank was quite overgrown with yellow gorse, and we passed more brilliant yellow fields which Betty told us were planted not with mustard but with rape, the seeds of which are crushed for oil for making margarine.

Felixstowe is a prosperous little port able to handle container shipments and increasingly busy since Britain's entry into the Common Market. We drove to the cliff north of the town where Betty and her friends have their 'chalet' looking out over the North Sea. It was quite calm but a bit cold and too hazy to see far. From time to time we could make out ships, some quite large, sailing mistily into view. A few sailboats close to shore were taking something of a tossing.

We unpacked the lunch and shortly thereafter our friends Winnie and Reg Bourne arrived. Both were looking quite well, though they have had a hard time looking after three aged parents who have all died in the past year. They are thinking of making a trip to the States now that they are free of family responsibilities – I do hope they will! Kate then appeared with Dougal, her very lively and inquisitive Jack Russell terrier who immediately made friends with David.

We had a lovely English-style lunch of cold meat and salad, sitting outside in the sun with our backs to the wind. We took a long walk on the beach and there was lots of talk about families, our differing ways of life, education and its deterioration, politics, and the Falklands War. Most British seem to be riding a wave of renewed jingoism and approve of Mrs Thatcher's handling of the war. Prince Andrew is quite the hero for his naval duty.

After a cup of tea we packed up and returned to Betty's house. Later we all went out to dinner at a nice hotel in Ipswich called the Crown and Anchor.

FRIDAY, MAY 14TH

We were ready to leave by 8.30 on a lovely morning. As Betty drove us to the station we passed and had a good look at Wolsey's Gate, a red brick Tudor construction which is the sole relic of the Cardinal's unrealized dream of founding an institution to train young Ipswich scholars for

Oxford, where he himself studied. It stands in an industrial area and is very dirty, shaken by decades of heavy traffic. There are some plans to move it to a safer, more scenic location where people can better appreciate its historical significance.

The train was on time and the ride back to London just as fascinating as the trip out. The shining fields of rape still amazed us. From Liverpool Street Station we managed the long subway ride to Heathrow, though in changing trains at Holborn we had to lug our heavy suitcases up steps and escalators. There was a long walk too from the subway to the car rental desk, where, eventually, we received a small red Austin.

1983

with the West Side Presbyterian Church Choir of Ridgewood N.J.

FROM HEATHROW TO CAMBRIDGE – CAMBRIDGE ENVIRONS – THE FENS

THURSDAY, JUNE 30TH

After a pleasant night flight we were through immigration at Heathrow in record time, though gathering every choir member's luggage took some time. We assembled at two buses where we met our guides Chuck and Susie Riley and shortly afterwards set out for Cambridge through wet and dismal streets. Our first view of England was, alas, a rainy one. The small row and semidetached houses that lined the streets were brightened to some extent by their tiny patches of brilliant green lawn, many of which were ringed with spectacular displays of roses of every hue. The cabbage-sized blooms were loaded with water and hung down in the rain. One house had a front path lined with tree roses, the heavy blossoms swooping low from the water burdening their petals. Some of the tiny gardens contained blue delphinium, pink lupin and a variety of border flowers.

Travelling east and north from the airport we went through an area of heavy industry. The traffic was congested in the early morning rush and was extra confusing to us Americans because of the left-hand rule of the road. Minute cars seemed to come perilously close to our mammoth bus. Industrial towns stretched endlessly one into another, with rows of houses interrupted only by the pubs – at one point I saw three in a row – churches black with grime, and schools. Most of the last were old buildings, though some had later additions, their vaguely ecclesiastical architecture typical of the time when schools were hastily erected to comply with the 1870 laws for universal education. The schools are still in session in England, and one infants school we passed had its doors wide open for the young students flocking in – the prettiest rosy-cheeked children you could wish to see.

One of the towns we went through was Denham, home of the J. Arthur Rank studios where many of the finest English films have been made. After going through Uxbridge we stopped at a restaurant on the M1 for breakfast. We were delighted with the quality and variety of the food, though service was slow and we were hindered by the difficulty of the strange choices and paying in dual currency. In one booth we noticed a girl with her hair dyed shocking pink. Though the news has made us aware of England's 'punk' generation, her appearance was nonetheless quite a shock and quite unlike our conception of the English. As we left the restaurant we noted a small station wagon, its back filled by two Pyrenean sheepdogs looking more like polar bears than any member of the canine family.

The countryside soon became less congested, with green fields, hedgerows and large trees more frequent. I was saddened by the sight of big elms, once the glory of the countryside, struck by rampant Dutch elm disease, their trunks and leafless limbs standing like gaunt sentinels. The roadside verges were overgrown with wild parsley (sometimes called cow parsley), a larger coarser variety than that which grows in America with the more attractive name of Queen Anne's lace. The hedges were full of profusely flowering elderberry shrubs, the flat white flowers made of myriads of tiny florets. In fall the bushes bear black-purple berries and country folk make wine from both fruit and flowers. We saw many beautiful horse chestnut trees, but with their candle-like blossoms over they were not as striking as when in full bloom. Wild, or dog, roses abounded in the hedgerows, their yellow-centred single flowers a delicate pink.

We passed a large lake with swimming swans mirrored in crystal clear water and came into a section of fine agricultural land. Most of it is under the plough, and we saw relatively few cattle and no sheep. The main crop is 'corn' – the English term that includes wheat, barley and oats rather than referring specifically to maize, or Indian corn, which does not grow well in the cool damp climate. We also saw fields of sugar beet and broad beans, the latter in bloom with black and white flowers that give off a delightful fragrance. The arable fields were dotted with large numbers of bright red poppies, soon to be joined by white daisies and blue cornflowers that will give the fields quite a patriotic appearance at harvest time. Around the town of Watford we went by many fields of barley, easily recognized by the bearded ears of the stalks. These fields supply the 'maltings' around Watford, the huge factories where beer is brewed and whisky distilled.

In one place I noticed a spur of chalkland covered in short springy turf. Horse jumps and stables indicated a racehorse establishment nearby. This is the area where several of the Home Counties – the counties which touch

London – meet, and we passed through parts of Surrey, Buckinghamshire, Hertfordshire and Bedfordshire. We went through Letchworth, Hatfield and Welwyn, three of the so-called Garden Cities. These are planned communities designed around long-established towns to provide homes for Londoners outside the city. Some of them were begun as far back as 1903. The movement picked up steam between the wars and after World War II, but it has been only partially successful because the towns were built on prime agricultural land and have created problems for farmers. While they have provided pleasant homes for thousands in the so-called 'Green Belt,' they have also caused mass transportation problems in and out of London. Hatfield is the site of Hatfield House where Elizabeth I was confined for much of her childhood and where she received the news of her accession to the throne. Unfortunately we could not see the house from the bus.

We went through one lovely village called Melbourn, with many fine thatched cottages. At one time a dying rural craft, thatching is now enjoying a revival. Years ago thatch was made in rural wheat-growing areas from the wheat straw. Modern reaping methods spoil the straw for this purpose, however, and the main material used today is the Norfolk reed.

As we approached Cambridge the land flattened out and the planting became more intensive. A large area near the town has been given over to experimental gardening under the aegis of the university. Closer to the centre of town the road passed between beautiful houses set in green lawns and gardens. Finally we came to the River Cam and the 'backs,' beyond which rise the majestic buildings of the university colleges. We drove to New Hall, the modern women's college where we were to be accommodated. We were assigned to quarters, spartan but adequate, a twin-bedded room sharing a bathroom with another bedroom.

After I had a short nap, my good friend Betty Glover arrived from Ipswich to spend some time with us. She visited us once while we lived in New Jersey and has been to West Side Church. She has also visited Chapel Hill twice. Headmistress, teacher, artist, writer, literary expert, amateur actress and world traveller, she is a lady of many talents. We jumped into her little car and sped downtown for tea in the Blue Boar Hotel, taking a quick look at Cambridge's many beautiful buildings on the way. The green grass of the quadrangles and the roses growing near the ancient stone glowing in the sun were essentially English and heartbreakingly beautiful. We watched the punters on the river, mostly girls, moving slowly and tentatively down the stream. We returned in time for dinner in the college dining hall. We were amazed by the levitation of the serving table up from the basement, and the meal of roast veal was well cooked. After getting directions for tomorrow, we retired to the lounge, and then Betty, David and I walked to a pub called the County Arms for a nightcap.

FRIDAY, JULY 1ST

I was awake very early after a good though hardly long sleep. Dawn was breaking, and the day came in bright and sunny with a brisk wind and nip in the air reminiscent of early fall in the U.S. After breakfast the choir met in the chapel for a rehearsal after which buses took people into town for walking tours of the city. Because I had been to Cambridge several times, Betty and I decided to go off on our own, and we headed out towards Trumpington and Grantchester, two villages just outside the city. Grantchester has retained its rural character more than Trumpington, which has almost become a suburb of Cambridge.

Trumpington has a beautiful church which despite restoration has kept its mediaeval character. The east window is of clear glass except for a centre panel consisting of a random mosaic of stained glass. The original windows were destroyed by Cromwell's Puritans, but enough fragments were found to make this panel. The timber roof has been cleaned, and its ornamental Tudor roses and other heraldic symbols have been painted in the bright colours of mediaeval craftsmen. The church's proudest possession is the second oldest brass in the country, that of Sir Roger Trumpington and dated 1289. The old verger who told us this was so proud that I was afraid to ask which church had the oldest (I later found out that the oldest is that of Sir John d'Abernon, dated 1277, in the church of Stoke d'Abernon in Surrey). Sir Roger reportedly died in France on his way home from a crusade, but he must have died at peace and in bed for his feet rest on a hound. The brass is kept locked and under glass, but for a small fee visitors can make a rubbing. Trumpington was also the home of Chaucer's miller, in whose tale two students from Cambridge attempt to seduce the miller's wife.

We drove on a couple of miles to Grantchester, a pretty village made famous by its connection with the World War I poet Rupert Brooke. Brooke was born in 1887 at Rugby, where his father was a master at the public school. In 1906 he came to King's College, where he lived in rooms in the college until he moved to the Orchard, a private house in Grantchester. He eventually moved to another house called the Old Vicarage because it was once the home of the village clergyman. About this house he wrote 'Grantchester', his best-known poem. He joined the army in 1914 in the flush of patriotic idealism that accompanied the outbreak of World War I. He wrote eloquently of love for England and of service and sacrifice. He died of blood poisoning on board a French hospital ship in the Mediterranean on April 23rd 1915 at the age of 27. He was buried on the island of Skyros beneath an olive tree in, as he himself wrote in 'The Soldier', 'a corner of a foreign field that is for ever England'. Winston

Churchill, the First Lord of the Admiralty, sent this telegram to his commander-in-chief – 'Endeavour to attend Rupert Brooke's funeral on my behalf. We shall not see his like again.' The war memorial in Grantchester churchyard bears his name among the village heroes and a quotation from his poetry – 'Men of splendid hearts'. Brooke had mentioned the church clock in the fine climactic lines of 'Grantchester':

> Stands the church clock at ten to three
> And is there honey still for tea?

As Betty and I were nurtured on the poetry of Rupert Brooke and his contemporaries, this was a meaningful pilgrimage for us. Full of sad thoughts we walked across the street for coffee in a fine hostelry that owes its prosperity to Rupert Brooke. Turning our backs on nostalgia we then drove back to Cambridge to meet David for lunch at the Blue Boar Hotel and then returned to New Hall to change for the concert in an Essex village called Earl's Colne.

I think we all enjoyed the 37 mile trip there, a ride through the leafy lanes of the Cambridgeshire and Essex countryside. As we drove southeast the flat land around Cambridge gave way to the gentle rolling land of Essex, some of the best agricultural land in the country. It is good for grain crops such as wheat and barley. The green of the latter was just assuming a faint tinge of yellow, the first sign of ripening before harvest, which is still some three or four weeks away. Some fields were planted with sugar beet, an increasingly important crop in England. The hedgerows were white with elderflower, and here and there we saw pink dog roses. Perhaps the most spectacular sights were fields of sweet peas in full bloom, planted in bands of colours shading from white to pink, lavender, coral, deep purple and dark red.

We passed through pretty villages with gardens ablaze with summer flowers. The plaster walls of some old houses were decorated with pargetting – designs in low relief – an ancient craft much practised in these parts. We passed through Haverhill, originally a small town but now greatly enlarged with housing estates built to ease London's crowding. According to Betty this particular migration from city to country is considered largely successful. On the horizon we saw the keep of the very old castle of Hedingham in a remarkable state of preservation.

As we approached Earl's Colne we were thrilled to see the Stars and Stripes flying in our honour atop the battlemented and buttressed church tower. The imposing church quite dominates the sizeable village. The vicar and our guides the Rileys were waiting to greet us, and we were ushered into the sanctuary to find our places for a brief warm-up. We then met our hosts and were taken in twos and threes to their homes for tea. Judging from our own experience and from the descriptions of the English delicacies I heard later, the ladies of Earl's Colne outdid themselves in providing for us. Certainly I enjoyed it for it was very much like the teas we had on special occasions when I was a child. I think my hostess may have been a little apprehensive about entertaining the only Englishwoman in our group – I hope I allayed any fears she may have had. We found much to talk about and discovered many common interests. Our host had been a timber merchant who had dealings with Chivers of Devizes and the Robbins, Lane and Pinnegar barge-building firm on the Kennet and Avon Canal, two firms with which my father had strong connections. Our hosts' home, which had once been a private school, was large and comfortable, its furnishings and appointments typically English. I saw prints of the Cries of London, of which I have a collection, hanging on the walls as well as some of my favourite Doulton figurines. It was unfortunate that our host had been discharged from the hospital the day before and was not at all well, and I hope our visit did not tire him unduly. But there was no mistaking the genuine pleasure our hosts showed in entertaining us, as well as their love of church, pride in their village, and happiness at playing their part in this 'hands across the sea' experiment.

We were due back at the church at 7.30. We assembled to robe in a school next to the church. The classrooms were hung with the work of infant and primary school pupils and evoked in me certain memories, not all of them pleasant, of my own experiences as a child and a young teacher, especially those of the wartime evacuations when I taught city children sharing space with local children in village schools.

I cannot begin to describe our concert. It was a melange of hymns, anthems, sacred songs and Negro spirituals. It bore the hallmark of crisp perfection that we take for granted from the choral direction and organ playing of Jack and Joanne Rodland. On this occasion we were encouraged and supported by a tremendously empathetic and enthusiastic audience.

We drove back to Cambridge in the darkening summer evening, broken now by rain and thunder. We were in bed by midnight, our packing done for an early morning start. I wrote part of this account before turning in, resolving to complete it before breakfast.

SATURDAY, JULY 2ND

We were up early and enjoyed a good English breakfast. It was raining, but lightening skies promised clearing, and I remembered the old adage, 'Rain before seven, shine before eleven'. We were delayed slightly by some luggage problems and then pulled away from New Hall at 9.15, travelling north towards Lincoln some two hours away. We were warned that there would be no rest stops until then.

The country is very flat here, and we could see for miles. Now and then the towers and steeples of village churches pierced the horizon. Most of the churches are old, of either late Norman or Early English architecture. Though some are no longer used for services, many have been wholly or partially restored. Both government money and voluntary giving play a part in financing such restoration, and there is a considerable tax advantage in undertaking such work. We noticed that brick was widely used as a building material – brick is made in this eastern part of England and became a popular building material in Tudor times. The interesting tower of the Earl's Colne church where we sang yesterday was partly brick.

We went through the edge of the Fen country. For centuries this was a remote wasteland of bog, quagmire and shallow pools, very sparsely inhabited by man but rich in otters, waterfowl, fish and other wildlife.

In the centre of the marsh a low hill of land rises like an island. Here a vast Norman cathedral was built, and a small town grew up around it. It was called Ely.

Reclamation of the Fens began about 1700 and is an ongoing project requiring constant maintenance. Using Dutch methods, drainage ditches and dikes have been constructed to dry out the rich black soil and make it suitable for bumper crops of potatoes (of which the British eat large quantities), sugar beet, wheat, barley, fruit and vegetables. Much of the sugar beet crop goes to nearby factories that use local fruit to produce jam. The fields here are the largest in England, and we saw huge tyre tracks indicating that heavy machinery is used for cultivation and fertilizing. The farming is intensive and we saw few cows or sheep. There is a good deal of farm-related industry such as milling grain into flour. Some coal and iron is mined, and there are huge steel mills at Scunthorpe. Around Peterborough, an old and important cathedral town, much brick is manufactured.

Just as the Romans built a network of straight roads through primeval territory, so modern man has constructed great multilane highways the length and breadth of England. The motorway we followed today traced the path of Ermine Street, an important Roman road linking the garrisons of London, Cambridge, Lincoln and York. Most secondary roads in England are crooked – Chesterton's 'rolling roads' that wind along property lines determined before the importance of straight roads became evident. We passed close to Huntingdon, birthplace of Oliver Cromwell, the revolutionary who executed a king and ruled in his place for 10 years, and Samuel Pepys, the diarist whose constant jottings give us a vivid picture of life in seventeenth-century England and London.

1985

VISITING IN IPSWICH – TUNBRIDGE WELLS – NEWBURY

WEDNESDAY, MAY 1ST

We left Marlborough early yesterday for the long ride to Ipswich to visit Betty Glover, going through Swindon, bypassing Oxford (somehow we always do!), through Aylesbury and around Colchester to Sudbury in Suffolk. Here we stopped, parking near the beautiful church surrounded with velvet lawns, tall trees and impressive arrays of tulips and daffodils. We saw the house where Thomas Gainsborough was born – an old Tudor house to which a Georgian front has been added. The house is now a museum but was closed at the time we were there.

We received a warm welcome at Betty's little house, where we had dinner with her friends, saw slides of their recent travels in Iceland and of course talked a great deal.

THURSDAY, MAY 2ND

Leaving Ipswich we were on our way to Tunbridge Wells by 1 o'clock. As we drove towards the Dartford Tunnel under the Thames we left the rural environment of Suffolk and entered the industrial development of the greater London area. Its outgrowth and encroachment into the countryside is quite daunting. Just prior to reaching the tunnel we stopped for petrol, and met a bitter wind mixed with rain as we got out of the car. As we drove on, however, an intermittent sun came out and warmed us up a little in the car. Our destination was a bed and breakfast house in Tunbridge Wells where we had reservations. We expected to have a few hours in the evening and possibly tomorrow morning in which to have a look at Tunbridge Wells, a spa I have long wanted to visit.

We negotiated the tunnel with no trouble, finding traffic lighter than we had expected, and soon began to pass through some pretty Kentish countryside, distinguished by orchards in full bloom, old brick farmhouses, and villages of ancient half-timbered cottages grouped around church towers and steeples. Lush and burgeoning, a picture-book England turned its pages before our eyes.

We saw many hopfields and oast houses. Between February and September the hop vines climb to about 14 feet – they were about half-grown at this point. In September the hops are picked, often by slum dwellers from London who make a working holiday of the task. The hops are taken into the oast houses, great round structures with asymmetrical chimneys where they are dried in great trays over charcoal fires. Heat passes out through the chimneys that turn with the wind. After several hours of drying the hops are cooled and packed in large sacks called 'pockets' and shipped to the breweries. Some growers are now replacing the traditional oast houses with less attractively housed oil-burners, and we were reminded of how in North Carolina the old log-cabin type of tobacco barns are being replaced by more efficient but far less attractive metal ones. Some oast houses still remain in use, however, and some have been converted into dwellings.

Traffic became very heavy as we skirted the industrial area of Tonbridge and grew heavier still as we neared Tunbridge Wells. The highway was lined with large houses of the Victorian era, homes then of the rich and prosperous but today looking somewhat seedy and neglected. Some have become offices, businesses or group homes for troubled people. We found the Firwood Hotel to be a large Victorian house, its conversion into a hotel almost complete. We are among its first guests. We were shown into a pleasant lounge and glimpsed the dining room, its decor, heavy on red with a melange of pattern, not to my liking. We were taken to a bedroom, large and tastefully decorated in blue with a king-sized bed and huge television set. A nicely equipped adjoining bathroom proved not quite so nice when six tiles fell into the bath that David had just vacated. The owner, when informed of the mishap, seemed only slightly chagrined.

We were anxious to see the town while it was still daylight, so we declined the offer of dinner in the hotel and drove into town. We found a parking place with no trouble in the almost deserted streets, made our way to the colonnaded Upper Walk paved in the famous 'pantiles,' and walked to the spring where we sampled the evil-smelling, foul-tasting water and picked up some pamphlets about the town and its history.

The town grew up around chalybeate springs discovered in 1606 by Lord North, who introduced their supposedly medicinal qualities to the society of his day. The word 'chalybeate' derives from the Greek for 'steel' and means to have a strong mineral taste. The water here gets its taste from deposits of iron, calcium and magnesium through which it percolates. There is a local legend that says St Dunstan met the devil near the bubbling springs of clear water. Being the patron saint of blacksmiths, he seized the devil by the nose with his red-hot tongs, whereupon Satan soothed his hurting nose in the waters, giving them the strong metallic taste they have had ever since. Be that as it may, the water has a bitter vitriolic taste. Nevertheless it became fashionable in the seventeenth and eighteenth centuries for the rich and famous to 'take the waters,' and, with its close proximity to London, Tunbridge Wells became a very popular spa for many years.

The full name of the town is actually Royal Tunbridge Wells. Though

Edward VII conferred the right to append 'royal' to the name only at the beginning of this century, the town's royal associations go back much farther. In 1630 the embryonic resort had a very important visitor in Henrietta Maria, the French queen of Charles I. She went there to recuperate after the birth of her son, who later became Charles II. The queen and her retinue had to live in colourful tents pitched on the downs overlooking the town, as at that time there were few houses and facilities. During the Civil War the town was strongly Royalist and was outraged at the execution of Charles I.

After the Restoration in 1660, Charles II made Tunbridge one of his favourite haunts and during his reign its popularity and attractions grew by leaps and bounds. Charles even sent his wife, Catherine of Braganza, there in the hopes of curing her barrenness. For centuries local countrywomen had come to drink the water to cure infertility. There are no records as to its efficacy – certainly Charles' queen never bore a child. In 1665 Samuel Pepys' wife took the waters, and when he visited her he wrote that she was 'not very well and looks almost the worst I ever did see her. It seems that drinking the waters did almost kill her before she could with most violent physique get it out of her body again.'

Despite – or perhaps because of – their bad taste, the waters developed a growing reputation for curing disease and easing the rheumatic pains that were well nigh endemic in England's damp cool climate. With the patronage of Charles II, the town became a social and entertainment centre as well as a therapeutic one. Coffee houses, assembly rooms, and a theatre were built, and the main street, known as the Upper Walk, was planted with a double row of elm and lime trees. Here the fashionable rich were wont to promenade. Shops sold lace, jewellery, fans, snuff boxes, wigs – anything that might catch the fancy of the idle rich. Gambling and dancing became popular pastimes, with dances often held outside in the summer. Charles II entertained several of his mistresses here, bringing with him a large retinue of courtiers. Often when the men returned to London the ladies would find consolation elsewhere, so that Tunbridge began to be called '*les eaux de scandale*'. Nell Gwynn, one of the king's favourite mistresses, may have visited the spa with a theatre troupe, and another actress, Peg Hughes, had an affair with the ageing Prince Rupert, Royalist hero of the Civil War.

The spa's royal heyday lasted well into the eighteenth century. Mary of Modena, second wife of the Duke of York – who succeeded Charles II as James II – went there to recover from a miscarriage in the company of her stepdaughter Anne, who later became Queen Anne. Like her uncle, Anne liked the place very much and its popularity extended into her reign. It was Anne, with her tragic history of children dying young, who was responsible for paving the Upper Walk with the pantiles, one of the most distinctive features of Tunbridge. Of her 19 children only one survived infancy. He happened to trip and fall walking on the unpaved surface, whereupon his panic-stricken mother ordered the walk to be covered in square clay tiles, some of which are still preserved.

The town never seemed to capture the imagination of the Hanoverian monarchs who followed Anne, especially after George IV built the Pavilion at Brighton. Beau Nash visited Tunbridge but preferred to develop Bath into a health spa that far surpassed it. Queen Victoria went there only occasionally, but there was some renewed interest shown in the reign of Edward VII. I suppose that today the town is an interesting anachronism, appealing mostly to people anxious to recreate the past. It holds a festival in July every year when for a brief two weeks it comes alive with concerts, plays and Morris dancing on the green.

On this cool darkening May evening we walked the famous pantile walk, distressed to see grass growing between the tiles. Glancing in the shops now lacking their one-time elegance, we made our way to the spring for a sip of the evil-tasting water. Then we were glad to duck into an ancient inn where a blazing fire and the prospect of food and drink offered a respite from the outside dreariness. Leaving its shelter we walked to the church completed in 1678 and dedicated to Charles the Martyr – Charles I who was beheaded in Whitehall at the end of the Civil War. We were lucky to be able to get in, for it is a beautiful church with a fine plaster ceiling designed and executed by Henry Doogood, Sir Christopher Wren's chief plasterer. The church was fortunately spared when a fire destroyed much of the town in 1687. We walked then to the High Street, which was quite deserted, though a small French restaurant was open where we got a passable meal before returning to our hotel for the night.

SATURDAY, MAY 11TH

We have left our shopping till the last day – Saturday, too, which is not a good day as crowds of bargain hunters are usually out as are those doing their weekly marketing. Like most Americans we are in search of sweaters and woollens at reasonable prices and generally find good quality bargains at the Marks and Spencers chain. When I was a child this store was more or less a dime store inferior in this regard to Woolworth, but since the war it has grown into a prosperous conglomerate selling clothing, dry goods and foods. It is very popular with Britons and foreigners alike. Following Joan Fulk's advice, we usually go to the shop in Newbury, 15 miles away in Berkshire, for it receives and distributes the latest lines and so there is more choice. We can easily find the large green and gold store in the High Street and in spite of the crowds can make our purchases quickly, leaving plenty of time for some exploring around the town.

Newbury is 15 miles from the River Kennet's confluence with the Thames at Reading, and the river here is considerably wider than at Marlborough. The river is paralleled by the Kennet and Avon Canal and is crossed by a narrow balustraded eighteenth-century bridge. With a population of some 20,000 the town is prosperous with a long and distinguished history. It is mentioned in Roman records, and part of its site is noted in the Domesday Book initiated by William the Conqueror. It was a very prosperous centre for wool and woollen cloth in early Tudor times due largely to the enterprise of a clothier named John Winchcombe who came to be known as Jack of Newbury. He built a fine house, part of which still remains, where he received Henry VII and Catherine of Aragon. He also built a fine church dedicated to St Nicholas, and in its tower we saw his memorial brass. In Tudor times the town became a royal borough. The Jacobean Cloth Hall, a beautiful building with wonderful woodwork and an overhanging upper storey, is now a museum. Prior to the advent of the railway, Newbury's suburb of Speenhamland was an important stagecoach stop.

Two battles were fought near Newbury during the Civil War in 1633 and 1644. The Royalists successfully defended the town in the first battle but the situation was reversed by the Parliamentarians in the second, which kept Charles I from reaching his headquarters in Oxford.

Newbury is built largely of brick introduced in Tudor times. Bricks can be dated by their shape and colour, earlier ones being smaller and browner than later ones. In the shopping streets of Newbury, if one looks above the garish modern shopfronts, the upper storeys are of charming harmonious brickwork, the bricks sometimes fashioned into curves and cornices.

Newbury has grown tremendously since the M4 opened some 40 years ago, partly from the influx of commuters and weekenders from London and partly from its own developing industry. There is an exceptionally beautiful racecourse to the east of the town, and the town is especially crowded and busy on race days.

1986

with Jane Sockwell & Betsy Newland

EGHAM AND GREAT FOSTERS HOTEL

WEDNESDAY, SEPTEMBER 24TH

As we approached London the build-up of traffic increased, but a new link in the network of highways helped us find our destination of Egham, where we had a reservation at Great Fosters Hotel. Egham today is a well-to-do suburb – a bedroom community for city businessmen – but it has a long history of prosperity as a community in the heart of a rich agricultural district in the Thames Valley. It is close to Runnymede where King John was forced to sign Magna Carta in 1215. Some of the barons who signed the document are buried and memorialized in Egham Church.

Great Fosters Hotel is well nigh indescribable. Originally a hunting lodge in Richmond Forest, it is a huge red brick Tudor mansion set in beautiful grounds and has been named an historic site. It belonged to and was much frequented by Henry VIII, and was later expanded into a house in the reign of Elizabeth I. It bears all the hallmarks of Tudor construction – brick, mullioned windows with diamond-leaded panes, curved tall chimneys, the 'E' shape loved by the Elizabethans, and a very impressive entryway. Close by and now attached is an enormous tithe barn, used today as the hotel restaurant. The parterre plantings of clipped yew and box feature larger yew trees clipped into geometric, animal, and bird shapes in the ancient art of topiary that enjoyed a vogue in Tudor times. The ground in between the low hedges is planted with many coloured flowers, their blooms massed together and creating the effect of a vast Oriental rug.

We were ushered into the baronial hall, its oak floor and furniture black with age and lustrous with frequent polishing. We entered through a small door that had been cut in a very large heavily studded portal. Massive chairs and sofas were covered in deep-piled dark red velvet. The huge stone fireplace cried out for a roaring fire of logs, for the room was cold in spite of the opulence around us. We were taken up a red-carpeted oak staircase to a big room aptly named the Tapestry Chamber, for the walls were hung with arras in true mediaeval style. The mullioned windows were heavily draped. Another huge fireplace – large enough to accommodate a tree limb – was unlit, and the room struck me as cold. All the furniture was heavily carved, and two throne-like chairs were covered in red and ivory damask. In one corner stood a cradle of heavy dark oak. The two beds were likewise carved. The linen sheets were faintly redolent of lavender, and the thick wool blankets were covered with bedspread and eiderdown. A television set seemed like an intrusion. The adjoining bathroom was large, almost cavernous, with the outsize bath raised on a dais in the middle of the room. A twisting staircase led from the bathroom to an upper room generally used as a nursery. Many celebrities have stayed in this room, among them Charlie Chaplin, whose many children used the nursery. The entire suite was cold and draughty, and it made us aware that our ancestors must often have been uncomfortable in the midst of opulence and luxury.

We drove then to the airport to check out the way along the maze of roads leading to it. We had lunch in the garishly modern Penta Hotel.

Returning to Great Fosters, we explored the grounds and then drove to Runnymede and Eton where –

> Wanders the hoary Thames along
> His silver-winding way.

We had an excellent dinner in the old tithe barn and were waited on by a waitress who looked like Princess Anne. Then to our splendid rooms to pack and repack for the morrow's flight back to the U.S. and home.

1987

WOBURN ABBEY – AGAIN TO IPSWICH AND FELIXSTOWE

SUNDAY, AUGUST 9TH

My 70th birthday! We left Marlborough early, taking the familiar road to Swindon and then going northeast to Oxford, which we bypassed. It seems we always do, though I visited it many times years ago.

We passed a side road with a sign pointing to Kingston Bagpuize, the village where my friend Sybil Beard was born and raised and where her father was the blacksmith. I wanted to go there since she has talked a good deal and done some writing about it, but David thought it would delay us too much. We continued on, skirting the towns of Aylesbury and Leighton Buzzard and arriving at Woburn about lunchtime. We pulled into the Bedford Arms where we booked a room for the night and had a good meal. The hotel is large and spacious, an architectural gem built by Henry Holland in 1790.

After lunch we went to Woburn Abbey, one of the great houses of England and principal seat of the immensely rich and powerful Russells, the dukes of Bedford. The abbey was founded in 1145 and was given to the Russell family at the time of the Dissolution. The present house was rebuilt on the old abbey foundations by Henry Flitcroft in 1747 but underwent considerable remodelling by Holland a few years later. It is set in a grassy park of some 3,000 acres full of magnificent trees.

An enterprising family, the Russells were among the first of England's peers to see the moneymaking possibilities of developing a large estate for public entertainment. Though they are among the richest families in the country, they, like other wealthy landowners, face a constant drain in keeping up their mansions from rising inflation and high death duties such as inheritance taxes. Very interested in animal conservation, one duke heavily funded nearby Whipsnade Zoo, established his own wildlife park to which he added an amusement centre, and opened the abbey to the public for guided tours. In 1900 the 11th duke brought 18 deer of the rare species called Père David in an effort to save them from extinction. Discovered in 1865 near Peking by the French missionary for whom they are named, they are no longer found in the wild but over 300 survive in the park at Woburn. They are large animals with many branched antlers. Other species close to extinction have been brought here and their herds replenished and built up, and visitors driving around the park see many deer.

But we were mainly interested in the mansion and indeed it was all we had time for. Though quite magnificent, its outside appearance I found less impressive than Chatsworth, which we visited a year ago. Inside it is filled with the accumulated treasures – rare and costly furniture, works of art and books – of a fabulously rich family, an embarrassment of riches so vast that we could take in only a fraction of what was there. One room was entirely devoted to the memorabilia of the 'Flying Duchess', a pioneer of women's rights as well as aviation. She disappeared on a flight in 1930, and I remember reading about her in the newspapers when I was young. The basement has been converted into a strongroom where family silver and jewellery are displayed, a fabulous collection that makes one wonder how one family could amass so much.

After the guided tour we drove around the park. On its outskirts we saw the entrances to the wildlife park and amusement centre. We went through the estate villages where the cottages occupied by servants and retainers were well built of stone and bear the carved monogram 'B' beneath the ducal coronet. Some of the houses have no front doors since one of the dukes objected to his tenants idly gossiping on the main street. Though the Bedfords looked after their people well and bountifully, in many ways they ruled them with the iron fist of the mediaeval feudal lord. The present duke, an entrepreneur and considered somewhat eccentric, is much more democratic than his forebears.

We returned to our hotel for a delightful dinner in a dining room filled with photographs and memorabilia of the Russell family. The service was impeccable, and we were left with the feeling that both hotel and town are still very much under the patronage of the owners of Woburn Abbey.

MONDAY AND TUESDAY, AUGUST 10TH AND 11TH

We left Woburn next morning going through Bedford – John Bunyan country – around Cambridge and so to Ipswich. We spent two days revisiting mostly places related in previous journals and ending as usual with a picnic on the cliffs of Felixstowe. The weather was beautiful and it was a relaxing restful time that included lots of talk of other times and places.

On our second day we left the picnic site after lunch and found our way through the Dartford Tunnel to Copthorne. There we spent the night in the attractive hotel we had discovered upon arriving, before being taken to the airport for our flight to North Carolina.

1989

WEST FROM GATWICK AND BACK FROM MARLBOROUGH

TUESDAY, SEPTEMBER 12TH

It was incredibly early when we touched down at Gatwick on a dry but murky morning with the temperature hovering around 60 degrees. British clocks pointed to 6.40 a.m., but our own timepieces told us it was still the middle of the night. Passport formalities were mercifully brief, our luggage was waiting for us, and we changed dollars into sterling quite speedily. By good luck, quick thinking and a loud whistle on David's part, we caught a bus to the Swan car rental office, where we quickly obtained a small white Vauxhall. The people there were pleasant and welcoming – an elderly man called me 'luv' and an efficient young lady was very nice to David. We then walked across the road to the Gatwick-Concorde Hotel, large, modern, expensively tasteless and right in the flight path, but a convenient spot to spend the night before our return. We made a reservation and stayed for breakfast. A diminutive waitress with the reddest hair and a delightful Irish brogue served us, but at £10 it was surely the most expensive tea and toast I have ever eaten.

The miles from Gatwick to Reading cannot be called a very scenic part of Britain. The topography is flat and uninteresting, with industry encroaching on previously agricultural areas and destroying much of the beauty of well-tended fertile land. Occasionally we glimpsed a big house or comfortable farm surrounded by large trees and lush meadows supporting herds of cows and flocks of sheep. We passed some great fields where the corn crops have now in September already been gathered in. A persistent early morning mist seemed to soften the ravages of industry, and the sight of Keats' 'mossed cottage trees' bending under bumper crops of fruit made me think of that poet's mellow fruitfulness. On our left we passed Windsor Castle rising wraith-like out of the mist, and then at Theale we saw swans swimming. Two of the graceful birds flew overhead, their wings beating in harmony and their long necks stretched taut.

MONDAY, SEPTEMBER 25TH

We were up early and after a last look at Marlborough's High Street and checking out of the hotel we left about noon for Gatwick, where we are spending tonight before tomorrow's flight home. Because we had plenty of time we elected to avoid the motorway and take the longer scenic route. In view of the beautiful weather it was a wise decision.

We said farewell to Wiltshire by going through Savernake Forest to Burbage and the Collingbournes, passing into Hampshire just past Ludgershall, a rather sad and depressing little place. We drove around the prosperous market town of Andover and towards Basingstoke. We escaped the mushrooming urban sprawl around that town by taking a side road leading through lush farmland and many pretty villages. We stopped in a village called Hurstbourne Priors for lunch at an inn called the Hurstbourne, where the landlord and barmaid were very friendly and the food very good. Harsh modern decor spoiled the interior of what once must have been a charming old place, and the music was loud, but certainly the welcome was warm.

Shortly after lunch we entered Surrey and for some miles west of Guildford we were on what is known as the Hog's Back. Here the downs narrow into a high ridge, both sides of which offer spectacular views. Beyond Guildford the downs broaden into wooded hills and commons. For awhile we followed the Pilgrims' Way, which begins in Winchester in Hampshire, enters Surrey at Farnham, and continues across the county along the ridge of chalk before ending in Canterbury. It was the route followed by Bronze Age traders and later by mediaeval pilgrims, Chaucer's among them, bound for Thomas à Becket's shrine in the cathedral at Canterbury.

We made a brief stop in Dorking, admiring its bow-fronted shops. Dickens stayed in one of the old inns here and is said to have set part of Pickwick Papers here. The town has associations too with Lord Nelson and is where John Keats completed his long poem 'Endymion.'

Leaving Dorking we entered the built-up area of London's outskirts. We reached Gatwick at last and, more by luck than judgement, found our way to our hotel, turned our car in, had a good meal, and went to our room for an early night, our stay in England over.

Great Gate at Blenheim Palace,
Oxfordshire

Chester – the Rows and Black and
White Architecture

Washington Old Hall, Durham

Sulgrave Manor, Northamptonshire. Homes of George Washington's
Ancestors

Coventry Cathedral – the Old and the New

Newstead Abbey – home of Lord Byron

Tunbridge Wells – the Pantiles

Flatford Mill and Willy Lott's Cottage

Canterbury Cathedral

Sissinghurst – home of Harold Nicholson and Vita Sackville-West

American Cemetery at Cambridge

Marlborough High Street

Marlborough College – famous public school

Tottenham House – ancestral home of the Marquess of Ailesbury in Savernake Forest

Devizes – Market Place, Bear Hotel and Corn Exchange

Castle Combe – often called the prettiest village in England

Stonehenge

St David's Cathedral, South Wales

Fettiplace Tombs at Swinbrook in the Cotswolds

Chapter Eight

WILTSHIRE, COUNTY OF THE MOONRAKERS

'That shire which I the heart of England well may call.'
Michael Drayton 1562–1631

Michael Drayton's words are about Warwickshire, but they seem appropriate for my feelings about Wiltshire. All my journeys begin or end – sometimes both – in the town of Marlborough in the county of Wiltshire. I will write a little first about the county before coming back to Marlborough, which for me is its focal point.

Wiltshire is in the southwest of England, a landlocked county bordered by Gloucestershire, Berkshire, Hampshire, Dorset and Somerset. Wiltshire falls physically into two sharp divisions – downland and lowland, with the latter occupying about one third of the county. The lowlands are mostly in the west and far north and far south, grouped around the central core of chalk downland, which, in spite of its name, is really upland. The division is often referred to as that between 'chalk' and 'cheese,' the latter referring to the dairy farming carried on in the lowlands.

It is however the chalk downs we think of first at the mention of Wiltshire. They have given the county its characteristic scenery, ancient history, and distinctive way of life. It is a dry upland country of smoothly rolling hills, the white soil covered in short turf good for little agriculturally except the raising of sheep. The only native trees are thorn and juniper, but here and there are great clumps of beech trees planted by farmers to act as windbreaks. The lowlands, merging in the west into the foothills of the Cotswolds and Mendip Hills, are lovely in their own way with well-wooded valleys, fertile farms, pretty villages and market towns built on streams and rivers, the waters of which are clear and limpid from the chalk soil in which they rise.

One of the most beautiful small cities in all England is in Wiltshire – Salisbury, its cathedral town. It is built in the low-lying meadows of the River Avon in the lee of Salisbury Plain, the great heartland of the downs, so that in Salisbury the two Wiltshires come together.

WILTSHIRE

GLOUCESTERSHIRE

BERKSHIRE

● Cirencester

● Highworth

● Malmesbury

Lydiard
Tregoze ● ● Swindon

● Wootton Bassett

Lambourn
●

● Castle Combe

MARLBOROUGH DOWNS

Hardenhuish ● ● Chippenham
R. Kennet
● Calne   Avebury
● Corsham   Axford Ramsbury
West Kennett ●   ● ●   Hungerford
● Lacock   Marlborough ●

● Box   ● Beckhampton

● Melksham   ● Bishops Cannings
Devizes   Pewsey
● Bradford-on-Avon   Alton ● Woodborough ● Burbage
● TROWBRIDGE   Urchfont ● ● Charlton

Bratton
●
Westbury ● ● Edington

SOMERSET

SALISBURY PLAIN

● Warminster

Tidworth ●

HAMPSHIRE

Stonehenge
●   ● Amesbury

● Stourhead

● Old Sarum

Chilmark ● Bemerton
Wilton ●   ● SALISBURY

R. Avon

DORSET

But Salisbury is young by Wiltshire standards, for eons before the cathedral was built in the thirteenth century the nomadic tribes of earliest man were wandering in search of food and shelter on the high downland where they were safe from the marauding wild beasts of the valleys. Here on the downs man built his first settled homes after learning to till the soil and grow crops, make pots, and use metals. Here he built, using methods still unfathomed, great stone temples to whatever gods he worshipped. All over the downs one sees the grave mounds of races long vanished while defensive earthworks frown down from the highest hills. The downs are still criss-crossed by tracks worn by the feet of the men of long ago, tracks of which the Ridgeway was the chief thoroughfare across the crest of the hills.

Wiltshire's story is not only of prehistoric times, however. The Romans came and went and Wiltshire became part of Wessex, the land of the West Saxons, and it was on the chalk downs that Alfred the Great fought his greatest battles against the Danes. Sheep farming flourished on the downs, and the wool from the sheep became the raw material of a cottage industry that flourished in the lowlands until the Industrial Revolution. Wiltshire has remained an agricultural county to this day, with Swindon as its only truly industrial town. Swindon developed with the advent of the railway and in spite of the railway's decline continues to experience phenomenal industrial growth today.

True Wiltshiremen speak in a rich dialect, soft and slow, which often gives the impression that they are not very bright. But it is only a veneer, for a shrewd wisdom underlies, as the origin of the term 'Moonraker' for an English man or woman born and bred in Wiltshire – among whom I am proud to count myself – demonstrates. The term dates from the smuggling days of the eighteenth century, when French brandy would be landed illegally on the south coast to avoid the heavy excise tax and then smuggled along a chain of conspirators to its final destination, usually London. The excisemen were often hard put to outwit the smugglers and those in league with them, and many confrontations arose between the lawmen and lawbreakers.

The story goes that one bright moonlit night the 'revenooers' were hard on the heels of smugglers, who in desperation tossed the contraband into a Wiltshire dewpond near a group of smock-clad yokels who were raking hay in the moonlight to take advantage of fine weather. When the excisemen rode up, panting hard and with their horses blown, they found the Wiltshiremen raking the pond rather than their hay. After asking for news of the smugglers, and receiving a false and negative answer, the excisemen asked why they were raking the pond. The Wiltshiremen, slow of speech and giving every indication that they were also slow of mind, pointed to the round yellow reflection of the moon in the water and said they were raking for the 'girt big cheese' that they could see at the bottom of the pool. The excisemen cried, 'Why, ye girt vools, that be the moon,' and laughing heartily at such stupidity, rode off into the night in search of the smugglers and the brandy. Whereupon the Wiltshiremen smugly retrieved the casks of brandy with their rakes and sent them on their way. By a show of slow stupidity – a characteristic still mistakenly and unfairly attributed to men of the West Country – they thus outwitted the authorities, and ever since all Wiltshire natives have been called Moonrakers.

Several places in Wiltshire lay claim to the pond where this incident occurred, Bishop's Cannings and Yatesbury among them. As a native of Devizes, I like to think it was in the Devizes pond known as the Crammer that the event took place, if indeed it did.

The small town of Marlborough lies in the lap of the chalk downs on the banks of the River Kennet. To the north lie the Marlborough Downs, to the east Savernake Forest, to the south the Pewsey Vale and Salisbury Plain, and to the west another spur of chalk, the Kennet valley, and the source of the river.

In common with most small towns in England, Marlborough has a long and distinguished history. The Arthurian legend appears in its Latin motto '*Ubi nunc sapientis ossa Merlini*' ('Where now lie the bones of the wise Merlin'). It is doubtful, though, if it is indeed the burial place of Arthur's wise mentor, and while some maintain that this is the case – with the name meaning the 'burgh' or town of Merlin – others think 'marl' refers to the chalky soil. Still others believe the name indicates the burial place of an ancient chief named Maerl, for there is a prehistoric mound, now within the college grounds, that rivals the nearby Silbury Hill in mystery if not in size.

Legend aside, the Romans had a settlement called Cunetio at nearby Mildenhall (pronounced 'Minal'). The Saxons built the first dwellings around the open grassy space known today as the Green. The Normans built a castle to the west that was especially beloved by King John (1199–1216), who accordingly granted Marlborough a charter making it a royal borough. Marlborough was mentioned in the Domesday Book, and in Norman times money was minted in the town, so that Marlborough pennies are valuable finds for collectors today. Henry III held his last Parliament in Marlborough in 1267 and a law known as the Statute of Marlborough was passed. It gave certain rights to small landowners and was an important adjunct to Magna Carta.

A grammar school was founded in 1550 by Edward VI, perhaps because his mother Jane Seymour, third and favourite wife of Henry VIII, lived close by at Wolfhall in Savernake Forest. During the seventeenth-century Civil War Marlborough was a Parliamentary stronghold, so that it was under attack several times by the Royalists. The town's heyday came with the coaching era of the eighteenth century, for it was a prime stopping place between London and Bath. Many famous people stayed at the Castle Inn, among them Pitt the Elder, Earl of Chatham and Prime Minister of England. The prosperity ended with the advent of the railway, for Marlborough was bypassed by the main line. About this time, however, Marlborough College was opened and after a rocky start grew into one of the most famous of public schools, so that the town's economy once again flourished.

Marlborough's outstanding feature is its very wide High Street lined with gracious houses and shops. The street slopes from north to south, so that natives refer to its 'top' and 'bottom,' often to the confusion of strangers. The lower side of the street parallels the waters of the River Kennet.

Marlborough is much grown and changed from the time I knew it as a child. Yet when I return I do not feel a stranger. The wide street, a church at either end with the Town Hall abutting into it remains the same and I feel I have come home.

1973

with Thomas & Margaret McKnight

THE RED LION AT AXFORD – REVISITING WARTIME HAUNTS – SALISBURY AND STONEHENGE – VISITING AND SIGHTSEEING AROUND MARLBOROUGH

SUNDAY, JULY 15TH

Leaving Windsor we drove through Reading, Newbury and Hungerford, where we left the main road and took leafy lanes to Axford in Wiltshire, some six miles out of Marlborough. Axford is the smallest of hamlets – a handful of houses, a war memorial cross, and a tiny inn on the banks of the River Kennet. The inn is the Red Lion, a small building of brick interspersed in true Wiltshire style with bands of flint. Small though it is, it is becoming a popular place for enjoying a drink and good bar food, its popularity due in no small measure to its proprietors, Joan and Oscar Fulk. Oscar is a transplanted American. After serving for several years during the war in Marlborough as a railway transport officer, he married a Marlborough girl and decided to remain in England, where he found his niche as an innkeeper. David and he knew each other in the army, and both are natives of North Carolina. Joan like myself was brought up in Marlborough and we both attended Marlborough Grammar School. The inn, small though it is, boasts several rooms for guests so it is very natural for us to stay there and partake of their hospitality when we visit Marlborough.

MONDAY, JULY 16TH

We were on the road by 10 o'clock driving first through Savernake Forest to Tottenham House. As children my sister and I often played and picnicked under Savernake's great oaks and beeches. Now the forest shows some deterioration from the green woodland I remember, change perhaps due to age, neglect and its use during the war. David was stationed in the forest when I met him and was billeted at Tottenham House, the great mansion belonging to the Marquess of Ailesbury. Tommy also had stayed in Tottenham at the time of our wedding.

We then drove towards Salisbury, stopping at the pleasant Castle Inn for lunch. This old hostelry is on the outskirts of the city, opposite Old Sarum, the ancient fortified town on the hill which in the Middle Ages was deserted for the new city site in the valley. From the inn we could see the distant spire of the cathedral piercing the sky.

Salisbury was planned by Bishop Poore on a grid system, the streets leading in and out of a spacious marketplace with the superb cathedral at its very heart. The great grey stone church with its tall tapering spire – the tallest in England – is surrounded by the green grass of its spacious close which in turn is ringed by a harmonious melange of beautiful houses of many designs and periods. To the south are the lush watermeadows of the River Avon, the whole forming the scene painted by Constable and immortalized in *The Compleat Angler* by seventeenth-century author Izaak Walton.

I have visited many of England's cathedrals and think Salisbury the finest. Perhaps it is because of my native ties to the area, or perhaps because it was built in one perfect architectural style and is set like a jewel in its emerald close. A notice in the nave announces proudly, 'The building composes perfectly from whatever view point,' and it has been called a key building for an understanding of English architecture. Inside the cathedral we found part of it closed off for a wedding already in progress. Once again as part of the wedding service we heard 'Be Thou My Vision.' After the ceremony the bride and groom, followed by their attendants, walked the length of the centre aisle, and from thence around the cloisters, which are large and exceptionally fine with great cedars of Lebanon growing in the enclosed lawn.

We took a few minutes – all too brief a time – to look around the cathedral, admiring the stained glass and the Chapter House and seeing one of the few existing copies of Magna Carta. There are many fine tombs in the nave and side chapel, some of them of Crusaders who can be identified by the crossed legs of their sculpted effigies.

Leaving Salisbury reluctantly, we drove on to Stonehenge, going first through Amesbury, an old grey town much associated with the legends of King Arthur. It was to the nunnery here that Queen Guinevere fled after the death of Sir Lancelot. Beyond Amesbury the huge broken circle of mammoth stones which is Stonehenge rises starkly from the green downland of Salisbury Plain. There is much ongoing discussion of why it was built, when and by whom. Most agree it was a temple for sun worship. How the stones were brought here from North Wiltshire and South Wales – some even say from Brittany in France – and how the large stones, some weighing 50 tons, were raised into the trilithon formation are subjects of endless speculation. The temple remains enigmatic and mysterious and is best seen at sunrise for its full dramatic effect. Today the monument is reached by an underground passage. Discreet markers indicate the place of missing stones. Fences have been kept to a minimum, and a twentieth-century shop and refreshment stand kept out of view, so as not to disturb the atmosphere of ancient awe and wonder.

From Stonehenge we went west through Potterne to Devizes. Potterne is a large village and we often visited friends and relatives there when I was growing up. We stopped to take pictures of the Porch House, a fine example of the half-timbered, black-and-white architecture much favoured in Tudor times. Devizes is an old and locally important market town with a fine marketplace. After stopping in the town for tea we drove back across the downs to Axford and then went to Marlborough for dinner in the Ailesbury Arms Hotel.

TUESDAY, JULY 17TH

We reached the Red Lion just in time to get ready for our date with friends at the Seven Stars in Bottlesford. En route there we drove through a village called Lockeridge and a stone-strewn area known as the Valley of the Rocks. These huge sarsen stones are often called 'grey wethers' because from a distance they resemble sheep. Stones were taken from here for building the Stonehenge and Avebury temples. The stones probably resulted from glacial deposits.

We got an excellent view of the Alton White Horse and a fine view too of the Pewsey Vale, a rich agricultural valley between two spurs of the chalk downs. We went through the villages of Alton Barnes, Honeystreet and Woodborough. This part of Wiltshire is the land of my forebears. My father lived in Alton Barnes and went to school there and in Woodborough. At the barge-building works at Honeystreet on the banks of the Kennet and Avon Canal, he worked as an apprentice under the eagle eye of his grandfather. Our friends the Turners live at the School House attached to the school in Woodborough, where Tig Turner is the village schoolmaster. When I was a schoolgirl I spent weekends and holidays there with my friend Molly Trollope, daughter of the then schoolmaster. The war took her to New Zealand as it took me to America.

We were a little late and our friends were waiting for us. Tig, his charming wife Nessa and I have been friends since after the war, when I met Tig at St Peter's School in Marlborough where I taught briefly while awaiting transportation to the States. After dinner the moonlight ride back over the downs was a rare treat, but we arrived at Axford very late and very tired after a full day.

FRIDAY, JULY 20TH

Tom and Margaret left very early for Stratford-on-Avon to spend the day with Shakespeare. David and I caught the 9.40 bus into Marlborough. The sun was shining brightly when we left but alas! it quickly clouded over and the day became the wettest we have had so far. From the bus we got an excellent view of houses, gardens and fields which from a car are hidden by high hedges. We had several errands, one of which took us into an old shop on the corner of Kingsbury Street as it turns in the High Street. My sister and I used to go there with Mother at Christmastime to buy Christmas cake decorations – crystallized violets, silver balls, tiny fir trees, reindeer and always a little Father Christmas on a laden sleigh. In my mind I could smell the tantalizing aromas of the shop's spices and fruits summoned up by these memories.

With the rain holding off for a brief period, we walked out to Preshute Church. The walk along the Bath Road and over the causeway across the watermeadows was quite nostalgic, but I was sorry to see the lovely horse chestnut trees severely cut back and the river choked with weeds. No fish, no moorhens, no water rats as we used to see. What a peaceful place this little country churchyard is. A hard shower drove us into the church, a small squat structure of flint and stone with the square tower typical of Norman design. Most likely the garrison church in the far-off days of Marlborough Castle, the church stands villageless beside the Kennet. King John was married here to Isabella of Gloucester and the children of his second marriage are thought to have been christened in the big black stone font of unusual design. There are two exceptionally fine brasses set in the floor hidden under matting put down to protect them from the feet of worshippers and visitors. They are dated 1518 and are memorials to John and Maryon Bailey, the Barton farmers of their day. We uncovered them so that David could see them.

After lunch in Marlborough we returned to Axford as the rain had become almost torrential. We had an afternoon of rest and supper at the inn and a jolly party developed with many friends dropping by. This is our last day at Axford and it has proved a good place and a nice experience for Tom and Margaret. I felt it was interesting to get three North Carolinians together all of whom had first come to England as soldiers. Joan is a charming hostess, and Oscar has become locally famous as a host known as 'the Yank from Axford'. Their success and popularity does not entirely make up for all the hard work and the exhausting schedule involved in keeping an inn.

Also I felt it was a real opportunity for the McKnights to see firsthand a sample of ordinary English country people at work and play. One funny incident happened while we were here. We were in the bar shortly after 6 p.m., when only the local regulars were there quaffing their before-supper pints. Tommy, genial and talkative as ever (he is an extremely good ambassador for the United States) entered into the general conversation talking about America and North Carolina. One very old man, who sat pipe in mouth in the chimney corner nursing his tankard of ale, suddenly said in his broad Wiltshire dialect, 'Ah, young feller I were thur 'fore you were barn!' He went on to tell how he had worked in an iron mine in Minnesota and a textile mill in North Carolina. I think it points up that, particularly in the years before World War I, the most surprising English people travelled and lived in many parts of the world.

1975

VIEWS AND VISITS ABOUT MARLBOROUGH – WILTON AND STOURBRIDGE – A DAY IN CHIPPENHAM
SATURDAY, JULY 12TH

En route to Marlborough from Heathrow, we picked up the A4 at Hungerford, then going through Froxfield and Savernake Forest and so to Marlborough. I love the view of Marlborough from the top of the London Road hill as we round the bend by Savernake Hospital.

We passed by my old home as we went to see our friends the Chandlers, where we had tea and all the fattening little delights that accompany it in England. Then we went to the Red Lion at Axford where we will be staying for the next few days.

SUNDAY, JULY 13TH

We were up for a late breakfast, after which I made some telephone calls and arranged meetings with old friends. Then we set off in the car for a little drive around Marlborough. We drove up Stitchcombe Hill, where David took some pictures of the Kennet valley with the Red Lion just visible in the distance. Two white swans were swimming in the river. We went on to Marlborough and thence to Preshute Church. The church cannot be reached by road so we parked the car and walked along the causeway across the watermeadows. Church was just coming out, a pitifully small group of worshippers. The churchyard is well-mown and all the graves well-tended. We returned to the inn at Axford to join several old friends for a dinner of roast pork and after a rest went back to Marlborough for supper with the Chandlers.

MONDAY, JULY 14TH

We were in Marlborough by 10.30 and stopped first at Elcot Lane to see the new premises into which our friends the Chandlers have moved their saddlery business. Here I also met an old friend and neighbour Humphrey Stone, now over 60 and working part-time in retirement. I had not seen him since the war. Always a handsome young man, he has become a good-looking, well-preserved older gentleman. He was a devoted admirer of my sister May, and we talked about her, her long illness and death, and also about his sister Betty, a schoolmate of mine and now an invalid.

The Chandler saddlery is a modern operation of a family business which has been in town for generations. It makes all kinds of leather goods though mostly riding equipment. We found the workrooms and showrooms quite fascinating. There was a pleasant old smell of oil and leather about the place that was somehow distinctive of an ancient trade requiring great skill and dexterity that cannot be entirely duplicated by modern machinery. The nearby racing stables provide much of the Chandlers' business, but their saddles and riding gear go also to Newmarket, England's racing capital, and to markets in Europe, particularly Germany, as well.

We then left for Wilton, the old Saxon town not far from Salisbury at the confluence of the rivers Wylye and Nadder. The morning was cloudy but dry, and the sun occasionally peeped through hinting at a nice afternoon. It is amazing how closely we watch the weather over here!

We took the road up Granham Hill and stopped briefly to admire the view of Marlborough, the College and Preshute Church, the Kennet a silver ribbon winding through the valley. We passed through Pewsey, centred around the headwaters of the Avon and a statue of King Alfred. It brought back memories of my sister May, who lived here most of her married life. We went on through Amesbury and turned off the Salisbury Road just before Old Sarum, taking a very narrow twisting road skirting the edge of Salisbury Plain and leading us into Wilton. Once the capital of Saxon Wessex and site of an important monastery, it gradually lost its importance during the Middle Ages to the 'new' town of Salisbury after a Bishop Bingham built a bridge across the Avon at Harnham which bypassed Wilton. The little town was then unable to compete commercially with her thriving neighbour.

In the streets of the town are many ancient stone houses, long low stores and unexpected narrow alleyways. The church is a surprise for it does not match the rest of the buildings, though it is nonetheless a church of great beauty and distinction. It was built some 150 years ago by Lord Herbert of Lea, a devotee of Italian art, and its Byzantine style is loosely modelled on the Italianate churches of Tuscany and Lombardy. Unlike most English churches, which face east, it has an unusual siting to the south. This is typical of Russian churches, and Lord Herbert positioned the church in this direction out of deference to his Russian mother. The interior is very ornate but dark, with only dim light filtering through coloured panes of stained glass in tall narrow windows. Flanking the altar are effigies of Lord Herbert and his mother, who were members of the Pembroke family from nearby Wilton House.

In the marketplace of the town is a very much older church, long the parish church. After falling into bad disrepair it was partially restored in 1937 through the generosity of the American ambassador Robert Bingham, who wished to honour the memory of his presumed ancestor Bishop Bingham – the very bishop who built the bridge which led to Wilton's decline and who was installed as bishop on the steps of the church. By the door there is a plaque which reads:

> Honouring the memory of his ancestor Robert
> Bingham, consecrated Bishop of Salisbury on this
> spot 27th May AD 1229, Robert Bingham,
> Ambassador of the United States to the Court of
> St James, caused the chancel to be restored. The
> Ambassador who died 18th December 1937 left in
> this country an honoured memory and many friends.

It is always a thrill for me to find in England links with the United States, and this one is special, for Ambassador Bingham was not only a distinguished American but a member of an old North Carolina family. In the Memorial Hall of the University of North Carolina in Chapel Hill, where we are planning our retirement home, there is a plaque honouring

Robert Bingham as a famous alumnus of the university and noting his contributions as ambassador to relations between England and America. It seemed to me a memorable coincidence.

Interesting as the churches are, the main attraction in Wilton is the great house which is the seat of the Earl of Pembroke. We were disappointed that the house was not open, as is often the case on Mondays at England's stately homes. So after lunch at a nice pub called the Greyhound we drove to Stourhead to see the famous gardens there, hoping the Palladian mansion belonging to the Hoare family would be open. We drove along leafy lanes passing through villages with fascinating histories, among them Chilmark, where quarries produced the stone for Salisbury Cathedral and where we saw a signpost for the East Knoyle birthplace of Christopher Wren, and the little stone town of Mere with its famous old inn the Ship.

The gardens at Stourhead were open but the house was not. The gardens are the chief attraction, however. They are very formal and stylized, a perfect example of the eighteenth-century craze for the picturesque. They were laid out beside and around a series of artificial lakes connected by a stream. The pretty little village of Stourhead is incorporated in them. There are many foreign and domestic varieties of trees and shrubs, most of which we could identify only from the visitors guide. Among the trees, and situated in the most favoured spots, are marble statues, pillared temples, arched Palladian bridges and gazebos. Those modelled on Greek architecture are very beautiful, while others like the caves and grottoes are the mere follies which so enamoured the age. There were no flowers except in the village gardens, a big disappointment to David who would have vastly preferred a garden brimming over with blossom and colour. No amount of Greek temples and statues could make up for the absence of flowers in his opinion. For my part, I must confess a certain fascination and satisfaction in the eighteenth-century taming and organization of nature. As we walked around the lake, I envisaged the world of Trollope's novel *The Last Chronicle of Barset*, the basis for the television series 'The Pallisers' which was filmed here and which we recently saw.

The house was built in 1722 by Sir Henry Hoare, a member of a wealthy and prominent banking family. It was designed by Colin Campbell, who followed the plans of an Italian villa. Later the house was altered and added on to greatly, largely to match the gardens designed by Sir Henry's son. Gutted by fire in 1902, it was completely rebuilt. The 6th baronet and his wife lived at Stourhead for 53 years and were greatly loved in the locality for their good works. He handed the property over to the National Trust a year before his death on March 25th 1947. His wife outlived him by only six hours, saying she could not live without him.

Leaving Stourhead in the late afternoon, we drove to Woodborough where we had a dinner date. Woodborough is a rather undistinguished village between Marlborough and Devizes that gained a little importance when the railway came through. We drove into Pewsey for dinner and back to Axford across the downs in moonlight.

TUESDAY, JULY 15TH

We arrived in Marlborough from Axford about 10 o'clock. I stopped to see Jo Chandler, and we drank coffee and admired the additions she and her husband have made to the old house they recently purchased on the London Road. It is a roomy old place, long and low, the outside hung with rosy red tiles. The enormous master bedroom runs the whole length of the house and overlooks the typically English garden where flowers of all kinds grow haphazardly in herbaceous borders. The house was cheerfully cluttered and untidy with books, magazines and children's gear strewn around, but its casual appearance said 'Welcome!' in the friendly English way.

After a short visit we left for our noon date in Chippenham with my cousin Gwen. We headed west along the Bath Road through the Kennet villages and past Silbury Hill, a huge artificial mound of mysterious antiquity which is part of the prehistoric temple at Avebury just to the north. I have climbed the hill in the past with my father but doubt if I could tackle its steep slopes now.

At the Beckhampton crossroads we took the right fork at the great brick house which belonged for many years to the famous racehorse trainer Fred Darling and is still the headquarters of a foremost racing establishment. Here we had to stop to allow a string of horses, some of them quite skittish and excitable, to cross the road. We pulled into a beech copse at the top of a rise to watch more horses exercising and galloping on the short turf of the chalk downs. While watching them a sudden storm blew up, the intense rain blotting out our view, but it was over as quickly as it started.

We drove through Calne and on to Chippenham. It is an old market town mentioned in Domesday Book. It was important in Saxon times because it was given by King Alfred to his daughter Elfrida as part of her dowry. Like so many towns in western England, it once had a thriving woollen industry, though little trace of it remains today.

We drove under the many-arched railway bridge built by Brunel, England's most famous railway engineer, and followed Gwen's directions to Hardenhuish (pronounced 'Harnish') Church. It is an elegant Georgian structure designed by John Wood the younger who, with his father, created some of Bath's beautiful crescents and terraces. Like Lord Herbert's church in Wilton, it looks a little out of place in rural Wiltshire. We turned to the right and shortly after found Gwen's bungalow in Riding's Mead, a modern development with only a name reminiscent of a mediaeval past.

Gwen is my first cousin, daughter of one of my mother's younger sisters. For years she lived a few miles from here in an old farmhouse known as Giddeahall but has sold that and moved to this bungalow typical of the housing that has proliferated in England since the war. Gwen heartily welcomed us. She is a practical nurse and is taking care of a Mrs Weaver, a very old lady from Lacock whose family is away on holiday. This Mrs Weaver is a little bird of a woman confined to a wheelchair but with a lively active mind. She was much interested in meeting us and asked all kinds of pertinent questions about President Ford, U.S. policies, and of course Watergate and Nixon.

Gwen's bungalow has an entrance hall, a good-sized living room, a glassed-in dining room off a modern kitchen, two bedrooms and a bath – a far cry from the inconveniences of Giddeahall, though the old house was certainly long on charm. The garden is small but Gwen, who comes from a farming background, cultivates it intensively.

Gwen also has quite a menagerie of pets, its most notable members two Jack Russell terriers. These small dogs were bred to go down rabbit holes like ferrets. They move like quicksilver, and are very pugnacious. They are popular as pets in country areas but need very energetic masters. Gwen's seem to spend most of their time trying to get at each other, while Gwen spends a lot of hers seeing that they don't. She only has to speak or look at one to send the other into paroxysms of jealous rage. Gwen also has four cats of varying sizes and colours, two birds, and three tortoises who live in the garden in the summer but spend the winter in a box of hay under the bed!

We had dinner when her husband Carl came in from his work in the fields. He is a slow-moving countryman with a real Wiltshire accent, very pleasant and hospitable. The meal was delicious – roast lamb, mint sauce, new potatoes, peas and carrots followed by gooseberry pie and cream. Such an English meal and so much like the way my mother cooked!

Gwen gave us a detailed tour of the garden, explaining everything in minute detail to David. Later she brought out a box of old photographs, and we had lots of fun – tinged with sadness – looking at family pictures of old places and relatives departed this life. Among Gwen's possessions is an artist's representation of Goody Two Shoes which I can remember in the little round house in Erlestoke where my grandmother Sharpe died, though I was only 4 at the time. Gwen also has some furniture and china that belonged to my grandmother.

We left about 4 o'clock after a most pleasant day. We stopped to see if the Bowood Gardens at Calne were open but they were not, so we drove on.

We passed through Calne, another little grey stone town, its economy almost entirely dependent on Harris's bacon factory. Charles Lamb called it 'sweet Calne in Wiltshire'. Over the downs we got a fine view of the Cherhill White Horse with the monument marking the boundary of the Lansdowne estate in the distance. And so on to Marlborough where we joined the Chandlers at dinner to help them celebrate their 39th wedding anniversary. We drank mead, the Anglo-Saxon drink made from honey, and had a lovely meal of boiled bacon and broad beans served especially for me. Surely today saw a surfeit of the English food I love so well but so rarely get!

1977

BRADFORD-ON-AVON – MARKET DAY IN DEVIZES – SAVERNAKE FOREST – ROUNDABOUT WILTSHIRE – A DOWNLAND RIDE

WEDNESDAY, OCTOBER 5TH

Off to Chippenham today to see my cousin Gwen Carpenter. The weather was still unsettled, on again and off again sunshine alternating with brief periods of sharp scudding rain. The downs look especially beautiful in this changeable weather, and when we stopped at our favourite hilltop beech copse we could see racehorses looking like tiny wind-up toys in the vast panorama of rolling fields and hills.

We found my cousin looking as usual bright, bustling and pleasant. She is much confined to the house. Her husband recently retired from the hard life of a smallholder and is increasingly housebound with arthritis, that plague of agricultural workers in Britain's damp climate. She also has assumed the care in her home of a 93-year-old bedridden lady. This type of home care is much encouraged by the National Health Service, and qualified people who undertake it are amply compensated. As a nurse Gwen finds it easier than going out to work, and she appears to have the right temperament for such work. She cares for her dogs, cats, tortoises, husband and invalid guest with great competence, brisk encouragement, and tender loving care.

We left shortly after lunch for Bradford-on-Avon, a very old and unusual town that was once an important and wealthy weaving centre. The houses are built in a series of terraces up the sharply rising banks of the Avon, giving it a Mediterranean rather than English appearance. Certainly it bears no resemblance to an ordinary Wiltshire town. Geographically, the town belongs to the Bath district, and indeed is often called 'little Bath'.

We entered the town down a very steep hill into a maze of narrow twisting roads to cross the river and find a parking place, after which we set out on foot to explore the town. The weather was grey and unwelcoming but at least remained dry. We went first to the little Saxon church of St Laurence, one of the most perfect remaining specimens of this early architecture. It is more than one thousand years old and is thought to have been built by St Aldhelm. It is as high as it is long and twice as high as it is wide with a very narrow chancel arch. Its presence was only realized after an observant clergyman noticed signs of it from a nearby hilltop and insisted on excavations that revealed the church within later built enclosures. Opposite stands the large and beautiful parish church, which is of Norman origin but has been added to and greatly restored. There are some interesting memorials and brasses inside, largely those of prosperous woollen merchants, among them the distinguished Methuen family who originally settled in Bradford but later moved to Corsham. The church is well-located on the banks of the river, and the terraced Georgian houses on the steep banks and hills form a striking background. We obtained a map of the town in the church and from it could see what a well-planned town Bradford is, and how prosperous it must have been at one time.

After tea in a gabled restaurant we drove out to the tithe barn, well-preserved and one of the largest in the country. In the year 1001 Bradford was given to the Abbey of Shaftesbury, and in the fourteenth century the abbess had this barn erected for the storage of crops paid to the church in lieu of taxes. Theoretically a tenth of everything produced had to be given to the church. The barn is enormous, with 14 bays, four projecting gabled porches, and a beautiful hammer-beam roof. To reach it we had to cross a very old pack horse bridge.

Back in town we crossed the main bridge over the Avon, likewise very old, with nine arches and a curious structure built first as a chapel for pilgrims en route from Glastonbury to Malmesbury and later used as the town lockup. There are many fine houses in and around Bradford built by wealthy clothiers. Today cloth manufacture has quite disappeared from the town, but other industries have come and brought their own prosperity.

As we left the sun came out to light up the rows of houses built of the honey-coloured stone native to the district, a quite lovely sight.

THURSDAY, OCTOBER 6TH

Thursday! Market Day in Devizes! We asked Joan Fulk to go with us, and, as she does not drive, she accepted with alacrity. Unfortunately it was raining but we have learned to accept rain with equanimity and carry on with our plans in spite of it.

We had long promised ourselves a day in Devizes on a Thursday. Devizes – the name relates to ancient divisions and boundaries of land – is the English town nearest and dearest to my heart after Marlborough since it is my birthplace. Just before leaving Chapel Hill, we saw the movie of Hardy's novel *Far From the Madding Crowd*. It was filmed in Devizes with supporting actors with authentic Wiltshire accents and whetted our appetite to go there once more. In the film, the hero was stationed at Devizes Barracks, the church in the wedding mix-up was St John's, the girl's coffin was drawn on a farm wagon through the marketplace past the Bear Hotel, and the Corn Exchange was the site of the farmers' selling and trading. The last-named reminded me of the music festivals I attended there as an elementary school pupil.

Devizes lies in the very heart of Wiltshire. It is built on the edge of the high chalk downs that overlook the green and pleasant and very fertile farmland of the Pewsey Vale, on the other side of which lies Salisbury Plain. It is almost in the centre of Wiltshire, and this location has given it much of its past as well as its present importance. At Southbroom, just to the north of Devizes, is a pond known as the Crammer. It is thought by many to be the place where the legend of the Wiltshire Moonrakers was born.

Today the town boasts one of the largest farm markets in the West Country. Since 1609 the market has been held on Thursday, and every week on that day the town is transformed in to a hive of bustling activity. Sheep and wool are brought in by the downland farmers, while from the low fertile valley land comes corn, root crops, cattle, milk and cheese. At a second market, a wide variety of stalls sells anything and everything imaginable. At one time an additional market was held on Mondays. Not very successful, the practice was discontinued but the street where it was held is still known as Monday Market Street.

The town itself goes back to Norman times, and its story really begins with its Norman castle, now unfortunately vanished though replaced by a modern facsimile. The original castle was one of the largest, strongest, and most important in southern England. The castle and the settlement that grew up around it were founded by Roger, a Norman churchman who became a bishop and Chancellor of England under Henry I, successor to William Rufus and third son of the Conqueror. Henry's reign was followed by a long period of civil war between his daughter Matilda (Maud) and his nephew Stephen. During this time Devizes Castle was attacked and besieged several times and was the scene of imprisonments, escapes and mediaeval atrocities before it finally surrendered to Stephen.

In 1142, during these hostilities, Matilda granted the town a royal charter that was later confirmed by Henry II, and the castle became a royal castle. King John was a frequent visitor and it was a favourite hunting retreat for his son Henry III. The castle played little part in the fifteenth-century Wars of the Roses, but in the Civil War between king and Parliament of the seventeenth century both the town and castle of Devizes were bitterly contested. Though many townspeople were sympathetic to the parliamentary cause, the Royalists won an important victory at Roundway on the downland some three miles outside the town. The castle was then held for the king until September 1645, when Cromwell captured the town and demolished the castle with his reorganized, well-trained army. Two centuries later, in 1860, a wealthy entrepreneur named Robert Valentine Leach built himself a country house in the form of a castle on the site of the old fortress. During World War II it housed Italian prisoners of war and has since been converted into flats, but nonetheless its walls and crenellated towers stand to remind visitors of the illustrious past of Devizes Castle.

Devizes went through a period of stagnation after the Civil War, but in the early part of the eighteenth century Daniel Defoe wrote of the town's prosperous cloth industry, which brought with it a spate of new building. Tobacco and snuff manufacturing also supported the local economy. Many mediaeval frame houses were replaced by elegant Georgian buildings as Devizes entered what might be called its 'Golden Age'. There are four particular Georgian houses that are especially charming. They are on a secluded street and share a neat garden in Lansdowne Grove and are said to have been built by the second Marquess of Lansdowne to house his four maiden aunts.

Devizes experienced another great change in 1810 when the builders of the Kennet and Avon Canal reached the town and encountered their greatest engineering challenge. The canal, which was constructed to link the Avon at Bath and the Kennet at Reading and so connect the Thames and the Bristol Channel, was masterminded by John Rennie, a Scottish engineer who was a contemporary of Thomas Telford. Rennie's canal faced a climb of 300 feet from the Avon valley to Devizes atop the downs, a hill that he surmounted by putting in 29 locks in a two-and-a-half mile distance. This flight of locks includes 16 in the Caen Hill area (this name is thought to be a reference to French prisoners from the Caen area of northern France who were imprisoned here during the French wars) and nine more past Devizes and beyond. The others in Devizes itself are very close together. With the completion of the canal, great wharves were built at Devizes. For the next 30 years, the canal was busy with great barges carrying cargoes of food, building materials, and other essentials. But in 1841, another great engineer, Isambard Kingdom Brunel, completed the London to Bristol railway, which bypassed Devizes going instead to the north through Chippenham. The canal then fell into disuse and disrepair, and Devizes experienced another period of depression as it reverted to merely a local agricultural and government centre.

Until recently the town was the headquarters of the one-time Wiltshire Regiment, now amalgamated with the Berkshire Regiment into the Duke of Edinburgh's Royal Regiment. An old Wiltshire ditty that was adopted by the regiment as its marching song gives a wonderful example of the Wiltshireman's accent, dialect, and humour:

'Twere on a jolly zummer's day, the twenty-fust o' May
John Scroggins took his turmut- [turnip-] hoe, wi' thic he trudged away:
Now zome volks they likes haymakin' and zome they vancies mowin' –
But of all the jobs as I likes best, gi'e I the turmut-hoein':

The vly [fly], the vly,
The vly be on the turmut –
'Tis all me eye
Fer I to try
To keep vly off the turmut.

The soldiers of the regiment were housed in huge buildings of red brick on the Marlborough Road known as the Le Marchant Barracks. With the recent disbanding of the regiment, these now stand sadly empty and abandoned in a state approaching dereliction.

Nearby are the more modern and functional buildings of the Wiltshire Constabulary, for Devizes is the headquarters of the county police. Also, for many years the county mental asylum was located here, so that the mention of Devizes conjured up for the ignorant ideas of derangement and lunacy and gave the beautiful town a reputation it did not deserve. Today the elderly and chronically ill are housed and treated in the Roundway Hospital, and it was here that my father died in 1964.

Devizes' main street widens into a spacious marketplace that is the very hub and centre of town. It is surrounded by buildings of several architectural styles, among them some fine Georgian houses (one of which must have been a doctor's house, since it bears a carving of the caduceus, the symbolic serpents entwined around Mercury's winged staff) and the Corn Exchange, its 1856 pediment topped appropriately enough by a statue of the Greek goddess of Plenty. There are also several fine old inns in the marketplace, among them the Black Swan, dated 1737 and much used in coaching days, the Elm Tree, and the Castle. Another inn, no longer in existence, was the Lamb, notable as the billet of General James Wolfe, the 1759 hero of Quebec, when he was stationed at Devizes Barracks to drill and inject a fighting spirit into stolid and apathetic Wiltshire recruits. His father, also a general, is believed to have stayed here en route to Bath to take the waters. At the north end of the marketplace stands the Town Hall and behind it can be seen the tower of St John's Church, a fine Norman building.

Of Devizes' inns, the Bear Hotel deserves special mention, for it holds pride of place among them. Over the centuries the hotel grew haphazardly into an establishment of some size and became noted for its warm welcome and efficiently offered services to all travellers regardless of their condition, circumstances or ability to pay. The Bear's growth and prosperity were due in no small measure to a succession of able and enlightened landlords. Chief among these hosts was Thomas Lawrence, who erected 12-foot-high white posts along the lonely desolate road across Salisbury Plain to guide travellers through the gloom of winter and hazards of snow and storm to the safe haven of Devizes. The posts were inscribed with a 'D' for Devizes on one side and an 'S' for Salisbury on the other for travellers going in the other direction.

Sir Thomas Lawrence, one of England's most famous portrait painters, was the son of this family. Growing up in the Bear, he was a true child prodigy who was able to memorize and recite long passages of poetry and at a young age displayed an ability to sketch and paint remarkable likenesses of any who sat for him. Legend has it that his father would introduce his talented son to hotel guests thusly, 'Gentlemen, here is my son. Will you have him recite from the poets or take your portrait?' Among the notables much taken by the Lawrence family as well as the clever boy was the novelist Fanny Burney on her way to Bath. Fanny was often accompanied by Mrs Thrale, for years the friend and confidant of Dr Johnson. In her journals Fanny noted the beauty and musical skill of the two older Lawrence daughters, but of young Thomas she went on to write:

But the wonder of the family was still to be produced; this was their brother, a most lovely boy of ten years old, who seems to be not merely the wonder of the family, but of the times, for his astonishing skill in drawing. They protest he has never had any instruction, yet showed us some of his productions that were really beautiful. I was equally struck with the boy and his works. We found that he had been taken to town, and that all the painters had been very kind to him, and Sir Joshua Reynolds had pronounced him the most promising genius he had ever met with.

The family left Devizes when Thomas was about 12, and he later attended the Royal Academy school in London. His portraits were noted for their courtliness and social elegance, and it became the fashion among the rich and powerful to have likenesses executed by him. He is best known for his portrait of Mrs Siddons and for the picture of a young girl clad in pink, affectionately known as 'Pinkie'. He was commissioned to paint portraits of persons who took part in the defeat of Napoleon, and these hang today in the Waterloo Chamber at Windsor. In Devizes he is remembered at the Bear in a room named after him, its walls lined with sketches and pictures executed in his youth.

Devizes also has a museum of local history housed in a Georgian house in Long Street. It contains a well-documented collection of archaeological finds and historical artifacts dating from prehistoric days. It was a favourite haunt of my father, who for many years went to Devizes every Thursday. After tiring of the market he would find refuge in the museum and indulge his passion for local history. He knew Mr Cunnington, for many years the curator of the museum and considered him one of the great scholars and historians of Wiltshire.

Today, as always on a Thursday, the town was crowded, and we had difficulty finding a parking place. The rain had stopped, but the weather remained cold and grey. We walked through the covered arcade leading to the open marketplace, stopping en route to buy fish, dog food and homemade goodies from sellers who rent space there. The open marketplace was likewise full of stalls selling everything from flowers and produce to household goods and apparel. Hawkers were crying their wares and housewives with dogs and small children in tow were jockeying for position in search of bargains.

We stopped in Strong's, a bakery in the marketplace to buy a real Wiltshire lard cake, a local delicacy they have produced for many years. I remember my mother talking of buying them when she lived in Devizes more than 60 years ago. Often, too, during my childhood my father would bring one home from his weekly Thursday trip to the market.

David got a good look at the Ruth Pierce monument and took a picture of the plaque telling the story of the woman who died with a lie on her lips – he had entertained some doubts as to its authenticity. Standing in the marketplace almost opposite the main entrance to the Bear, the ornate cross was given to the town in the mid-nineteenth century by a Mr Addington, later Lord Sidmouth, the town's parliamentary representative for 20 years out of the affection he bore the town. Upon erecting it, however, the town fathers immediately attached a stone slab to it on which was engraved the story of an unusual tragedy that had taken place in the marketplace in 1753. The tale is that of Ruth Pierce and three other women from Potterne who together purchased a sack of wheat in the market and were to share its cost. When the time came to pay, one share – obviously Ruth's – was lacking, but Ruth protested that she had paid her contribution and invoked Almighty God to strike her dead if such were not the case. The words were hardly out of her mouth when she did indeed fall dead, with the money found clutched tight in her hand. The monument and her story always attract a great deal of attention and remain as a warning to all future liars, but they have also overshadowed the service of Lord Sidmouth, who became quite forgotten while the humble Ruth became immortalized through the moral lesson of her tale.

Later we had a sherry and buffet meal in the Bear Hotel, standing at the bar cheek by jowl with farmers and dealers clad in tweed jackets and corduroy breeches smelling of damp wool, tobacco and beer – probably Wadsworth's, the favourite beer of Wiltshiremen that is made in Devizes by a brewery that dispenses a rich warm aroma in its vicinity. The men were noisy, vociferous, joking, perhaps clinching deals in their broad accents, all full of the high spirits engendered by 'market day in Vize!'

After lunch we stopped in Tytherleigh's, a beautiful china shop of which my mother sometimes spoke. With its delicate stock and high prices it seemed somehow out of character in the town today given over to agriculture and rural shoppers, yet it has survived and prospered for many years. Then to St John's Church where I was christened and where we met a friendly and informative clergyman. We stopped in a nearby narrow alley lined with half-timbered houses with upper storeys projecting over those below. I bought some nice prints of the church and street in a gift shop, and then after a short visit to Devizes Museum we returned to Marlborough.

In the evening we dined with friends at their cottage on the banks of the canal at a hamlet called Honeystreet. The cottage was one of a number built to house employees of the barge-building business owned by Robbins, Lane and Pinnegar. I have some special feelings about the canal, for my father's family were barge builders at Honeystreet and as a boy my father was apprenticed in the barge shops. When Mother and he were courting and when they were first married they often walked the towpath beside the canal at Devizes, and later they would take their two small girls – my sister and myself – there on fine Sunday afternoons.

Regrettably I have not explored the canal at Devizes in recent years, but should I do so I would find the wharf once more a busy place with shops, restaurants, and a small theatre. In 1962 a trust was established to resurrect and revitalize the canal and make the waterway accessible to holiday makers and pleasure boats. On Good Friday of every year a race for canoeists from all over the world begins at Devizes Wharf and ends at Westminster. It is a gruelling experience that demands great skill and stamina. In addition to the paddling the canoes are portaged around the locks, and sometimes the contestants are attacked by nesting swans who for all too long have had the canal banks and waters to themselves.

After dinner the rain cleared and we drove back to Marlborough across Alton Hill and past the Valley of the Rocks in Lockeridge in bright moonlight.

FRIDAY, OCTOBER 7TH

I had my hair done in a shop in Marlborough High Street, from the window of which I got a fine view of the town fair going up. Later we went to lunch with our old and dear friends Ro and Jess Chandler at the Savernake Forest Hotel, now enlarged, modernized and refurbished since the days we stayed a few weeks there shortly after our marriage in 1944. After a very good meal we took a little walk past what used to be Lady Wright's Riding School and across the canal and railway bridges. The environs of Savernake have changed somewhat since the branch railway line has fallen into disuse. Though express trains still roar through the little station, they no longer stop. Ro was brought up in the forest in a lodge nearby and was able to add details of interest about life there long ago. Her father was a keeper employed by the Marquess of Ailesbury but was killed at Gallipoli in World War I. The marquess allowed her mother and family of six to continue living in the Leigh Hill Lodge, the gatehouse at the Burbage end of the forest on the Salisbury Road.

We then drove to St Katharine's Church, a pretty steepled structure of some size very close to Tottenham House. This was built in the latter part of the nineteenth century by a marchioness named Mary Caroline as a memorial to her mother, the Countess of Pembroke. The marchioness, a daughter of the Herbert family of Wilton House, is buried along with her husband under a massive white cross surrounded by an inscribed curbing. Other members of the Ailesbury family are interred nearby, and inside there is a handsome memorial brass to the marquess given by the clergy of his estates in Yorkshire and Wiltshire. The noble family worshipped here in the old days with all their retainers present at the services. Now I doubt there are ever more than a handful of people in the congregation, and the church today shares a minister with another church also suffering from a falling off of membership. We next drove back to Marlborough down the Grand Avenue, now alas not so grand.

Back in the High Street the work of setting up the fair was going on apace. Dark-skinned swarthy men and heavily-bejewelled women in vibrant colours were setting up rides and stalls, while along the lower side of the street the caravans were drawn up, allowing us occasional glimpses of gipsy domesticity. Marlborough's two fairs, the second a hiring or Mop Fair, have been held in the High Street since the Middle Ages. The privilege to hold the fairs here on the two Saturdays before and after the 11th of October was granted by special charter. The town merchants and residents who live in the High Street would like the fairs moved to the Common, but so far the tradition, bolstered by its charter, has held good, and the fairs – noisy, disruptive and dirty though they may be – remain in the wide High Street.

SATURDAY, OCTOBER 8TH

We woke up to sunshine and felt somewhat encouraged at this improvement in the weather, but it was short-lived as rain started to fall about 9 o'clock heavier than ever. This is sad for the fair people as rain makes their work much harder and drastically cuts their profits.

David drove me up to Cold Harbour to visit with some old friends, Flo and Marjorie Slade. They are sisters, now both retired from long teaching careers in Marlborough and Bath. They are members of an old Marlborough family and proud of the fact that their great-grandfather was a drummer boy at the Battle of Waterloo in 1815. Flo taught me, and I got to know Marjorie when I was teaching for a short while in Bath during the war. They remain active in the life of the town, working tirelessly in church and hospital activities. They are two of my favourite people, and Marjorie is my most faithful Marlborough correspondent. We found as always lots to talk about.

Later we met the Turners for lunch at a very nice inn called The Seven Stars in the village of Bottlesford and then set out on a nostalgic tour of villages in the Devizes area – Alton, Manningford Bruce, Worton, Erlestoke and Great Cheverell – where my parents had lived in their younger days. Our first stop was Urchfont, a pretty village where the houses and towered church cluster about a grass-fringed pond where ducks and swans swim. In a side street we found the Lamb Inn, where an aunt and uncle of mine had lived and where I spent several summers before my aunt died at a relatively early age.

On we then went to Erlestoke, to the little round house where my grandmother had lived with her large family after her husband's early death. My grandparents had left Herefordshire around the turn of the century to come to Wiltshire where my grandfather was the estate manager for a wealthy man named Mr Watson Taylor for two years before dying suddenly of appendicitis. By the grace and favour of Mr Taylor, my grandmother and her family were allowed to live in the cottage. Mr Taylor lived at Erlestoke Park, a great house set in a beautiful park full of rare trees and an ornamental lake that I can dimly remember as covered with exotic waterlilies. Now the mansion has been converted into a prison and the only remaining trace of lake and lilies are a few tall bulrushes. The church, small, not especially old and of no architectural pretension, is opposite the house where we used to visit my grandmother, who died when I was 4. I remember bantam cocks and hens scratching around the door and my father showing me the lake and an enormous tulip tree in the park. In the church, on October 31st 1911, my father Joseph Frank Biggs married my mother Hilda Sharpe – we found the entry in the register – and in the grassy churchyard found the stone memorializing my grandmother Harriet Sharpe and her daughter, my Aunt Nan. My grandfather James is buried in the neighbouring church of Great Cheverell.

Sad and thoughtful, we went on to Worton but could not locate the grange where my mother had worked for a well-to-do couple named Hume. We then headed back to Devizes through Potterne, where I saw the cottage high on a cliff in which the village blacksmith William Burden lived. His wife was an old, old friend of Mother's, and she often had my sister and myself stay with her for a week during our summer holidays. I remember the unmistakable smell of the oil stove on which she cooked and the wonderful food that she produced from it. 'Aunt Beat', as we called her, was very religious, and she took us to interminable Sunday services in the old Norman church so close opposite the cottage that the sound of the bells almost deafened us as they called the villagers to worship every Sunday morning.

The rain, heavy most of the day, curtailed our sightseeing somewhat and saddened my glimpse into the past. We drove home from Devizes with night falling on a stormy sky. We stopped to try to take a photograph in the fading light of the Wansdyke, a mysterious rampart of probable Saxon origin that snakes across the road, through a farmyard, and up and over the downland slope. Sad and downhearted we resolved to have an early night but found an old friend waiting for us at the hotel, and dinner with him lifted my spirits.

In the street outside, the fair was bravely trying to carry on, but the crowds were sparse and the few fairgoers were wet and dispirited. But the show must and did go on till the stroke of midnight.

SUNDAY, OCTOBER 9TH

Up early to sunshine and not a trace of the fair left in the High Street. After a leisurely breakfast we left for a last look at the downs. We leave Marlborough tomorrow and will not return to Wiltshire on this trip.

We started out across the common to Rockley, a tiny isolated village that was the unlikely scene of riots against the introduction of agricultural machinery over a century ago. The downs bisected by the straight Roman road looked especially beautiful in bright sun under a heavenly blue sky dotted here and there with puffy white clouds. We descended the steep escarpment of Hackpen Hill, crossing the grassy prehistoric track known as the Ridgeway at its top. We came to the old market town of Wootton Bassett, where David took a picture of the half-timbered town hall built on stilts in the middle of the street, a reminder of the town's wool-based prosperity before the Industrial Revolution.

We drove around the growing industrial complex of Swindon and passed through many pretty villages, among them Wanborough, its church always a distant landmark for us as children when we drove from Marlborough to Swindon. What makes the rather imposing church unusually interesting is the fact that it has both a tower and a steeple. An unlikely local legend explains that this odd feature resulted from a compromise between the two wealthy sisters who built the church, one of whom wanted a tower and the other a steeple as the church's crowning glory.

A few miles beyond Wanborough we passed from Wiltshire into Berkshire en route for Lambourn. On our right we could see Ashdown House, its high centre flanked by lower wings standing starkly out, its singular early classical shape lonely among its grounds. After years of neglect the house is now in the hands of the National Trust, but unfortunately on this fall Sunday morning it was not open. The building of the house tells a sadly romantic story. It was designed and built for Elizabeth of Bohemia, daughter of James I and his queen Anne of Denmark and wife of Frederick, Elector Palatine and King of Bohemia. This lady, exiled for many years, inspired love in the hearts of many men, among them William, Earl of Craven, who worshipped her from afar. He built Ashdown House for her in the hope that she would one day enjoy its lonely splendour. The Winter Queen, as she came to be known, never did live at Ashdown but she died in Craven's London house and left him many of her possessions and papers which are now, appropriately enough, displayed in Ashdown's rooms. It was a disappointment not to see the interior of the house. We must return in future.

We came next to Lambourn, an old and pretty place noted for its racing stables. As we drove past them we could see horses' heads peering over the half doors of their stalls, but met none on the road and saw none exercising on the gallops – perhaps a concession to Sunday morning tradition. Dick Francis, a successful jockey and even more successful mystery writer, lives here. I eagerly read every one of the books he produces annually in collaboration with his wife.

We saw signs to Uffington and its famous White Horse. This is an area of Saxon and Danish legend, as opposed to Celtic and Arthurian, and we saw signs to Wayland Smith's cave. Wayland – from the Scandinavian Volundr and German Wieland – Smith figured in Scandinavian mythology as a maker of weapons that always brought victory to those who used them. His 'cave' is a remote and mysterious cromlech, and legend has it that any horseman with a mount needing a shoe could leave horse and money overnight nearby and would find in the morning that his horse had been shod. There is also a great sarsen stone nearby with a hole in it, which when blown into supposedly summoned ancient warriors to fight against their enemies. Perhaps ancient Britons responded to its call to resist the Saxons, or the Saxons to resist the Danes – most likely the latter, as this is King Alfred country. I had been here with my father many years ago and today would have liked to have gone again with David, but time was short. I recounted these legends instead of visiting the places of their origin, a poor substitute I fear.

We detoured slightly to go to Inkpen Hill, which at almost 1,000 feet above sea level is the highest point of the chalk downs. It is also the place where Wiltshire, Berkshire and Hampshire come together. The sinister Combe Gibbet crowns the summit, left at first as a warning to would-be criminals and now an interesting anachronism.

We drove through small villages, their houses built of clunch, which is hardened chalk, and their farmyards surrounded by thatched walls of the same material. We then descended into the Kennet valley. As we returned to Marlborough by way of Chilton Foliat, Ramsbury and Axford a sharp rain shower came up and spoiled our view.

Back in Marlborough we had tea with Joan and Oscar. Dinner with the Chandlers then followed, rather too closely for appetite and digestion. We said sad farewells to our friends. Ro and Jess expect to make a trip to the States in the spring, but his health is precarious and we wonder if he will be able to undertake the journey.

1982

HEATHROW TO WILTSHIRE – CHARLTON – A FAMILY REUNION IN BRATTON – SERVICES AT ST JOHN'S IN DEVIZES – KINGTON ST MICHAEL – WILTON – SIGHTSEEING WITH DAVID'S SISTERS – MARLBOROUGH MARKET DAY – PRESHUTE CHURCHYARD – CHURCH IN ST MARY'S – SWINDON – WEST KENNETT LONG BARROW – CALNE AND MILDENHALL

FRIDAY, MAY 14TH

We got out of the environs of the airport quite easily and stopped for an indifferent lunch at a large pub called the Peggy Bedford.

I was quite relieved when at last we reached the exit for Hungerford and the gentler A338, a secondary highway. The Berkshire scenery was beautiful with stretches of downland, pastoral valleys, and tree-enshrouded parks and estates. We saw yellow fields of blossoming rape and smelled its sweetly pungent aroma as we drove along the edges of fields.

We came to Hungerford and instead of bypassing the main street for the road to Marlborough drove through the busy centre of the ancient town. The townspeople here today maintain manorial rights such as common grazing and fishing privileges granted them by John of Gaunt, Duke of Lancaster and third son of Edward III, in the fourteenth century. Outside the town we stopped on the brow of a hill and looked over to the swelling height of Inkpen Down crowned by its ancient gibbet. In the valley we could see the tiny village of Shalbourne clustered around its church and framed by – what else? – a dazzling field of rape. The sky was clear and the air was cool and fresh. At my feet were tiny blue flowers called bird's eye, and the soil was white! I had come home to the chalk country from whence I came.

Driving on we passed through the large villages of Burbage and Pewsey where we took the Devizes Road. From there we could see across the valley to Alton Hill with its fine white horse carved in the escarpment. The valley was a patchwork of greens and browns and bright yellow, the seams of the quilted pattern stitched with the dark green of hedgerows. We stopped at an ancient pub called the Charlton Cat to take a picture of the scene. This old pub has a long history and for me some personal memories. I remember having a meal here with my sister May and her husband Bill. She was then in a wheelchair, and I recall the difficulties getting her in and out of the tiny parlour. It was not long before she died, and it was the last time I saw her with even this limited mobility. I remember too, though I'm afraid imperfectly, something my father told me about the inn sign. Executed by an untrained local artist, it was supposed to be a leopard but turned out looking more like a cat.

The village of Charlton was home to Stephen Duck, one of the so-called 'ploughman poets' of the first half of the eighteenth century. He began his working life as a farm labourer and was almost entirely self-educated. He took to writing verse and eventually came under the patronage of Lady Hertford of Marlborough and to Queen Caroline's attention. He took Holy Orders, but the strain proved too much and he drowned himself in the Kennet in a fit of despondency. He and his poetry are remembered annually at a dinner for threshers held at the Charlton Cat. His verse is read aloud, and 13 men drink from a chalice known as the Duck Goblet. The meal is hosted by the Chief Duck who wears a tall hat decorated with duck feathers. Rent from a field given in Duck's honour in 1734 by Lord Palmerston provides the funds for the feast.

Charlton was among several Wiltshire villages where bloody riots took place when mechanical threshers were introduced to the farms. Farm labourers, poorly paid as they were, feared virtual starvation would follow the loss of their jobs and protested violently against the machines that could replace them.

At last we pulled into the marketplace of Devizes, finding it very busy on the late Friday afternoon. We were lucky enough to find a parking place outside the Bear. Again there was no porter to greet us, and we had to struggle with our bags up the many uneven and unexpected steps of the old inn. David especially had to watch his head on the low ceilings and doorways. Our room looks out on to the marketplace and is well-furnished in keeping with its age, and we are delighted with it.

SATURDAY, MAY 15TH

This reunion of my cousins on my mother's side was the brainchild of Victor Sharpe, who made all the arrangements. He lives in Vancouver, British Columbia, and it seems odd that the one who lives farthest away is the one who made all the plans. Perhaps the need to get back home and meet long separated relatives is greater for those who live abroad.

We woke to a bright sunny morning which augured well for our party. At breakfast local field mushrooms, for which the area is noted, supplemented the bacon and eggs. I found them most enjoyable. I made a hair appointment, and then we set off on a walking tour of Devizes, the town quite crowded with Saturday morning shoppers. We went into a bookstore specializing in books about the local area and talked about the book about Marlborough that I have written and hope to get published. After a light lunch in the bar of the Bear I went to the hairdresser where three delightful girls attended me, one to shampoo, one to set, and one (possibly a learner since she mostly watched) to take the rollers out. They were very interested when I told them I had been born in Devizes, and their Wiltshire accents delighted me. One was slim and blonde with poppy-red cheeks, reminding me of the way I looked when I was a young Wiltshire girl. A lovely yellow Labrador retriever was also in the shop and reminded me of Ginger back in Chapel Hill. 'Labs' are such friendly creatures and so anxious to like and be liked.

After a short rest and nap we set out for Bratton rather chagrined at a sharp little shower in progress. Following directions we drove through many pretty villages, among them Potterne, Erlestoke, Great Cheverell, and Worton. In Bratton we missed the turning to Lower Road but eventually found the house belonging to my cousin Greta, hostess for the party.

Bratton is a good-sized village nestling at the foot of Bratton Down, a steep escarpment at the edge of Salisbury Plain. It is close to the small market town of Westbury, and one of the famous white horses of Wiltshire is cut into the down exposing the chalk underneath. The horse's white figure is quite realistic and positioned well in a fold in the downs. It is perhaps the most famous of all the chalk horses which are the very symbol of Wiltshire and is certainly the oldest in the county. It is believed to mark the site of Alfred's great victory over the Danes in AD 878 in the Battle of Ethandune (sometimes called Edington). After that the Danes were confined to the north and east of England while Wessex and the south remained under Saxon rule.

We were given a warm welcome by my assembled cousins. Two were missing, their whereabouts unknown. Among the company was my Aunt Win, widow of my Uncle Percy. She is an apple-cheeked country lady with a delicious accent and full of country lore long lost to most people today. I have another aunt in Vancouver, also the widow of an uncle, and these two ladies are the sole survivors of my mother's generation.

Greta's 300-year-old home is a commodious farmhouse which she and her late husband bought when they were married and have spent a great deal of time and money fixing up. It is long and low with doorways that were a constant threat to David and Vic who are both over six feet tall. There are steps in unexpected places, uneven floors and very steep stairs, but it exudes charm and looks warm and lived in. The house is set back from the road and hidden from view by a high hedge. Behind there is a big lawn with many flower beds and a large vegetable garden. At the bottom of the garden runs a fast-flowing millstream, its bank covered in spring flowers. Pansies were flowering profusely along borders of rose beds heavily in bud but not yet blooming. In the corner of the lawn was a spreading apple tree covered in pale pink blossoms and just beginning to scatter petals on the grass beneath. On the south side of the house is a greenhouse where seeds are started and tomatoes ripen.

And the food! The last time I saw food even closely resembling today's fare was in 1954 in my Aunt May's tiny stone cottage a few miles away in Ford. Tea today was served about 4.30 along with biscuits and fruitcake, but it was only a preamble to the real meal which followed. We were led to the large table in the kitchen, a groaning board where we found ham, turkey, sausage rolls, quiche, salad, pickled pears, devilled eggs, crusty bread and yellow farm butter. And then the sweets came – sherry trifle, strawberry trifle, fresh fruit and cream, brandy snaps, lemon pudding, and cakes of several varieties, all made by two of my cousins.

What a nice gathering it was, and how grateful we should all be to Vic for masterminding it. I have loved being part of David's family and have always been most welcome, but for once it was nice to be with relatives of my own instead of being the perennial in-law. We left about 12.15 and drove back to Devizes in the clear cool night.

SUNDAY, MAY 16TH

We had breakfast in the Bear dining room about 9 o'clock, an English feast of lambs' kidneys, wild mushrooms, Wiltshire ham and eggs, and thick-cut bitter marmalade, all unusual delicacies for Americans. Afterwards we walked in rain the short distance to St John's Church for Matins at 11 o'clock. St John's is a lovely old church of some size with a tower that still bears cannon shot marks from General Waller's siege of Devizes during the seventeenth-century civil war. Much of the church dates from early Norman times, as seen in its round arches and dogtooth decoration typical of the era's architecture.

We could not have chosen a better Sunday, for today happened to be Rogation Sunday, a celebration of special prayers, litanies and processions held on the Sunday closest to Ascension Day. It is an ancient service recently revived and incorporated into the Church's calendar. On this beautiful spring morning in the old Norman church the mayor and corporation of the town were to process in ceremonial robes and worship with the congregation. The procession was led by the town crier looking like a huntsman in his bright red coat and peaked velvet hat. He was followed by an official bearing the town maces. Next came the mayor, a short grey-haired man clad in a red fur-trimmed robe and wearing a heavy gold chain around his neck, both insignia of his office. Following him were the town councillors in black robes, and bringing up the rear was the bewigged town clerk. For a time before and during World War I, my father worked as a chauffeur for the town clerk of Devizes, then a wealthy landowner named Mr Grant-Meek who had estates at Manningford Bruce and Devizes.

I was disappointed in the music of the service. The reedy pipe organ seemed to be competing with the loud and strident bells, and the choir consisted of four small boys and one young girl. Nonetheless we joined lustily in four familiar hymns, and the rector's sermon was thought-provoking, his diction perfect, and the psalms and chants touched chords of memory in me. An elderly lady sitting next to David assiduously helped him find and keep his place in the order of worship and after the service welcomed us and chatted kindly. We introduced ourselves to the rector as we left the service, and I told him that I had been born in Devizes and christened in his church.

We walked back to the hotel in brilliant sunshine, the morning rain quite dissipated. After lunch we set off for Kington St Michael, a small village near Chippenham for a visit with my cousin Gwen. This is a very old village, part of the royal demesne of early Norman times and, along with its mill, is mentioned in Domesday Book. Old records indicate that the village was decimated by an attack of the plague in 1666, the year following its last great visitation upon London. It is said that grass grew in the main street, so short was the village of able-bodied men. The nearby hamlet of Easton Piercy is the birthplace of John Aubrey, a seventeenth-century antiquary, historian and biographer whose writings tell much about the Wiltshire of his time. Once while out hunting with his hosts from Marlborough, he came to Avebury, where the stones of the great temple fascinated him so much that he undertook extensive research into the prehistoric site, carefully recording his observations. On this sunny Sunday afternoon the countryside was unbelievably beautiful, so much so that my heart ached that I had left it yet was comforted by the reflection that my absence helps me appreciate it all the more when I return.

We found Gwen's house, a small brick attached house in a new development in Kington St Michael known as the Ridings. I wondered if the name had mediaeval connotations. We approached it through a greenhouse and tiny fenced garden as pretty as any. At long last the British have learned how to build small houses with modern conveniences such as central heating and efficient use of space. Gwen and her husband Carl are comfortable and content there, though he is very sick with cancer and makes great demands on her. But Gwen is Gwen – 'our' Gwen as her younger brother Philip calls her in his broad Wiltshire accent – calm, serene, efficient and uncomplaining. I envy her composure as I admire her fortitude and acceptance of their situation. She has the grey hair and sharp features of the Sharpes and looks very much like her mother. I can also see a resemblance to my mother.

She produced some very old photographs of the Lane family – Lane was Grandmother Sharpe's maiden name – and we spent some pleasant time looking through them. Grandmother was the oldest of several girls and probably had the hardest life, since she was widowed and left with nine children to raise. One faded photo showed her with three children – Edie (who died at the age of 10), my mother Hilda as a toddler, and my Uncle Jim as an infant in her arms. After a cup of tea we left feeling sad for Gwen. Of all my cousins I feel closest to her.

On our way to Pewsey we next drove along a road through a vale of rich agricultural land at the foot of the downs and passed two white horses cut into the green hillsides. The sun was shining brilliantly from a bright blue sky, the rain sprinkles of the morning completely gone. Every little cottage flaunted the bright colours of many flowers, and every village seemed a cluster of houses around a towered or steepled church. We saw big houses – every village boasts several – small schools and of course the pubs which seem to have superseded the churches as centres of village life.

We reached Pewsey about 5.30 where we had arranged to call on Nessa and Tig Turner, friends from my teaching days in Marlborough. We were just in time to share the last cup of tea. We sat in the garden under a blossoming apple tree and met Annee, the Turners' French daughter-in-law, her mother visiting from Paris, and two little granddaughters named Stephanie and Jessica. The Turners' young son Paul was there too. We saw for the first time and admired the small bungalow which Nessa and Tig have bought for their retirement and old age. They seem happy and content.

We drove back to Devizes in the lee of the downs – a lovely ride in the westering sun. The rounded curve of the chalk lay against the sky paradoxically hard yet soft, harsh yet gentle, and quite peculiar to the county of chalk and cheese, sheep and corn. We had a light supper in the Lawrence Room back at the Bear and then to bed after a lovely day.

WEDNESDAY, MAY 19TH

Entering Wiltshire from Dorset we passed segments of the great walls of the 'Gothick dream palace' which William Beckford began building in 1796. Beckford celebrated Britain's 1798 victory over the French at the Nile with Nelson and Lady Hamilton in the partially completed mansion, but the megalomaniacal enterprise was never finished. The central tower collapsed, and Beckford lost much of his money and retired to Bath. Only a few sections of wall and a gateway remain of the vast project.

We passed through the village of Fovant on the edge of Salisbury Plain. Here soldiers stationed during and between the world wars cut their regimental badges into the green turf exposing the white chalk beneath. Australian soldiers left a map of their land and a huge kangaroo pale against the downland.

A short while later we arrived at Wilton, the stately home belonging to the earls of Pembroke. The great grey stone mansion, entered through imposing gates atop which stands an equestrian statue of Marcus Aurelius, is built on the site of a Saxon religious house. When Henry VIII dissolved the monasteries he gave the land to the Welsh knight Sir William Herbert, who was later created Earl of Pembroke by Edward VI. Herbert married the sister of Catherine Parr, Henry's last wife, and became the progenitor of one of England's most distinguished families. In 1573 Queen Elizabeth visited Wilton, finding it a 'merry and pleasant' place. She left a lock of her hair which, hidden in a book, was not discovered till years later.

Herbert was related by marriage to Sir Philip Sidney, the soldier-poet who epitomized Elizabethan chivalry. Sidney is believed to have written much of *Arcadia* at Wilton. Other writers, Shakespeare possibly among them, also met at Wilton House, in keeping with the custom of rich families encouraging and sponsoring the arts. It is believed that either *Twelfth Night* or *As You Like It*, or perhaps both, may have been produced here for the first time. Shakespeare's statue stands in the front hall to remind visitors of his associations with Wilton.

After a fire partially destroyed the Tudor house in the seventeenth century, the mansion was restored and enlarged to the plans of Inigo Jones and his son-in-law John Webb. They designed the elegant Double Cube Room with its impressive 60 ft × 30 ft × 30 ft dimensions. The house is built in the form of a huge square around a central courtyard and is filled with one of the finest private art collections in England. It numbers Vandykes, Rembrandts, Rubens, Lelys and Dürers among its treasures. The collection was begun by an earl living in the time of Charles I, who, we are told, was fond of the excellent trout fishing in the chalk streams of the valley.

During the war Wilton was the secret headquarters of the Southern Command, the nerve centre where invasion plans were made. Fortunately the secret was well-kept and the house never bombed, for the famous art was never removed. In the cloister we saw Winston Churchill's painting of the Palladian bridge over the River Nadder which flows through Wilton's grounds. Perhaps General Eisenhower, another amateur artist, also drew some inspiration from the Old Masters all around him. Wilton also houses an impressive collection of armour which includes the suit worn by the Earl of Pembroke when he fought with the Spanish against the French during the reign of Mary Tudor.

Just as the spacious close adds to the beauty of Salisbury Cathedral, so the grounds of Wilton frame the mansion. The park is noted for its spreading Lebanon cedars, and there are fine oaks and horse chestnuts, both pink and white, in bloom at this time of year:

> The stately homes of England!
> How beautiful they stand,
> Amidst their tall ancestral trees,
> O'er all the pleasant land.

Of England's stately homes, Wilton is certainly among the finest.

We took tea in the restaurant and had the pleasure of seeing the present earl drive up and greet some of the sightseers. We then drove back to Marlborough by way of Salisbury. In Marlborough we checked in at the Castle and Ball, the old coaching inn in the High Street now run as a Trust House. Our room is not as nice as the one we had in the Bear, though it is considerably more expensive. After phoning and seeing some of our friends, we were in bed fairly early to get ready for a long day tomorrow.

THURSDAY, MAY 20TH

We were up at 5.30 for our 60-mile trip to Stratford-on-Avon to meet David's two sisters, both widows from Greensboro, North Carolina, who are in England on a tour. We had arranged to pick them up in Stratford and bring them back to Wiltshire to show them places meaningful to David and myself.

After tea and biscuits in our room, we got downstairs only to find the gates to the High Street still locked, so we were delayed a bit getting out the back exit. It was beginning to get light on a wet misty morning. The sun never did appear, but somehow the downs looked very right and English in the fog and drizzle. The roads were deserted, and we made good time on the straight Roman road to Swindon, though there we missed a turn causing another slight delay. We reached Stratford without further trouble and found Jane and Betsy's tour group at breakfast in the Hilton Hotel – very posh and American, a far cry from the Stratford Shakespeare knew. We joined the group for breakfast, very good but no bargain at four pounds each.

The four of us then set out for Marlborough via the Cotswold country, going through the Gloucestershire show villages of Broadway and Bourton-on-the-Water. We stopped in the latter and walked along the clear sparkling waters of the Windrush running alongside the main street of the village. Quaint old houses and shops built of the yellow stone which is the hallmark of the Cotswolds line the street.

We went on towards Cirencester driving along stretches of the old Roman road known as the Fosse Way. We did not go into Cirencester itself but could plainly see the great tower of its famous 'wool' church. Cirencester was an important military town in Roman days and in the Middle Ages became the centre of a thriving wool industry supplied by the sheep of the Cotswold Hills. We drove for miles along a road paralleled by the immense walls of Cirencester Park, created by Lord Bathurst in the early part of the eighteenth century. This nobleman was an enthusiastic gardener and landscaper who mingled art and utility in his vast projects. He was a friend of Alexander Pope, and the poet's letters to him and others praise Bathurst's 'great and noble works, worthy of a large mind and fortune.' We named the trees and bushes – many flowering profusely at this time of year – identified wildflowers, talked of crops and explained odd bits of history for our guests.

We passed into Wiltshire and the true chalk downland a few miles north of Swindon. We proceeded through Marlborough on the wide High Street, past the college to Avebury. Jane and Betsy were quite amazed at the huge sarsen stones of the ancient temple, and I endeavoured to tell them as much as I could of its history and purpose. We had a drink in the Red Lion, the inn in the very heart of the village and temple, but decided it was too crowded for lunch. So after a browse in the National Trust gift shop we drove the mile or two to Beckhampton for a pub lunch in the old coaching inn called the Waggon and Horses.

Next we drove around the villages of the Pewsey Vale, Oare, Pewsey, Burbage and into Savernake Forest. We pointed out the little hotel in the forest and the keeper's house where we had spent a few weeks early in our marriage. We then went on to Tottenham House, ancestral home of the Marquess of Ailesbury, where David had been billeted while on duty in the forest. The long straight drive to the mansion is now pitted and rutted. Even at slow speed the car scraped bottom, and when a lone cyclist appeared Jane had to tell David to keep left instead of right. The house, no longer the residence of the now impecunious Marquess, is instead a prep school for boys, but it appears dilapidated and in disrepair. To the left we saw horses and foals grazing in meadows where herds of deer once roamed. The forest, though still beautiful to people seeing it for the first time, shocks me today, for it is quite unlike the great green park full of towering beeches and sturdy oaks that I remember. It is distressing to see giant beeches lying fallen on the ground with the rotting centres of their silver trunks obscenely exposed. The famous Grand Avenue is no longer like a green nave in a forest cathedral but like any other tree-lined country road, while Iron Gates, the avenue's stately entrance, stands rusting and derelict, its stone walls and pillars broken and crumbling.

We drove back down London Road – such a lovely view of Marlborough – past my old home, into the High Street, past the Castle and Ball and on to see Ro and Jess Chandler, who warmly welcomed our visitors. We walked through St Mary's churchyard and into the church where we were married, meeting the rector there and telling him our story. We then went on to Herd Street to see the Fulks, now retired from the Red Lion at Axford where we have spent so many happy times. Their house in Herd Street is a fine example of a very old house restored, renovated and appropriately decorated with antique furniture and treasures. Joan's pug Charlie complements her own sleek and suave appearance and manner, while Oscar, his accent a strange mixture of the American southern drawl and the broad tones of Wiltshire, seems the odd one out in the trio.

Joan served us tea in the correct English way, after which we set out on the return trip to Stratford. Again as we drove we pointed out sights of interest. Occasionally the sun peeped out with the rain falling lightly off and on. It was clear enough to see something of the valleys and hills, the chequerboard patterns of fields and hedges, and the rape fields adding patches of brilliant yellow to the kaleidoscope of greens and browns. When we reached the Cotswold town of Burford we stopped and found an ancient inn called the Bull. It was a happy find – after drinks in the bar panelled in dark oak we had a delicious meal quickly and graciously served. The menu offered English cuisine at its best – steak and kidney pie, mixed grill, roast beef, and grilled trout, followed by a dizzying array of desserts.

We made it to Stratford and left Jane and Betsy at their hotel about 8.30, and we set out again for our return to Marlborough in a dark and drizzling night. Fortunately we met little traffic and made good time, but we were both very tired when at last we reached the Castle and Ball. We had driven well over 300 miles, a long way for an American driver on the narrow twisting roads of England. But it had been a most rewarding day and an unusual opportunity for a get-together with our American family in Marlborough.

MAY 21ST–MAY 26TH

We remained in Marlborough for the rest of the trip, seeing friends, visiting and revisiting places of local interest, and spending a good deal of time driving along the country roads of Wiltshire. To avoid repetition of places and activities, I include only a few excerpts from my journal of these days.

Wednesdays and Saturdays are market days in Marlborough. Stalls are set up in the wide High Street where local farmers sell their produce and travelling cheapjacks, flea market operators, and craftsmen set out their wares. Buyers are out early and in force to hunt for bargains and get the best buys. On this sunny Saturday morning we enjoyed walking up and down, inspecting what was for sale, and watching both the local people and those in from the surrounding country. Since Britain's entry into the Common Market, the greengrocers' stalls present a lesson in practical geography, with local produce now supplemented by new potatoes from France, oranges from Cyprus, strawberries from Spain, and grapefruit further afield from North Africa. Even Wiltshire Moonrakers are eating internationally these days!

By 1 p.m. the stalls in the High Street had all been taken down and the space as usual was filled with parked cars. After lunch we walked out to Preshutes Church. Looking around at the graves of centuries past, one experiences a sense of timelessness, a feeling that our greatest concerns are unimportant and infinitesimal in the universal scheme of things. Chestnut trees, the river with its moorhens and water rats, the often submerged meadows, the small church with its sturdy tower, the churchyard white with snowdrops or daisies, the ancient yews, the moss- and lichen-covered gravestones sunken and tilted with age – all make up a picture I hold forever in my mind.

On Sunday we went to church for a service almost a repeat of that which we attended last week in Devizes, for the Marlborough mayor and town corporation were to attend in full official regalia. We were there early, and while David remained outside to take pictures I went in and sat in a pew that I found extremely uncomfortable, something I had forgotten or else did not notice when I was young. The procession came up the aisle led by the town crier wearing his blue ceremonial dress; then came the mace-bearers, and the mayor robed in fur-trimmed scarlet followed by his black-clad councillors. The churchwardens came next and took their places in the front pews as the rector began the service. The congregation was sparse and the sermon short, but the hymns were sung with vigour with the national anthem added because of the Falklands War. For me the use of the revised liturgy spoiled the service. Perhaps modernizing it makes it more readily understood, but it also discards the beauty and cadence of language, and I craved for the familiar words of the past. I felt a stranger and only saw two people I knew. Afterwards, however, we had coffee in the church hall where our friend David Chandler, one of the town councillors, introduced us to the mayor and other important people.

Early Monday morning we picked up Joan Fulk and drove to Swindon, the only industrial town of any size in Wiltshire and the best place in the county for the shopping Americans want to do while in England. The ride to Swindon across the downs is one I never tire of. Off to the left I saw the houses of the Ogbourne villages built around their churches and on the right, carved into the swelling downs, the lovely golf course of a Swindon club. Swindon has changed greatly since the war. Regent Street has been transformed into a shopping mall known as the Brunel Centre, named for the brilliant engineer of the Great Western Railway who made Swindon the nerve centre of that line and built it into an important industrial city. David went off to browse in the Railway Museum, which he found of great interest, while Joan and I shopped, buying mainly gifts for me to take home. We went into McIlroy's, a large department store, which brought back some memories for me. It was indeed a rare treat when as a child I was taken to McIlroy's to buy a dress or coat and to have tea in the restaurant there. We met David at the car about 1 o'clock, stopped at the Plough Inn for lunch and then went on to Richard Jefferies' birthplace, now a museum but unfortunately closed today.

Late in the afternoon we drove out along the Bath Road as far as Silbury Hill, parked the car and took the long walk across the downs to the West Kennett long barrow. It was a long uphill pull over a rough and rutted track, and I kept a wary eye on nearby cows. But the object of our climb was well worth the effort involved. The Kennet valley contains about 20 of these long barrows, which are thought to be the burial places of the ruling families of Neolithic tribes. This is one of the most accessible as well as the largest, measuring about 300 feet long, 100 feet wide and 20 feet high. It is built of the sarsen stone found in quantity in nearby Lockeridge, with a dry walling of oolitic stone. A gallery leads to a single chamber inside containing many burial sites. It is a gloomy place, cold and dank inside, and I was glad to get outside.

From the entrance there was a fine view of Silbury Hill and the sweep of chalk downland unbroken except for clumps of beeches planted as windbreaks. We walked back to the car finding it easier going down but still keeping a weather eye open for the cows, who seemed to move with us. We then drove around the Avebury circles and as far as we could up Windmill Hill along a heavily rutted track marked 'Unsuitable for Motors'. This was the home of the ancient 'Beaker' people – so named for their skill in pottery – and now is the site of extensive archaeological excavations that have uncovered much pottery, jewellery and weaponry, most of which is now in Devizes Museum.

We met Joan and Oscar in the Conservative Club for drinks and then drove to Calne for lunch at the Lansdowne Arms. We saw no racehorses at Beckhampton as we usually do but got a fine view of the Cherhill White Horse cupped in the green folds of the downs. On the horizon we could see the tall obelisk of the Lansdowne monument piercing the sky.

The little stone town of Calne has received a major economic blow with the closing of Harris's bacon factory due to family decisions and economic problems. The processing of bacon and related pork products started here in 1770 when the first shop was opened by Sarah Harris to sell her home-cured bacon and sausage. The operation grew rapidly, especially after the introduction of American methods of refrigeration. The factory came to dominate the town and was always the major employer. It was granted a warrant as a provisioner to the royal family in 1929. Now the great buildings stand empty and idle, but Calne's gardens today still blossomed bravely in the spring sunshine. The big old hotel called the Lansdowne Arms has received a facelift and some modernization. The hotel is named for the local peer, the Marquess of Lansdowne whose ancestral home, beautiful Bowood, is just outside Calne. We had an excellent meal there, and there were many customers, mostly farmers and local folk from the area racing industry.

We returned to Marlborough and picked up Ro and Jess Chandler and drove out to Littlecote near Hungerford, hoping to get into the lovely Tudor mansion which has recently been opened to the public. It was closed, however, so we had to settle for admiring the rosy-red brick house set in beautiful gardens from afar. The house has a long history of war, murder and intrigue, and is said to be haunted. A Roman mosaic has been uncovered nearby, and we were able to see this. We then went on to the village of Mildenhall, which was the site of a Roman settlement known as Cunetio. Here we stood on a bridge over the Kennet and looked into Black Field, where ploughing has uncovered many Roman coins and other artifacts. We returned to Marlborough along the narrow lane known as Chopping Knife which follows the lee of the hill marking the edge of Savernake Forest.

1983

with the West Side Presbyterian Church Choir of Ridgewood N.J.

STONEHENGE AND SALISBURY – BRATTON AND EDINGTON

MONDAY, JULY 11TH

It was a very hot night in Bath, and we awoke to the threat of a very warm day ahead for the long journey to London. Our last view of Bath was of the lovely city of golden stone sweltering in an early morning heat haze, its houses rising up the terraced hillsides that surround it. At a distance and half-hidden in the mist, its beauty lay unmarred by the rubbish and graffiti that to my shock and dismay the carnival weekend had produced. Even though I suppose I am by now more American than English, I still want my native country to look its best and to give foreign visitors no cause for criticism or complaint.

We drove through a corner of the county of Avon – Bath used to be in Somerset but in 1974 it became part of Avon – into Wiltshire en route to Stonehenge. I was born and brought up in Wiltshire but further north than where we went today. This southwest corner of Wiltshire has creamy stone buildings, lush meadow land, great trees, and leafy lanes. Old towns such as Westbury and Warminster owed their early prosperity to wool manufacture.

From this 'cheese' country, we passed into the 'chalk' country formed by the high exposed plateaux of the Salisbury Plain and the Wiltshire Downs of rounded hills stark against the ever-changing sky. The downs are treeless except for occasional clumps of beech trees planted as windbreaks. Their turf is so closely cropped by sheep that the white chalk soil is often exposed. Such are the 'downs', which are not down but up, and known, loved and remembered by Wiltshire folk wherever they may be.

We drove up the steep hill from the valley to the escarpment that is the edge of Salisbury Plain, the chalk plateau which was home to early man through the Palaeolithic, Neolithic, Bronze, and Early Iron ages. Here on the high bare uplands he was safe from the marauding wild animals of the valleys, while in the chalk he found bands of hard yet malleable flint to chip and fashion into rough weapons and utensils. Here he buried his dead in the grassy mounds known as barrows, providing them with articles he must have considered essential in the life hereafter. And here he built his mysterious temples of which Avebury in northern Wiltshire and Stonehenge in the south are prime examples.

Everyone in the bus was bemoaning the fact that owing to vandalism the stones of Stonehenge are off-limits to the public and can only be viewed at a distance from behind a fence. Actually, I thought the restrictions an improvement, for instead of seeing the stones surrounded by people one now sees them more nearly as they originally were – silhouetted against the downland sky, lonely, remote, and mysterious, and evocative of early man's need to reach out to a Supreme Being he could articulate in no other way. I have seen Stonehenge many times, but my first view of its pristine isolation behind its ditch and vallum on the far reaches of the plain is my clearest and best-remembered. Thus Tess must have seen it in her agony in Hardy's novel and also Samuel Pepys, who wrote that 'it was prodigious so as to fright me to be alone in it at night.' In spite of recent theories based on solar and astronomical data, the stones and the adjoining burial sites remain an enigma.

Leaving Stonehenge we drove the 10 miles or so to Salisbury, passing Old Sarum on our right. Sarum is the Latin name for Salisbury, and Old Sarum was first a prehistoric settlement, then a Roman fort, and then a small town that was finally abandoned in the Middle Ages. It remained, however, one of the infamous 'rotten' boroughs that continued sending representatives to Parliament until the passage of the Reform Bill in 1832 eliminated this practice. The foundations of a sizeable cathedral had already been laid – and can still be seen – at Old Sarum when Bishop Poore decided in 1102 to leave the hilltop site because of an inadequate water supply.

Salisbury has at its heart the glorious grey stone cathedral with the highest spire in the country, a landmark that can be seen for miles. This jewel of a cathedral is greatly enhanced by the velvet green lawns of a spacious close. On the far side the cathedral green merges into the watermeadows of the Avon, the view that Constable painted.

We wandered around the cathedral in silence. We admired the old stained glass as well as the more recent blue windows at the east end. We noted the lovely sculpture of the many tombs and walked in the cool serenity of the cloisters in the centre of which huge Lebanon cedars grow. We saw with dismay that the marble pillars supporting the spire have buckled under its weight and noted the efforts underway to strengthen them and save the spire. We grouped on the chancel steps and sang 'Come Ye Who Love the Lord', while a canon of the cathedral played with and for us. Later Jack and Cathy played the great organ. Salisbury is my favourite cathedral – perhaps because I have visited it more often than any other, perhaps because I was confirmed by its bishop, or perhaps because I really do think it is the most beautiful. I was happy this day to see it again in the company of so many of my friends. As choristers and music lovers we were happy to learn that Handel had written part of 'Messiah' in Salisbury.

LATE JULY

We had an overnight stay with my cousin Greta in Bratton and while there we visited the neighbouring village of Edington to see what is thought to be the finest country church in Wiltshire. This miniature cathedral, built in the fourteenth century by one William of Edington, Bishop of Winchester, is a cruciform building with a massive central tower. It was built near a monastery belonging to Augustine monks of the Bonhommes order, a monastery that was sponsored by no less a personage than the Black Prince, knightly son of Edward III. The monastic buildings fell into ruin at the Dissolution, though traces of them remain. In the churchyard there is an enormous yew tree that reminded me of the one we saw at Selborne in 1977.

The interior is large and beautifully proportioned with a cool uncluttered atmosphere. There are many interesting tombs and a rood screen intricately carved in wood. There is a monument to Sir Edward Lewys, who died in 1630, and his wife Lady Anne Beauchamp. They lie side by side on a high table tomb while the figures of five of their children kneel in grief. Above is carved:

> Since children are the living cornerstone
> Where marriage built on both side meetes in one
> While they survive our lives shall have extent
> Upon record in them our monument.

One of the stained glass windows is very old, an original depicting the Crucifixion. It is very dark but its colours glow richly.

In 1449 a terrible murder took place at Edington. A group of Wiltshire yokels broke into the church while Thomas Ayscough, Bishop of Salisbury, was at the high altar in the very act of celebrating mass. They dragged him away, took him to the top of a nearby hill, and dashed his brains out. It is thought that the men may have been incensed by the rural disturbances which preceded the short-lived 1450 Kentish rebellion of Jack Cade. In 1629 a happier event took place in the church. George Herbert of Bemerton, priest, scholar, poet and musician, was married to Jane Danvers of a locally prominent family. It seems appropriate that in modern times Edington hosts an annual music festival in which choirs from all over the country participate.

Once a year Edington also plays host to the parishioners of the tiny isolated village of Imber in the far reaches of Salisbury Plain. It was destroyed during the war by army gunner training. The villagers were scattered but rare church services are still held in what is left of the village as well as the annual one at Edington.

1985

BOOK-SIGNING IN MARLBOROUGH – RADIO INTERVIEW IN BRADFORD-ON-AVON – VE DAY IN MARLBOROUGH AND RAMSBURY – GLOUCESTER – SPEAKING TO THE WOMEN'S INSTITUTE

[This trip was dictated by the publication of *Recollections of a G.I. War Bride* in late 1984 and included a book-signing at the White Horse Book Shop in Marlborough; interviews and photography sessions with newspaper reporters; a visit to publisher Alan Sutton in Gloucester; several talks to local organizations; and a radio interview in Bradford-on-Avon. We stayed with Oscar and Joan Fulk in their charming house in Herd Street, and I met with many friends and acquaintances from the past who seemed well-pleased with my descriptions of life in Marlborough between the two wars and during the second. All these activities cut into our time for sightseeing and visiting in other parts of England, though we managed to fit in visits to see a cousin in Wyke, Dorset, and friends in Suffolk. From Ipswich we drove west along the south coast as far as Sidmouth before returning to Marlborough.

The spring timing of this visit also distinguished it from our usual high summer or early fall trips. The April and May weather, unfortunately, was quite disappointing, wet and cold most of the time, though the spring flowers, nothing daunted, were quite magnificent.

It was only after we arrived in England that we realized we would be in Marlborough on May 8th, the 40th anniversary of VE Day, to be marked by solemn military ceremonies of remembrance in every small town and village and an occasion that would make my small chronicle of those times doubly appropriate. Unfortunately I arrived with a very bad cold that plagued me most of the time we were in England.]

SATURDAY, APRIL 27TH

We were warmly welcomed on our arrival in Marlborough by Joan and Oscar Fulk, in whose charming house in Herd Street we will be staying. After a good meal and much exchange of news we climbed the narrow twisting staircase of uneven steps to our low-ceilinged bedroom under the eaves. We slept in featherbedded comfort and woke to blue sky, bright sun and an apple tree heavy with blossom waving its pink branches outside our window. In the distance we heard the bird that is the true herald of the English spring – 'cuckoo, cuckoo, cuckoo'.

At 10 o'clock in the morning I appeared at the White Horse Book Shop in the High Street for a book-signing. It was a new experience for me, heady and fascinating. It was a thrill indeed to come back to Marlborough after 40 years to be greeted as something of a local celebrity. I was very busy all morning meeting friends and others I had known in the past, some of whom I could recall and some of whom were now strangers. My small book is one among many about Marlborough in the store, for there is apparently today a great interest in books about particular localities, and many beautiful and informative books have been written for local consumption. My work's greatest attraction seems to be that it is about Marlborough in the twenties and thirties and speaks for all G.I. brides from the town and area and their adjustment to life in the U.S.A.

MONDAY, APRIL 29TH

After spending yesterday at morning services at St Mary's and visiting cousins in Bratton and Kington St Michael, we were on our way out of Marlborough early today for a 10 o'clock radio interview in Bradford-on-Avon. We had been told to meet our interviewer outside the small Saxon church of St Laurence. It was cold and windy, and I got quite chilled waiting. My voice turned husky, and it was quite apparent that I was suffering from a very heavy cold. Bradford, which on a sunny day is a most attractive town, looked grey and uninviting. We had some time to wait, but eventually a lady with a microphone turned up, and I was interviewed then and there on the bridge over the Avon. I answered lots of questions about my childhood in Marlborough and life in the U.S.A. and what prompted me to write a book about my experiences. I never did hear myself on the radio, but friends who did said I came across quite well.

When it was over we walked across the old three-arched bridge into the main part of the town. Men wearing high hip waders were working in the river, and I thought how much colder they must have been than I was. We took refuge from the cold in the old and historic Swan Inn. Its Georgian facade has been added on to a much older part, behind which is an open space once known as the Bull Pit, a yard given over years ago to the cruel sport of bull-baiting. In the bar sitting by a blazing fire, a whisky and soda followed by a good meal restored me somewhat so that I felt much better on the drive back to Marlborough.

WEDNESDAY, MAY 8TH

We were at the Marlborough War Memorial at 11 o'clock for the very simple wreath-laying ceremony performed by members of the British Legion. My old friend Philip Garside officiated as president of the local legion branch. Though his voice was drowned out in the bitter wind and noise of traffic, he offered a few words of gratitude for victory and remembered those who gave their lives in its cause. A similar ceremony will be held in August for VJ Day, but the main tributes will come on Remembrance Day, the Sunday following November 11th. David, Oscar and myself were the only Americans present, and afterwards we studied the names engraved on the memorial of the fallen from both wars. Many of them were known to me, and some from World War II had been friends or schoolmates.

We then walked across the Green to the Legion Club where many had gathered to continue reminiscing, mostly asking 'And where were you on May 8th 1945?' Quite a few were on their way to the Pacific theatre of the war and knew nothing of the victory for several days. These Marlborough men served their country in varying capacities, and all were wearing medals and ribbons indicating the campaigns they were involved in. Several wore a heavy gold medal hanging below the others – this was presented by the French government to men who served in the British Expeditionary Force in September 1939 and were involved in the Dunkirk evacuation. One man, Chappie Green, wore an oak leaf cluster on one of his ribbons, indicating a mention in Dispatches for special service. John O'Keefe, now the chief coxswain on the *Queen Elizabeth II*, wore the medal and blue-green ribbon of England's most recent war in the Falklands.

We had a good lunch in the Wellington Arms with Oscar and Joan after which David and I drove to Bowood, home of the Marquess of Lansdowne on the Bath Road between Calne and Chippenham. It somehow seemed appropriate on VE Day to visit a stately mansion of a family that had helped make England great and to see their way of life that was twice in a lifetime saved by the heroic sacrifices of ordinary Englishmen. The Lansdownes made their sacrifices too – the seventh marquess was killed in Italy in 1944 just a few days after his younger brother died in France. And in World War I the fifth marquess lost his younger son at Ypres in 1914.

The weather had warmed up a little and the wind had dropped. We turned off the road into the drive leading to the house, a drive through deep woods carpeted with bluebells and starred with primroses. We saw many pheasants, generally in pairs, the cocks in bright springtime plumage. The house is surrounded with velvety lawns that slope down to a shimmering lake. They are dotted with immense oaks, beeches, chestnuts and several superb Lebanon cedars. Daffodils were blooming abundantly, some planted in formal beds but many more growing naturally as if wild. A series of terraces with ornamental flower beds frame the house. Roses were in bud and will be spectacular in a few days. In the distance we could see a Greek temple, one of the follies of eighteenth-century taste.

The house itself is one of the smaller of England's stately mansions, deliberately made so by a former marquess. It nonetheless is an example of pure architectural symmetry. The rooms on display are very fine and because of their smaller size are less grand and more intimate than those in many great mansions. The family has amassed a fine collection of art, and there is a display of watercolours of Oriental scenes painted by a Major-General Matthew Gosset. The walls of the chapel are hung with priceless pictures of Biblical scenes. In another room we saw the collections of valuable objets d'art presented to a marquess who was at one time Viceroy of India.

In the late eighteenth century Bowood was the centre of a literary circle, and many important writers and thinkers met here from time to time. Among them were Samuel Johnson, David Hume, Oliver Goldsmith and Benjamin Franklin. We were taken into the library in which the chemist and philosopher Joseph Priestley – then the librarian at Bowood – discovered oxygen. Later the poet Thomas Moore lived at Bowood in a grace-and-favour cottage for many years.

As at many other great houses, the owners of Bowood have had to find ways of making their estate self-supporting. Bowood charges a fee for house and garden tours and operates a gift and garden store and a playground for children. In the shop we noticed frozen pheasants ready for the table, presumably bred in the woods for this purpose. The house is the residence today of the Earl of Shelburne who is heir to the marquess.

We were back in Marlborough by 6 o'clock to get ready for the church service in Ramsbury commemorating the victory of 40 years ago. We drove there in the calm of the evening through Mildenhall, Stitchcombe and Axford. Ramsbury is a large village – more like a small town, actually – built around a very large and ancient church once a bishopric and recently restored to that status. Nearby is Ramsbury Manor, a beautiful Georgian mansion that was long the seat of the Burdett family until it was recently purchased by a wealthy tycoon. Littlecote, home of the Darrells and Pophams, is not far away. The church contains many fine memorials to these families, though unfortunately some have been recently vandalized.

There was a goodly number in the congregation though the enormous building was by no means full. It was very cold, the warmth of the late afternoon not having penetrated the chill of the stone interior. The people gathered looked typical of any English village – mostly middle-aged, the men red-faced from their farming work looking a little uncomfortable in their Sunday suits and ties, and the women stout and motherly in their suits and dowdy hats so loved by English ladies on solemn occasions. Though mostly ordinary country folk, they gave the impression of solidity, modest prosperity, and belief in themselves and their country, their pride perhaps representative of the national character that defied Hitler and helped achieve the victory now being celebrated 40 years later.

The service followed the usual liturgical progression of hymns, Scripture readings and prayers, with members of the congregation reading from the Bible and leading in prayer. The hymns played on the reedy old organ were familiar tunes, but some words had been updated; I suppose to make them more meaningful in today's context but disappointing to me. All denominations were represented in the ecumenical service. A surpliced priest of the Church of England led the service, while a Methodist minister who had been a padre in the war preached the sermon. His discourse was liberally sprinkled with references to his service days.

Afterwards there was a brief wreath-laying ceremony at the cross in the churchyard commemorating the dead of the two world wars. Again we studied the names engraved thereon, and I wondered where these Wiltshire lads lie – some no doubt in the cemeteries of northern France; some farther afield in Singapore, Thailand or Libya; others resting in graves unknown. But many are remembered not as soldiers, sailors or airmen but as the boys of their home places, known and loved as the individuals they were, and some in the congregation left the churchyard with tears in their eyes.

We crossed the road to the British Legion Hall where food and drink and good fellowship awaited us. The sandwiches, sausage rolls, and bread and cheese prepared by the ladies of the Legion were very good. Simple and wholesome, it was the typical food of village occasions. There were raffles and competitions and drinks were sold at 1945 prices. But the merriment was overlaid with a persistent air of sadness that would not go away, and the talk was mostly of the war, of victory and the price paid for it.

On the way back to Marlborough we stopped at the thatched pub in Mildenhall for further celebrations. I had known the landlord when I lived in Marlborough and was a classmate of his cousin Stuart Goldsworthy, a flier killed in the war. We had much to think about, but there was a festive air in the small crowded pub. Licensing hours had been extended, and the beer flowed freely. In the spirit of the evening Oscar produced and put on his American uniform – alas! it was too small – and the company broke into song, the songs of the war years being rendered with great enthusiasm if little musicality. As this was probably the last victory celebration I will experience, I felt indeed fortunate to be in England for it, a memory I will treasure for the rest of my life.

THURSDAY AND FRIDAY, MAY 9TH AND 10TH

We made a quick trip yesterday to Gloucester to see Alan Sutton and get a report on sales of *Recollections of a G.I. War Bride*. It was a nice sunny day, and we enjoyed the ride through the country in its spring glory. We had a quick look around the city but needed to get back to Marlborough in good time, for I had a date to speak at the monthly meeting of the Women's Institute. My niece Rachel drove up from Weymouth for the occasion, and we had lunch with Ro Chandler, who looked after Rachel when she was orphaned at the age of 13.

The meeting was held in the Church Hall in the Green, and there were many people there who either knew me or my parents or my sister May, Rachel's mother. May had been an enthusiastic member of the Institute when she lived in Pewsey, and during her long illness friends she had made through the organization were of great help and support. Many were interested to see what a beautiful young woman her daughter Rachel had grown into.

The Women's Institute is a British organization of rural women with an interesting history. In 1897 an organization was formed in Ontario, Canada, for women to get together socially to combat loneliness and isolation and to receive some instruction in farming, household management, and domestic science to make their lives more meaningful. It enjoyed immediate success, and, at the beginning of World War I, a Mrs Alfred Watt spoke in England about it and broached the idea that a similar organization should be started in Britain. In September 1916 a first meeting was held in a corrugated iron hut beside an old toll gate in Llanfairpwllgwyngyll (understandably shortened to Llanfair) on the Isle of Anglesey off the north coast of Wales. From this humble beginning the organization spread like wildfire, establishing chapters in villages and small towns. At first leadership was supplied by educated women – squires' wives, doctors' wives, rectors' wives and the like – but soon the ordinary women of the country began to take over. It became a tradition to open every meeting with the singing of 'Jerusalem', Blake's apocalyptic poem that was set to music by Sir Hubert Parry in 1916. Because many of the early meetings were given over to farm wives' domestic concerns, the somewhat opprobrious epithet of 'Jam and Jerusalem' was applied to the organization's activities. During World War II the government did indeed put the W.I., as it is known, in charge of jam-making, but it branched into other rural handicrafts, animal husbandry, and, over time, into matters relating to housing, health, roads and education. Eventually the organization came to wield much influence on legislation in such areas. It has established a college named for Lady Gertrude Denham, its first president, to teach women leadership and business skills and is now one of the most respected of such organizations in the world. There is some concern, though, that membership will fall off because so many young women are entering the labour force, but I feel adjustments will be made and the W.I. will continue to thrive.

The meeting at which I had the privilege to speak was very well-attended and though tea was served very little time was given over to social chit-chat. The women were mostly clad in ordinary workaday clothes, and business was dealt with quickly and efficiently. I followed a speaker from one of the local headquarters, and after I spoke a question-and-answer period followed. I told them how I had come to write the book and how I had always been interested in Marlborough's history. It seemed to me that they liked what I had written about the war and my descriptions of local people known to most in the audience. For myself I found the experience most rewarding.

1986

with Jane Sockwell & Betsy Newland

KINGTON ST MICHAEL AND BRATTON

SATURDAY, SEPTEMBER 13TH

On the previous Thursday David drove to London, changed to a large Austin station wagon and picked up Jane and Betsy to take them to Limpley Stoke in the West Country near Bath. Oscar Fulk meanwhile drove me to Kington St Michael to spend two nights with my cousin Gwen Carpenter.

David, Jane and Betsy spent Friday 'doing' Bath, and this morning drove around to towns such as Bradford-on-Avon, Trowbridge, Lacock and Chippenham. They got lost for awhile in Trowbridge, a fairly large town that serves as the county town of Wiltshire. It has a fine parish church where the poet George Crabbe was rector for many years in the early nineteenth century, and Sir Isaac Pitman, inventor of a shorthand system, was born in the town. Lacock is a show village entirely under the auspices of the National Trust. It has many black and white houses in half-timbered style, an old inn called the Angel, and a hunting lodge frequented by King John. Its most notable building is the abbey, which has been a private house since the dissolution of the monasteries in the reign of Henry VIII. It was the home of William Henry Fox Talbot, a pioneer in photography.

David, Jane and Betsy arrived at Gwen's house about 12.30, and after a good lunch we left for Bratton village a few miles away where another cousin lives. Rain had unfortunately started and was coming down steadily and inexorably, so that our drive through the countryside was to some extent spoiled. We detoured through Castle Combe, like Lacock a show village sometimes called the most beautiful village in England, though many others also lay claim to this title. Castle Combe was brought to the notice of the general public when it was chosen as the locale for the film

Dr Doolittle. Since then it has been a constant tourist attraction, crowded with people in the summer months, though on this Saturday afternoon the streets were deserted in the heavy bone-chilling rain. The steep road leading to the village in the valley was like a dark green tunnel through thick woods dripping heavily with rain. The houses of the yellow-grey lichened stone are built around an ancient poultry cross, and a street lined with mediaeval weavers' houses follows the twisting course of the By Brook, a babbling stream spanned by a three-arched bridge of weathered stone. The village church tower seems to stand watch over all.

We passed through several other very attractive villages, most notable among them Steeple Ashton. In its centre rises the tall steeple of the church, visible for many miles. The tower was built with 'wool' money and has many pinnacles and much crenellation. We noticed several half-timbered houses, some black and white and others the less common black and red.

Jane and Betsy had been quite taken with Gwen's small house typical of today's working-class homes. They liked her tiny fenced garden, complete with venerable pet tortoise, her 'conservatory', pleasant living room and sunny functional kitchen. Now in Bratton they were to see a very different house – Portaway, a 300-year-old farmhouse that Greta and her late husband bought and modernized, decorated and furnished appropriately. They cleared the wilderness surrounding it, transforming it into a beautiful garden sloping down to a millstream. Unfortunately the heavy rain prevented us from taking a tour of the garden, which was in full fall bloom and colour, but we did get into the greenhouse to see the ripening tomatoes.

A warm welcome awaited us at Portaway. Plump smiling Greta and her sister Pauline greeted us. Their mother, my Aunt Win, was there. She has lived with Greta since having a stroke two years ago. It is sad to see this strong-minded, resourceful apple-cheeked old countrywoman with her stricken right side struggling gallantly around and climbing the steep and narrow stairs of the old house. Though her speech has not been affected, she was very quiet just when I was hoping Betsy and Jane would get to hear a real Wiltshire accent. Greta's younger son William was there. Young, slender, curly-haired, he was very much at ease and charmed us all with his quiet self-assurance, sangfroid, and the way he helped his mother dispense tea. He is a graduate of London University in environmental science and lectures at a college near London in addition to broadcasting and writing occasional articles. Greta showed us a picture of him receiving his degree at the hands of Princess Anne. The perfect English tea was served with several kinds of tiny sandwiches, hot scones, jam, a variety of small cakes and a special kind of fruitcake called a Dundee cake. All had been made by Greta herself.

We left soon after tea. Greta directed us out the driveway into the narrow road with Aunt Win and Pauline waving until we were out of sight. Following William's directions we reached Limpley Stoke without getting lost. Limpley Stoke is a village built on the slopes of the high hills just outside of Bath. The Kennet and Avon Canal flows nearby. We are staying at the Cliffe Hotel, a big old house of Bath stone, Victorian in style and furnishings though some discordant modern touches have been added. The host is a genial Scotsman. We find stairs in unexpected places – five for instance lead from our bedroom to our bath.

1987

HEATHROW TO MARLBOROUGH – MARLBOROUGH FLOWER SHOW – BOOK-SIGNING – MARLBOROUGH ROTARY CLUB AND MARLBOROUGH COLLEGE – LITTLECOTE – EAST WILTSHIRE VILLAGES

[This trip was dictated by the publication of *Marlborough Revisited and the War Remembered*, my second book. Its writing had been inspired by the services we attended in 1985 commemorating the 40th anniversary of VE Day. After writing an account of that day in Marlborough and Ramsbury, I felt it should be made available for the residents of those towns for whom it would mean much. But how? As news it had lost its immediacy and it was either too long or too short for any other form of publication. So around it I wrote the story of the town and its environs, adding memories of growing up between the wars and my experiences during the war. The book amplifies, without repeating, what I had set down in *Recollections of a G.I. War Bride*.

Though much of our time was taken up by book business, we nonetheless were able to revisit places near and dear to us and discover corners of the county hitherto unknown. It was a rich experience seeing people and places, and we were fortunate to be blessed with extremely good weather.]

FRIDAY, JULY 31ST

We landed at Heathrow early in the morning in pouring rain and found the crowds overwhelming as usual. We picked up our car at Copthorne, west of the airport, at a beautiful hotel and convention centre fashioned out of an ancient half-timbered manor house. We breakfasted there, booked a room for the night before our return flight, and then set out on the M4. When we arrived at Marlborough we found the sun just beginning to shine on a wet drenched world.

We booked into the Castle and Ball, the town's only first-class hotel now that the Ailesbury Arms is being converted into the central building of a shopping mall and office complex. It is hard for me to comprehend such changes for Marlborough, and I grieve for the demise of the hotel, which, over a long and distinguished history, served travellers and clients with a kind of shabby elegance that seemed typically English.

After making some phone calls and having lunch we went to the town hall where the judges had just made their final decisions at the local flower show. Many people were there, and in the crowd I met friends and acquaintances who were happy to see me and excited about my new book. David was much interested in the fruits, vegetables and flowers on display – great heaps of shining red and green apples, purple plums, giant marrows, foot-long runner beans, potatoes, bouquets of pastel-shaded sweet peas, gaudy dahlias, and shaggy asters repeating the sweet pea colours. All were of the highest quality betokening good soil, cooperative summer weather, and unstinting care and toil. In Marlborough, as in most country towns and villages, the flower show is an important late summer occasion. My father, I remember, though not a gardener, always displayed his honey and sometimes his beautiful wood carving and always received commendations for both.

Afterwards we walked through St Mary's churchyard to Herd Street to see Joan and Oscar Fulk. Oscar is seriously ill with leukaemia. We had been told of his condition at Christmas and found him looking quite sick today, even though now, after much treatment, the disease is in remission. He and Joan were delighted to see us, and he was quite thrilled with what I have written about them in my book. We plan to spend as much time with them as we can. As the Yank who chose to settle in Wiltshire he has become very popular in the town. Farmer, publican, and bartender at the British Legion and Conservative clubs, he is a veritable Marlborough institution.

SATURDAY, AUGUST 1ST

The morning was taken up with the book-signing party at the White Horse Book Shop. Interested people, some known to me but many strangers, came to buy a book and meet the author. Several former mayors came, along with one young man who had been educated at Marlborough College and then went on to become a Morehead Scholar at the University of North Carolina in Chapel Hill. I met Mr Harraway, by now very old and retired from his drapery store 'along the Parade', where I often went as a child to purchase reels of cotton, papers of pins and yards of elastic for my mother. One old lady, Mrs Large, hobbled in on two canes, thrilled that I had mentioned her as well as her husband and her sister, both now deceased. It was a happy occasion, inevitably mixed with sadness, longing for youth and a wish that I could have spent more time with and perhaps done better by these people from the past.

The party was over by noon, and we met Joan and Oscar and drove out to one of the Chute villages for lunch at the Hatchet, a delightful old pub. Long, low and thatched, it has been discreetly modernized inside. The food was of high quality, and Oscar knew the innkeeper so we were treated as very special guests. The whole area and the three Chute villages seemed so appealing that we resolved to come back later for a closer look and to go on to Vernham Dean, a village I often visited with my parents.

SUNDAY, AUGUST 2ND

We spent the day in Bournemouth but drove back to Marlborough, arriving in time for evensong at Preshute Church. We were shocked to find a congregation of eight, ourselves included. However the service followed the order of worship faithfully with a short sermon, and we sang several hymns accompanied on an old piano by one of the ladies from the congregation. We were greeted warmly by the minister and worshippers, but I remembered with sadness services of long ago when the church was filled and how on summer evenings my sister and I walked through the watermeadows to Preshute to attend evensong with our mother.

MONDAY AND TUESDAY, AUGUST 3RD AND 4TH

On Monday we left early for Gloucester where we had a meeting with publisher Alan Sutton.

Back in Marlborough by evening, we had dinner with Dr and Mrs Dick Maurice at their beautiful home in Stonebridge Lane. Dr Maurice belongs to a large and distinguished local family that is one of the largest medical dynasties in England and has supplied Marlborough with doctors for several generations. Dr Dick – there have been so many doctors with the last name Maurice that they are known by their given names – is the son of Dr Walter, who attended my family for many years. We thus found much to talk about.

Tuesday we spent a leisurely morning in the town until 1 o'clock, when I was the speaker at the monthly meeting of the Rotary Club. It came as something of a shock to realize that I was an old lady to this group of mostly middle-aged men. In fact I had once taught two of them at St Peter's School when I did a short stint there while waiting for transportation to the States. Some too remembered my father. I met a very interesting old gentleman from Aldbourne and the young doctor from Burbage who is the president of the local club.

Afterwards we took a walk around the grounds of Marlborough College, following Dr Maurice's suggestion of the previous evening. He and many of his family were educated here. When I was growing up in Marlborough, the college was strictly off limits to the townspeople, but today there is much more exchange and communication. For the last few years a summer school that attracts townspeople and visitors alike has been held there.

We entered the grounds through the imposing gates opposite St Peter's Church and strolled through tree-lined walks and around grassy lawns to a tree-shrouded mound. At the base of the mound is a marker informing that here the eighteenth-century pastoral poets Stephen Duck and James Thomson were wont to write their bucolic verses. They were sponsored by Lady Hertford who lived in the Seymour mansion and gathered a literary coterie around her in the fashion of the age. The mound itself is akin to the larger and more famous Silbury Hill five miles away down the Bath Road. The origin, meaning and use of these mounds are unknown, though they are the subject of much speculation. Some historians think they were mounts of ascent from which priests or rulers gave out laws to tribesmen assembled below.

We next went to the beautiful chapel, opened in 1886 and dedicated to St Michael and all Angels. It is built of grey sarsen stone in the decorated style and graced with a slender spire. We walked around the gardens of the Memorial Hall, a semicircular assembly building erected in memory of Marlburians killed in World War I. It was built in the 1920s and considered at the time very avant-garde for Marlborough. It was then one of the few college buildings where townspeople were welcome. We went to many evenings of dramatic presentations known as 'Penny Readings,' often simple plays performed by college boys and staff. They were among the few cultural opportunities that we were exposed to while growing up.

Last we walked up the wide straight drive to 'C' House, once the Seymour mansion and later, in the coaching days of the eighteenth and early nineteenth centuries, a famous hostelry known as the Castle Inn. Its name came from a Norman castle much frequented by King John that once stood nearby. Today 'C' House is the college administration building.

FRIDAY, AUGUST 7TH

We were back in Marlborough by noon, ready for an afternoon visit to Littlecote, a house only a few miles from Marlborough the grim story of which has fascinated me since I was a child. Privately owned by the Wills family of tobacco wealth, it was not then open to the public, and we have never before managed to fit a visit into our busy Marlborough schedule.

The house is in Wiltshire close to the Berkshire line, not far from Ramsbury and the pretty village of Chilton Foliat. It is a long low Tudor mansion of rosy brick, gabled roofs, mullioned windows and tall twisted chimneys, set in a green park hard by the River Kennet. Some years ago archaeologists uncovered a very fine piece of tessellated pavement on the banks of the river. This Roman mosaic, preserved in almost perfect condition and which we saw several years ago, is accessible from the house by a short railroad.

The manor was first owned by the Darrells and later by the Pophams, both West Country families of wealth and distinction. In 1922 the Popham owner sold it to the Wills, of tobacco wealth, who made it their private residence until they recently sold it to an entrepreneur who is developing it into a tourist attraction. Today its facilities include shops and restaurants, a display of antique farm machinery, a pets farm for children, a demonstration of falconry, and lists for jousting in the tradition of mediaeval knights. The house remains largely untouched, and, because the surrounding park is so spacious, it is not encroached upon by the additional building. House tours are available during certain hours though not all the rooms are open.

Beautiful as it is, the house has a dark history and is said to be haunted. The story goes that in 1575 Littlecote was owned by William Darrell, who was described by a contemporary as 'a man of evil and ferocious countenance' and whose wild escapades and wicked deeds earned him the sobriquet 'Wild Bill'. One windy rainswept night Darrell sent a messenger in haste to the village of Shefford some miles away with instructions to bring to Littlecote a midwife known as Mother Barnes to attend a woman in labour. The midwife, a woman of some repute and skill, rode pillion behind the messenger and was blindfolded so that her destination would be unknown. On reaching Littlecote she was taken to an upstairs chamber where in due course she delivered a baby to a woman who was a stranger to her. Immediately after the birth Wild Bill entered the room and ordered the midwife to throw the baby into the fire roaring on the hearth. She demurred and pleaded to keep and raise the child herself, but Darrell seized it from her and cast it into the flames himself, prodding the little body with his foot until it was quite consumed. The midwife was then blindfolded and returned to her village. But, outraged at the cruel deed she had witnessed, Mother Barnes had the presence of mind to snip a small piece of bed hanging and hide it on her person before leaving. She also noted the time the journey took and its general direction. She eventually eliminated all possible locations and decided that Littlecote must have been the scene of the bloody crime and, with the snippet of cloth as evidence, a charge of murder was brought against Darrell. In spite of the damning evidence, Darrell went free. The case was tried by Judge Popham, a distant cousin of Darrell, and bribery was suspected but never proved. The chamber where the murder took place is said to be haunted, and some strange feelings and apparitions have been recorded therein. Unfortunately this room is not included in the guided tour of the house.

Shortly after this incident Wild Bill Darrell met his death in a fall from a horse at a place near Littlecote known to this day as Darrell's stile. Upon his death the house passed into the possession of the Pophams, who became prominent in legal circles with one becoming Lord Chief Justice of England. During the Civil War, Colonel Alexander Popham fought for Parliament against the king. Roundhead soldiers were stationed in the house. Later, however, disillusioned with Cromwell's rule, the same man helped restore the Stuarts to the throne, and in 1663 Charles II dined with Popham at Littlecote. Later in 1688 William of Orange met with his advisers first at the Bear Inn in Hungerford a few miles away and then at Littlecote before taking over the throne from the abdicating James II.

We took the guided tour of the house, going first into the magnificently panelled great hall, the walls of which were hung with the buff uniform coats of Roundhead soldiers along with their armour breastplates and weapons. The firearms and blunderbusses looked very clumsy and unwieldy, though they were deadly in the hands of Cromwell's dedicated followers. The windows were of stained glass and decorated with armorial devices. One small instrument of torture was brought to our notice by our guide – a fingerpress used by the owners of the house on any disobedient, lazy or otherwise intractable servants. One small room had panelled walls painted with scenes of Dutch life in honour of William of Orange, who used the room as an office and study. Perhaps the gem of the house is the chapel. Plain and austere in Cromwellian style, it is unique. There is no altar, its place taken by an elevated pulpit from which in days gone by lengthy discourses of hellfire and damnation thundered. Here and there in certain rooms and hallways are tableaux with wax figures in Puritan dress. I was unsure whether I liked them, but they did seem a valiant attempt to bring history alive.

The gardens are magnificent and quite untouched by recent developments. Wide lawns are enclosed in brick wall and flower borders, and there was a fine display of late roses. On one wide lawn a man in mediaeval garb was demonstrating the sport of hawking with falcons of different sizes and species leaving his wrist and returning to him on signal. We went on to watch the jousting in a wide grassy area of the park some distance from the house. Here horsemen clad in cleverly simulated armour rode gaily caparisoned horses and engaged in tilting at the quintain and hand-to-hand combat like knights of old. Occasionally one would be unhorsed but none sustained any injuries. The younger people in the audience were wildly enthusiastic. We stayed for a while and then went on to browse in the attractive shops that have been opened in the former stables.

SATURDAY, AUGUST 8TH

I spent about an hour in the White Horse Book Shop signing and selling books and meeting many people. I am very grateful for the interest shown. After saying goodbye to Joan and Oscar over morning coffee we left for a long day of local sightseeing, going first to Chute as we had promised ourselves and then on to Vernham Dean and the villages where my father spent much of his early life.

On the way to Chute we went through Great Bedwyn and Oxenwood where we took a road known as the Chute Causeway, a high road that follows the crest of the downs in a great semicircle for about five miles. On either side were magnificent views – Berkshire and Hampshire to the east and Wiltshire to the west – with the farmland on this late summer morning lush and ripe. The causeway itself is a spur off the old Roman road running between Winchester and Marlborough. At the southern end lie the three Chute villages hidden in an isolated pocket of the remains of Chute Forest. Far off the beaten track, they have been passed by, but the Hatchet Inn is now an attraction for people who discover them. In one of the villages stands the ivy-covered St Mary's Church, unused today but still beautiful.

Leaving the Chutes we followed a signpost to Vernham Dean in Hampshire, just across the Wiltshire border. Many a Sunday afternoon long years ago my family would come here in the motorbike and sidecar that was then our proud conveyance, my sister riding pillion behind my father while Mother and I were packed into the bullet-shaped sidecar. My father, deep in his latest hobby of beekeeping, was going to see a friend and mentor named Larry Pearson, one of the foremost beekeepers in the country. Public-school educated, Mr Pearson was the youngest of 10 children born to a clergyman who for many years was chaplain to Queen Victoria. He was a bachelor and lived with his sister, the oldest of the family, in a square stone house with a garden near the grassy banks of a crystal pond around which the village clustered. I was always delighted to go to see the Pearsons for I was made much of and always given little presents and fed lemonade and cakes. They opened a new world for me, a world in which art and music and good books were important, and I will never forget them.

This morning I was excited about seeing this place of happy memories, so that I was very shocked to be able to find neither the house nor the pond. Quite bewildered, we approached a pleasant young couple who were weeding their garden and who told us that the pond had been drained several years ago and the house I wanted was next door. It was so overgrown with shrubbery, hedges and tall trees as to be nearly hidden from view and unrecognizable. I did not have the courage to introduce myself to the house owners, but our kindly informants asked us in and told us they had heard that many years ago the house had belonged to a beekeeper of some distinction. Without its pond the village looked very ordinary, and I left feeling somewhat dejected.

After a pleasant lunch at a pub restored me, we drove to Pewsey, stopping at the bridge over the Kennet and Avon Canal not far from a funny little pub named the French Horn. Once dark and poky but charming with age, it was modernized some years ago and lost much of its attraction as it gained more space and light. It was a favourite haunt of my brother-in-law Bill Nutley, deceased now these many years, and David has some good memories of sharing a few pints with him and the locals on several occasions.

On the canal a boat filled with sightseers was just leaving the wharf. Such trips help bring in a little money for the ongoing work of restoring the canal, which was once a thriving waterway full of action but is now calm and stagnant. There was a refreshment stand manned by volunteers nearby, and we stopped to talk to the ladies and sample their homemade goods. Then we drove on to Honeystreet, now an undistinguished cluster of houses on the banks of the canal. Grouped around the timber yard of Robbins, Lane and Pinnegar, Honeystreet was once one of the most important stops on the canal, for here the flat-bottomed barges that transported goods of all kinds were built. The business began in 1812 through the enterprise of three young engineers named Samuel Robbins, Ebenezer Lane and Samuel Pinnegar, and expanded rapidly to build narrower barges for the Midland canals and craft for the Severn River. It employed many workers who were housed in terraced dwellings built with stone from the dismantled stables of Tottenham House. My great-grandfather, Benjamin Biggs, was a foreman in the works and, although he had never built a house before, designed and built the Barge Inn on the banks of the canal to meet the needs of the workers and boatmen. A sign on the inn attests to this. We wandered around the outside of the inn, which at this hour was closed in accordance with the licensing laws. It looked forlorn and lonely, but I believe it attracts good crowds on summer weekends in spite of its remote location. When I was there some years ago I was shown a pane of glass in one of the windows in which my father had cut his name many years ago.

We went next to Alton Barnes, the small village where my father had lived with his grandfather. He was a lonely clever child who became the star student in the village school until circumstances forced him to leave at 12. Some years ago I gave a talk to the pupils in the school about life in America, but the school is closed now.

We went down a narrow farm lane leading to the manor farm and tiny village church next door. The little building is dedicated to St Mary and is much restored. It stands on Saxon foundations, as indicated by the narrow dimensions of the nave and chancel. During the late eighteenth and early nineteenth centuries, this church had two distinguished scholars from Oxford as incumbents, Drs William Crowe and Augustus Hare. Dr Hare and his wife Maria wrote much for and about the church, providing much valuable research material for historians today. Their family correspondence was published in 1849 under the title *Memorials of a Quiet Life* and tells a delightful story of village life at Alton. Both the rector and his wife were extolled for their devotion and good works. They provided medical as well as spiritual help for their parishioners and, since the village had no shop, established a Saturday market that sold goods at cut-rate prices. When in 1830 farmworkers rioted outside the rectory and the farm next door against the introduction of agricultural machinery, Maria Hare recorded how 'some 200 peasants descended on the cottage to break the machines on the farm.' The militia from Devizes had to be called out to quell the riot, throughout which Dr Hare impressed everyone with a brave and determined demeanour in the face of great danger. A farmer named Pile was shot and killed in the riot. Later in the century a man of the same family masterminded the cutting of the chalk horse on Milk Hill, the largest and one of the finest of the Wiltshire White Horses.

In the church there is a bust of Dr Hare, who is buried in Rome next to the poet Keats, having gone there for health reasons. There is a picture of Dr Crowe, who is buried in a tomb beside the chancel wall. On an outside wall there is a memorial to Crowe's infant son with the touching inscription:

> Blessed little lamb, before that thou couldst roam,
> The Shepherd's bosom claimed thee, caught and carried home.

There are several other memorials to members of the Crowe family, some of whom served and died in the farflung outposts of the Empire. In more recent times a descendant, Sir Colin Crowe served as Britain's permanent representative to the United Nations.

Another notable buried in this tiny out-of-the-way village is Sir Eric Phipps, ambassador to Paris at the beginning of World War II. So many well-known people, yet the grave that mattered most to me was that of a schoolmaster named Butler, who is buried here along with his wife. A teacher at Alton for many years, he provided something of a warm home environment for my father, and it was he who opened up opportunities for reading and encouraged the thirst for knowledge that stayed with my father all his long life.

We next drove the few miles to the Manningford villages where my father was chauffeur to the Grant-Meek family in the years before World War I. Manningford Bruce has an interesting old church. Its architecture is a mixture of Saxon, Norman and Romanesque and lacks ornamentation both in and out. After the Battle of Worcester in 1651, Charles II remained hidden, supposedly playing cards, for several days in the rectory before escaping with the help of the rector's wife, Mary Nicholas (nee Lane, a prominent local family). As a reward the family was allowed to add the three lions of England to its coat of arms. This story is told on Mary Nicholas' tomb, dated 1686.

Our next stop was East Grafton, another village of happy childhood memories. Here we often visited a local artist named Richard Marshall and his family in their thatched cottage overlooking the wide triangular village green. The church here was built about 150 years ago by the Marquess of Ailesbury. During its construction there was a serious accident in which a workman lost his life and the heir to the marquess only narrowly escaped.

From East Grafton we drove on through the long straggling village of Burbage to the Salisbury Road and then back through Savernake Forest to Marlborough.

1989

SAVERNAKE AND ENVIRONS – LYDIARD TREGOZE – BEMERTON AND WILTON – VISITING AROUND WILTSHIRE – A TRIP TO BOX – AVEBURY, CALNE, CHIPPENHAM AND PRESHUTE – MUSEUM IN DEVIZES – CORSHAM COURT

TUESDAY, SEPTEMBER 12TH

It wasn't until we turned off the motorway at Hungerford that I felt we had really arrived in England. We drove down a leafy winding lane to connect with the A4, formerly the main road to London from the west. We turned on the A4, bypassing the main street of the ancient town of Hungerford and going past the Bear Hotel and through a commercial area given over almost entirely to antique shops. As we passed from Berkshire into Wiltshire we noted huge fields unbroken by the green hedgerows of former days, indicative of the rise of 'prairie farming' on great sweeps of open land where modern machinery can operate most efficiently. We entered Savernake Forest at what used to be Puthall Gate. As always it pained me to see the deterioration of the forest from the green verdure and giant beech and oak groves I remember from my childhood. Passing Iron Gates, we rounded another curve past Savernake Hospital, the view of it from the road unchanged, and then Marlborough in the valley below came into sight. I rejoiced at the sight of the little town that nurtured me, though some of the memories it arouses are sad ones of lost youth and departed family members and friends.

We passed my old home and following directions to the Ivy House Hotel we drove through a small development of delightful little houses tucked away off the Pewsey Road. The neat detached dwellings have postage stamp-sized lawns and a profusion of blossoming flowers, and over them the tower of St Peter's Church stands sentinel. We parked under a spreading copper beech and made our way into the hotel where we were expected and welcomed. The Ivy House Hotel is a foursquare Georgian building with a brick facade covered with ivy. Some 250 years old, a school for boys was opened there in 1780 by a Mr Davis and his son-in-law Mr Gresley. Boys from the school cut the white chalk horse on Granham Hill, and brothers who were pupils there, Thomas and Walter Hancock, attained some minor fame in the development of, respectively, the steam engine and India rubber. Later the house became a private dwelling and eventually a residential hotel that was both exclusive and expensive, its services unavailable to the general public. The Best Western hotel chain recently acquired the hotel and has modernized and refurbished it, so that it is now challenging the Castle and Ball as Marlborough's premier hotel. We were rather chagrined to find that we will not be housed in the hotel proper but in the Vine, as the annex across the street is known. However our room is delightful – large and well-appointed with windows that command a wide view of the High Street. We unpacked, rested briefly, and then wandered across the street to the Wellington Arms, one of Marlborough's old pubs, where we ate sandwiches in the crowded bar. We were greeted enthusiastically by one of the barmaids who remembered us from previous visits. She announced that she is leaving tomorrow for sun and fun in Florida! We made a few purchases in the town shops and then retired for a long nap. The travelling and time change seems to have upset us more than usual – could it be that we are getting old?

Rested and relaxed, we had dinner in the dining room of the hotel. It is developing a reputation for haute cuisine, but to our tastes the meal, though very expensive and elegantly served, was not exceptional. The Palladian-style dining room was beautiful in pink and white with pale green accents and highlighted by exquisite floral arrangements. The windows look out on the herbaceous borders of the garden backed by ancient brick walls while above rise the higgledy-piggledy roof lines and chimney pots that to me spell Marlborough.

WEDNESDAY, SEPTEMBER 13TH

We awoke to rain, a disappointment after all we have heard about the summer's glorious weather. We have decided to spend most of our two weeks in England visiting old friends in and near Marlborough and sightseeing in the area, so after breakfast we called on several friends and then in the early afternoon drove to Lydiard Park near Swindon 11 miles to the north.

In order to avoid the traffic around Swindon – said to be the centre of the fastest-growing industrial complex in Western Europe – we took the longer more scenic road that winds up, down and finally over the Marlborough Downs. The rain had stopped but a mist shrouded the distant reaches of spectacular views. We drove across Marlborough Common, past the town cemetery and the forbidding-looking buildings that successively housed the workhouse and isolation hospital, the latter the scene of my traumatic bout with scarlet fever at the age of five. Most of the common is now part of a golf course, once the subject of acrimonious town disputes over whether land that from time immemorial had belonged to all the residents of the town should be used for a golf course for the sport of the privileged few. At the far end of the Common we saw the circle of larch trees known as the Clump surrounding a slight eminence thought to be an ancient tumulus. Very often in days long gone the Clump was the destination and turning back point of Sunday afternoon walks with my father.

Beyond the Common we faced the great sweep of downland ahead, some of it ploughed in readiness for winter sowing but most of it providing grazing for great flocks of sheep that wander at will over the vast unfenced stretches of close-cropped grass. Here and there we saw occasional outcroppings of white chalk through the green. In the sky above birds wheeled and soared, the curlews among them uttering plaintive cries eloquent of emptiness and loneliness. The smooth contours of the hills are broken occasionally by clumps of beech trees. Seemingly wedded to the chalkland, these trees are not indigenous but were planted by enterprising farmers long ago to act as breaks and barriers against the winds that howl across the downs in the winter. In fact the busy and ubiquitous Capability Brown has been given some credit for the introduction of beech to chalk.

At one of the highest points we crossed the ancient road known as the Ridgeway, a track made by the feet of ancient man as he went on his nomadic journeyings following the high land and avoiding the perils of the jungle-like valleys. We stopped and savoured the view of the valley below, though the distance was shrouded in the persistent mist. We descended the steep and winding road of Hackpen Hill into the villages of Broad Hinton and Broad Town, the latter the site of the Broad Town Charity, a school for poor Wiltshire boys founded in 1686 by the same duchess of Somerset who built the almshouses at Froxfield and endowed Marlborough Grammar School with scholarships to Oxford University. As we neared Wootton Bassett, a small market town of great antiquity, we passed a huge St Ivel factory where dairy products are processed. I recalled that some Double Gloucester cheese that I recently bought in Chapel Hill came from this very plant. Going into the town we turned right on the main street, leaving on the left the mediaeval half-timbered town hall built on stilts in the middle of the street. Shortly after leaving the town we turned right down the narrow road for Lydiard Park.

The writer John Buchan once said that every street corner in London is peopled with ghosts from history and literature, and it is a remark that is just as applicable to every village in England. I recalled it as we made our way through flat farming land to a hamlet, mansion and church once important historically and full of artistic treasures but buried in obscurity before being rescued from near ruin in this century by the forward-looking borough of Swindon.

The story of the estate and the family that owned it is a singular one. The name Lydiard is mentioned in Domesday Book as land belonging to Alfred of Marlborough, about whom little is known. The Tregoze family settled here in the twelfth century from Troisgots in Normandy – whence the name Tregoze. By the middle of the fifteenth century the estate passed through the female line to the St John (pronounced 'sinjon') family, who were related to the Tudors. They were to hold it for 500 years and build the mansion during the Georgian era. In the eighteenth century the title of Bolingbroke was conferred on the head of the family, although only at the level of viscount. About this time the family began to live most of the time in London, spending only portions of the summer in the country house or using it as a refuge in times of plague. Tenants farmed the land and sent the produce to London for the family's use. Under these circumstances the estate began a slow decline that intensified as the Bolingbrokes gradually lost both money and prestige. The mansion fell into disrepair and ruin, and it is said that its last occupants, an elderly viscountess and her son, moved from room to room as ceilings collapsed one by one around them.

Ultimately the town of Swindon bought the estate, which by this time was within its growing boundaries. The mansion has been restored, the church preserved, and a modern conference centre added. The land has been converted into a park and recreation areas for public use. The work of restoring and refurnishing the beautiful Georgian house is ongoing. Several rooms are completely furnished, and there has been some success in retrieving furnishings and objets d'art belonging to the St John family. The plaster ceilings in the beautifully proportioned rooms are especially fine, and in one small dressing room of the master bedroom there is a stained glass window of unusual design executed by a master Dutch craftsman named Abraham van Linge. The house looks on to a wide expanse of lawn dotted with some big trees, one an exceptionally fine Lebanon cedar. In the distance is a lake and a driveway marked by an avenue of lime trees planted to replace elms that have fallen victim to disease. The original small village has completely disappeared, though archaeologists have found traces of its existence.

The thirteenth-century church stands behind but very close to the mansion. It is entered through a churchyard full of mossy barely decipherable tombstones tilting at crazy angles. Except for the mowing of the grass and edging of paths, no attempt has been made to alter the ravages of time. We noted the reddish stone of the church's exterior and that its tower shows filigree decoration unusual in a small village church.

But it is the interior, filled with heavily carved dark oak box pews, that is unique and of great interest to all who like and study ecclesiastical design and monuments in out-of-the-way places. The monuments to and effigies of the St John family especially strike the visitor, while the stained glass east window of the church, also by van Linge, traces the descent of the manor to Sir John St John through the ages. The church was enlarged and improved in the fifteenth century, and in 1633 the south chapel became the burial place for family members. Sir John, who lived from 1585 to 1648, was responsible for the church's fine memorials, and in 1670 the noted antiquarian John Aubrey wrote, 'for modern monuments it exceeds all the churches in the country.' Such memorials are rarely seen in parish churches such as this.

The chief and rarest treasure is the painted triptych begun in 1615 to honour the parents of Sir John. The outer sides of the dark green central panels display heraldic tables of the family, and these panels open to reveal painted representations of the honoured man and woman kneeling upon a coffin and flanked by their children, a son and six daughters. We unfortunately were not able to see the triptych in position, for it had been disassembled and a team of artists and restorers were repainting it. Nonetheless it was interesting and instructive to watch them working painstakingly at such difficult detailed work.

In the chapel we saw the marble effigy memorializing Sir John. His recumbent figure, skilfully carved in lifelike representation, lies between his two wives, one clasping an infant to her breast. At the head kneel five boys while at the foot are three girls. Sadly three of the boys died before their father. The last of these, and his father's favourite, was killed fighting for his king at the second Battle of Newbury in the Civil War. The grieving parent erected a spectacular bronze gilt statue as his memorial. Standing in the church to this day, it has become known as the Golden Cavalier. Another marble monument memorializes a daughter and husband. The figures face each other as if talking, so it has become known as the Conversation Piece. Four other figures commemorate children who died as infants. We saw coats of arms and family trees as well.

We left the church, stopping at the gate to enjoy the view of the modern town of Swindon below and to our right. The sun had finally cleared away the fog, and we could see the vast industrial complex below. As we walked back to the car in bright sunshine we watched the antics of four young Labrador dogs, two black and two yellow. They were wet from swimming in the lake and were drying off by chasing and retrieving a stick, each in competition with his fellows. There were also several parties of young people and families, proof that the park provides a needed recreation area for the growing town.

By this time it was too late to return via the Richard Jefferies museum at nearby Coate, as I had hoped we would be able, so we returned to Marlborough the same way we had come. In the clearer atmosphere we had full views of the vistas around us, though these are better appreciated while descending rather than ascending the steep curving roads.

Back at the hotel we rested briefly before going to dinner with Dr Dick Maurice and his wife Anne at their beautiful house called 'Welland' at the top of Stony Bridge Lane. An interesting company was assembled, among them a cousin of Anne's and her husband, a Scottish doctor who had practised for many years in Richmond, Virginia. Now retired, they live in Andorra though spend much time travelling. A young lady named Vanessa, daughter of a Jamaican father, was along too. Very bright and attractive, she was educated at Marlborough College, and has a university degree in economics. She has taken a year off to travel around the world. Another gentleman present was a retired solicitor who was a classmate of Dick's at Marlborough College. I was the sole representative of Marlborough's 'other' school – the grammar school founded by Edward VI in 1550 and long a rival establishment of the college. After drinks in the study we had a delicious dinner of roast lamb followed by gooseberry fool for dessert. Conversation was delightful throughout the evening. I was surprised that when we related our visit to Lydiard Tregoze, the Maurices knew little about it – it does seem that local places of great interest are often unknown to people who live nearby!

We left about 10.30 for Bemerton near Salisbury. It was a cool grey morning with low clouds threatening rain. We drove through the forest and the village of Burbage, across the canal and railway bridges, and on through the twin villages of Collingbourne Kingston and Collingbourne Ducis. On either side of the road lay wide stretches of the high exposed chalk downland that is Salisbury Plain. Some of the land is used for cultivation and sheep raising, but much of it is reserved for military installations and troop exercises. As we approached Tidworth, a large sprawling military town half in Wiltshire and half in Hampshire, we saw many warning signs for tank crossings. We bypassed Amesbury and Stonehenge, passed on our right the grassy hilltop fortification of Old Sarum, and at last came to Salisbury. The landmark spire of the cathedral was wreathed in scaffolding for much needed repair, and reinforcement work has at long last begun. We then took the road west to Bemerton, a tiny village lying low in the watermeadows of the Avon and now encroached upon by the city's growth.

Bemerton would have been doomed to obscurity but for the three-year tenure of George Herbert as rector from 1630 to 1633. Herbert was the wealthy scion of a noble family and a gifted intellectual and scholar. After much thought, however, he renounced his worldly possessions and ambitions and became the rector of a tiny primitive church in the poverty-stricken village of Bemerton. In his brief priesthood he endeared himself to his parishioners with his humility, energy and charity. A keen musician, he was accustomed to walk twice weekly in all weather through the marshy meadowland to hear the choir singing in the cathedral that he once called 'Heaven upon earth.' The choir in turn came to sing at Herbert's funeral in Bemerton after his death at about the age of 40 from tuberculosis in 1633.

Several years before coming to Bemerton Herbert married Jane Danvers in the large and beautiful church at Edington, and she became his constant companion and helpmeet in his parish duties. Herbert wrote a book called 'The Country Parson' in which he laid out the duties not only of the clergyman but also the clergyman's wife, and Jane did her best to live up to her husband's demands. They lived in the Rectory, a dour forbidding-looking house separated from the church by a road so narrow that today only one car at a time can proceed. Though they had no children they adopted two orphaned nieces.

Both church and rectory were built of flint, a common enough material in that area, where bands of the silica nodules run through the chalk. The church appears smaller than the rectory and stands within a walled graveyard full of ancient tombstones half-buried in the ground, covered in moss and deep in grass, their inscriptions rendered illegible by time and weather. Inside it was dark and dankly cold, and I wondered if the damp of the house and church and their location in flat often waterlogged land had contributed to Herbert's early death. On the wall to the left of the altar is a modest stone with his initials and the date of his death. The east window of stained glass seems to brighten the sombre interior just a little, and its inscription 'Greater love hath no man than this' seems to serve as Herbert's epitaph. The altar is covered with a heavily embroidered cloth recently executed by needlewomen from the See of Sarum to illustrate his poem 'The Flower,' but to me the bright colours seemed a bit garish and discordant.

For three years Herbert ministered to his flock, preaching and praying and wrestling with his own soul until illness overtook him. As he lay struggling for breath and dying in an upstairs room of the rectory he could look across the river meadows to the cathedral he loved and whither he had walked for clerical meetings and the musicales that inspired him. He left behind a wealth of writings, both prose and poetry but especially the latter. His verse is straightforward, pure, practical, simple and sometimes melancholy, yet it hints of mysticism and the metaphysical. It is touched with joy and the light of genius. His manuscripts were left to Nicholas Ferrar, a friend from his days at Oxford University, with instructions to publish them if he thought they might 'turn to the advantage of any dejected soul' but otherwise to burn them. He told Ferrar that the poems represented 'a picture of the many spiritual conflicts that have passed betwixt God and my soul before I could subject mine to the will of Jesus my Master.' Some of his simpler poems are sung as hymns today, and scholars still ponder the meaning and subtleties of his mystical writings. I remember one hymn in particular that we used to sing as children at school:

> Teach me, my God and King
> In all things Thee to see,
> And what I do in anything
> To do it as for Thee.

By this time, the rain that had been threatening all day started in real earnest. The rectory was closed and because of the rain we could not explore the grounds, though I would dearly have liked to see the medlar tree Herbert wrote of. Sadly and meditatively I left this place I had so long wanted to see, and we headed for Wilton. On our way we passed the much larger Victorian church built in the nineteenth century as a tribute to

Herbert, yet it is the primitive little church of St Andrew that remains his true memorial and the shrine to which his admirers come.

We drove the short distance to Wilton through heavy rain that showed no sign of abating. We passed the imposing entrance to Wilton House and stopped on the outskirts of the town at the Pembroke Arms, a gracious hostelry where we had lunch and warmed ourselves by a roaring fire. We drove through the narrow streets of the small town to the imposing church, outside which we were able to leave the car along a brief stretch of straight and wide road.

A little town today of no great importance but for its agriculture and manufacture of carpet, it is hard to believe that once Wilton was the capital of Saxon England and for many years rivalled Salisbury as Wiltshire's premier city.

The nineteenth-century church comes as a big surprise in this ancient town, for not only is it very large and comparatively modern, but its Byzantine architecture and Italianate design seem oddly at variance with the rest of the town. Designed by the famous architect T. H. Wyatt, it was built by a younger brother of the Earl of Pembroke, Lord Herbert of Lea, who was Minister of War at the time of the Crimean campaign and a close friend and patron of Florence Nightingale.

One enters the church by an impressive flight of steps. Its body is tremendous, very ornate in Byzantine style, and the stained glass windows are exceptionally fine. The altar was a gift of the townspeople, and the carpet was donated by the employees of the Royal Carpet factory. Two beautiful recumbent statues commemorate Sidney Herbert – distantly related to George of Bemerton – and his Russian mother. On this dull dark day the interior was in a state of confusion because a new heating system was being installed. But in spite of pipes, water and workmen, we were able to appreciate the ornate decoration, the coloured glass of the windows, and the many artifacts of unusual design and great beauty. We were especially interested in the organ, as our Chapel Hill organist and choir director Allen Harris played it with great enthusiasm earlier this year. Truly it is a gorgeous church unrivalled in rural England, yet, as its slender bell tower fashioned after an Italian campanile rises over the grey gabled roofs clustered below, it does not seem to fit its Anglo-Saxon surroundings.

We returned to the car and to the marketplace where we walked to the 'other' church in Wilton, the much older, smaller and half-ruined church of St Mary. The little church was locked, but a note said the key could be obtained from the ironmonger in the marketplace. In view of the now torrential rain we decided against going after it, however.

Next we drove to the Royal Carpet factory, the oldest in England, to take one of the hour-long tours offered. We were disappointed to learn that the last tour of the day was solidly booked. Instead we looked around the complex of creeper-covered buildings and read a pamphlet that told us that the manufacture of carpets was begun by an earl of Pembroke who smuggled French weavers over in large wine casks. There are still local Wilton families in existence with obviously French names, descendants perhaps of these arrivals from France. The carpets manufactured here are of the highest quality and are world famous. I remember going into a mosque in Johore Bahru, Malaysia, and finding chandeliers made of Waterford crystal and carpets made in Wilton.

Quite disgusted by the rain, we decided to return to Marlborough by way of Devizes so we could visit bookshops in an effort to locate copies of *Recollections of a G.I. War Bride*, my first book now out of print having sold nearly all copies. We drove across a very desolate stretch of military land on Salisbury Plain, and then left the plain to go through Shrewton and West Lavington. Usually pleasant and placid Devizes was both wet and crowded in the aftermath of market day, and we got very wet searching out the bookshops but finding no books. It was nice however to be greeted by the booksellers as the author of two locally popular books. We left Devizes and drove fast back to Marlborough, the downland road very bleak and desolate in the driving rain. Back in the hotel a drink, hot baths, and a change of clothes restored us, and we spent an enjoyable evening over dinner with our old friend Phil Garside.

SATURDAY, SEPTEMBER 16TH

Rain yet again! I spent the morning visiting my old family friends the Chandlers – Ro, the widow of Jess who was instrumental in getting my books published, and her daughter and son-in-law and young grandchildren. Over coffee we shared photographs and stories about children, books, gardens and all the other things old friends talk of when they are briefly together.

In the afternoon we drove to Kington St Michael to visit my cousin Gwen Carpenter. As she grows older she bears a striking resemblance to my mother. She lives in a tiny house in a development along with a lady friend who is a retired farmer. Daisy is 81 but looks younger with the ruddy complexion and strong Wiltshire accent of the countrywoman. The house, though small, is well-planned with all modern conveniences and a sunroom they call the conservatory. Gwen's tiny garden is well-tended and full of flowers and is still the home of a very elderly tortoise soon to be taken inside for his long winter sleep. These housing developments, duplicated in practically every village in England, represent a great improvement for the rural labouring class, which formerly lived in scenic cottages that often hid deplorable living conditions.

We left after lunch and drove westward towards Bath on the main road.

En route we could just see the pinnacles and turrets of Corsham Court beyond the lengthy grey stone wall enclosing its grounds. This is the home of Lord Methuen. No longer a cloth-making centre, Corsham is now economically dependent on important naval installations, and it is a matter of local pride that Prince Philip was stationed here when he became engaged to Princess Elizabeth.

As we drove on, a spur of the Cotswold Hills was to our right, the steep slopes cut up into tiny irregular fields of many shades of earth tones, seamed together by the dark green of hedgerows into a landscape quilt. Both sheep and cattle were grazing in the pastureland. We soon reached our destination, the long village of Box stretching for a mile or more along the main road. Nearby are quarries that mine the fine Bath stone. The village is the site of the 2-mile long Box tunnel connecting Box and Corsham, one of the railway engineering masterpieces of Isambard Kingdom Brunel, the great Victorian engineer whose bridges, tunnels, railway cuttings and viaducts are all over the West Country.

Today Box has become something of a prosperous bedroom community for Bath and Bristol. We were looking for the house of one Hillary Foord, a Marlborough lady who began corresponding with me after she read my books and whose brother Timothy Williams lives in Chapel Hill. After wandering around the steep hills surrounding Box we eventually found her house. She proved to be a most attractive lady, and we had a fine visit talking of Marlborough past and present, of writing, and of people we both knew. We found her house and garden very interesting too – in fact it is one of the nicest modern English houses that I have been in. Her bird feeders were attracting a variety of birds, and we enjoyed a close look at warblers, tits and chaffinches. We were served a proper English tea before leaving for Marlborough. As we drove we got a fine view of the Cherhill White Horse in the watery westering sun, for the rain had briefly stopped. The chalk figure cut in a fold in the downs was framed between a beech copse on the left and the tall Lansdowne monument on the right – an essentially Wiltshire scene.

Later we drove the few miles to Axford to have dinner at the Red Lion, the small country pub that was the scene of many past good times when Joan and Oscar Fulk were landlords there. Altered and enlarged since those days, it is not quite the same except that Mrs Kirby is still there, blonde and stylishly dressed, happy to see us, and attentive to our needs. The steak and kidney pie was excellent. We returned to Marlborough in a pitch black stormy evening.

SUNDAY, SEPTEMBER 17TH

We awoke again to rain, the sky heavy and threatening. We decided against going to church and instead elected to visit and revisit local places near and dear to us. We drove first through Savernake Forest, and once away from the main roads I was happy to see the forest looking much better. Much clearing has been done so that the giant oaks and beeches that remain can be seen in all their majesty. The stone posts of Iron Gates marking the entrance to the Grand Avenue have been restored though the gates themselves have been removed. The avenue now cannot be compared with the road I remember, when it was lined with tall beeches evenly spaced, their grey trunks straight like soldiers at attention and their leafy tops meeting overhead in a green cathedral arch. The replacement trees are well-tended, however, and the road has been recently paved.

We passed the converging point of the Eight Walks and then saw in the distance on our left the great grey bulk of Tottenham House. It aroused many memories, not this time of my childhood but of the war, for it was in this stately home of the Marquess of Ailesbury that David was stationed when we met and courted. No longer affordable as a residence for the marquess, it is now a boys school. We observed the 'No Trespassing' sign and did not go up the long straight driveway to the imposing entrance, a drive that goes through the centre of what used to be the deer park but is now given over to grazing sheep. In the distance opposite the house we could see the top of the Column, and finding a side road leading in that direction we drove to the monument. In a brief rainless interval we got out to read the rather singular inscriptions. Originally put up to honour an early marquess, a tablet was added several years later to thank God for George III's recovery from madness.

We looked up the broad carriageway now grass-covered to the mansion and sensed what a magnificently planned estate this was in its heyday. This section of the forest has many of the giant beech trees for which the forest has always been noted, and we passed one grove of exceptionally fine old oaks, their gnarled sturdy trunks a contrast in strength to the slender elegance of the beeches. Waist-high bracken was growing freely in any open space, its fern-like fronds now beginning to brown in the late summer. Once frost comes the bracken will die down until its resurrection next spring. We saw no deer, though road signs tell us some still remain from the great herds of both red and fallow deer that were once the pride of Savernake.

We drove then down country roads narrow and lined with high hedges to Great Bedwyn, a sizeable village of some importance in early times and in the Victorian age, when the railway and Kennet and Avon canal both ran through the area. Beside the canal there were great noisy flocks of Canada geese and waterfowl that rushed up when we stopped the car in hopes of being fed. Bedwyn has a fine old Norman church, and services had just finished as we passed the cassocked rector standing at the gate talking with his flock. Sir John Seymour, father of Henry VIII's queen Jane is buried here. Nearby is Lloyd's stonemasonry, the yard a hodgepodge of headstones and monuments, carved angels, saints and mythological figures. It reminded me as always of Thomas Wolfe and his stonecarver father in *Look Homeward Angel*.

Some miles further on we came to Wilton Water, a wide expanse of water fed by natural springs that supplies much of the water used in the canal. In a building in nearby Crofton are the steam engines once used for pumping the water out and transferring it to the highest point of the canal at the Bruce Tunnel at Savernake. Made in 1812 and 1845, these engines are unique, and David, who finds such things fascinating, climbed into the pumping station to see them while I stayed in the car and admired the view. Electricity drives the engines now, but on occasion they are still steamed. On the banks of the canal and around the edges of the lake we saw fishermen huddled under umbrellas but still intent on their pastime.

Down the road we came to Wolfhall, once a part of the Seymour estate and site of the wedding feast of Henry VIII and his third wife Jane, but now a decaying farm with a yard littered with old machinery. The tithe barn where the ageing monarch and his youthful bride danced the night away has been destroyed by fire, but through the trees we could catch a glimpse of rosy brick Tudor chimneys, a hint of past glory and prosperity.

We stopped for lunch at the Savernake Forest Hotel, renovated and updated into a very attractive country inn and thus rather different from the modest hostelry where we lived briefly when first married. It was built by the Marquess of Ailesbury in an oddly isolated spot to house travellers to Marlborough who had to get off the train at Savernake and wait for transportation for the six or so miles into town. The marquess had refused permission to build the railway through the forest to Marlborough, a decision that brought some economic hardship to the little town. Eventually a branch line was built, but all passengers to and from London had to change at Savernake if they wished to get to Marlborough.

After a brief return to Marlborough we drove to Bratton, to visit a cousin and her mother. We had a delightful tea and then made a stop in Devizes to see another acquaintance. We drove back across the downs in the darkening evening of what had been a very wet day. But the rain at last stopped and a full moon came out, bathing the downs in its silvery light and adding to their mystery.

MONDAY, SEPTEMBER 18TH

We had planned a quiet day to go to Calne and Chippenham in search of books. We were fortunate to find two in Chippenham. It was our first dry day, but a cold wind was blowing and it remained cloudy. En route to Calne we stopped at Avebury, site of the largest prehistoric stone temple in England. We have both been there many times before, and many years ago I spent a college summer studying and writing a paper about it. Braving the elements we climbed ditch and vallum to get a good view of the concentric circles and avenue of single sarsen stones. There were many groups of exuberant school children there studying prehistory and enjoying themselves hugely in the process. We were glad to escape the bitter wind and take refuge in the National Trust shop where we found a plethora of historical data and many attractive gift items.

A few miles further on we lunched at the Black Horse Inn at Cherhill. The food was disappointing, but it is an old historic spot that was once the headquarters of a gang of highway robbers who carried out their nefarious deeds naked, partly to terrify their victims and more importantly to escape recognition.

Calne, the 'sweet Calne in Wiltshire' of Charles Lamb, is today a rather sad little town of grey buildings huddled around an enormous parish church. It is still reeling from the economic disaster brought about by the closure of Harris's bacon factory. Chippenham, a very old market town, by contrast exudes an air of prosperity as it is an important agricultural centre and the site of several recently established factories.

Returning we stopped at Preshute Church in the watermeadows on the outskirts of Marlborough to visit my parents' graves, a sad little pilgrimage I always make. My heart is cheered somewhat by the peace and beauty of their resting place in the grassy churchyard beside the limpid waters of the Kennet.

SATURDAY, SEPTEMBER 23RD

Marlborough was very busy with shoppers on this bright sunny morning. The usual stalls were set up in the High Street, and they seemed to be doing a brisk business offering all kinds of produce and bargain goods. We left for Devizes in the late morning, the ride across the downs enjoyable as ever. We saw a string of the Beckhampton racehorses returning to their stables at a sedate walk after galloping no doubt at great speed for their training exercises. Devizes was busy, and after parking the car we stopped for a sandwich lunch at a very old pub called the Elm Tree. The beamed ceilings were low, the floors uneven, and the glass in the windows wavy, and I felt that it had probably not changed much since the days when General Wolfe stayed here while training Wiltshire recruits.

After lunch we walked to the Long Street Museum where we spent a pleasant hour or so learning about the flora and fauna, history, and prehistory of the county. We were especially interested in the models of Avebury and Stonehenge and the documentation of the theories set forth about the origin and meanings of these stone temples. This is an admirable museum and the headquarters of the Wiltshire Archaeological Society.

We drove next to Corsham to visit Corsham Court and see the noted art collection there. Corsham is another of southwestern Wiltshire's old woollen towns, more akin to Gloucester's Cotswold country than the chalk uplands of the major part of Wiltshire. There are many beautiful old stone weavers houses here built in Flemish style by imported master craftsmen in the Middle Ages. The upper storey windows are larger than those below to let maximum light in on the looms as the weavers worked on intricate patterns. The dominant noble family here is that of Methuen, descendants of Flemings arrived long ago. The Methuen family was very successful in the publishing field and one, whom I remember my parents talking about, had a distinguished military career, reaching the rank of Field Marshal.

Acquiring wealth and power through innate ability and skill, the Methuens became the owners of the great house and its surrounding park known as Corsham Court and began assembling an art collection that is considered one of the best in the country. The core of the gracious house was built in Elizabethan times but added to in the Stuart and Georgian eras. Capability Brown planned the gardens and, in a departure from his usual landscaping work, also designed some of the additions to the house. The house is built of the honey-coloured stone quarried locally. The grounds contain some enormous trees and two delightful 'follies': a tiny little Gothic bath house and the Bradford Porch, which came from a house owned by a family ancestor in Bradford-on-Avon. The extensive stone-walled park is now the home to large flocks of grazing sheep. As we entered the great gates to the house the old spired church was on our right and a great cedar tree of indeterminate age spread its branches over clumps of tiny pink cyclamen tentatively putting out their blossoms in the bright sun in spite of the cold wind.

The house and the art collection are open to the public, and we were able to purchase a very complete and informative guidebook describing the pictures and many of the furnishings. The most valuable paintings are hung in the enormous hall known as the Triple Cube. Among them are masterpieces by Lely, Reynolds, Van Dyck, Fra Lippo Lippi, Rubens and other well-known painters too numerous to mention. There were no professional guides, but the house was policed by Methuen employees who, judging from their broad Wiltshire accents, live or work on the estate or in the town. They were very knowledgeable and willing to answer questions, doing so with quite a proprietorial air that I found touching and endearing, perhaps a trace of remaining feudal loyalty.

Chapter Nine

1992

WILTSHIRE, WEYMOUTH, STROUD, PORTSMOUTH, CHICHESTER, ARUNDEL, IPSWICH, WORKSOP, RIPON, APPLEBY, KNUTSFORD, SOUTH WALES, THE COTSWOLDS

We believe, perhaps with some pessimism, perhaps with a common-sense acceptance of advancing years, that this will be our last trip to England. Consequently, we planned it carefully to see as many people and places as possible. We elected October as the time to go because of home commitments, budget and hopes that the weather would be as good as it was in 1977. In this we were disappointed, for we experienced colder weather than I had expected, with much overcast cloud and drizzle though fortunately with no extended periods of heavy rain.

We decided to avoid hotels as much as possible, staying with friends or relatives or in bed-and-breakfast establishments. It was a decision that paid off in more than the saving of pounds and dollars, for we cemented old friendships and made rewarding new ones.

OCTOBER 2ND TO 9TH

IN AND AROUND MARLBOROUGH

For the first week of our three-week stay we enjoyed bed and breakfast at Cadley House near Marlborough. It was an unforgettable experience of gracious living and excellent amenities provided by our hosts, a charming couple named Julian and Antonia Wethered. The large brick Victorian house lies just off the Salisbury Road in the heart of Savernake Forest. It is close by little Cadley Church, now no longer used for services, and is opposite the tiny school closed these many years. A wide circular drive approaches the house, which is surrounded by gardens and lawns set against a backdrop of the venerable forest's towering beeches and sturdy oaks. Marlborough, about two miles away, is easily accessible.

Our first week we spent visiting friends in Marlborough and other places described in my earlier journals. We enjoyed the drives through familiar fields and forests, downs and dales, villages and small towns, all tinged with the colours of early fall and especially bright when the sun deigned to shine. We made a trip to Weymouth on a cold bright day with blustery wind whipping the waves into foam-tipped breakers and blowing sand across the road along the sea front. The Georgian town was quiet, the beaches deserted, and few shoppers were out, making us realize that Weymouth along with other holiday towns had had a bad summer and has been badly hurt by the severe recession. The greatest change we saw was in our three great-nieces, for in three years one had become a pretty teenager and the others at the ages of 9 and 6 no longer babies but enchanting little girls.

WEDNESDAY, OCTOBER 7TH

STROUD, GLOUCESTERSHIRE

We spent the early part of the morning driving around the villages of Pewsey and Wilcot. In Wilcot we drove along the canal – still and covered in green algae – trying to find Rose Cottage, where my sister had lived many years ago. Then we left for Far Thrupp, a village outside of Stroud in Gloucestershire, to see my publisher Alan Sutton. We drove the straight Roman road across the downs toward Swindon, then through the flat waterlogged land where the Thames rises, and then on to Cirencester with its imposing church tower. Built at the intersection of three roads, Cirencester is believed to have been the largest Roman town in Britain after London. In the Middle Ages it became an important woollen centre and held the largest cloth market in the West. We drove for many miles along the walled boundary of Cirencester Park, part of which has been taken for the Royal Agricultural College. We saw many blue-jeaned, T-shirted, long-haired young men and women presumably destined for careers in farming and related industries. Leaving the lush woods of the estate we went through a high, desolate area that appeared to be used in some spots for farming and in its more open spaces for gliding. We came at last to a shabby rundown inn called the White Horse where, despite appearances, a hospitable innkeeper provided the food and drink we needed.

As we drove on after lunch, the land became hilly, with village houses clinging to steep slopes and swift streams coursing along valley bottoms. We were nearing Stroud, from which five such valleys radiate. They were once known as the Golden Valleys for the prosperity they brought to the cloth manufacturers and dyers of the town and surrounding area. The fast-flowing streams provided power for the mills and pure water for dyeing, and the soil provided fuller's earth for whitening. Much of the cloth was exported to Europe, and even today Stroud still makes and dyes cloth. Some mills remain in the valley villages, though most are used for purposes other than weaving. It was in such a village, Far Thrupp, almost a suburb of Stroud, that we found the Alan Sutton publishing offices housed in a former mill.

After our meeting we drove home fast to arrive in time for a little party with Mr and Mrs Wethered and a Mrs Winkleigh, who had once lived in Cadley House. She is the widow of an army officer and the mother-in-law of the Earl of Cardigan, heir to the Marquess of Ailesbury.

FRIDAY, OCTOBER 9TH

PORTSMOUTH, CHICHESTER, ARUNDEL

We left Cadley reluctantly. We could not have been more comfortable or made to feel more welcome. Our destination was Portsmouth, the great naval port of the South Coast that has been home to the Royal Navy for some 500 years. A city at the forefront of naval tradition, Portsmouth has witnessed many historic occasions. The first tobacco and potatoes arrived on the docks here from Raleigh's Virginia, and Portsmouth was the last view of England for thousands of convicts bound for Botany Bay in Australia, including those later known as the Tolpuddle Martyrs of Dorset. In 1944 Portsmouth was a departure point for D-Day invasion troops. The city's greatest hero, however, remains Lord Nelson, who sailed from Portsmouth in 1805 for Trafalgar, where he met victory and death. Its greatest shrine is Nelson's flagship, prophetically named Victory, now restored and immaculately preserved. It is still a fully commissioned ship flying the flag of the Commander-in-Chief of the Naval Home Command.

The sleek steel-grey ships of the modern British fleet could be seen in a marvellous panorama of maritime strength. We followed signs for the 'Historic Ships' dockyard, home to H.M.S. *Warrior*, the *Mary Rose* and H.M.S. *Victory*. The *Warrior* was an ironclad and the pride of Victoria's fleet, while the *Mary Rose* was King Henry VIII's favourite ship. It was sunk with few survivors in the Solent on July 19th 1545, during Henry's French campaigns. She remained in her watery grave for over 400 years before excavation efforts raised the wreck and recovered her treasure, now displayed along with the ship in a special exhibition hall.

Today we had time only for H.M.S. *Victory*. After a hurried lunch we

joined a tour led by an old sailor who proved an excellent guide –
knowledgeable and humorous and able to make history come alive. He
took us first to the officers' quarters, contrasting them with the dark,
cramped mess decks where the crew lived, ate and slept. We saw the spot
where Nelson fell early in the battle, now marked by a shining brass plate.
He was picked off by a French sharpshooter, perhaps because he insisted on
wearing his many medals and decorations into battle. Mortally wounded, he
was carried below to the cockpit where he died, first ordering his face to be
covered with a kerchief lest his sailors lose heart at his falling. He lived long
enough to know that victory was assured and that his last command,
'England expects this day that every man will do his duty,' had been carried
out. His body was transported to England in a cask of brandy and given a
hero's burial. After the French fleet was destroyed at Trafalgar, Napoleon
was never again able to consider an invasion of England.

The Admiral's cabin was luxuriously furnished in highly polished
mahogany furniture. In war, the cabin became a battle station, and the
furniture was packed in canvas bags and placed in a lighter that was towed
behind the ship. This was common practice for friend and foe alike, and
there was a gentleman's agreement to save the precious furniture if possible.
In the cabin we noticed three portraits, one a pastel of Lady Emma
Hamilton, Nelson's mistress and the love of his life, a pale watercolour of
Horatia, their unacknowledged daughter, and an oil of Nelson himself.
Nelson, a very short man of 5 feet, 3 inches in height, is made to appear
very tall in relation to the background. In reality he appeared very short
indeed, especially next to Hardy, the *Victory*'s 6-foot 4-inch captain who
was Nelson's close friend and in whose arms Nelson died. I have recently
read the very fine biography of Lady Hamilton by Norah Lofts, so all we
saw today seemed especially interesting.

We left for Chichester, a cathedral city some miles to the east. Chichester
was first of all a Roman settlement and military camp built at the
intersection of two important roads, a point which is marked today by a
large ornate Butter Cross erected in the sixteenth century. On this bright
but very windy and cold day many chattering uniformed school boys and
girls were gathered around the cross, which apparently is a popular meeting
place. We went into the lovely cathedral, built on a Saxon foundation but
mostly Norman in style. The nave is one of soaring beauty, and the spire is
a landmark for miles. We saw the site of the shrine of St Richard of
Chichester, bishop from 1245–1253 who was canonized in 1262. Until it
was destroyed by order of Henry VIII, the shrine rivalled that of St Thomas
à Becket at Canterbury in the numbers of pilgrims visiting it. It was
St Richard who gave us the beautiful prayer still sometimes sung as anthem
or introit:

O most merciful Redeemer,
Friend and Brother
May I know Thee more clearly,
Love thee more dearly
And follow thee more nearly.

While in Chichester I was able to meet a correspondent named Joe Jennings for the first time. Joe, a Marlborough native like myself, and I have been corresponding for some time, so it was a pleasure to spend some time with him.

Leaving Chichester after a restorative cup of tea, we drove further east towards Arundel in search of a hamlet named Lyminster where we had reserved room at a bed and breakfast house located in a vineyard. The way was scenic but made long by a detour around extensive road works. We glimpsed the great castle at Arundel but in the gathering dusk had some difficulty finding the house we wanted. We drove for what seemed a long way along the edge of tall green vines, some with grapes not yet harvested. People may be surprised to hear of grapes growing and wine being made in England's cold northern climate, but in fact the Romans grew grapes and made wine here long ago, perhaps attempting to bring something of their Mediterranean homeland to their sojourn in a wintry land. Later monks of the Middle Ages made wine for their own and travellers' use, though this ended when the monasteries were closed. Wine was then imported from the Continent and its use restricted to the upper classes. Only in recent years has winemaking made a comeback, though most operations are small because the climate is not suitable for grape cultivation on a large scale.

We finally reached our destination, where we were welcomed heartily by our hostess. She and her husband have their own small winemaking operation, and she described the hard work involved in cultivating, harvesting and pressing the grapes, and in producing, bottling and marketing the wine. She also provided a welcome cup of tea and directions to a nearby village called Burpham (pronounced 'burfam') where the public house, the St George and the Dragon, served us a gourmet meal in a building of great charm and antiquity.

SATURDAY AND SUNDAY, OCTOBER 10TH AND 11TH

ARUNDEL, IPSWICH

We left our vineyard early after a good night and an excellent breakfast of finnan haddie delicately cooked in butter and milk. We stopped briefly in Arundel, a small West Sussex town built on the banks of the lovely river Arun. The town's streets and houses climb the river banks to the battlemented walls and towers of a massive castle that flies the flag of the Duke of Norfolk, premier duke of England. The castle was built by Roger Montgomery, Earl of Shrewsbury, shortly after the Norman Conquest. Situated in a magnificent park, it has been added to through the centuries and was heavily damaged by Cromwell's forces during the Civil War and then later restored. We were disappointed that both grounds and castle, normally open to the public, are closed on Saturdays. The castle is full of treasures, furniture, china, silver, portraits and pictures by the Great Masters, and it also houses some personal possessions of Mary, Queen of Scots.

The Norfolk title was conferred on Sir John Howard in 1483 by Richard III and retained through the Tudor years. Lord Howard of Effingham, commander-in-chief of the fleet that defeated the Spanish Armada in 1588, was a member of the same Howard family. Henry Howard, Earl of Surrey, heir to the dukedom until his execution in 1547, was an important poet of the pre-Elizabethan period and is remembered for establishing the English form of the sonnet and as the first poet to publish in blank verse. He gave us such lines as:

> Content thyself with thine estate
> Neither wish death nor fear his might.

Two of Henry VIII's queens, Anne Boleyn and Katherine Howard, were nieces of the third Duke of Norfolk. Henry beheaded both on charges of adultery. The dukes, who are Roman Catholics, own the hereditary office of Earl Marshal of England and are responsible for overseeing all royal ceremonies such as coronations, weddings and funerals.

As one looks across the river valley to the castle, the beautiful nineteenth-century, French-Gothic Roman Catholic church of St Philip Neri adds to the richness of the scene. It adjoins the fourteenth-century church of St Nicholas, the church of England parish church. There is a dividing wall separating the Fitzalan Chapel, where the tombs of the Catholic Howards are located, from the nave of the Protestant church, a unique situation in which Catholic and Protestant worship under the same roof.

We waited for the sun to come out so we could take a photo of a lovely lime avenue beside the castle grounds, then drove east towards the Thames, crossing at Dartford via the tunnel beneath the river. We saw for the first time a graceful new bridge spanning the river, which is reserved for southbound traffic. We bypassed the cities of Chelmsford and Colchester and went on through the flat fertile fields of Essex, eventually reaching Ipswich. My friend Betty met us and led us through a maze of city streets to her small house, where we spent the rest of the day with good food and conversation.

The next day continued in this fashion, the weather being too wet, cold and windy for sightseeing. In the afternoon we went to a concert in the impressive city hall, a rare performance by the Budapest Symphony Orchestra of works by Kodaly, Beethoven and Dvorak.

MONDAY, OCTOBER 12TH

EN ROUTE FROM IPSWICH TO WORKSOP

We left Ipswich early seeking less-travelled roads through Suffolk and Norfolk, going through the pretty old town of Ixworth and several small villages. The fields in this part of the country are big and flat, and the red-brown soil, much of it newly ploughed and ready for the sowing of winter wheat, looks very fertile. Other fields are green with sugar beet, an important crop in the region. Many of the village houses are washed in pale colours and decorated with the ancient local art of 'pargetting,' raised patterns in the clay from which they are built. The villages have towered or steepled churches that are grey with antiquity and sometimes covered with silvery lichen or Virginia creeper, now crimson with the onset of fall, and most are treasure troves of history, though much of it unexplored.

We drove past walled estates with lodges at their entrance gates, but few had names and most of the big houses were hidden behind walls. One of the largest and most notable of these mansions is Euston Hall, seat of the dukes of Grafton. We drove down the long street of the village of Euston lined with black and white half-timbered houses. The village church is located within the park grounds surrounding the hall. Undoubtedly the church was there first and the big house was built near it for the convenience of the landed family. Many big houses often had private chapels built within them, but retainers and servants were expected to worship in the parish church under the feudal eye of the gentry.

Passing into Norfolk we stopped at a park on the outskirts of Thetford to see Thetford Castle, actually more of a prehistoric earthwork than a mediaeval fortress, and then entered the town along a fine avenue of chestnut trees. Thetford is a prosperous market town that started as a Roman settlement at the confluence of the Thet and Little Ouse rivers. Here the Icknield Way crossed the stream by a ford, now replaced by an arched bridge. Later Thetford was the site of an important priory that is now in ruins but was a see of an East Anglian bishop in Norman times. The town is best known today as the birthplace of Thomas Paine, whose writing did much to foster the American Revolution. His statue stands in the town centre.

Thetford is the chief town in a rather desolate area known as Breckland that lies between Suffolk and Norfolk. It is made up of tracts of heathland that are good for only marginal farming, but it is also the site of some of ancient man's earliest attempts at agricultural and settled, non-nomadic life. Many relics have been found near the site of a Neolithic flint mine known as Grimes Graves. One of the pits is open to the public. Flint axes and arrowheads are found in abundance, and the grave mounds known as barrows are scattered throughout the area.

An area of woodland known as Thetford Park Forest extends for many miles around Thetford. Much of it is planted by the Forestry Commission with both deciduous and coniferous trees. It has become popular as a vacation spot with fine facilities for picnicking and camping. We pulled off into one of these with the unusual name of the Lynford Stag, so called because of a large metal stag erected by local landowner Sir Richard Sutton. An expert marksman, he was prone to practise his aim on the model beast. The stag still stands proudly at the far end of an open space cleared for sports activities and can be seen from the road by those who pass.

A few miles on we came to a village called Mundford and there we took a side road directing us to Lynford Hall, an impressive mansion built in decorative brick work and approached through a series of courtyards. We found it to be a country club and hotel and no longer the seat of the aristocratic Suttons. On this cold Monday morning it seemed quite deserted with no sign of life.

Leaving the forest we drove through desolate country along roads lined with pine trees. We detoured again at a village called Cockley Clay where there were signs for an Iceni village, but we decided not to explore as time was running short.

We drove through the lovely old town of Swaffham, its most famous citizen one John Chapman, known as the Pedlar of Swaffham. He is said to have gone to London to seek his fortune but was directed in a dream to return to Swaffham because he would find treasure in his own backyard. Discovering a pot of gold under a tree, he used the money to enlarge the church.

We came next to Fakenham down a pretty wooded road, passing a sign pointing to Raynham Hall, the home of Viscount Townshend. Townshend was a prominent politician of the eighteenth century and brother-in-law to prime minister Sir Robert Walpole. He is best remembered today for his interest in scientific agriculture. He promoted the rotation of crops and encouraged turnip growing, earning him the nickname of 'Turnip' Townshend. Fakenham seemed a busy little market town with a fine church and a scenic old mill next to a fine hotel where we got a good lunch.

We then took country roads to Sandringham, the royal estate of 7,000 acres purchased by Edward VII in 1861. Both house and gardens were closed to the public as of September 30th, but we took a photograph of the large wrought iron gates emblazoned with the royal coat-of-arms. The park encompasses several parishes and we saw the church in West Newton where the royal family worships when in residence.

We came shortly to King's Lynn, the great and ancient port where the Great Ouse empties into the Wash, and drove through much of its industrial and mercantile complex. Though silting has diminished its importance as a trading and fishing port, it remains busy and seems to have recovered some of its former prosperity, and the area should grow more as England's ties to Europe become stronger.

To the west of the town the flat marshy fenland begins, stretching into Lincolnshire. We passed the village of Walpole St Andrew from which King John in 1216 sent wagons loaded with royal treasure across the Wash to escape from his French enemies. They were trapped in the quicksand of the treacherous water to be lost forever. John died shortly afterwards.

We seemed to drive endlessly through the depressingly flat land of Lincolnshire. Bitter winds howled across the huge diked and ditched fields which are grey, drab and bleak at this time of year. Dwellings and farm buildings seemed lost in the inhospitable landscape. We passed the Royal Air Force Officers College at Cranwell, where so many World War II pilots were trained in the flat fields ideal for flying exercises.

We entered Nottinghamshire and crossed the Trent, one of England's most important rivers, at Newark. Here we got lost at a roundabout where the exit we needed was closed. Losing precious time we found ourselves in a pretty village called Coddington, where a young fresh-faced boy delivering newspapers gave us excellent directions to the A1 north in accents we could decipher only with difficulty.

After a few more miles we reached Worksop and beyond it to the north the village of Carlton-in-Lindrick, now almost a suburb of the town. We found my cousin's house and were heartily welcomed by him and his wife.

TUESDAY, OCTOBER 13TH

WORKSOP, CLUMBER PARK, SHERWOOD FOREST, NEWSTEAD ABBEY

Worksop, an industrial town in the coal-mining area of north Nottinghamshire is a surprisingly pleasant and historically interesting place. The unattractive sounding name is a very ancient and honourable one that developed into its modern form from the Saxon 'Werchesope', going through, it is said, some 60 different spellings before arriving at Worksop. Uncertain of the meaning, most etymologists believe it means 'fortified hill'. The Domesday Book of 1081 indicated it was already a prosperous settlement. In the succeeding centuries it was often visited by kings and queens as it is located on the fringes of Sherwood Forest, a royal hunting preserve. In 1542 the fifth Earl of Shrewsbury, Lord of the Manor of Worksop, was given the priory lands in return for providing a glove to support the sovereign's right hand as it held the royal sceptre at coronations, a custom that endured for centuries. At the time of the Industrial Revolution vast deposits of coal were discovered nearby, mining became very important, and the town grew rapidly. Related industries were chairmaking and beer brewing. Despite the fact that now the mines are mostly outworked and closed, many citizens were incensed at the arbitrary closure of many of the country's remaining mines, a decision announced within the past week and later modified.

Founded in 1103, Worksop's ancient Priory, now the parish church, is the town's chief glory. The gatehouse, where visitors were received, made welcome, fed and sheltered, is the oldest part of the building. Inside the church is a 140-foot-long nave, its roof supported by huge columns. The stained-glass windows are exceptionally beautiful, and there are many tombs and effigies of notable people. The east end of the church was added to in the last century, making the church a beautiful meld of ancient and modern and telling the story of church and town life down through the ages.

We could only spare a few brief moments for the Priory before going on to Clumber Park. The surrounding countryside, gentle and wooded, is called the Dukeries because it comprises the estates originally owned by dukes and earls making up the titled families of the area. Clumber, the best known of these estates, was formerly owned by the dukes of Newcastle but today belongs to the National Trust. It is a fine park of about 4,000 acres with forest walks, rare trees and shrubs, rhododendron displays, and a great lake well-stocked with fish. The great ducal mansion is no more, though its outline can still be traced on the greensward where it stood. Partially destroyed by fire, it was demolished in 1937. The nearby Gothic chapel built by one of the dukes in 1886 is open for visitors, and services are regularly held in it. Its spire points heavenwards among the great trees surrounding it. The fall is probably the best time of the year to view Clumber and we were fortunate in the weather, for it was a warm, sunny, windless day with a cloudless blue sky. We walked along the woodland paths and the lakeshore walk known as the Lincoln Terrace. We saw the miniature cannon pointing lakewards with which one of the dukes used to shoot toy boats he sailed on the water, and among the trees on the distant shore we could see Greek temples erected during the time when such follies were in fashion. Clumber gave its name to a special breed of dog, the

Clumber spaniel. One of the dukes, believing that the barking of hounds alerted the game and so spoiled the chase, developed through selective breeding a spaniel that could not bark and so remained silent during the hunt.

We left Clumber and drove through part of Sherwood Forest to Edwinstowe where we lunched at an inn called the Royal Oak. On the way we passed a very large and ancient oak, its limbs propped against the ravages of time. It is known as the Major Oak and is believed to have been the meeting place for Robin Hood and his Merry Men. The church at Edwinstowe is likewise believed to have been the wedding place of Robin and Maid Marian.

Our next stop was some miles away at Newstead Abbey, once the home of Lord Byron and his ancestors. The abbey was built by Henry II in 1170, in part to atone for the murder of Thomas à Becket. Byron spent part of his childhood and young manhood there, but was forced to sell it in 1817 to pay his debts. The great house was built around the ruins, part of which remain and lend romantic beauty to the setting. The house is set in an extensive park and surrounded by lovely gardens, full of fall blooms and resident peacocks. The house is filled with Byron memorabilia but today was unfortunately already closed for the season. We saw the statue to Bo'sun, Byron's dog, and the poem he wrote eulogizing his beloved pet. Byron loved Newstead Abbey, though he thought the surrounding country a 'region of dullness.' He is said to have flooded the monks' mortuary to make a bathing pool for himself and his dog. Sometimes he and his friends would dress up as monks and carouse far into the night. This reminded me of Sir Francis Dashwood and his 'monks of Mendmenham' and the orgies of the Hell-Fire Club. Byron is buried nearby at Hucknall Church. Dying a hero's death in the swamps of Missolonghi fighting for Greek independence, his body was returned to England but denied burial in Westminster Abbey. There is a bust of him in the chancel of the church, a lamp burns eternally in his memory, and a brass wreath of laurels given by the King of Greece is set in the floor of the church.

Returning to Worksop we went through Mansfield, a town that figures prominently in the Robin Hood legends but is known principally today for shoe manufacture. After tea and a short rest we drove to a village called Wellow, where we had dinner at the Red Lion. Opposite the inn stands what is believed to be the tallest Maypole in England. The traditional dances are held every May Day, and the sleepy village comes alive with mediaeval festivity. Our dinner in the tiny pub was delightful, and we were waited on by a gentle girl whose beauty seemed to typify that of an unspoiled English maid.

WEDNESDAY, OCTOBER 14TH

EN ROUTE TO APPLEBY, TADCASTER, RIPON, AND THROUGH
YORKSHIRE TO CUMBRIA

We drove north, going through the pretty old village of Blyth along what was once the main road between London and York before getting on the more modern highway. We passed from Nottinghamshire into Yorkshire, along the way crossing several of that county's famous rivers – the Ouse, Wharfe, Nidd, Swale and Ure – as we followed the A1 north to Scotch Corner. We passed a sign to Harewood House, home for many years to the late Princess Royal, Countess of Harewood, only daughter of George V, but felt that a diversion there would be too time-consuming with only a remote chance that the house would be open.

Having travelled this road on previous occasions, we noted many familiar names. We detoured to a place called Tadcaster, where we thought the Wharton family may have once owned estates. We also hoped the originals of the family effigies we had seen in Kirkby Stephen would be located in the local church, but we were disappointed. It seemed a sad little town, principally taken up by two large breweries, 'Tower' and 'Magnet', which dispensed an overpoweringly rich aroma. Both the old church and the library were locked up and we could find no one to take our enquiries. Returning to the highway we could see the misty purplish hills of the Pennines in the distance on our right.

Some miles further on we took a side road to Ripon to see the cathedral there. It was an isolated narrow way through high moorland country, and we stopped to get some lunch at a run-down inn called the Blackamoor. Getting out of the car we encountered a strong and bitter wind, making us grateful to get inside to warm ourselves at the smoky fire burning in the lounge.

Ripon is a small country town with a cathedral that ranks with York and Beverley as one of the first centres of Christianity in the north of England. Though the cathedral is not especially large, it appears spacious as it is open and uncluttered. The first church was built in AD 672 by St Wilfred and dedicated to St Peter. This church was destroyed by the Vikings in AD 860, although they spared the Saxon crypt. The present building has evolved since 1180 with many additions and, after a damaging storm in 1450, much rebuilding. The heavily carved choir stalls were made between 1489 and 1494 by unknown craftsmen of unusual skill. The Misericord, tiny half seats against which old or invalid monks could prop themselves during the interminable services, are carved in patterns half humorous, half minatory, and are among the great treasures of Ripon.

We were fortunate to be present at the rehearsal for a hymn festival to be presented by the combined choirs of several district high schools. It was a joy to listen to fresh young voices raised in the lofty nave to the glory of God and to watch the intent expression of young boys and girls trim and neat and shining in their school uniforms.

We returned to the main road, continuing north and passing Catterick Camp, a huge army installation sprawling in desolate moorland. It is built very close to the site of a Roman military base, traces of which remain. At Scotch Corner we took the west road leading into Cumbria and so at last reached Appleby and Bongate House, where we had made reservations for dinner and the night. Bongate proved to be a pleasant Georgian house, and we enjoyed an excellent dinner featuring English dishes of steak and kidney pie and bread pudding. Afterward we spent an hour in a firelit lounge talking to three elderly Yorkshire couples who were fellow guests. Though their accents were those of rural Yorkshire, they had travelled much and had some pithy down-to-earth comments on the state of the world in general. When they heard our name was Wharton, they talked of the local family of that name, and one of the men said he had received one of the Wharton Bibles when he was at school. Such Bibles were then, and still are, presented to local schoolchildren by a trust set up by Lord Thomas Wharton many years ago.

THURSDAY, OCTOBER 15TH

APPLEBY, KIRKBY STEPHEN, KIRKBY THORE

We woke to a very cold morning and at breakfast actually saw a few snowflakes. We stopped in Appleby's wide street to buy a newspaper, parking opposite the old Moot Hall built in the middle of the street and still used for council meetings. Prior to the local government changes of 1974, Appleby was billed as the smallest county town in England. The main street rises from St Michael's Church at one end to Appleby Castle at the other. The grammar school, which originally stood near the church, is of interest to Americans because George Washington's brother Lawrence and other family members were pupils there.

We then drove to Kirkby Stephen, our third trip to what we believe was the home of Wharton ancestors. On this cold damp morning the town, lively enough in summer, looked very depressing. We parked behind the church, which is surrounded by a hodgepodge of buildings of great antiquity but in a state of some disrepair, their stone walls dank and dripping and the ground a mass of half-frozen mud. Walking into the main street we were met by blasts of bone-chilling cold, so we took refuge in a bookshop that yielded no new information about the Whartons. We then went out to the dairy farm Wharton Hall has become. While the ruins remain as they were on our previous visits, the inner courtyard has been made habitable and looks quite attractive, its grey stone walls and mullioned windows surrounded by the greenest grass. A short chat with a farmworker told us nothing we did not already know, and we returned to Appleby for lunch and a quick look at Appleby Castle. The weather remained very cold and windy with rain and bright sun at intervals, and once we were treated to one of the most colourful and complete rainbows I have ever seen.

Appleby Castle is now the site of a farm that breeds rare animals, and as we drove around we indeed saw cattle, sheep and other domestic animals that were strange to us. But we were more interested in the castle itself, which has a strong Norman keep that has been restored and is remarkably well-preserved. A good deal of restoration was completed after the Civil War by Lady Anne Clifford, one of the dominant women of her age. She was a great benefactress to Appleby, building a hospital and restoring the church which holds her tomb. The Great Hall was open to the public and we spent a little time there admiring the fine furniture and objets d'art of the Clifford family. There are many fine pictures, among them many portraits of the Cliffords. Most notable is the Great Picture, a triptych covering the fortunes of the family over several decades. It was commissioned by Lady Anne to commemorate her final acquisition of the Clifford estates.

Still in search of Wharton roots, we drove north to Kirkby Thore where we believed some ruins of a hall once belonging to a branch of the family would be found. It turned out to be a depressed unprepossessing village, with a gypsum mining operation nearby. We explored the lanes around the village and saw a sign pointing to Great Musgrave and Warcop, and we remembered that the name Musgrave appears in the records at Kirkby Stephen. We found the church but it was locked. It was built of sandstone, badly eroded in places, and seemed in a generally bad state of repair. It was too cold to spend much time looking at the headstones in the churchyard and we saw no Wharton names. An elderly man working in his garden told us of a farmhouse called Kirkby Thore Hall. Approached by an avenue of trees, it was comparatively modern but could have been the site of an earlier house possibly belonging to one of the Whartons. Like the church, it was built of sandstone perhaps taken from a nearby Roman fort.

Disenchanted we left the village driving as fast as possible to link up with the M6 en route for Sculshaw Willows near Knutsford in Cheshire, our next port of call.

FRIDAY, OCTOBER 16TH

SCULSHAW WILLOWS, THROUGH WALES TO SOLVA

Our bed and breakfast near Knutsford was rather special, for it belongs to Elizabeth Grayling, a great friend of a great friend of ours who lives in El Paso, Texas. We were treated as honoured guests and enjoyed a delightful dinner courtesy of the house. Afterwards we sat in the drawing room by a blazing fire and found much to talk about while two lively Jack Russell terriers frolicked at our feet or sat in our laps. We left early in the morning as we had many miles to go.

We crossed into Wales at Trewern at noon after making a brief stop in a town called Whitchurch for some film. It was an old place of narrow streets, unattractive looking in the hard rain that was falling. We crossed the Severn and detoured around Shropshire's county town of Shrewsbury. We were delayed getting through Welshpool, the gateway to mid-Wales. The town centre was crowded with people, the streets narrow, crooked and undergoing road work that caused detours. But the rain had cleared, the sun was out, houses on the outskirts of the town had pretty gardens of fall flowers, and the roads were lined with trees just assuming their autumn colours. We drove diagonally across country to Machynlleth, traversing the wide main street, which appeared unchanged since our last visit in 1986, and continued westward toward the coast. How green were the valleys, how blue the sky and how bright the sun, how white the sheep dotting the mountain sides and how wild the sudden brief storms that in an instant transformed a bright world into frightening greyness only to be followed by a rainbow with its eternal promise and the reappearance of the sun. We stopped at a wayside inn, The Brigand, for lunch. Fishermen were there in their stockinged feet, but they had caught nothing and the larder was empty of the local salmon billed on the menu. On then past Aberystwyth to catch our first glimpse of the sea near Cardigan – a happy meeting of green field, blue sky, white-capped waves, grey rocks and fleecy sheep. At Fishguard we got to a bank with three minutes to spare to cash travellers' cheques for the weekend and only then could we turn our attention to the lovely port to and from which ferries between Wales and Ireland regularly sail. In 1797 a party of French soldiers sent to attack Bristol were blown off course to land near Fishguard. They mistook Welsh women clad in red shawls for grenadiers and hastily capitulated. It was to be the last time forces of a foreign enemy landed on British shores.

We were on the last leg of our long journey through Wales and dusk was fast falling. We were lost so we stopped at a telephone to call my old, old friend Babs who came out to find us. We were in Solva, a delightful village perched above a winding inlet where fishing boats and yachts were anchored. Babs led us through a narrow maze of lanes seemingly for miles before we reached her isolated farmhouse. We climbed the stone steps, where a mother cat was nursing several kittens, into the warm haven of the kitchen. I was seated in a corner by the 'Aga', or stove, and given a cup of tea and 'lard' cake, a West Country delicacy for which our home county of Wiltshire was famous in the old days when we were children together. I can say little about our visit except that we talked nonstop about the past and the different directions our lives had taken. Babs had become a farmer's wife and the mother of a very large family, coping with hardship, illness and widowhood, while I had been a cosseted protected American wife. Our common ground I suppose is writing. Babs has contributed a column to the *Farmer's Weekly* for many years, while I have set down some of my life's experiences. We talked into the wee hours, going to bed at last up under the eaves. It was, for me, the most rewarding experience of this whole trip.

SATURDAY, OCTOBER 17TH

ST DAVID'S AND THE WELSH COAST, EN ROUTE TO MONMOUTH

We awoke to a cold bright morning with a view from our window of the distant Preseli Mountains. These hills, rising only to 1,760 feet, are the centre of a national park. From here came the altar stone and the 33 'blue' stones that form the inner circle of Stonehenge about 100 miles away. The stones for the Wiltshire temple were undoubtedly transported in wood and skin boats along the coasts and up the rivers. From this historians deduce that the Welsh countryside was sacred to the priesthood of the period 1600–1440 BC. Many minerals came from here, including lead, copper and gold, and there was some trade even at that early date between Wales and Ireland. In the mountain areas there are many signs of prehistoric life – standing stones, stone circles, gravesites, camps, and earthworks. Centuries later early Celtic Christians kept the rituals of their religion alive in the remote vastnesses of the mountains.

Babs provided us with a hearty breakfast and then drove us the several miles to St David's, the smallest cathedral city in the country and the site of one of the oldest and most interesting of cathedrals. The first sight of the cathedral is surprising, for it is built in a valley so that the higher town looks down upon it at eye level with the top of the strong sturdy tower. While the present building is thought to date from the twelfth century, its origins are much older. In the Middle Ages St David's was the destination for countless pilgrims, and two pilgrimages to St David's were reckoned to have the religious merit of one to Rome. The great church is built of a purplish sandstone quarried locally, and nearby, lower still in the valley on the banks of a stream, are the very impressive ruins of the mediaeval Bishop's Palace, which at long last is undergoing extensive renovation and reconstruction.

The cathedral is dedicated to St David, the patron saint of Wales. He was a Celtic monk, abbot, and bishop of the sixth century and the most important of the early saints who helped spread Christianity throughout the tribes of far western Britain. He founded a monastery on the banks of the stream where the cathedral and palace now stand. Many legends are told about him, and he was believed to have visited the Holy Land. Many wells are attributed to him because he was always very concerned about a fresh water supply for his people. He is believed to have died on March 1st, AD 589, and is buried in the grounds of his monastery and what is now the cathedral. March 1st has become a secular and patriotic holiday in Wales and is known as St David's Day. Welshmen wear the leek – a type of green onion that grows wild in Wales – on his day, recalling how he ordered Welshmen to wear it to distinguish friend from foe in a skirmish. Shakespeare refers to the wearing of the leek in *Henry V.* Visiting his Welsh soldiers on March 1st the king himself wears a leek 'for a memorable honour, for I am Welsh you know.' In the nineteenth century the daffodil, which grows wild in Wales and blooms in March, partially superseded the leek as the country's emblem, probably because of its better wearability.

The cathedral inside is large and open with beautiful windows, carvings, and a blue and gold tower lantern, the latter a faithful copy of the original done during the extensive restoration work done by Sir George Gilbert Scott. There are some fine tombs, among them a brass marking the grave of Edmund Tudor, Earl of Richmond, father of Henry VII. St David's last words were believed to be 'Brothers and sisters be cheerful and keep your faith and belief and do the little things you have heard and seen through me.' These words are often repeated by Welsh people to keep his memory alive and bring him close despite the 1,400 years that have elapsed since his death.

St David's is the only British cathedral where the reigning monarch is a member of the Chapter. The sovereign's stall is the first in the choir and is marked by the royal coat of arms. The only monarch to have occupied this First stall is Queen Elizabeth II.

We returned to Solva for lunch, after which Babs drove us along the coast, wildly beautiful with yellow gorse still blooming on the sheltered side of the hills. We drew into a gateway where curious cattle viewed us suspiciously and from which we could see the dim outline of the Irish coast across the sea.

We left Babs sadly in the early afternoon to make our way to the village of Mitchel Troy near Monmouth, where we had made a reservation for the night. We drove through the Dyfed county seat of Haverfordwest, a handsome market town where we got on to A40 towards Carmarthen. I had wanted to stop at Laugharne with its many associations with Dylan Thomas, but there was not enough time. Carmarthen is the burial place of Sir Richard Steele, Irish essayist and friend of Addison. We took the southern road towards Swansea and Cardiff along the edge of coal fields marked by industrial structures, mines, and coal tips, and then bypassed the area by turning north. At last we reached Monmouth, where we drove around for a look at the town before seeking out our billet in the village of Mitchel Troy.

Monmouth is built at the confluence of the Monnow and Wye rivers and lies in a lush green valley. The town was the birthplace of Henry V in 1387 and a statue of him stands in Agincourt Square, named for his 1415 victory over the French. Nearby is another statue, this one of C. S. Rolls, pioneer airman and the Rolls of Rolls Royce. His father Lord Llangattock lived near the town. There are some fine old houses and a unique fortified Norman bridge with a gatehouse.

It had grown dark by now and we had difficulty finding our lodging. It proved to be an old, old farmhouse, half-timbered with heavily beamed ceiling, fireplaces big enough to walk in, and steep uneven stairs. It had only been partially modernized but was comfortable enough. Our hostess was a very pleasant young woman who directed us to a local pub for dinner. The food was good, but being Saturday night a rock group was playing and it was rather too noisy for our old-fashioned tastes.

SUNDAY, OCTOBER 18TH

EN ROUTE TO BOURTON-ON-THE-WATER – ABERGAVENNY,
RAGLAN CASTLE, ROSS-ON-WYE, CHELTENHAM

Before heading east into Gloucestershire, we retraced our steps to visit Abergavenny, a town in Wales of some interest to me. On Friday, September 1st, 1939, I, along with several other teachers, arrived there from Birmingham in charge of evacuated schoolchildren seeking safety from bombs expected to fall as soon as war was declared. I remember very well the emotional scenes as parents said tearful goodbyes to their children at New Street Station in Birmingham, the long slow ride to Abergavenny, and our reception at the railway station by the mayor and a committee of ladies chosen to conduct the children to their billets. Another teacher and I were put up in the house of the mayor, a short stocky man with a florid face who was a cattle dealer and local entrepreneur. Saturday we were busy settling the children in their new homes and attempting to iron out the problems that inevitably arose. Sunday – the fateful 3rd – was a beautiful late summer morning. Some of us were free to explore our surroundings and we took a walk into the hills outside the town. And so it happened that at 11 am we were standing outside a row of miners cottages when we heard Neville Chamberlain, in solemn measured tones, announce over the wireless that we were at war with Germany. The next few days are now a blur in my mind, as we had long hectic days of arranging school space for the newly arrived children, organizing recreational activities, and dealing with the children's homesickness and host family difficulties. As the weeks of the 'phony' war dragged on and no hostile attacks came, a slow return of evacuees to their homes began, and early in 1940 I was recalled to Birmingham, never to return to Abergavenny until now. Our arrival at the Abergavenny railway station those many years ago remains clear in my mind, as does the vivid memory of Chamberlain's declaration of war. I also remember the kindness of the mayor and his wife.

Otherwise, however, the town today seemed unfamiliar, and we had only the briefest time to look about. Because of its location at the mouth of the Gavenny river, the town is often called the Gateway to Wales. The town is guarded by hills on either side, with the river leading into the Brecon Beacons National Park. Down through the ages the area was the site of sporadic warfare between the Welsh and English over the border marshes, and in 1177 the town was the scene of a notorious massacre of Welsh nobility by William de Braose.

Departing the town we stopped for a quick look at Raglan Castle, an impressive ruin with a large gateway and machicolated towers. It served as a fortress during the Wars of the Roses and became the home of the earls of Worcester. During the Civil War the earl held it for the king for 10 weeks before surrendering to Cromwell's forces.

We continued on through magnificent country and past the famed beauty spot known as Symonds Yat ('gate') in the valley of the River Wye. The Wye is considered one of the most beautiful rivers in Britain as it travels over rocky beds and through gorges, meadows and woodland to join the Severn in its run to the sea. We bypassed Ross on our right, marked by its tall slender church spire, which reminded me of childhood visits to the area, for we had friends there and the Wye Valley was one of my father's favourite spots.

A few miles further on we crossed into Gloucestershire, with the great cathedral of Gloucester marking the skyline on our right, and thence to Cheltenham, where the road we wanted led us through the heart of that beautiful city. The sun was shining as we drove along the tree-lined streets, and the changing leaves were touched with gold and red. We passed the

Ladies College and the Queens Hotel set in gardens blooming with fall flowers, and drove up the Promenade lined with elegant Georgian and Regency buildings. Many of these buildings date from the eighteenth century, when the town grew famous as a spa thanks to the ingenuity and enterprise of a sheep farmer named William Mason. In 1716 Mason noticed pigeons gathering regularly in one of his fields to peck at crystals of salt near a spring of pure mineral water. He began to bottle the water and sell it, and its perceived medicinal qualities became locally popular. In 1740 a brick edifice was constructed over the spring and a pump installed, and so the spa was born. George III came to take the waters in 1788, and others of the upper classes soon followed along with the construction of many of the town's beautiful buildings. Cheltenham's reputation was further enhanced in 1816 when the Duke of Wellington, hero of Waterloo, was cured of a liver ailment after taking the Cheltenham waters, and the town soon rivalled Bath as England's premier spa. Though modern medical treatment has now superseded treatment by curative waters, the town is still an important educational and cultural centre as well as a retirement locale for wealthy people.

Beyond the town we reached Andoversford, where we took the high road to Bourton-on-the-Water. The route followed the spine of the Cotswold Hills, giving us remarkable views on either side, until we reached the new home of our friends Sybil and Norman Beard.

SUNDAY AND MONDAY, OCTOBER 18TH AND 19TH

THE COTSWOLDS

Our two days in the Cotswolds were a melange of visiting, talking, eating and sightseeing. We were fascinated by our friends' accommodation in a retirement community in Bourton-on-the-Water. A few months ago they moved from a dream cottage in East Harptree near Bristol where we had visited them on previous occasions, so this was our first opportunity to experience retirement living British-style. It is a relatively small complex of carefully designed living units built in clusters around a central garden of the creamy Cotswold stone that melds unobtrusively into the town's beautiful architecture. The complex is walled with gates to which residents are given a key that provides a measure of security, and there is a caretaker-manager living on the premises. Apart from this there are no other services such as meals or health care. There are, however, excellent restaurants and shops of all kinds within very easy access. The two-storey houses, though small, are extremely well-planned and have all the amenities. We were a little surprised that the two-floor accommodations for elderly people are not supplied with elevators. Our friends have added a conservatory that looks out on to a tiny walled garden reminding me of similar ones we have seen in Charleston and Savannah in America's Southeast. Sybil's antique furniture, pictures, objets d'art and Laura Ashley covers combine to make a miniature showplace.

Bourton is built beside the River Windrush, the clear waters of which flow between lawns alongside the main street and beneath graceful stone bridges. The old houses are built of the local stone with its yellowish cast and many have roofs covered with silvery lichen. At one end of the street there is a mill and behind the New Inn, not new of course, is a model of the village built of the same stone to exact specifications. We had a delightful dinner at the New Inn.

The Cotswold country is perhaps the most visited part of England, especially by Americans. The hills, not high as hills go but none the less giving an impression of height, occupy parts of Wiltshire, Oxfordshire, and Somerset, though their heart lies in Gloucestershire. The area is distinguished by sheltered honey-coloured villages contrasting with higher exposed towns such as Stow-on-the-Wold 'where the wind blows cold'. The hillsides are steep and often covered in beechwood, and the flocks of snowy-fleeced sheep grazing in the meadows remind us that in Shakespeare's day this was the very centre of England's lucrative sheep-raising and cloth-making industry, from which came many beautiful manor houses and churches. The streams are clear and fast-flowing, and the Thames rises near Cirencester and rapidly develops into England's premier river. Houses, farm buildings, manors and churches are all built of the yellowish limestone mined locally, and it has become the distinguishing feature of the Cotswold country. J. B. Priestley, a writer associated with Yorkshire, remarked on the faint luminosity that the buildings give off even in the absence of sunlight and claimed that this is at the heart of the Cotswolds' mysterious loveliness and enchantment.

Most people have heard the famed Cotswold names of Broadway, the Slaughters, Snowshill, Bibury, Minster Lovell, Burford, Swinbrook, and so on. At some time or another I have visited or passed through most of them, the villages of the local stone looking as if they have grown naturally from the ground like the trees surrounding them. Some are strung out along babbling streams where swans and ducks swim, with churches, manor houses, and old inns nearby.

On this bright sunny but cold Sunday afternoon our hosts took us for a ride around the villages. We stopped to visit the church at Swinbrook, famous for monuments to the Fettiplace and Mitford families. The Fettiplace family was very wealthy from riches accumulated over 400 years, but it died out soon after the Civil War. In the church of St Mary are six recumbent marble effigies of family members lying in groups of three in a shelf-like arrangement. Resting on one elbow, they look remarkably uncomfortable. Three are dressed in Tudor dress, while the other three wear the clothes of the later Stuarts. The Fettiplaces were very rich as is borne out by the following rhyme:

> The Tracys, the Laceys and the Fettiplaces
> Own all the woods, the parks, the places.

At the death of the last baronet the manor was sold to a Mr Freeman from London, who led the life of a wealthy country squire until he was discovered to be the much sought head of a gang of highwaymen who had been terrorizing travellers in the countryside around. After his arrest by the Bow Street Runners, the estate fell into ruin and the big house crumbled. The Fettiplace family is still remembered locally by certain charities they established for indigent old people and local schools. They also provided funds to send two poor boys annually to Christ's Hospital in London for training as doctors.

Lord Redesdale – the family name is Mitford – lived in a large house in the village in the 1920s. He moved his large family here from a more attractive house in nearby Asthall and it is believed that his son and several daughters were not happy with the change. The Redesdale daughters, known as the Mitford girls, were beautiful, gifted and with one exception controversial. Two of them, Nancy, a writer of note, and Unity, an admirer of Hitler, are buried near the door of the church. Unity, the youngest of the girls, died several years after a botched suicide attempt at the end of the war. Their grey stone headstones bear inscriptions made almost illegible by time and erosion. Inside the church is a memorial tablet to the only son and heir, who was killed in World War I. The title passed to a male cousin who lived in London and Northumberland rather than Gloucestershire. A few years ago we got to know one of this Lord Redesdale's daughters slightly while she was a Morehead Scholar at the University of North Carolina.

Later on we drove through Batsford, another estate once belonging to the Redesdale family, the park of which comprised an entire village. We then drove on to Burford, passing from Gloucestershire to Oxfordshire, crossing the Windrush over a narrow bridge from which we got a fine view of the spired church across the watermeadows. We went on to Minster Lovell, also on the Windrush, where there are the ruins of a manor house to which are attached two tragic legends. One went into song and story as *The Mistletoe Bough* and tells of the disappearance of a bride who was playing hide and seek with her guests as part of her wedding festivities. Seek as her playmates would, they could not find her, but years later a skeleton still clad in marriage finery was discovered in an old oak chest. What is purported to be the chest can be seen today at Grey's Court near Henley-on-Thames. When I was young we sometimes sang the folk song and it often made me cry:

> At length an oak chest that had long lain hid
> Was found in the castle. They raised the lid,
> And a skeleton form lay mouldering there,
> In the bridal wreath of the lady fair.
> Oh! Sad was her fate, in sportive jest
> She hid from her lord in the old oak chest,
> It closed with a spring and her bridal bloom
> Lay withering there in a living tomb.
> Oh! The mistletoe bough!
> Oh! The mistletoe bough!

The other legend concerns a man named Francis Lovell who during the reign of Henry VII after the Wars of the Roses supported a pretender to the throne named Lambert Simnel. Simnel, in an ill-advised attempt to make himself king, claimed to be one of the 'princes in the tower', whose fate had never been ascertained. Francis hid in a secret room from which there was no exit in his manor house looked after by a faithful servant. When the servant died unexpectedly the prisoner slowly starved to death. In 1718 during work on the house, the hidden chamber came to light and in it there was indeed the skeleton of a man seated at a table.

Two Cotswold villages named Barrington provided some of the stone for the rebuilding of St Paul's Cathedral after the Great Fire of London. A local stonemason named Strong was asked by Sir Christopher Wren to lay the foundation stone of the cathedral. Blocks of stone were shipped from the Cotswolds on flat-bottomed boats down the Windrush to the Thames and so to Ludgate Hill.

We spent Monday morning shopping in Bourton and going to the model village, an exact replica of the town in miniature but large enough for people to walk through, giving an effect of Gulliver in Lilliput. Warmed by sunlight, we had lunch in the conservatory and then left for a tour of Sudeley Castle near Winchcombe. Though a very cold wind was blowing, the sun was shining from a cloudless blue sky, adding to the incredible beauty of the landscape. We went by way of villages with fascinating names such as Guiting Power and Temple Guiting, wishing we could stop and explore them. We drove along high roads with banks of red poppies, yellow charlock and white daisies. Along the way we passed a family of gipsies in two horse-drawn caravans, their backs ajingle with pots and pans and tinkers' tools, while alongside marched a motley group of swarthy men, women, and children, the likes of whom I had not seen since my childhood.

We approached the small grey town of Winchcombe down a lovely avenue of beech trees, their green touched by autumn's copper shimmering in the sunlight. The town was once a place of some importance, but now seems passed over and withdrawn. It was the site of a Benedictine abbey founded by a king of Saxon Mercia and then dissolved and razed in the reign of Henry VIII. The fifteenth-century church contains two stone coffins believed to be those of Kenulf, king of Mercia, and his son. An altar cloth is thought to be the work of Catherine of Aragon, first wife of Henry VIII, and the church boasts 40 gargoyles to keep it free from evil spirits. Like many other Cotswold churches it was built by rich wool merchants, for Winchcombe was at one time a prosperous centre for cloth manufacture.

Sudeley Castle is on the outskirts of the town. It is today the family home of Lord and Lady Ashcombe and its present form dates from the mid-fifteenth century. At one time it was the home of Sir Thomas Seymour, brother to Jane Seymour, Henry VIII's third wife. When Henry died leaving his sixth wife, Catherine Parr, a widow, the lady married Sir Thomas and came to live at Sudeley Castle, though within a year she died in childbirth. Her very beautiful tomb, surmounted by a colourful effigy, is in the castle chapel, which now serves as an additional church for the community. The castle contains much fine furniture, pictures, glassware, tapestries and a fine lace collection. The gardens are its greatest glory, however, and they looked especially beautiful today with the greenest of velvety lawns, flower beds rife with autumn blooms and towering yew hedges bordering the walks, all clipped in precise perfection. It was a photographic opportunity and David took full advantage.

TUESDAY, OCTOBER 20TH

We woke to pouring rain, quite the wettest day we have seen. We said sad goodbyes to our dear friends, wondering if and when we will see them again. We left after breakfast, going through the Oxfordshire Cotswolds, their views obscured by the drenching rain. We stopped for lunch in Thame, parking with difficulty and walking through the rain to an indifferent pub. It is a wide-streeted town of some antiquity where important markets and fairs are held and a large imposing church stands beside the river Thames. It has a famous old grammar school, where John Hampden, leading parliamentarian and friend, relative and supporter of Oliver Cromwell, once was a pupil. We drove on to Hemel Hempstead where we spent our last night with a widowed cousin of mine. An old town in a valley in the Chiltern Hills, Hemel Hempstead formed the nucleus of a 'new' town developed to house Londoners in the so-called 'Green Belt', and since 1947 has grown by leaps and bounds.

Early on Wednesday morning we made our way to Heathrow for our return journey. It was a harrowing ride of bumper-to-bumper traffic on the M25, though fortunately the rain was over and gone. We had plenty of time but were glad to board our plane for an uneventful flight home.

Chapter Ten

POSTSCRIPT – 1994

At the beginning of my 1992 journal I made the rather gloomy prognostication that that trip would most likely be our last visit to England. Yet June 1994 did indeed see me 'going home' once more and we have just returned from one of the pleasantest holidays we have ever spent there.

After a direct flight we drove from Gatwick to Marlborough on a dull almost cold morning. We had chosen to stay the entire three weeks at Cadley House, the delightful bed and breakfast establishment in Savernake Forest that we had discovered in 1992. Here we were treated as friends and honoured guests by the charming proprietors Antonia and Julian Wethered.

We arrived on June 3rd amidst all the preparations for the 50th anniversary of D-Day. We watched the Portsmouth and Normandy ceremonies on BBC television, while on the evening of June 6th we attended the service of commemoration held at the War Memorial in Marlborough, a ceremony which would be mirrored in every village and town in England. The service was followed by a gathering at the British Legion Club of veterans, all wearing their medals, some of whom had participated in the landings on Gold, Juno or Sword beaches. Here I met friends and acquaintances from the past and we were welcomed as the only Americans present. D-Day brought back many memories – a hectic time for David, an officer in an Ordnance Company readying and shipping ammunition from Savernake Forest where it was stored to the invasion areas, while I was living in a keeper's cottage in the same forest waiting to see him whenever possible. During the night of June 5th and all day on June 6th I remembered how the sky was filled with planes, many of them towing gliders, droning their way south and we knew then that the long-awaited invasion had begun and prayed for its success. It seemed fitting to be back in Savernake Forest fifty years later.

For the rest our time was spent almost entirely in Wiltshire with only brief forays into the neighbouring counties of Dorset to see my niece in Weymouth, Berkshire for shopping in Newbury, Avon to see Bath once more, Somerset for Wells and Glastonbury, Gloucestershire to Stroud to see my publisher and to see friends in Bourton-on-the-Water. The weather was delightful. We had only 2 wet days out of 21 and most of the others gave us blue sky, bright sun, warm temperatures and gentle breezes. We found most of our friends at home and ready to entertain us.

The countryside was at its June best. As we drove the highways and byways the hedgerows were lined with the flat creamy white flowers of blossoming elderberry, with the pale pink of dog roses and sweet-smelling honeysuckle, while the verges flourished with white ox-eye daisies, red poppies and blue speedwell. Occasionally a rabbit would cross our path and we saw several hares, a badger, a hedgehog and deer in Savernake Forest. Here we saw giant silver-trunked beech trees and great gnarled oaks crowned with the fresh green leaves of early summer. The bracken, many of its pale green fronds still curled, had not yet reached its full height and I saw something I had never before seen in Savernake — great patches of foxgloves with their red and white blossoming spikes 5 or 6 feet tall.

While I love the thatch and flint villages, the lush green meadows centred by great shade trees, and bisected by a silver stream, the ancient storied market towns, yet it is the downs that are to me the essence of Wiltshire — 'our blunt, bow-headed, whale-backed downs' as Kipling called them. The downs give us wide vistas, springy turf, white roads, windbreaks of beeches, valleys of arable fields and pastureland enriched by clear streams bordered by villages grouped around their ancient churches. Add to this sheep everywhere, white horses cut through the shallow turf, prehistoric earthworks, camps, barrows, stone temples, British tracks, Roman roads, Saxon settlements and modern training grounds for armies and racehorses.

One sunny morning in June 1994, we stood in the same spot we had in 1961 and 1975, on a hill on the edge of Savernake Forest overlooking the Kennet valley. Except for seasonal variations it was unchanged from the earlier years. Marlborough was just out of sight, but could be reached by a bridle path. Beneath us to our left was the village of Mildenhall (Minal), in the distance its toy-like houses identified by its church and octagon-towered schoolhouse. In the centre was the farm complex of Stitchcombe, a gracious house with barns, outbuildings and labourers' cottages nearby, and on our right was the hamlet of Axford, the Red Lion Inn barely discernible in the distance. The three were linked by the winding silver ribbon of the river, while the land rose beyond the valley to the swell of the Marlborough Downs. The valley and hillside fields were a medley of many shades of green and brown, their odd shapes outlined with the darker green of hedges, and were accented with patches of brilliant yellow — rape in full bloom. Haymaking was in full swing in some fields, cows and sheep grazed in others.

This valley scene, unchanged in a changing world beset by problems, conveys a sense of peace and stability, giving reassurance that as long as such places exist there will always be an England. It made a sight I will long remember.